WRITE WITH
JANE AUSTEN

WRITE WITH JANE AUSTEN

MASTERCLASSES WITH THE MASTER STORYTELLER

KATHERINE COWLEY

Pointe Press

Pointe Press, 2025.

ISBN: 979-8-9993134-0-9 (paperback)
ISBN: 979-8-9993134-1-6 (hardcover)
ISBN: 979-8-9993134-2-3 (e-book)

Cover design by Michelle Williams Design.

Publisher information: Pointe Press, kathy@katherinecowley.com, PO Box 145, 3885 S 9th St, Kalamazoo, MI 49009-9997.

Printed and bound by IngramSpark.

Australia: Ingram Content Group AU Pty Ltd, Melbourne, Victoria. US: Lightning Source LLC, La Vergne, Tennessee/Allentown, Pennsylvania/Jackson, Tennessee, United States. UK: Lightning Source UK Ltd, Miton Keynes, United Kingdom. Europe: Lightning Source UK Ltd, with facilities in Germany, France, and Spain.

The authorized representative in the European Economic Area is Lightning Source France, 1 Av. Johannes Gutenberg, 78310 Maurepas, France. compliance@lightningsource.fr

This book is printed in accordance with commercial printing standards.

to the teachers who have taught me the most
about writing: Daune Spritzer, Lynn Krumvieda,
Gideon Burton, and of course, Jane Austen

CONTENTS

INTRODUCTION

I n October 1798, Jane Austen came very near to losing her writing. As she explained in a letter to her sister Cassandra,

> After we had been here a quarter of an hour it was discovered
> that my writing and dressing boxes had been by accident put
> into a chaise which was just packing off as we came in, and were
> driven away toward Gravesend in their way to the West Indies.
> No part of my property could have been such a prize before, for
> in my writing-box was all my worldly wealth.[1]

The writing box contained both Austen's tools for crafting words—the paper, the ink, the quill pens—and her words themselves, the products of her creation. She seems unworried by the loss of her dressing boxes—her writing box was the prize. At this point, she had not yet received recognition for her writing: It would be more than a decade before the publication of *Sense and Sensibility*, in 1811. Yet publication and recognition were irrelevant; she treasured her writing more than any other possession.

---

1. Jane Austen to Cassandra Austen, October 24, 1798. *Letters of Jane Austen*.

Jane's writing box, which is held by the British Library.[2]

Fortunately, Jane's fears did not last long. A man was dispatched on a horse, and in about thirty minutes, her writing box was back in her possession.

From this experience, I have learned an invaluable writing lesson: It is absolutely necessary to back up your work in multiple places.

I'm sure that if Jane lived in the digital age, she would agree.

Of course, there is much more we can learn from Jane Austen than the value of keeping hold of your work. Regardless of what style or genre you write, regardless of whether you are a beginning writer or a seasoned professional, regardless of your nationality, race, or gender, there is much we can all learn from Austen about storytelling. She is a master of character and plot, dialogue and setting, form and function. By considering her writing techniques and applying them, we can hone our craft and better tell our own stories. And as readers, a better understanding of Austen's craft will lead to a greater appreciation for her work.

Thousands of years ago, the Greeks and the Romans touted imitation of the masters as one of the primary ways to learn to

---

2. Details on image sources and licenses can be found in the back matter, in the Image Sources section.

write. Jane herself engaged endlessly in imitation. Scholar Rachel M. Brownstein has written about how both Jane Austen and her contemporary, Lord Byron, learned to write through imitation; Lord Byron was encouraged to imitate the classics at school, while Austen imitated contemporary fiction out of her own initiative. Brownstein explains, "By imitating the styles and voices of writers before them, recognizing and rehearsing established tropes and tricks, writers may develop their distinctive ... styles and learn in the process to engage with readers." While Austen's imitations, now available in her *Juvenilia*, were largely parodies, burlesques, and satires, through them she mastered storytelling techniques and developed her own style and approach to writing. Brownstein writes, "Jane Austen started out mimicking fiction to show up its mindless falseness, and learned in the process how to mimic the minds of whole neighbourhoods so as to make them seem ridiculous and real."[3]

Just as Jane Austen learned to write through imitating others, we can learn to write better by imitating her. The goal, of course, is not to write exactly like Jane Austen or to adopt her voice and style. Rather, the goal is to write *with* Jane Austen—to learn from her techniques and her mastery of storytelling and the English language, and by doing so to develop our own mastery.

Jane Austen has transformed my own abilities as a storyteller. My first exposure to Austen was when I was eleven years old. My mother handed me a copy of *Pride and Prejudice*, and I liked it so much that I read it twice that year. Like Austen, I've enjoyed writing since I was very young, and I wrote many short stories throughout my youth—though none nearly as entertaining as Austen's juvenilia. In college, I earned a master's degree in Rhetoric and Composition, focusing on what makes writing work and how to teach writing to others. But it was only after graduating that I began to take my fiction seriously. In the following years, I wrote many short stories and novels across various genres—contemporary, literary, historical, and fantasy. A number of my short stories were published, and I could tell that I was improving as a writer, but I also knew my skills hadn't developed as far as I needed them to in order to tell the stories of my heart.

---

3. Brownstein, "Endless Imitation," 128, 133.

For years I had been thinking about Mary Bennet and what could give her purpose and meaning—what could allow her to live a life beyond the confines of her family and society's expectations. I decided to write a novel titled *The Secret Life of Miss Mary Bennet*, and doing so forced me to immerse myself in Austen's craft.

Even though I was writing a work inspired by *Pride and Prejudice*, I didn't want to directly imitate the voice of Austen's narrator. But I desperately needed to understand how Austen weaves supporting characters throughout her plots, how she uses foreshadowing, what makes her relationships feel real, and how she adds nuance and depth to her conclusions.

After studying Austen's craft, I ended up publishing three Mary Bennet novels (the first of which was nominated for the Mary Higgins Clark Award), a number of award-winning short stories, and an essay that was nominated for the Pushcart Prize. On my blog and at writing conferences, I began teaching other writers the techniques I'd learned from Austen that apply to any genre. Ultimately, I decided I wanted to turn what I had learned from Jane Austen—these masterclasses she gifted me—into a full book.

Write with Jane Austen will provide lessons on writing based on Austen's six complete novels and her shorter and unpublished works, with occasional references to other Austen-inspired texts. There are numerous editions of Jane Austen, many of which have made changes to the original text. Some update early nineteenth-century British English to modern British English usage; some editions use American spellings; many modernize Austen's punctuation to match contemporary conventions. For the purposes of this book, quotes from Austen's six novels will be taken from the Project Gutenberg editions, which stay very close to the original texts.[4] Because of the many editions, specific page numbers will not be cited.[5]

We will begin by looking at story as a journey—both internal and external—through analyzing Austen's use of plot structure and

---

4. There are a few exceptions when I use other editions. These will be noted in the text. Also, the Project Gutenberg edition of *Persuasion* omits the periods after "Mr." and "Mrs." However, I will include the periods in order to match Austen's original editions and to match the Project Gutenberg editions of the other books.

5. Life is too short and this book is too long for me to include exact citations for quotes from Austen's novels. Besides, do you *really* want two thousand references in the footnotes when you can find the exact location of the quotes by searching online? (However, if you are into references the way I am, then you will enjoy the index locorum, which does include all the references to Austen's works, organized by book and chapter.)

character arcs. We will then consider creating characters, crafting the beginnings of stories, and choosing an overall stance for the work. Next, we will focus on applying pressure to characters through antagonism and the rising action, as well as how to construct key turning points and use foreshadowing. From there we will learn Austen's techniques for planting emotional clues, using dynamic settings to impact a character's journeys, crafting compelling relationships and relationship arcs, and creating engaging dialogue that forwards the story. Then we will explore Austen's approaches to style, humor, and irony, and how we can apply what we learn to our own distinctive writing styles. Finally, we will consider how Austen created a space for writing in her life and how we can do the same.

Throughout these lessons, I include writing exercises. Like the Greeks and the Romans discovered long ago, and countless modern researchers have reconfirmed, I have found that one of the very best ways to learn to write is to actually write. I've taught writing classes as an adjunct faculty member at two universities and one community college, and my students and I always learn so much through exercises—short pieces that are not necessarily intended for publication but are a type of focused practice. Writing exercises help us develop specific techniques and skills in a contained medium; these techniques then become familiar tools that can be applied as needed to your future projects.

In this book, you will find four main types of writing exercises.

1. **Short scene prompts.** These prompts include directions for writing a short scene using specific techniques that we find in Austen's stories. Doing these exercises is like practicing scales on an instrument or running drills in a sport: It is an opportunity to learn, refine, and internalize certain skills.

2. **Analysis.** This type of exercise asks you to find and analyze other works of fiction, whether literature, film, or other media. Analyzing masterful storytelling trains your mind to think analytically; truly understanding the tools of storytelling and different ways to implement them will make these tools more comfortable and useful in your own hands.

3. **Personal experience.** The third type of exercise requires you to draw upon your own life, and your own experiences

with people and settings and tension, in order to learn and apply storytelling principles. Our lives are filled with story and meaning, and noticing the stories about ourselves and those around us can help us connect to these techniques on a more personal level, as well as understand why these techniques resonate with readers.

4. **Current projects.** This final type of exercise focuses on applying the lessons from Austen to your current writing projects, whether you are brainstorming a short story, drafting a screenplay, or revising a novel. Ultimately, we need to take the techniques that we learn and apply them to our polished writing that is intended for a wider audience.

As you read this book, you can choose to do the writing exercises sequentially, you can focus on exercises in certain chapters, or you can revisit the exercises later. You can do all the exercises in a chapter or select a few that seem most relevant to the skills you want to improve. Feel free to modify the exercises to suit your needs. Regardless of how you choose to use the exercises, it is through applying and practicing these techniques that you will improve your writing and your storytelling.

It has now been 250 years since Jane Austen's birth. Endless writers have eloquently expressed her impact, both on themselves personally and more generally on culture, society, and the literary world. Dozens of films have brought Austen's work to the screen, and dozens of scripts have brought her work to the stage. Memes, gifs, and spin-offs apply her storytelling in new directions and invite us to participate in the worlds and words she crafted. And so we return, again and again, to her words and her brilliance. As you read this book, I invite you to spend a little more time with Jane Austen, the master storyteller.

CHAPTER ONE

THE JOURNEY

"I wish as well as everybody else to be perfectly happy; but, like everybody else it must be in my own way."

—*Sense and Sensibility*

In Jane Austen's first published novel, *Sense and Sensibility*, Edward Ferrars receives constant pressure from his family to conform to their expectations for him—they want him to seek greatness by pursuing success and wealth. From their perspective, doing so will grant him (and, by extension, his family) happiness. He does desire happiness, but as he says, "it must be in my own way."

In fiction, each character must seek their own happiness, and each character must do so by following their own distinctive journey. This includes two parts: an *external journey*, an interaction with the world, also known as *plot*; and an *internal journey*, a changing and progression of the self, also known as *character*. The external and internal journeys, plot and character, must be addressed at every stage of the writing process and at every moment in a story.

Throughout Austen's work, a single underlying principle distills both character and plot, creating the intersections between internal and external journeys: **A main character must want something.**[1]

In Austen's novel *Emma*, the title character, Emma Woodhouse, wants to bring others happiness (and herself entertainment) by playing matchmaker. At the beginning of the story, she sets herself on this path while speaking of her success in finding a husband for her dear friend and governess, Miss Taylor:

> "I made the match myself. I made the match, you know, four years ago; and to have it take place, and be proved in the right, when so many people said Mr. Weston would never marry again, may comfort me for any thing."
>
> Mr. Knightley shook his head at [Emma]. Her father fondly replied, "Ah! my dear, I wish you would not make matches and foretell things, for whatever you say always comes to pass. Pray do not make any more matches."
>
> "I promise you to make none for myself, papa; but I must, indeed, for other people. It is the greatest amusement in the world! And after such success, you know!"

THE WANTS OF A CHARACTER REVEAL THEIR INTERNAL CHARACTER AND PERSONALITY.

Emma wants to be a matchmaker because she believes she understands people better than they understand themselves.[2] Not only does she consider herself superior to others, but she is used to getting what she wants.

Her internal journey focuses on the question: Can she change? In other words, can she learn to look outside herself? Can she give others the same autonomy that she possesses?

A character's want may assist them on their internal journey, or it may interfere with that journey. Ultimately, the character's want will be a catalyst for change, whether positive or negative.

---

1. This seems obvious, but if I ever have a story that's not working, this tends to be the problem. On a smaller scale, in every single scene, each character should want something. Kurt Vonnegut famously wrote, "Every character should want something, even if it is only a glass of water." Emily Temple, "Kurt Vonnegut's Greatest Writing Advice."

2. You probably have an Emma in your life (either with or without the matchmaking aspect). Most people do.

Emma bringing Mr. Weston and Miss Taylor together.
Illustration by C. E. Brock, 1909.

THE WANTS OF A CHARACTER CREATE PLOT.

Emma's desire to make matches leads to most of the action (and comedy) of the novel, such as her prolonged attempt to match her friend Harriet Smith with the vicar, Mr. Elton.

She constantly strives for this goal, and this striving creates struggle and conflict, an essential element of plot. At various points, Emma progresses toward her want, and at other points she experiences failure. As we near the end of the novel, her want shifts:

She rejects matchmaking, for she sees all the trouble it has caused both herself and others. Yet even once she stops interfering in the romantic lives of others, her previous actions continue their domino effect, impacting the final plot events.

Ultimately, a want will influence how a character interacts with other characters and the world. In traditional Western narratives, a want drives the external journey.

How do you show character wants?

One of the simplest ways to show what a character wants is through their **dialogue**, as seen in the above example from *Emma*. As we will discuss in Chapter 9, dialogue is not just about communication: It is a tool we use to assert our identities in the world, to create change, and to influence other characters.

What a character wants should also be shown through **action**. Emma arranges endless opportunities for Harriet and Mr. Elton to spend time together. At one point as she walks with them, she intentionally breaks her shoelace so she can fall behind, giving them the opportunity to be alone.

A further method that can be used to show character wants and motivation is through **description**. Emma notices every time Mr. Elton looks in Harriet's direction, and the description reflects her motivation and hopes.

Finally, wants are manifested through **emotion** and **internal thoughts**. As we see in the previous passage, Emma delights in the results of her behavior. Later, when we see her internal thoughts, it is clear that her perspective is not a complete view of the situation; it's a lens, pointed in a certain direction and controlled by her past experiences and beliefs.

Throughout the rest of *Write with Jane Austen*, we'll see how wants are manifested in both the internal and external journey. And in this chapter, we'll further explore what external journeys and internal journeys look like for characters. But first, a few writing exercises.

Exercise 1.1: Character Manifesto

Whether you're writing a novel, a short story, or a picture book, your main character should want something. One method of discovering and/or refining what your character wants is through expressing their wants, from their perspective, in the form of a manifesto—a public declaration of intent or motivation.

Write a manifesto from your main character's point of view about what they want, why they want it, and what they are willing to do to get it. This could be a single paragraph or a full page.

Exercise 1.2: Two Character Wants

Write a short scene featuring two adults who, after a decade apart, experience a chance meeting at a park. In addition to considering how these characters might interact at this sort of reunion, make sure to give both individuals a strong character want (such as being a matchmaker, getting home in time for a basketball game, selling a product, etc.). The character wants should impact the dialogue, the action, the description, and the characters' emotions and thoughts.

Exercise 1.3: A List of Fictional Wants

Set a timer for five minutes. During this time, think about characters from books, movies, and other stories. Write down a list of as many characters and their wants as you can before the time goes off.

THE EXTERNAL JOURNEY: PLOT

For many readers, *Pride and Prejudice* is their first experience of Jane Austen, as it was for me. Its plot captivated me from the start—a family with five daughters and an uncertain future. Each daughter has a distinctive personality, but I especially liked Elizabeth, with her independence and her wit. Elizabeth and her family attend balls, forge and fracture relationships, and try to make their way in the world. And in the end, we find out their fates.

The story uses a classic structure, which Aristotle detailed over two thousand years ago in *Poetics*. For something to be a story, he explains, there must be a beginning, a middle, and an end.[3] This movement through the beginning, middle, and end of a story typically takes the form of a **complication** followed by an **unraveling**. In the complication, difficulties build on each other, the characters seek the things they want, and relationships shift and change. In the unraveling, difficulties resolve, the characters either achieve or fail to achieve their wants, and relationships solidify.[4]

If we skip ahead to the nineteenth century, we meet Gustav Freytag, a German playwright and novelist. He expands on Aristotle's sense of complication and unraveling, using the visual of a pyramid to explain a plot as **rising and falling action**.[5] While Freytag describes a plot and its structure in detail, he points out that he doesn't intend for his structure to act as "a dictator." He wants plot structure to be "an honest helper"—a tool that helps us be creative and tell effective stories.[6]

The classic plot moments that make up Freytag's pyramid occur in so many stories because they are effective at powerfully conveying conflict and tension and action to an audience. Looking at how Austen uses narrative structure can help us at multiple stages of the writing process: when planning, while writing, and during revisions. Let's first analyze the plot structure of *Pride and Prejudice*. We'll consider how the plot takes Elizabeth Bennet and Mr. Darcy on an external journey, as they interact with the world and with each other.

---

3. It seems basic, but it's classic for a reason. Many of my early attempts at storytelling—and perhaps some of yours—were missing one of these three elements.

4. Aristotle, *The Poetics of Aristotle*.

5. Freytag, *Technique of the Drama*, 115.
In German, Freytag's book is titled *Die Technik des Dramas*. In English it's often translated as *Freytag's Technique of the Drama*. He focuses on full-length plays, but his work applies well to novels. Many of the modern approaches to plot and plot structure—including three-act structures, four-act structures, seven-point structures, and the hero's journey—build off of the work of Freytag, so we are going to use it as our basis for examining plot.

6. Freytag, *Technique of the Drama*, 5.

Plot Structure:
Pride and Prejudice

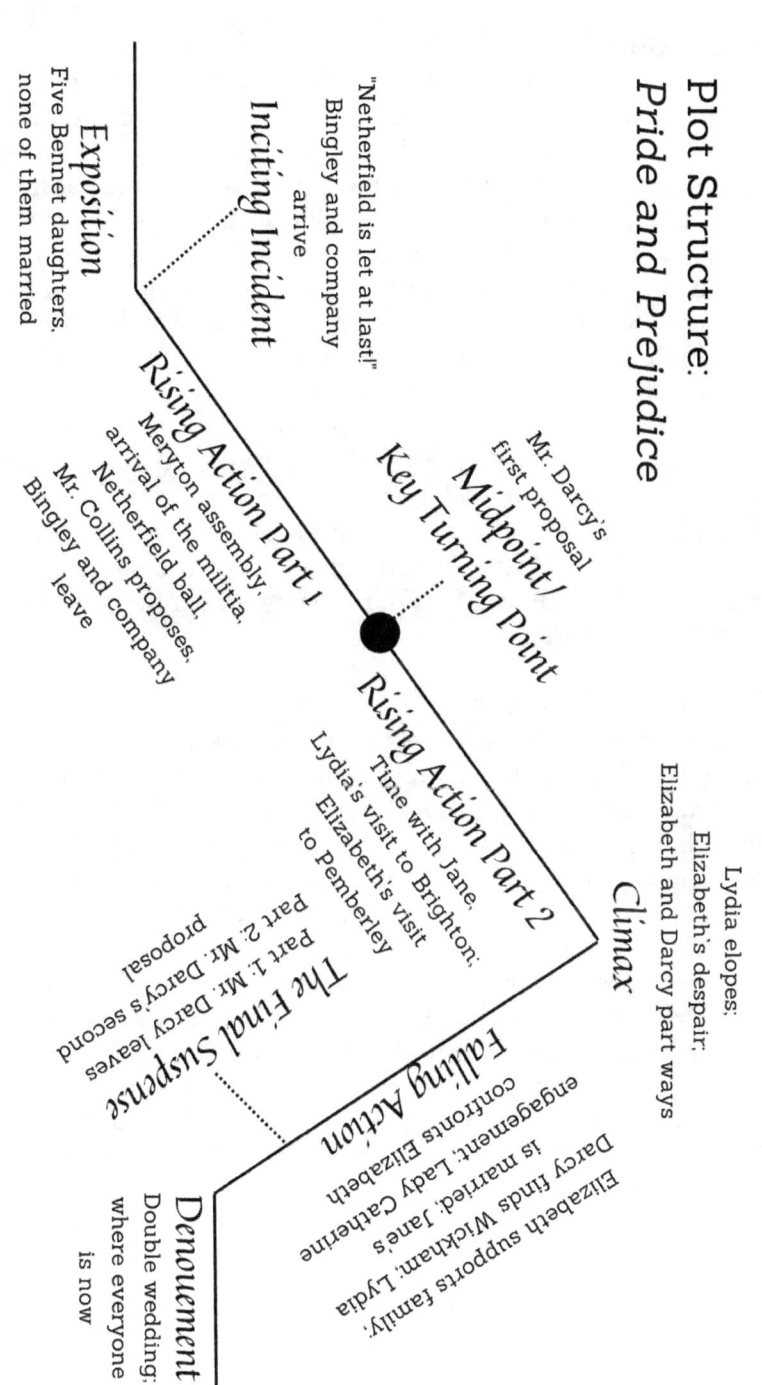

Exposition
Five Bennet daughters,
none of them married

Inciting Incident
"Netherfield is let at last!"
Bingley and company
arrive

Rising Action Part 1
Meryton assembly,
arrival of the militia,
Netherfield ball,
Mr. Collins proposes,
Bingley and company
leave

Midpoint/
Key Turning Point
Mr. Darcy's
first proposal

Rising Action Part 2
Time with Jane,
Lydia's visit to Brighton,
Elizabeth's visit
to Pemberley

Climax
Lydia elopes;
Elizabeth's despair;
Elizabeth and Darcy part ways

The Final Suspense
Part 1: Mr. Darcy leaves
Part 2: Mr. Darcy's second
proposal

Falling Action
Elizabeth supports family;
Darcy finds Wickham; Lydia
is married; Jane's
engagement; Lady Catherine
confronts Elizabeth

Denouement
Double wedding;
where everyone
is now

THE EXPOSITION

The exposition is the story world before the true story begins. The world is in stasis—it's still—and the inciting incident, the event that gets the plot moving, hasn't happened yet. Generally, the exposition is trying to paint a "picture of the situation," helping us to understand characters, relationships, the time, and the place.[7] There's no set length for how long an exposition should be: In some books, it takes several chapters, and in others, only a few sentences. Some stories skip the exposition and start immediately with the inciting incident, and then little pieces of exposition are woven in throughout the beginning of the story.

In *Pride and Prejudice*, not much time is spent on exposition at all—news of the inciting incident is delivered on the very first page. Yet in the opening chapters, the backstory is still made clear. We understand who these characters are, quickly grasp the nature of Mr. and Mrs. Bennet's marriage, learn of the entailment, and understand Mrs. Bennet's goal: to marry off her daughters so they don't die in poverty.

THE INCITING INCIDENT

An inciting incident is an event that sets the plot in motion, changing things for the character and starting them on both their internal and external journeys. This incident carries weight for the main character and creates the opportunity for change, both internally and externally. It often introduces forces outside of the main character's control. This disruption requires the main character to adapt and grow and interact with others in new ways. It often also sets up the main themes and conflicts of the story.

In *Pride and Prejudice*, the inciting incident is Mr. Bingley's arrival. Mrs. Bennet sets her sights on him marrying her eldest daughter, Jane, which becomes one of the major threads of the novel. Mr. Bingley also brings his sisters and his good friend Mr. Darcy to Meryton. When Mr. Darcy and Elizabeth meet, they are immediately antagonistic to each other. Ultimately it's their pride, their prejudice, and their romance that create the main external journey of the novel.

---

7. Freytag, *Technique of the Drama*, 118.

Mr. Bingley arrives at Netherfield.
Illustration by Hugh Thomson, 1894.

RISING ACTION PART I

After the inciting incident comes the rising action of the novel. To use Aristotle's term, this is the complication. This is the middle, with all the interesting scenes and incidents and relationships that help and hinder the characters. Through the rising action, we become more interested and invested in the characters and their stories. The themes of the novel are explored and developed. The rising action also introduces any remaining characters and subplots that will be important in the climax and falling action.

In the first half of *Pride and Prejudice*'s rising action, we experience some of the most memorable scenes: two balls, meeting the Bingleys and Mr. Darcy, the introduction of Mr. George Wickham, Mr. Collins's visit and failed proposal, and Elizabeth's trip to visit Mr. and Mrs. Collins. Elizabeth and Mr. Darcy's relationship develops, and circumstances change for many of the other characters (for instance, Jane falls in love with Mr. Bingley; then, when everything is looking good for their relationship, he leaves).

Themes and issues are raised—the role of love in marriage, the importance of financial security, and the tensions between individuals and society.

In a memorable scene during the rising action, Mrs. Bennet sends Jane to Netherfield on horseback because she knows that it will rain. Illustration by Hugh Thomson, 1894.

THE MIDPOINT/KEY TURNING POINTS

The midpoint is an event at or near the center of the story in which the core aspects of the character's journey are brought under a lens.[8] The character typically experiences either a major victory or a major defeat. In either case, the main character has not experienced a full transformation; they have not completed their internal journey. The midpoint generally highlights this, either providing

---

8. This is where I diverge a little from Freytag's model—he doesn't specifically discuss midpoints or turning points within the rising action. However, he does discuss different stages of the rising action, which clearly implies the existence of turning points.

tools the main character will need to make it through the climax and falling action, or emphasizing what the main character must still learn.

The midpoint in *Pride and Prejudice* is Mr. Darcy's first proposal to Elizabeth. Both Mr. Darcy and Elizabeth display their pride and prejudice in full force. Mr. Darcy tells Elizabeth all the many reasons he has resisted proposing to her (her family's status and behavior, and her lack of connections). Elizabeth refuses him. She verbally attacks him for his pride, accuses him of splitting up Mr. Bingley and Jane (which he did), and states that he caused Mr. Wickham's ruin (a falsehood, which shows the pitfalls of Elizabeth's prejudice). Then, in a follow-up scene, which is arguably part of this same sequence, Mr. Darcy writes a letter to Elizabeth, explaining his choices and perspective. He also tells her the story of how Wickham attempted to seduce his young sister in order to gain her fortune.

The midpoint is a key turning point that marks a major shift for the characters, often causing them to change both internally and externally. After Elizabeth's refusal, Mr. Darcy begins to treat others with more kindness; later, he explains,

> "I have been a selfish being all my life, in practice, though not in principle. As a child I was taught what was right, but I was not taught to correct my temper. I was given good principles, but left to follow them in pride and conceit."

After reading Mr. Darcy's letter and reflecting on it extensively, Elizabeth begins to question her preconceived notions and opens herself up to forgiveness and new perspectives.

Several *Pride and Prejudice* adaptations move Darcy's first proposal from the midpoint to the climax of the story. This often leads to substantive plot and character changes, because everything after the climax is falling action. (An example of this is Kate Hamill's theatrical adaptation of *Pride and Prejudice*.) However, in the original text, Mr. Darcy's first proposal happens almost exactly at the midpoint of the novel, and many film adaptations follow suit. (For instance, in the 1995 BBC adaptation, the proposal occurs at the end of the third episode, with three episodes remaining for the rest of the rising action, the climax, the falling action, and the denouement.) Other adaptations use his first proposal as a key turning point yet push the moment back so it occurs further along in the rising action; however, these versions keep Austen's original climax scene—the news of Lydia and Wickham—as the story climax. (This is the case in Melissa Leilani Larson's theatrical adaptation; the proposal occurs about two-thirds of the way through the script and acts as a key turning point.)[9] It's my personal belief that the exact placement of this sort of key turning point is less important than the structural and thematic roles it plays in the story.

While visiting Pemberley, Elizabeth spends several minutes looking at Mr. Darcy's portrait. Illustration by C. E. Brock, 1895.

9. This is one of my favorite adaptations because of the way it humanizes supporting characters like Mr. Collins and Mary Bennet, rather than using them solely for comic effect. I think Jane Austen would approve.

RISING ACTION PART II

After the midpoint, the action continues to rise toward the climax. The stakes—what can be lost, and what can be gained—are higher and more personal for the characters than they were in the first segment of the rising action.

During this section of the novel, Elizabeth engages in much reflection and soul-searching that has been triggered by the midpoint—the proposal and letter. Elizabeth returns to her home and decides not to expose Wickham's true character, even when her younger sister Lydia travels to Brighton with the militia. Elizabeth then takes a trip to Derbyshire with her aunt and uncle, and they visit Darcy's home, Pemberley. While they are there, Darcy's servants testify of his true character, and Darcy appears. He has changed—he goes out of his way to be friendly and polite to Elizabeth's aunt and uncle. Elizabeth wonders if she made the right decision in rejecting him, and they spend time together.

THE CLIMAX

In the climax, all the themes and conflicts of the novel come to a crisis, and it seems impossible for the characters to get what they want. Freytag writes that in or after the climax there should be a "tragic moment or force."[10]

In *Pride and Prejudice*, the tragic moment or force is when Elizabeth receives Jane's letters and learns that Lydia has run off with Mr. Wickham. This truly is a crisis, and the scene it causes is the climax of the novel: the point of greatest intensity, when everything the characters care about is at risk. The entire Bennet family will likely be ruined when word of this gets out, and Elizabeth will lose any chance of a good marriage. Further, she believes that now Mr. Darcy must despise her—everything he disliked about her family before pales in comparison to this. Mr. Darcy immediately leaves, and Elizabeth is certain that she will never see him again.

FALLING ACTION

The falling action is when all the final conflicts, questions, relationships, and subplots are addressed. Now the characters are fully put to the test: Can they resolve the problem of the climax and the larger problems of the narrative? Can the main characters create

---

10. Freytag, *Technique of the Drama*, 115.

a satisfactory resolution for themselves and others? Will they be able to use what they have learned throughout the story to address both internal and external challenges?

In some genres, the falling action includes a big final battle. Austen may not use an actual battle, but the stakes are just as high, and the circumstances challenge the characters to their limits.[11]

In *Pride and Prejudice*, Darcy proves himself in the falling action by finding Lydia and Wickham, pressuring them to marry, and providing them with financial support—all without taking any credit. He also brings Bingley and Jane back together.

Elizabeth returns home and provides support for her family members. Then, when Lady Catherine de Bourgh visits in an attempt to intimidate Elizabeth into submission (by requesting a promise never to enter into an engagement with Mr. Darcy), Elizabeth uses her pride in a useful way, to defend herself and stick to her principles. This event ultimately leads Darcy to realize that he still has a chance with Elizabeth.

THE FINAL SUSPENSE

In most stories, the falling action leads the characters in a particular direction, toward either success or tragedy. But then, as part of the falling action, they encounter what Freytag calls the final suspense. For Freytag, the final suspense is "a new, slight suspense; a slight hindrance ... thrown in the way of the already indicated direction of the end." In a tragedy, this final suspense could be "the distant possibility of a happy release."[12] In a comedy, drama, or any story with a happy ending, the final suspense throws a positive outcome into question—it seems possible, and perhaps even likely, that a happy resolution will not be achieved.

A final suspense is not a required component of the falling action, but it's generally helpful. Often, in this scene or sequence of scenes, other main questions and arcs are resolved. The final suspense can occur at any point within the falling action.

The falling action of *Pride and Prejudice* tends in a positive direction. In the external journey of the plot, we've seen good results for the entire Bennet family—Lydia married, Jane engaged, peace restored, ruin avoided. We've also seen good results for Darcy's and

---

11. The adaptation *Pride and Prejudice and Zombies* does use an actual battle. I find the film version absurdly delightful.
12. Freytag, *Technique of the Drama*, 130.

Elizabeth's internal journeys: They've changed and demonstrated internal strength. The final suspense, then, is the last test of their characters. Can Elizabeth and Darcy let go of their pride one last time and be fully reconciled to each other?

While some stories use a single moment of final suspense, Austen uses a sequence of scenes to throw Elizabeth and Darcy's relationship into question.

Mr. Bingley and Mr. Darcy return.
Illustration by Hugh Thomson, 1894.

When Mr. Bingley returns to Netherfield (and ultimately proposes to Jane), Mr. Darcy joins him. Elizabeth *knows* that it was Darcy who saved Lydia (and thus their entire family), so she hopes that Mr. Darcy might still be open to a relationship. Yet even though Elizabeth and Mr. Darcy spend time with each other—during a social call and during a sort of party at her home—he hardly speaks with her. After the first scene, Elizabeth asks herself, "Why, if he came only to be silent, grave, and indifferent ... did he come at all?" During the second scene, she says to herself,

"If he does not come to me, *then* … I shall give him up for ever."
After these two scenes, Mr. Darcy leaves, traveling to London. Mr.
Darcy's return to Meryton made Elizabeth think that perhaps he
might still like her, but now he is gone. Surely if he still had feelings
for her, he would, at the very least, have held a true conversation
with her. As part of the final suspense, it seems that Elizabeth and
Darcy will not find a happy ending.

This is followed by the previously mentioned chapter in which
Lady Catherine visits Longbourn in an attempt to persuade Elizabeth to break off her supposed engagement with Mr. Darcy.
Elizabeth admits that she is not engaged, but she refuses to agree
never to marry him. Lady Catherine leaves in a rage. In the next
chapter, Elizabeth reflects that if Mr. Darcy still feels anything
for her, then Lady Catherine will surely convince him to abandon these positive sentiments:

> If he had been wavering before, as to what he should do, which
> had often seemed likely, the advice and entreaty of so near a rela-
> tion might settle every doubt, and determine him at once to be
> as happy as dignity unblemished could make him.

*Lady Catherine informs Mr. Darcy of her conversation with
Elizabeth. Illustration by Hugh Thomson, 1894.*

A few days after Lady Catherine's visit, Mr. Bingley brings Mr. Darcy with him to Longbourn. While taking a walk, their group breaks into smaller parties, leaving Elizabeth and Darcy alone. This is the culmination of the final suspense: Will they, once again, not actually talk to each other?

Elizabeth takes the initiative and thanks Darcy for what he did for Lydia. Darcy expresses regret that she has discovered his role in helping the Bennets, and then he confesses, "I thought only of *you*."

The suspense is extended due to Elizabeth's reaction:

> Elizabeth was too much embarrassed to say a word.

Will Mr. Darcy interpret her silence as disdain or disgust? If so, their relationship might fail permanently. After a short pause, Darcy says,

> "You are too generous to trifle with me. If your feelings are still what they were last April, tell me so at once. *My* affections and wishes are unchanged; but one word from you will silence me on this subject for ever."

Elizabeth explains that her feelings have changed, and she accepts his proposal. This proposal, and Elizabeth's acceptance, contrasts strongly with the original proposal: They have let go of their prejudices and made themselves vulnerable to each other. This is the final resolution, a resolution that resolves the remaining core questions of the story.

DENOUEMENT

The denouement ties up loose ends, and the main characters end up better off than they were at the start of the novel. (The exception is tragedy, in which they end up worse off.) This section of the story often shows us a closing scene (or scenes) between the characters. In *Pride and Prejudice*, the narrator describes what happens next for everyone. The denouement is often short and should focus on the essentials for the characters and the story.

The denouement of *Pride and Prejudice* consists of two marriages: Jane to Bingley, and Elizabeth to Darcy. Other minor things are wrapped up: Kitty, we find, becomes "less irritable, less ignorant, and less insipid." Lady Catherine is "indignant," but ultimately "condescend[s] to wait on [Darcy and Elizabeth] at Pemberley." We learn of Mr. and Mrs. Bennet, the Collinses, the Wickhams, and the Gardiners, and we receive a glimpse of Elizabeth and Darcy's married life. And then we've reached the end of the story.

COMPLICATION AND UNRAVELING

The majority of *Pride and Prejudice* is spent on the complication, the rising action. Elizabeth Bennet strives to find her place in the world and navigate her relationships with others. She wants to make her own way, on her own terms, and she wants marriage only if accompanied by love and mutual respect. Characters are introduced, a series of situations and challenges arise, and she learns and grows. Then all comes to a crisis, and in the unraveling, all of the conflicts and character strivings are resolved in one way or another.

For Freytag, while plot and character are two very different forces, they must come together in the structure of the story. He writes,

> The structure of the drama must show these two contrasted elements of the dramatic joined in a unity, ... the accomplishment of a deed and its reaction on the soul, movement and counter-movement, strife and counter-strife, rising and sinking, binding and loosing.... What the drama presents is always a struggle, which, with strong perturbations of the soul, the hero wages against opposing forces.[13]

Understanding this big-picture plot structure and its overall movement is useful as we craft our stories. Throughout this book, we'll spend more time considering different moments within this external journey and what we can learn from how Austen crafts these moments. In Chapter 3, we'll dive more deeply into beginnings, exposition, and the inciting incident. In Chapter 6, we'll consider the rising action in more depth. And in Chapter 12, we'll focus on the climax, the falling action, the final suspense, and the denouement.

Not all stories use this narrative structure, and as previously mentioned, while Austen often uses this general structure, at times she breaks or plays with it (see *Northanger Abbey* and *Mansfield Park*). Yet it's a useful construct that helps us understand what

---

13. Freytag, *Technique of the Drama*, 104.

Elizabeth and Mr. Darcy converse after they become engaged.
Illustration by C. E. Brock, 1895.

readers expect from stories and what techniques are often effective at creating an external (and related internal) journey for the main character. The rising action, the sense of building, engages the reader. We become more and more invested in the story, and as a result, the falling action leaves us feeling satisfied.

Exercise 1.4: Charting Structure

Reread one of your favorite books or rewatch one of your favorite films, this time paying attention to structure. Plot the major events on a Freytag pyramid. If possible, include when the events occur within the story (by listing the page number for a book or the number of minutes into the film).

Exercise 1.5: A (Very) Short Story with an External Journey

Take something that happened during your day, an incident that was either positive or negative. This could be an interaction at work, the process of cooking something, a conversation with a child, etc. Write this as a very short story (maximum three paragraphs) with a beginning, middle, and end. Make sure to include an inciting incident, rising action, a midpoint, some sort of crisis, and then falling action, final suspense, and denouement. After writing, label the story elements by adding brackets with descriptions such as [Inciting Incident].

Exercise 1.6: Outline or Revise Using Freytag's Pyramid

Outline or brainstorm a story idea using Freytag's pyramid. You don't need to include every plot event, but make sure to include the key moments. (Even if you prefer to write without outlining, this can be a useful exercise to help internalize plot structure.)

If you already have a full draft of a novel, use Freytag's pyramid as a revision tool. Write the major plot points you've included on the pyramid and list the page numbers where these events occur in your manuscript. To take it up a notch, write down the characters' emotions and/or internal struggle at each of these key events.

Now analyze your pyramid:

- Are there any events that would be more effective if moved to a different part of the pyramid?
- Does the main character face enough struggle?
- At the climax, have you successfully put the main character in a spot where it seems impossible for them to succeed?
- Does the main character use what they have learned during the rising action to solve their problems during the falling action?

THE INTERNAL JOURNEY: CHARACTER ARC

Novels allow the reader insight into the human mind—it has been said that we can know the characters of well-written stories better than we can ever know anyone in real life. This insight into character is why we care about fiction.

As seen in the discussion of the plot of *Pride and Prejudice*, it is almost impossible to talk about an external journey without also discussing the internal journey. Without the internal journey, the external journey would be impossible—the characters would be unable to overcome their challenges. The inverse is also true: Without an external journey, pressure would not be applied to the character, and they would be less likely to experience internal change.

In a novel, the internal journey, or character arc, constantly intersects with the external journey. A character arc is not a straight line of progress. It includes failures and successes, embracing and resisting change. Ultimately, though, **our characters should learn and grow.**

As you create a character arc, consider how this arc is influenced by:

- What happens to the character
- The choices and decisions made by the character
- Moments of resisting change and moments of progress
- Who the character needs to become by the end of the novel

All of Austen's completed novels contain excellently crafted character arcs: Her main characters change, develop, and transform.

One example of transformation is Catherine Morland in *Northanger Abbey*. In the introduction to the Broadview edition, scholar Claire Grogan explains that over the course of the story, "Catherine becomes an adept reader not only of texts but also of people and of situations."[14]

---

14. Grogan, introduction to *Northanger Abbey*.

Catherine Morland reading. Artist unknown, 1833.

At first, Catherine is innocent and naive, which allows her to be manipulated by others, including by her friend Isabella's brother, John Thorpe. Even though Thorpe consistently interferes with her desires and other friendships, Catherine does not see him for who he is.

When Catherine meets John Thorpe, she is "fearful of hazarding an opinion of [her] own in opposition to that of a self-assured man." She finds herself constantly frustrated by Thorpe's speech and behavior, yet she distrusts her own judgment and does not read anything truly wrong into his character:

> These manners did not please Catherine; but he was James's friend and Isabella's brother; and her judgment was further

bought off by Isabella's assuring her, when they withdrew to see the new hat, that John thought her the most charming girl in the world.

As their relationship progresses, Catherine consciously decides to *not* read into his character, to ignore his flaws, and to allow him to override her plans. In this, she **resists change and development.**

> Little as Catherine was in the habit of judging for herself, and unfixed as were her general notions of what men ought to be, she could not entirely repress a doubt, while she bore with the effusions of his endless conceit, of his being altogether completely agreeable.

In this particular scene, Catherine spends extensive time with Isabella and John Thorpe. When she returns to her residence in Bath, she learns that doing so has caused her to miss an opportunity to spend time with her friend Miss Tilney and her romantic interest, Mr. Tilney. This leads her to conclude that "John Thorpe himself was quite disagreeable." Yet even though she reaches this conclusion, she still does not change how she interacts with him.

A few chapters later, Catherine plans a walk with Miss Tilney, but it happens to be at the same time as an outing arranged by John Thorpe. Jealous and vindictive, Thorpe ignores Catherine's wishes, goes to Miss Tilney, and cancels Catherine's walk.

When Catherine learns of this, she **takes action in a way that begins her path toward transformation and growth:** She decides to trust her own judgment and act decisively. Disregarding all of Isabella's and John's entreaties, she declares,

> "This will not do.... I cannot submit to this. I must run after Miss Tilney directly and set her right."

Catherine proceeds to do so. Throughout the rest of the novel, she gains more practice reading people and situations. Sometimes her judgment leads her false (as when she searches for clues of Mrs. Tilney's supposed murder), but over the course of the novel her ability to read situations improves and she allows this reading to inform and change her behavior.

Exercise 1.7: Creating a Character Arc

Pick a name for a character, and choose one of the following attributes:

- Courage
- Willingness to sacrifice for others
- Ambition
- Persistence
- Resourcefulness
- Thriftiness
- Ability to forgive others

Set a timer for ten minutes, and in that time make a list of the following four events to create a basic character arc for this character:

1. An event that shows that the character does not yet possess this attribute
2. An event that shows the character learning this attribute
3. An event that shows the character resisting or failing at the implementation of this attribute
4. An event that shows that the character has learned to incorporate this attribute into their lives

Exercise 1.8: Analyzing and Charting a Character Arc

Read a book or watch a movie, and as you do so, take notes on the main character. How do they change over the course of the story? What do they learn and how do they develop? How do they resist change? On a piece of paper, plot out the main points of their character arc. Visually, what type of line or arc would you draw to show their development?

Exercise 1.9: Your Character's Arc

Choose a story of your own that you are currently writing or revising. Write two or three sentences describing who the character must become by the end of the story. Then write two or three sentences describing who the character is at the start of the story.

Now, evaluate your character. A few things to consider:

- There needs to be enough distance between who the character is at the beginning of the story and who the character is at the end. In a novel, this distance will need to be much greater than in a short story.
- The character may need to learn multiple things.

- If your story is part of a series, the character needs to change or develop in new ways in each book.
- As the character develops and grows, the goal is not to make them "perfect" or eliminate all of the negative attributes that are a core part of their character.
- Often, more than one character has a character arc, and these arcs can intersect with each other, parallel each other, or interfere with each other.

THE EXPERIENCE OF THE JOURNEY

We read and listen to and watch stories because of their power: Stories can transport us outside of ourselves. Most of Austen's heroines love to read, from Elizabeth Bennet in *Pride and Prejudice* to Catherine Morland in *Northanger Abbey*. In *Mansfield Park*, Fanny Price's favorite books are those recommended by her cousin Edmund, and she tries to bring joy and expanded possibilities to her younger sister by introducing her to literature. In *Sense and Sensibility*, after Marianne's heartbreak and illness, she resolves to read for six hours a day, and in *Persuasion*, Anne sees prose as something that will assist Captain Benwick in moving forward from his personal tragedy and finding new purpose in his life.

Each of these characters turns to literature because its journeys provide a map for our own. When we read, we step out of ourselves and trust a narrator with our time and our thoughts and our emotions. Often as we read, we want what the character wants, or, in books like *Emma*, we're enraptured by Emma's attempt to get what she wants, even as we question the wisdom of it.

In the coming chapters, we'll consider crafting characters and the beginnings of stories, but as we go in depth into these topics, it is important to remember the larger internal and external journey for both your characters and your readers.

CHAPTER TWO

CHARACTER

"May I ask to what these questions tend?"

"Merely to the illustration of your character," said she, endeavouring to shake off her gravity. "I am trying to make it out."

"And what is your success?"

She shook her head. "I do not get on at all. I hear such different accounts of you as puzzle me exceedingly."

—*Pride and Prejudice*

E lizabeth spends much of *Pride and Prejudice* attempting to make out Mr. Darcy's character. We read, in large part, to do the same. As mentioned in the previous chapter, while in real life it can be difficult to truly understand those around us, through fiction we can see people's essence, their motivations and goals, and the ways in which these components of character influence their choices.

In a letter to her sister Cassandra on January 29, 1813, Austen wrote of her character Elizabeth, "I must confess that I think her as delightful a creature as ever appeared in print."[1] In another letter, she wrote that "Fanny's praise [of *Pride and Prejudice*] is very gratifying. My hopes were tolerably strong of her, but nothing like

---

1. Jane Austen to Cassandra Austen, January 29, 1813, *Letters of Jane Austen*.

a certainty. Her liking Darcy and Elizabeth is enough."[2] Austen understood that fascinating, compelling, and unusual events can occur in a story, yet as readers we don't care about the plot unless we care about the characters. But what makes her characters work, and why do we care about them? Further, how can we apply these techniques to our own stories?

It's easy to describe the notable character traits of both Elizabeth and Darcy. Elizabeth plays the pianoforte, likes reading and walking, is good at dancing, and is clever, witty, and judgmental. She is the second of five daughters and has little inheritance to speak of. She has a positive outlook on life and gets along well with those in her community and family. Mr. Darcy is rich, he likes reading, he's good at letter writing, and he's uncomfortable around people he doesn't know. He's a caring brother and a loyal friend. He is proud and unforgiving, and he expects much of others. He has a close relationship with Mr. Bingley and a complicated history with Mr. Wickham.

While these traits create a sketch of these characters, they don't capture the full essence, nor do they explain why readers feel attached to Darcy and Elizabeth. In the book *Story: Style, Structure, Substance, and the Principles of Screenwriting*, Robert McKee argues that the core component in a round or three-dimensional character is inner contradiction.[3] Contradictions make a character complex and compelling; they create a need for an internal journey.

Here are five types of contradictions that Austen uses to create multifaceted characters:
1. Contradictions between a character's wants and needs
2. Contradictions between the character's inner self and the world in which they live
3. Contradictions between how the character interacts with some characters and how they interact with others
4. Contradictions between the simultaneously held ideals of a character
5. Contradictions between a character's ideals and how they live

Elizabeth and Mr. Darcy both possess a number of contradictions.

---

2. Jane Austen to Cassandra Austen, February 1813, *Letters of Jane Austen*.
3. McKee, *Story*, 377–9.

Elizabeth	Mr. Darcy
Is critical of Mr. Darcy's pride but holds fast to her own	Is prideful, yet kindhearted and generous
Wants to avoid Mr. Darcy, yet finds herself drawn to him	Despises spending time with people he does not know, yet willingly attends events with Mr. Bingley because of their friendship
Only wants to marry for love, yet is pressured by society and her mother to accept any eligible match	
Instantly trusts Mr. Wickham and accepts his story, yet distrusts and judges Mr. Darcy's words	Feels the need to save Mr. Bingley from a connection to the Bennet family, but is unwilling to do the same for himself
Wittily expresses views that are not always her own	Expects Elizabeth to see and accept his virtues, yet says hurtful things to her

As I've crafted my own stories, I've found that a single contradiction can do more to build a character than a dozen characteristics. This works in both novels and short stories. I've written a number of flash fiction stories—all less than 1000 words—where the main characters feel multidimensional. In one, the reader only learns two things about the character: 1. She absolutely loves listening to live vocal performances; 2. She applied multiple times to vocal performance degrees in college, was rejected each time, and has since given up on singing. A contradiction is created between her love of music and her rejection of her own musical self, and this contradiction sets the stage for the story.

Authors craft characters using a multitude of methods. Some thoroughly plan their characters, filling out worksheets about their histories, characteristics, and preferences. Some writers focus on a few key details, like a contradiction or a character want, and develop the rest of a character while writing. Other writers discover their characters as they write. There's not a right or a wrong way to create characters, yet by the time we've finished revisions, our characters must be endowed with life.

Exercise 2.1: Create a Contradiction

Choose one of the following characteristics, attributes, or skills that could belong to a character: charitable, athletic, loves reading, hates traveling, good at cooking, prone to procrastination.

Create a contradiction related to this characteristic or attribute. (For ideas, see the list of types of contradictions.) Then reflect on how this contradiction could play out in a story.

Exercise 2.2: Finding the Essence

Set a timer for three minutes. During that time, brainstorm at least twenty details about a character. This could include their name, physical appearance, age, hobbies, occupation, family, past life events, character traits/personality, etc.

Next, take the character that you brainstormed and write a short description that attempts to capture **their essence.** What details are most important about them? Do they have any inner contradictions? What is their greatest want or desire? What makes them feel complex and nuanced? As you define the character's essence, you are welcome to make changes to your initial brainstorm.

CHARACTER NEEDS

In the first chapter, we discussed how character wants can drive the forward movement of the novel. Yet in addition to wants, characters also have needs. Often, a character is complex—or contradictory—because of a misalignment between their wants and needs. Even when a character's wants and needs align, the needs—the deeper problems and gaps in a character's life—give weight and consequence to their wants.

In *Emma*, Emma Woodhouse **wants** to be a matchmaker. This is her conscious desire.

Yet Emma is coming from a place of loss—she has lost her dear governess to marriage; previously, she lost her mother to death and her older sister to marriage. Now she is alone, with a hypochondriac father.

What Emma really **needs** is friendship and connection. Despite being one of the richest members of her community, she desperately needs to feel important and of value.

All characters have conscious wants and needs, things they actively seek. But they also have underlying wants and needs, which are often subconscious. Whether or not they are aware of these needs, they are a driving factor for the character's behavior.

Emma watches Harriet Smith speak to Mr. Robert Martin.
Illustration by Hugh Thomson, 1896.

Early in the novel, Emma befriends Harriet Smith and plans a match for her, to Mr. Elton. But then Mr. Martin, a farmer, proposes to Harriet.

On the surface level, if Harriet accepts Mr. Martin's proposal, Emma fails at getting what she wants: Her matchmaking will have come to naught.

But it is not just Emma's overlying want that is threatened, but also her underlying need, and we see this play out in the scene in which Emma manipulates Harriet into refusing Mr. Martin's proposal. As Harriet begins to conclude that she should reject Mr. Martin, Emma uses all her rhetorical powers to reinforce this decision:

At last, with some hesitation, Harriet said—

"Miss Woodhouse, as you will not give me your opinion, I must do as well as I can by myself; and I have now quite determined, and really almost made up my mind—to refuse Mr. Martin. Do you think I am right?"

"Perfectly, perfectly right, my dearest Harriet; you are doing just what you ought. While you were all in suspense I kept my feelings to myself, but now that you are so completely decided I have no hesitation in approving. Dear Harriet, I give myself joy of this. It would have grieved me to lose your acquaintance, which must have been the consequence of your marrying Mr. Martin. While you were in the smallest degree wavering, I said nothing about it, because I would not influence; but it would have been the loss of a friend to me. I could not have visited Mrs. Robert Martin, of Abbey-Mill Farm. Now I am secure of you for ever."

Harriet had not surmised her own danger, but the idea of it struck her forcibly.

Emma's need for friendship, connection, and self-importance drives this scene as much as her desire for matchmaking. To a certain degree, she recognizes her need, admitting that she opposes the marriage because she would lose Harriet as a friend. In prioritizing her own needs, she refuses to recognize or allow for Harriet's wants and needs.

When constructing characters, in addition to making sure they want something, you should also make sure that they have deeper, underlying needs.

One way to think about character needs is through the lens of psychology. Abraham Maslow writes about what motivates human behavior by focusing on what humans need.[4] He talks extensively about a **hierarchy of needs**, and others helpfully turned his model into a visual pyramid. Near the bottom of this pyramid are needs for **basic survival**—food, water, sleep, shelter, safety, and financial security. Further up the pyramid are needs related to **love and belonging**, whether that's a sense of connection or friendship, true intimacy or family, or being a true part of a community. Then Maslow talks about **esteem**—this could be respect from others,

---

4. Maslow's work is complicated, full of nuance, and does not necessarily present a complete picture from a modern social science perspective. It's often critiqued for its rigid order. Yet it can still be a useful model for discussing needs.

self-respect and self-esteem, public recognition for one's accomplishments, or a feeling of strength and wholeness. At the top of the pyramid is **self-actualization**—becoming one's fullest self, achieving one's potential, and expressing oneself creatively.[5]

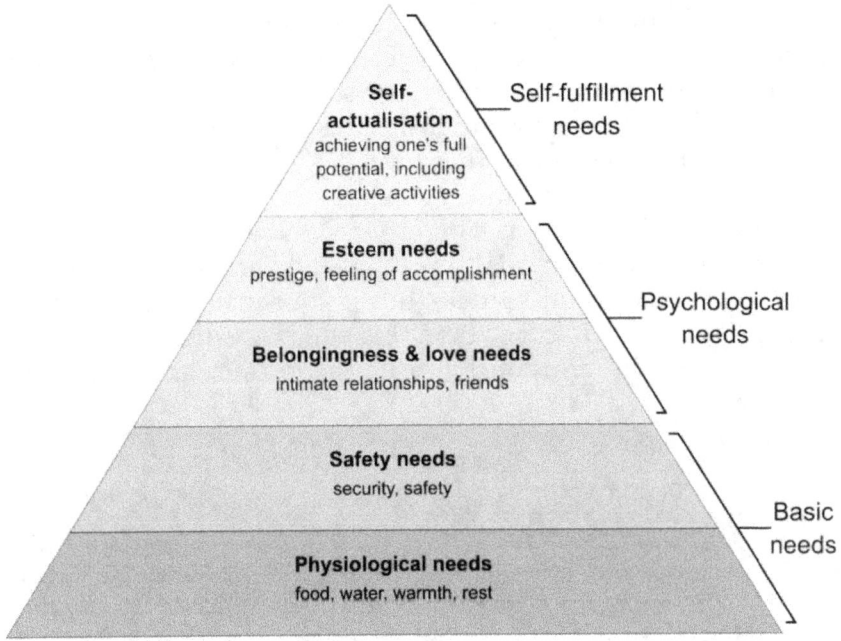

Maslow's Hierarchy of Needs.

In order to seek higher needs, often basic needs must be met. For instance, Maslow explains that "A person who is lacking food, safety, love, and esteem would most probably hunger for food more strongly than for anything else."[6] Basic survival trumps other needs. Yet as long as basic needs are met adequately, people may also seek after their higher needs, and many of our actions are motivated by needs on multiple levels of the pyramid.

These are not the only needs. Maslow also talks about personality needs—needs that derive from an individual's characteristics and the way they think about the world. Another common need

---

5. Maslow, "A Theory of Human Motivation."
6. Maslow, "A Theory of Human Motivation."

is "the desire to know and to understand."[7] Some needs are based on our cultures and on societal expectations. Your character may have other needs that don't fit neatly into Maslow's hierarchy but are just as essential.

Any intrinsic human need can be used to motivate your story's characters. Typically, you should choose one or two overarching needs that most drive your character. Your character may be aware of these needs, or the need might be subconscious. Sometimes, a character doesn't recognize their need at first but becomes aware of it through the course of the story.

Other smaller wants and needs may be manifest in individual scenes and interactions with other characters—Maslow argues that most people are "partially satisfied and partially unsatisfied in all of [our] wants" and needs[8]—but if your main character has a core want and a core need, then this will shape the overall arc of the story, both in terms of their external journey and their internal journey.

Exercise 2.3: A Need to Win

Teresa wants to win this year's chili cook-off. This is her **driving want** throughout a story. But **what does she need**? Choose one of the needs from Maslow's hierarchy. Is she trying to get recognition—and if so, why? Does she need acceptance, friendship, love? Will the prize money help her pay her rent?

Once you have chosen a need, write a short scene—probably two or three paragraphs—in which Teresa's actions, dialogue, and thoughts are influenced by both her want and her need. This scene could be when she signs up for the chili cook-off, when she's buying ingredients, as she's cooking, or during the judging.

Exercise 2.4: Analyzing Wants and Needs

Choose one of your favorite books or films. What is the main character's driving want in the story? What is the main character's driving need? How do the want and the need interact with each other—does the quest for one ever interfere with the quest for the other? Does the want or the need shift over time?

---

7. Maslow, "A Theory of Human Motivation."
8. Maslow, "A Theory of Human Motivation."

Exercise 2.5: Revising for Wants and Needs

Take a scene that you have written and analyze it for character wants and needs. Use one color to highlight lines or phrases that relate to the character's want(s), and another color to highlight lines or phrases that relate to the character's need(s). Some lines may be highlighted by both colors. How could you revise the scene with wants and needs in mind?

ACTIVE CHARACTERS

In 2012 I created a daily video blog. Every single day I posted a short video (5–30 seconds) of something interesting. As I worked on this project, I realized that I could only use certain types of videos:

1. A still shot (the camera not moving) with something moving inside the frame
2. A moving shot (the camera moving) with something moving inside the frame
3. A moving shot (the camera moving) with still objects

The only other option—a still shot with nothing moving—was not actually an option because that would be a photograph, not a video.

After a few weeks, I discovered that the best videos fit in categories 1 or 2. If something was moving in the frame, it attracted interest, regardless of what I did with the camera.

Our eyes are drawn immediately to things in motion. Our eyes, and often our hearts. This is the power of using active characters. Readers are drawn to active characters. Active characters are doing. Outside things may happen to them, but they are not just observers or reactors. They do not let themselves be pushed around or be determined by others. They go, they do, they strive.

Making your protagonist an active character creates a powerful story. This propels them on an external journey through the plot, with all its outward struggle and growth. It also propels them through an internal journey, facilitating character development, with its inner struggle and growth.

Both of the female leads in *Sense and Sensibility*—the two oldest Dashwood sisters—are active characters. The eldest sister, Elinor, actively steers her mother away from renting too expensive of a house, and she does much to ease the pain of others and make their cottage a home. Marianne actively refuses to let others play matchmaker for her and is guided by her own opinions and philosophies. Unlike Elinor, she is unafraid of offending others and is less circumscribed by a sense of decorum. She energetically attempts to find and make beauty in the world.

Their cottage is in an idyllic countryside, and on a somewhat blustery day, Marianne encourages her younger sister Margaret to walk with her:

> They gaily ascended the downs, rejoicing in their own penetration at every glimpse of blue sky; and when they caught in their faces the animating gales of a high south-westerly wind, they pitied the fears which had prevented their mother and Elinor from sharing such delightful sensations.
>
> "Is there a felicity in the world," said Marianne, "superior to this?—Margaret, we will walk here at least two hours."

Their walk, however, is cut short by the driving rain. Marianne is an active character, in charge of her own destiny, but even she cannot prevent the weather. Yet even in reacting to the weather, she resists passivity:

> Chagrined and surprised, they were obliged, though unwillingly, to turn back, for no shelter was nearer than their own house. One consolation however remained for them, to which the exigence of the moment gave more than usual propriety,—it was that of running with all possible speed down the steep side of the hill which led immediately to their garden gate.

Marianne is delightful because of her energy, her joyous outlook on life, and her refusal to do things in a simple, boring way.

As a result of her action, she hurts her ankle on the hill and is rescued by a charming gentleman, Mr. Willoughby, who carries her home.

*After her injury, Marianne is approached by Willoughby.
Illustration by Chris (Christiana) Hammond, 1899.*

Over the coming chapters, Marianne becomes quite attached to Willoughby. This worries Elinor, who *actively* encourages Marianne to be more careful with her affections. Marianne *actively* resists Elinor's advice.

> "You are mistaken, Elinor," said she warmly, "in supposing I know very little of Willoughby. I have not known him long indeed, but I am much better acquainted with him, than I am with any other creature in the world, except yourself and mama. It is not time or opportunity that is to determine intimacy;—it is disposition alone. Seven years would be insufficient to make some

people acquainted with each other, and seven days are more than enough for others. I should hold myself guilty of greater impropriety in accepting a horse from my brother, than from Willoughby. Of John I know very little, though we have lived together for years; but of Willoughby my judgment has long been formed."

While different in temper, disposition, and behavior, Elinor and Marianne are both active characters. An active character can be bold or shy, outspoken or quiet, and their actions can be grand or minute. Their key characteristic is that they are internally driven. An active character:

- Reaches for their goals or wants
- Engages in purposeful dialogue that attempts to have impact, persuade, or create change
- Takes actions—large or small—with purpose
- Asserts themselves and does things their own way when reacting to outside events

Yet no character is fully active. As writers, we shouldn't consider it a strict dichotomy between active and passive. No character is active all of the time—nor should they be. Moving a character along the spectrum of active and passive can be a part of their internal journey and a powerful storytelling technique.

Later in *Sense and Sensibility*, Marianne falls into a deep depression and becomes a largely inactive character. Her moments of activity—like taking a walk in bad weather—do her more harm than good. Her illness forces further inactivity upon her: At this point it is the doctor's treatment, the attentions of those who care about her, and fate that determine her future.

Yet the fact that Marianne is generally an active character both drives the story forward and creates audience investment. In her periods of passivity, we still root for her.

PASSIVE CHARACTERS

At times it can be useful to keep a character relatively passive for the entire story. Yet choosing to write a passive character—whether for a portion or the entire novel—is challenging. It is easier to effectively write an active character than a passive one, because interest and empathy are automatically given to active characters and must be gained in other ways by passive characters.

Austen's novel *Mansfield Park* features a generally passive main character: Fanny Price.

Fanny has spent years living with her aunt and uncle, the Bertrams. But then, they decide Fanny should live with her terrible aunt, Mrs. Norris. Fanny is surprised and upset, but she does not actively attempt to change her fate, though she does make a small complaint to her cousin Edmund. Fortunately, she is saved by outside forces: Mrs. Norris does not want her.

Later, the old horse she uses for exercise dies. This event happens *to* Fanny, and Fanny does nothing—in fact, because of her precarious situation, she cannot act. If she complains or attempts to create change, she risks losing her home.

Once again, someone else acts: Edmund eventually notices what this loss has done to Fanny and takes it upon himself to put things right.

After the arrival of the Grants and the Crawfords in the neighborhood, the narrator directly comments on Fanny's passivity:

> And Fanny, what was *she* doing and thinking all this while? and what was *her* opinion of the newcomers? Few young ladies of eighteen could be less called on to speak their opinion than Fanny.

Many readers find *Mansfield Park* more challenging to read than Austen's other novels. I would argue that this is in part because Fanny is a passive character for much of the novel, which makes it a bit less accessible. Fanny doesn't have a strong, forward-moving want or desire; at the beginning of the novel, she simply wants to be left alone. Fanny's passivity is essential for her internal journey, and she eventually finds a place for herself. And the external journey—the plot—focuses on what it means to be a character without power.

In many ways, Elizabeth Bennet actually begins as a passive character at the start of *Pride and Prejudice*. While she is active within scenes, and has interesting interactions and dialogue, it is Mrs. Bennet's want that drives the early movement of the story. Mrs. Bennet fervently desires to marry off her daughters, and in each of the early chapters, this want is manifest. As the story progresses, Elizabeth's wants become clearer. She wants to form relationships on her own terms. She wants to understand people and express her voice. And she wants to help those she cares about—especially Jane and Charlotte—in their relationships.

Just as Mrs. Bennet drives the forward movement at the start of *Pride and Prejudice*, other characters and events drive the forward movement in *Mansfield Park*: They organize a visit to Mr. Rushworth's estate and decide to stage a theatrical; Sir Thomas Bertram suddenly returns; Maria Bertram becomes engaged; Henry Crawford decides to pursue Fanny.

While in *Pride and Prejudice*, Elizabeth quickly becomes a more active character, in *Mansfield Park*, Fanny does not truly take action until the climax of the story (which we'll discuss in Chapter 12). Since Fanny is passive, Austen uses other techniques to maintain interest and forward movement.

1. INSTEAD OF A STRONG WANT, CREATE LARGE AND ESSENTIAL CHARACTER NEEDS.

At the beginning of the novel, some of Fanny's basic survival needs are not being met. She sleeps in a small room in the attic that does not have room "for walking about in and thinking." She can use one other small, unwanted room, but the Bertrams do not allow her to light a fire in it, even during the winter. She also lacks basic security: Mrs. Norris regularly reminds her that at any point, she could be thrown out for a transgression as small as expressing distaste for acting in a play.

As we move up Maslow's hierarchy of needs, we find that Fanny also possesses psychological needs: She needs basic kindness, she needs acceptance, she needs friendship. (While Edmund is her friend, many of his behaviors cause her harm; in Chapter 5, we will discuss how he sometimes acts as an antagonist.) Finally, Fanny needs love.

Fanny's needs create sympathy from the reader; we want her situation to improve.

2. MAKE PASSIVE CHARACTERS SYMPATHETIC AND/OR COMPETENT.
In the long-running, Hugo Award-winning podcast *Writing Excuses*, author Brandon Sanderson talks about an approach to characters that he calls character sliders.[9] For him, there are three sliders, or components, of character:

- Proactivity
- Sympathy/Relatability/Niceness
- Competence

Fanny Price and Mary Crawford.
Illustration by C. E. Brock, 1908.

9. *Writing Excuses*, season 9, episode 13, "Three Pronged Character Development."

These sliders are like sound mixing. When combined, they create characters. One slider may be set low and then move higher; another slider component may stay steady; one of the sliders may start high and then lower over the course of the novel. If a slider is really low—for example, if a character is extremely passive—then the character should probably be higher at one or both of the other sliders. Typically, the sliders do move up and down throughout the course of the novel.

In *Mansfield Park*, we sympathize with Fanny not only because of her situation but also because she has a high level of competence in a particular area: her sense of morality and her innate goodness. Because she is sympathetic and competent, we like her even though she is often passive.[10]

3. MAKE A PASSIVE CHARACTER'S THOUGHTS AND INTERIOR EMOTIONS REVEALING AND INSIGHTFUL.

Fanny's interiority is original and compelling. For example, as her cousins and their friends plan the theatrical, Fanny's internal thoughts engage the reader and provide additional insight:

> Fanny looked on and listened, not unamused to observe the self-ishness which, more or less disguised, seemed to govern them all, and wondering how it would end. For her own gratification she could have wished that something might be acted, for she had never seen even half a play, but everything of higher consequence was against it.

4. USE PASSIVE CHARACTERS AS A THEMATIC CHOICE OR TO PROVIDE SOCIAL COMMENTARY.

Fanny has few choices, and her situation forces passivity. Yet through it all, she finds inner strength and ultimately asserts herself, sometimes with dire consequences. Many readers who love *Mansfield Park* see part of themselves in Fanny; they admire her quiet steadiness and find her slow resistance both inspiring and empowering. Truly, in many life circumstances we don't have control. In Fanny Price, other readers see a critique of the slave trade and slave owners like Sir Thomas Bertram.

---

10. There are numerous techniques for creating sympathetic characters; we'll talk more about them in a few pages.

Whether you write a main character that is predominantly passive, or write an active character that experiences passive moments, passivity can be a powerful tool to give insight into the human experience. Shifts between passivity and activity can also be used to help create a compelling internal journey and show character growth.

Exercise 2.6: Purchasing an Antique or a Used Book

Write a short scene featuring a character in an antique store or a used bookstore. By the end of the scene, the character should purchase an item. Within the scene, the character's level of activity/passivity should change. They could:

- Start the scene active and become passive
- Start passive and become active
- Start passive and become even more passive
- Start active and become even more active
- Move back and forth several times between passive and active

Exercise 2.7: Favorite Active and Passive Characters

Select both a favorite active character and a favorite passive character from literature. These can be major or minor characters. Write down what makes them active or passive and why you like them. For the active character, list an example in which they are partially or fully passive; for the passive character, list an example in which they are partially or fully active. What is the impact of these moments on the story? If the character is always fully active or fully passive, how does this affect the narrative?

Exercise 2.8: The Active/Passive Scale

If you've drafted a novel or a short story, analyze each scene or chapter for where your main character falls on the spectrum from active to passive. Assign each scene or chapter a number from 1 to 10, with 10 being extremely active and 1 being extremely passive.

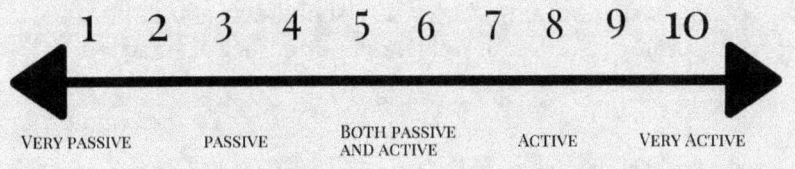

| 1 | 2 | 3 | 4 | 5 | 6 | 7 | 8 | 9 | 10 |

| VERY PASSIVE | PASSIVE | BOTH PASSIVE AND ACTIVE | ACTIVE | VERY ACTIVE |

What sort of arc or movement is created by the main character's shifts along the passive-active scale? Are there scenes in which your character should be more active or passive? How should the active and passive moments connect to the character's internal and external journey?

SYMPATHETIC CHARACTERS

In a letter to her niece Fanny Knight in March 1817, Jane Austen mentioned that she had a new novel, nearing readiness for publication: "You will not like it, so you need not be impatient. You may perhaps like the heroine, as she is almost too good for me."[11]

Jane Austen died a few months after her letter, but her family published the novel posthumously. That novel is *Persuasion*, and its heroine, Anne Elliot, is—despite Austen's self-deprecating comments—a true gift to readers.

Anne Elliot is a prime example of a sympathetic character. She broke off an engagement with Captain Wentworth almost eight years before the start of the novel, and now he is back in her life. She wonders—and we wonder, with just as much desperation and longing—if she will have a second chance with him.

A **sympathetic character** is a character who we feel compassion for and connection to. It is a character that we find likable. We want good things to happen to sympathetic characters.

The *Oxford English Dictionary* (*OED*)—the largest English dictionary in the world—goes into great depth in defining the word **sympathy.** One of the first definitions is as follows:

> A (real or supposed) affinity between certain things, by virtue of which they are similarly or correspondingly affected by the same influence, affect or influence one another, ... or attract or tend towards each other.[12]

---

11. Jane Austen to Fanny Knight, March 23, 1816. *Letters of Jane Austen.*
12. *Oxford English Dictionary*, "sympathy (n.), sense 1.a."

The OED cites an example from 1601 that talks about the sympathy between iron and lodestone—in other words, sympathy is like a magnet and a paperclip. There is some inherent similar quality that creates an attraction between them.

One of the main reasons we turn to literature is because **stories create feelings of sympathy.** We see ourselves in literature. **Stories change us.** We become part of the experience in the text, and the text becomes part of our own experience.

In the latter half of *Persuasion*, Anne attends a concert with her family. Captain Wentworth is present. Anne and Wentworth have a nice conversation before the concert, but during the concert Anne is seated next to another man, Mr. Elliot. We see ourselves in Anne as she tries and fails to catch Wentworth's eye. We feel Anne's frustrations with Mr. Elliot's flirtation; like her, we cannot truly be interested in him. We are one with Anne as she manages to change seats, placing her at the edge of a row, with the possibility of talking to Wentworth.

Anne and Captain Wentworth speak before the start of the concert.
Illustration by C. E. Brock, 1909.

Captain Wentworth leaves before the concert is over.

> "He must wish her good night; he was going; he should get home as fast as he could."
>
> "Is not this song worth staying for?" said Anne, suddenly struck by an idea which made her yet more anxious to be encouraging.
>
> "No!" he replied impressively, "there is nothing worth my staying for;" and he was gone directly.
>
> Jealousy of Mr. Elliot! It was the only intelligible motive. Captain Wentworth jealous of her affection! Could she have believed it a week ago; three hours ago! For a moment the gratification was exquisite. But, alas! there were very different thoughts to succeed. How was such jealousy to be quieted? How was the truth to reach him? How, in all the peculiar disadvantages of their respective situations, would he ever learn of her real sentiments? It was misery to think of Mr. Elliot's attentions. Their evil was incalculable.

A character is sympathetic when we as readers can understand the character's perspective and/or relate to the character's motives and actions.

Anne is an especially sympathetic character in this scene. The scene is in Anne's point of view, and the narration makes it easy to understand Anne's perspective on the situation, her history with Wentworth, and her desires. We are aided by internal thought as the narration slips into Anne's mind and thoughts. We'll talk more about these techniques in Chapter 4, on stance, and in Chapter 7, on emotion.

This scene also helps us understand Wentworth's perspective. While he is not the point-of-view character, his **perspective is revealed through his dialogue and behavior**. We can understand him as a person, and we feel a shared humanity with him.

In this scene, we relate to Anne's **motives**, especially in her desire to fix things between her and Wentworth. Her **actions** are logical for the situation.

As a reader, I personally don't always relate to Anne. For example, early in the novel, Anne avoids an in-depth conversation with Captain Wentworth. I would probably act differently in the situation. Yet because I can understand *why* she's making her choices, I still find her sympathetic.

Another definition of sympathy from the OED is "a favourable attitude of mind towards a party, cause, etc.; disposition to agree or approve."[13]

We feel favorably when characters take actions that we can agree with or approve of, and as people, we generally approve of kind, good, and self-sacrificing acts.

Jane Austen often critiqued stories written by her niece Anna. In one letter, Jane recommends that a character perform a specific, outwardly good action that would help the reader sympathize more with the character:

> What can you do with Egerton to increase the interest for him? I wish you could contrive something, some family occurrence to bring out his good qualities more. Some distress among brothers and sisters to relieve by the sale of his curacy! ... If you could invent something spirited for him, it would have a good effect. He might lend all his money to Captain Morris, but then he would be a great fool if he did. Cannot the Morrises quarrel and he reconcile them?[14]

Later writers have given similar advice. In the screenwriting book *Save the Cat!*, Blake Snyder talks about the need for the audience to feel sympathy for the main character early on. He encourages writers to include a **"save the cat"** moment.[15] In some films, the main character literally saves a cat, but any good, kind, self-sacrificing act can serve the same purpose.

Near the beginning of *Persuasion*, Anne has a strong "save the cat" moment. Anne's nephew is ill, which will prevent her sister Mary from dining out at another family's house. Mary vocally and desperately expresses her desire to attend the dinner—she does not want to miss out on a social gathering. Anne has what could be considered better desires to attend: She could see Captain Wentworth, who she hasn't seen since breaking off their engagement.

Anne decides to care for her nephew to help her sister:

---

13. *Oxford English Dictionary*, "sympathy (n.), sense 3.d."
14. Jane Austen to Anna Austen, September 28, 1814. *Letters of Jane Austen*.
15. Snyder, *Save the Cat!*

She knew herself to be of the first utility to the child; and what was it to her if Frederick Wentworth were only half a mile distant, making himself agreeable to others?

A "save the cat" moment can help create sympathy for any character, major or minor. For instance, if you want to develop sympathy for an antagonist, have them do something good or kind for another character.

Early in the novel, Captain Wentworth does something kind for Anne by helping her with her nephew. Illustration by Hugh Thomson, 1897.

There are a number of other techniques that can be used to create sympathy.

We find characters sympathetic when we can commiserate with their struggles.

The OED also defines sympathy as "the quality or state of being thus affected by the suffering or sorrow of another; a feeling of compassion or commiseration."[16]

In *Mansfield Park*, we sympathize with Fanny Price because of the poor way others treat her. Generally, readers sympathize with suffering (though too much suffering can make a character feel pitiable, and readers may find it too hard or uncomfortable to sympathize).

We like to root for underdogs, for people who have to prove themselves.

Anne Elliot is undervalued by her father and sisters; in the opening scenes of the novel, they dismiss her ideas and advice. Further, we see Anne suffering when Wentworth pursues another woman, and we feel for Anne in these moments. These scenes make Anne sympathetic.

We sympathize with characters who have flaws.

In literature, characters are often better than ourselves: They are a little more consistent, a little more understandable. They can be better examples of certain virtues or ideologies.

Yet if characters are too good or too perfect or too smart or too capable, we stop sympathizing with them. In real life, we often don't like people who seem too perfect; we feel more distance between us and characters that seem so much greater or better than us, because they are not like us.

Sympathetic characters must be like us; they must have weaknesses. They must try and they must fail, repeatedly, because it is trying and failing and trying again that makes us human.

Anne's weaknesses are plenty: She is easily persuadable. She veils her emotions. She does not stand up for herself. And because of this, she feels real and we sympathize with her struggles and failures and attempts to achieve her goals.

Sympathetic characters model traits we see as admirable, especially in times of difficulty.

---

16. *Oxford English Dictionary*, "sympathy (n.), sense 3.c."

In *Pride and Prejudice*, Elizabeth is sympathetic largely because of the way that she deals with negative situations and difficult people. One challenging person in her life is her mother. At various points, Mrs. Bennet does all of the following:

- Insults Elizabeth and makes statements that favor Jane and Lydia
- Commandeers events and gatherings in order to find marriage partners for her daughters
- Acts in ways that embarrass Elizabeth
- Is overly dramatic and easily upset
- Becomes angry when Elizabeth refuses Mr. Collins, even threatening to disown her

Despite the constant provocations, Elizabeth consistently reacts to her mother in a levelheaded way. She doesn't match her mother's extreme emotions. At times, she attempts to help her mother, and at other times, she holds her ground. She uses humor and wit in difficult situations, rather than falling into despair.

In the podcast *Writing Excuses*, the hosts argue that characters are sympathetic when they are self-aware, open, and vulnerable.[17] Elizabeth is aware of her prejudice against Mr. Darcy and for Mr. Wickham, and this self-awareness makes her prejudices—and resulting actions—more powerful. Elizabeth is open about her emotions and thoughts to her sister Jane and at times to her friend Charlotte and to other characters. Once again, this creates sympathy for her. And her vulnerability—like the times when she feels personal pain at Jane's pain—also makes us sympathize with her. Her self-awareness, openness, and vulnerability are admirable, sympathetic traits.

ॐ ☙

A character does not need to possess all possible positive traits in order to be found sympathetic. Elizabeth Bennet responds to struggle with humor; Anne Elliot does not. One reader might relate to Anne's story of lost love; another reader might relate to Elizabeth's close relationships with her family members. Yet both characters are sympathetic.

---

17. *Writing Excuses*, season 9, episode 25, "Adjusting Character Sympathy."

Like with active and passive, there is a spectrum between sympathetic and unsympathetic characters, and characters typically move up and down this spectrum over the course of a story. Whether your character is mostly or only occasionally sympathetic, it helps the reader connect to the story. We root for these characters and are excited to travel with them on their journeys.

UNSYMPATHETIC CHARACTERS

In order to make characters unsympathetic, you often use the reverse techniques, including:

- Giving the character unrelatable motives and actions
- Giving the character an unrelatable perspective (in the case of a non-viewpoint character, sometimes the elements that form the character's perspective—their background and their situation—are unknown to the reader, which makes it more likely that we will perceive the character and their choices as unsympathetic)
- Having the character act in unlikable ways. At times, they might be cruel, unkind, or selfish. If they hurt others, they are particularly unsympathetic (we especially dislike when characters hurt a different character, animal, or object that we care about as readers)
- Making the character too perfect or too imperfect (or too miserable in their circumstances)
- Having the character not learn from their mistakes and forgo opportunities to improve
- Making the character not self-aware

It is challenging to effectively write an unsympathetic yet engaging main character, yet Austen does so in the title character of *Emma*. The techniques she uses can be applied to writing unsympathetic protagonists, antagonists, or supporting characters; these techniques can also be used for characters who are unsympathetic for a portion of the story.

As Emma befriends Harriet, she learns of Harriet's romantic interest in Mr. Martin, whom Emma considers inferior. One day, as Harriet and Emma take a walk, they see Mr. Martin, and Harriet speaks with him briefly. Afterward, an excited Harriet asks Emma,

> "Well, Miss Woodhouse, is he like what you expected? What do you think of him? Do you think him so very plain?"
>
> "He is very plain, undoubtedly—remarkably plain:—but that is nothing compared with his entire want of gentility. I had no right to expect much, and I did not expect much; but I had no idea that he could be so very clownish, so totally without air. I had imagined him, I confess, a degree or two nearer gentility."
>
> "To be sure," said Harriet, in a mortified voice, "he is not so genteel as a real gentleman."

Emma's words are almost shockingly cruel. Her unsympathetic words and actions derive from her faulty judgment, her selfish motives, her wants, and her needs. She truly believes she is saving her friend. Though we understand Emma's perspective, we are not meant to relate to it, and instead, we latch on to Mr. Knightley's criticism of Emma's behavior.

REDEEMING QUALITIES

Though Emma consistently acts in unsympathetic ways, we keep reading because of her redeeming qualities:

- She is witty and intelligent
- She can be humorous (and the narrator is particularly funny)
- Others in the community respect and like her
- She is active and engaging

These redeeming qualities create some level of sympathy for Emma. **In most cases, unsympathetic characters should still have sympathetic qualities, especially if they are the protagonist.**

Even though her judgment can be faulty and her actions unkind, sometimes Emma shows good judgment and an awareness of the needs and desires of others. For instance, Emma's father hates marriage and is upset that Miss Taylor has become Mrs. Weston:

"Poor Miss Taylor!—I wish she were here again. What a pity it is that Mr. Weston ever thought of her!"

"I cannot agree with you, papa; you know I cannot. Mr. Weston is such a good-humoured, pleasant, excellent man, that he thoroughly deserves a good wife;—and you would not have had Miss Taylor live with us for ever, and bear all my odd humours, when she might have a house of her own?"

In this moment, Emma's good judgment contrasts with the poor judgment of her father. This draws attention to this redeeming quality. **We become invested in unsympathetic characters when they are more sympathetic (in one or more areas) than their fellow characters.**

Mr. Woodhouse laments that Miss Taylor has married. Illustration by Chris (Christiana) Hammond, 1898.

SELF-AWARENESS

Giving Emma a small dose of self-awareness is another way Austen makes this unsympathetic character just sympathetic enough. If Emma were completely self-aware, she would realize the terrible consequences of her actions much earlier in the novel. Yet despite her many blinders, even early on she shows a certain level of self-awareness, particularly in her animosity toward Jane Fairfax, a long-time acquaintance who has come to stay in Highbury. Here's an excerpt from a rather lengthy passage (with emphasis added):

> Emma was sorry;—to have to pay civilities to a person she did not like through three long months!—*to be always doing more than she wished, and less than she ought!* Why she did not like Jane Fairfax might be a difficult question to answer; Mr. Knightley had once told her it was because she saw in her the really accomplished young woman, which she wanted to be thought herself; and though the accusation had been eagerly refuted at the time, there were moments of self-examination in which her conscience could not quite acquit her....
>
> *It was a dislike so little just—every imputed fault was so magnified by fancy, that she never saw Jane Fairfax the first time after any considerable absence, without feeling that she had injured her;* and now, when the due visit was paid, on her arrival, after a two years' interval, she was particularly struck with the very appearance and manners, which for those two whole years she had been depreciating. Jane Fairfax was very elegant, remarkably elegant; and she had herself the highest value for elegance.

Emma is aware of her own unfairness, and she recognizes that her dislike is unjust. Yet as the scene progresses, she continues to justify her negative thoughts and actions, placing much of the blame on Jane. She won't sit with her self-awareness and allow it to change her behavior, but the awareness she shows makes readers more willing to listen to her unfair complaints and judgments.

REASONS TO CREATE AN UNSYMPATHETIC CHARACTER

As writers, we often want our characters to be likable and good, yet unsympathetic characters create tension, drama, and conflict. Humans do unsympathetic things all the time, and it's inherently interesting to explore this aspect of human nature. Unsympathetic characters have a greater potential to grow and change. When sympathetic characters behave in unsympathetic ways, it creates contrast with the key scenes of internal triumph, when the character makes admirable, sympathetic choices that we can really root for.

Emma's internal journey is about her rethinking her place in the community, learning to be kinder, and allowing others to choose what is best for themselves. She shows tremendous growth over the novel, in large part because she begins as an unsympathetic character.

Exercise 2.9: Sympathy Reversal

Write a brief scene of a character doing something that we generally find unsympathetic (e.g., taking a toy from a young child, ripping up a student's paper, etc.). Write this scene in a way that will make a reader feel sympathy for this character.

Exercise 2.10: Sympathy Analysis

Take a short story or a novel and choose two characters, one sympathetic and the other unsympathetic. Find specific passages that make these characters feel sympathetic or unsympathetic. What tools does the author use to achieve these effects?

Exercise 2.11: Fairy Tale Swap

Choose a classic fairy tale and select two characters: one who is generally seen as sympathetic (e.g., Cinderella) and another who is generally seen as unsympathetic (e.g., the wicked stepmother). Write a scene between these two characters, but in this scene reverse who is sympathetic and who is not.

EXPERIENCING THE CHARACTER

Character is our window into the story world: We experience the characters' journeys with them. Like the characters in our favorite stories, we, as readers, are filled with contradictions. We have wants and needs. At times we are active players in our lives, and at other times we are passive. We behave in both sympathetic and unsympathetic ways. And so, as we read, we see ourselves on the page.

Gustav Freytag wrote that "the dramatist compels the listener to repeat his creations. The whole world of characters, of sorrow, and of destiny, the hearer must make alive in himself."[18] While Freytag was writing specifically about playwrights and theatergoers, this applies to all storytellers and their audiences. The words we write on the page are repeated in the minds of our readers; our characters and other creations become alive in the imaginations and hearts of the audience.

In the next chapter, we'll look in more depth at the beginnings of stories. We'll find that characters are often introduced in moments of tension, action, and dialogue. We'll see the role of disruption in sending the characters on their journeys, so both the characters and the audience can experience transformation.

---

18. Freytag, *Technique of the Drama*, 93.

CHAPTER THREE

BEGINNINGS

"If adventures will not befall a young lady in her own village, she must seek them abroad."

—Northanger Abbey

In *Northanger Abbey*, the narrator spends the first chapter cheekily setting up Catherine Morland as an unexpected heroine who must seek out adventures. For these adventures, Catherine has developed many incredibly useful traits. For instance, despite being unable to write sonnets, "she [can bring] herself to read them," and while she can't transport "a whole party into raptures" through her skills at the pianoforte, "she [can] listen to other people's performance with very little fatigue." She has also filled her mind with novels, poetry, and Shakespeare, so she is ready to draw upon "quotations which are so serviceable and so soothing." The narrator promptly gives us a list of these quotations, which includes a passage from Shakespeare that explains that squished beetles feel as much pain as dying giants. If that's not a serviceable and soothing reference, then what is? The first chapter also establishes her childhood, her love of playing cricket and baseball, and, perhaps most importantly for the story, the fact that she has never experienced romance:

> She had reached the age of seventeen, without having seen one amiable youth who could call forth her sensibility, without having inspired one real passion, and without having excited even any admiration but what was very moderate and very transient. This was strange indeed!

The function of the beginning of a story is to establish the story, engage the reader, and set up expectations. In other words, the author presents a **reader-writer contract**, an agreement between the reader and the writer. In the opening chapters, the writer has an opportunity to make promises: the chosen genre, the main conflict, the themes, the storytelling stance, the point of view, the role of the narrator, and the sorts of characters and plots the reader will encounter. If the reader chooses to continue reading, they expect the contract to be carried out. When promises are kept, it creates a fulfilling experience; if the promises made at the start of the story are not kept, the reader may feel betrayed.

I've always loved *Northanger Abbey*, but some readers dislike it because it feels different than Austen's other novels. It's humorous and witty, but if you're expecting *Pride and Prejudice*, you will be disappointed. In essence, *Northanger Abbey* sets up a different reader-writer contract. Yet the contract is still clear—this story will be a humorous pastiche (an imitation) of the Gothic novel, with the narrator commenting on the conventions of the genre and at times even speaking directly to the reader.[1] The story will contain a romance, and Catherine will experience adventures abroad. Catherine Morland is established as an unexpected heroine, naive, inexperienced, and with much to learn.

In Chapter 1, we talked briefly about beginnings and the role of exposition and the inciting incident in the plot. In this chapter we'll consider them in more depth. We will explore different options for when to start a story and analyze Austen's techniques for setting up key information and starting the character's journeys.

---

1. While at times *Northanger Abbey* seems to parody the Gothic novel, it ultimately embraces and redeems the form.

EXPOSITION

Story is about change. But in order for us to see change, we must experience the characters and their world before the change occurs. This is the **exposition**—characters, relationships, situations, and settings in stasis. The exposition provides the background information the readers need to know about the characters, their history, and their world. The situation can be good or bad. The characters may already have wants and needs, though these will often change with the inciting incident. The protagonist existed as an individual before the start of the plot; the exposition gives us a window into that existence before it is disrupted and put on a new trajectory.

According to the *New Oxford American Dictionary*, the word exposition comes from the Latin verb *exponere*, which means to "put out, exhibit, [or] explain."[2] Freytag writes that the exposition must "set forth what [is] naturally prerequisite to the action."[3]

In *Emma*, the first four paragraphs provide the exposition, beginning with the following opening lines:

> Emma Woodhouse, handsome, clever, and rich, with a comfortable home and happy disposition, seemed to unite some of the best blessings of existence; and had lived nearly twenty-one years in the world with very little to distress or vex her.

This quickly paints an image of Emma's character, her place in society, and her general satisfaction with life.

In the second paragraph, the narrator brings up key details from Emma's past and sets up the world and her place in it:

- Emma is the second daughter.
- Her sister is married and gone.
- She is the mistress of the house (or basically, the female manager of it).
- Her father is "affectionate" and "indulgent."
- Her mother died when she was very young.
- Her governess loved her as much as a mother would.

---

2. *New Oxford American Dictionary*, "exposition," 611.
3. Freytag, *Technique of the Drama*, 31.

That's a lot of information for a two-sentence paragraph: Austen manages to swiftly set the stage.

The third paragraph provides more details about Emma's governess, Miss Taylor, in order to demonstrate the disruptiveness of the inciting incident:

- Miss Taylor has been with the family for sixteen years.
- She is more of a friend or sister figure than a governess.
- She does not restrain or direct Emma (and has not for quite some time).
- "They had been living together as friend and friend very mutually attached, and Emma doing just what she liked; highly esteeming Miss Taylor's judgment, but directed chiefly by her own."

Then, the fourth paragraph **raises the themes and issues that will be explored throughout the story**. In this case, it's a look into Emma's flaws and how these flaws will drive the narrative:

> The real evils, indeed, of Emma's situation were the power of having rather too much her own way, and a disposition to think a little too well of herself; these were the disadvantages which threatened alloy to her many enjoyments. The danger, however, was at present so unperceived, that they did not by any means rank as misfortunes with her.

By the time we reach the fifth paragraph, all the essential details have been explained, and we are prepared to learn of the inciting incident: Miss Taylor's marriage.

We learn more backstory as the novel progresses—details about the past and about Emma's relationships with others in her community—but these are not included in the initial exposition because they are not essential for setting the stage. Freytag warns that "the exposition should be kept free from anything distracting," and that the writer "must take heed that he simplify it as much as possible."[4]

Stylistically, it's more common today to present the exposition in a scene rather than as a narrator's commentary and summary. In this case, the summary works because of the narrator's distinctive

---

4. Freytag, *Technique of the Drama*, 120 and 28.

voice and role in interpreting the story. Yet this same information could be conveyed through character interactions, action, conflict, and dialogue; film adaptations generally present the exposition of *Emma* in scene. Austen's other novels take different approaches to the exposition, some presenting it in scene, while others use a mixture of scene and summary. We'll discuss choices about scene and summary in the next chapter, but regardless of how the exposition is presented, it sets the stage for the story and orients the reader.

Exercise 3.1: Exposition Snapshot

Write a few paragraphs that introduce a character and their world. The character should be traveling somewhere, using any form of transportation (metro, bus, car, bike, etc.). Try to quickly set the stage by using as little information as possible while still evoking complexity and life. In this exposition snapshot, include the following:

- A few details about the setting that reveal something about the character
- A few salient physical characteristics or outward behaviors that, once again, reveal character
- A brief yet insightful interaction with another character
- A brief reference to a past event that informs who the character is today

INCORPORATING BACKSTORY

While exposition provides the essential information about the world and the characters before their journeys begin, **backstory** is the entire history of the characters, their situations, and their communities. Exposition is most often incorporated at the start of the story, while backstory can be included at any point. If backstory is a set of twenty encyclopedias, exposition is a snapshot of a present moment, which often includes a few references to the encyclopedia.

Backstory is important—it provides weight and context, and it helps the reader understand the characters' motives, relationships, and various aspects of the plot. For example, the exposition of *Persuasion* introduces Sir Walter Elliot and sets up his relationships with various family members, neighbors, and friends. One of the most important relationships for the story is with his daughter Anne:

> Anne, with an elegance of mind and sweetness of character, which must have placed her high with any people of real understanding, was nobody with either father or sister; her word had no weight, her convenience was always to give way—she was only Anne.

A little backstory is then provided to show how their relationship reached this point:

> A few years before, Anne Elliot had been a very pretty girl, but her bloom had vanished early; and as even in its height, her father had found little to admire in her, (so totally different were her delicate features and mild dark eyes from his own), there could be nothing in them, now that she was faded and thin, to excite his esteem.

These brief sentences paint a revealing picture of Anne's role in the family, and the backstory helps us understand that her subordinate place is not a new event. She does not possess—even at her most attractive, she did not fully possess—the traits found valuable in her home. As such, she has no ability to persuade or influence her family; she has no power. Her initial powerlessness is essential for understanding her character and behavior, especially in the first third of the story.

Most backstory is never mentioned in a story—readers don't want or need to know the thousands of past events that inform the character and their community. And most writers create backstory selectively: You don't need to have figured out every aspect of a character's life or a town's history in order to create a story. However, it is often useful to figure out more backstory than will be needed on the page—understanding the characters' lives and their pasts will inform your choices in subtle yet essential ways.

When backstory is included, it should be included in moderation in order to avoid an **infodump**, an excess of information

Sir Walter admires his personal appearance.
Illustration by C. E. Brock, 1909.

that pulls the reader out of the narrative. When large quantities of backstory are given to the reader all at once, none of the information has purpose or weight, and the reader loses interest in the story. An infodump feels like a pile of trash on the beach: We want to either avoid it or dispose of it.

Instead of creating a pile of information, consider how to incorporate individual elements of backstory. A soda can might feel like garbage in a trash pile on the beach, but if we encounter it on its own, it can have weight. We might see someone drinking it—it might bring up an interesting recollection of a past event or situation. Or if it's abandoned next to a sandcastle, we learn things about the person who drank from the can.

The author Jo Walton talks about the benefits of what she calls **incluing**, or "the process of scattering information seamlessly through the text, as opposed to stopping the story to impart the information."[5] Austen is a master of incluing, of weaving moments of backstory throughout both the exposition and the entire story.

As mentioned in the previous chapter, much of *Persuasion* focuses on Anne Elliot's relationship with Captain Wentworth. Yet the exposition does not include any information about their backstory. Instead, the exposition provides information about the Elliots' financial troubles.

In order to remain financially solvent, the Elliots decide to rent out their home, Kellynch Hall. This is the inciting incident, the force of disruption and change. In the third chapter, they discuss a possible tenant: Admiral Croft. When Sir Walter speaks negatively of the Navy, Anne replies,

> "The navy, I think, who have done so much for us, have at least an equal claim with any other set of men, for all the comforts and all the privileges which any home can give."

This is subtle backstory—it's something she says in the moment, in response to her father's prejudice. Yet it reveals her attitude toward those who serve in the Navy.

A few pages later, Anne is able to share specific details about Admiral Croft's career: He fought in Trafalgar and has been stationed in the East Indies. **Once again, this provides key backstory.** We learn that Anne knows much more about the Crofts than anyone in her family, yet we don't yet know why she knows this information.

A few pages later, another character mentions that years ago, a visitor to the area had some sort of connection to Admiral Croft. After a pause, Anne volunteers a single detail.

> "You mean Mr. Wentworth, I suppose?" said Anne.

Her hesitation and lack of detail hint further at a connection between Anne and this family.

---

5. Walton, "Thud: Half a Crown & Incluing."

Ultimately, Sir Walter Elliot decides that he will allow Admiral Croft to rent the estate. The third chapter ends with this sentence:

> No sooner had such an end been reached, than Anne, who had been a most attentive listener to the whole, left the room, to seek the comfort of cool air for her flushed cheeks; and as she walked along a favourite grove, said, with a gentle sigh, "a few months more, and *he*, perhaps, may be walking here."

In this moment, we see Anne's current emotions and thoughts, but backstory is also revealed: We sense that her past includes a love lost.

At many points throughout the third chapter, Austen could have provided an infodump, and it might have even felt natural. Yet by spreading the information, piece by piece, it allows the scene to build, provokes our curiosity, gives crucial insight into Anne's character, and prepares us for the next chapter, when we are given a larger amount of backstory:

> *He* was not Mr. Wentworth, the former curate of Monkford, however suspicious appearances may be, but a Captain Frederick Wentworth, his brother.

The narrator then describes Captain Wentworth's situation years before and how he and Anne met and fell in love. It tells us of their short engagement, as well as how Sir Walter and Lady Russell had convinced Anne to break it off.

This is a lot of backstory, but by this point, we care about Anne, and this backstory has meaning for us. It doesn't feel like an infodump—by this point, we are thirsting to know. Austen uses several additional techniques to weave in backstory.

PROVIDE ENOUGH CONTEXT TO ORIENT THE READER, THEN ADD INFORMATION AND BACKSTORY AS THE CHARACTERS INTERACT WITH PRESENT EVENTS.

For example, the town of Uppercross is mentioned on the very first page of the novel, for Sir Walter writes that his daughter Mary has married "Charles, son and heir of Charles Musgrove, Esq. of Uppercross, in the county of Somerset." This provides our initial context and orientation for both Uppercross and Charles.

A few chapters later, we learn more about Charles, but this is raised because of a present occurrence: Wentworth has returned, which leads Anne to think about him, as well as about others who have sought her heart. Though years have passed since Anne's broken engagement, the narrator explains that "no one had ever come within the Kellynch circle, who could bear a comparison with Frederick Wentworth." This includes Charles Musgrove, who first proposed to Anne; when she refused, he proposed to her sister Mary.

As Anne's family prepares to move to Bath, Anne wants to find a way to stay behind. As often occurs, her sister Mary feels ill. Mary "entreated, or rather required [Anne], for it was hardly entreaty,

The ill Mary Musgrove greets her sister, Anne Elliot.
Illustration by C. E. Brock, 1909.

to come to Uppercross Cottage, and bear her company as long as she should want her." This provides the information we need to know about where Anne is staying and why, once again orienting the reader.

A few pages later, as Anne arrives at Uppercross, we receive a brief description of the "moderate-sized village." While this description could have been provided before, it's stronger here, when she's interacting with the village. More details are given on a need-to-know basis, as they provide context, unravel character, forward the plot, and provide insights into the emotions of the characters:

> Here Anne had often been staying. She knew the ways of Uppercross as well as those of Kellynch. The two families were so continually meeting, so much in the habit of running in and out of each other's house at all hours, that it was rather a surprise to her to find Mary alone.

Through these interwoven moments of backstory, we appreciate and understand Anne's connections to Uppercross, Mary, and Charles. Austen tends to provide enough backstory in advance to orient readers and then save further backstory for when it comes up naturally, when the characters are in action.

USE BACKSTORY TO BUILD MOMENTS OF EMOTIONAL IMPACT.
When Captain Wentworth visits Uppercross, he becomes friends with Anne's hosts, which means that Wentworth and Anne must interact frequently.

> They had no conversation together, no intercourse but what the commonest civility required. Once so much to each other! Now nothing! There *had* been a time, when of all the large party now filling the drawing-room at Uppercross, they would have found it most difficult to cease to speak to one another. With the exception, perhaps, of Admiral and Mrs. Croft, who seemed particularly attached and happy, (Anne could allow no other exception even among the married couples), there could have been no two hearts so open, no tastes so similar, no feelings so in unison, no countenances so beloved. Now they were as strangers; nay, worse than strangers, for they could never become acquainted. It was a perpetual estrangement.

This emotional backstory reveals Anne and Wentworth's former similarities and connection: "There could have been no two hearts so open." While this could have been revealed previously, saving it until now creates a greater emotional impact because the backstory is juxtaposed with their current relationship, creating a strong contrast between then and now.

While saving some backstory can heighten the emotional impact, it's important to not overwithhold in order to craft a shocking revelation. Saving large amounts of backstory does create surprise when it is finally revealed, but it can also cause confusion, create distrust in the narrator, and lessen the emotional impact. For instance, if we didn't learn about Anne and Wentworth's broken engagement until this particular scene, the news would surprise us. Yet we would also be overwhelmed and bogged down by information, and perhaps confused about why this was not previously mentioned. Instead of noticing the contrast between old and new interactions, the reader's focus would be on the new knowledge of the broken engagement. Anne and Wentworth's former similarity would no longer create the same emotional impact.

I often don't incorporate the backstory properly in a first draft. Sometimes I include too much; other times too little. I often realize that I've saved too much backstory for emotional scenes, so I place more backstory earlier in order to provide the proper context. Then, in the emotional scene, I incorporate only the most poignant and relevant backstory. For me, using too much or too little in early drafts is not a fault—it's part of the process of discovering the characters, their world, and their story. Often, the act of putting backstory on the page—whether or not it's the right amount or in the right place—helps me learn the best way to tell my story.

Backstory often provides history and facts, as well as insights into the character's mind, perspective, experience, and emotions. At the beginning of the story, it's essential to carefully weave in backstory in order to set the stage for the rest of the book.

Exercise 3.2: Fear of Water

Read the following paragraph:

> Ingrid stood at the edge of the dock, staring into the water. She could hear the other teenagers behind her, their laughter, their utter unconcern, as if this meant nothing. This meant nothing to

them. They didn't fear the water. She dipped her toe into the lake. She would be fine. She could do this. She closed her eyes, sucked in a breath of air and courage, and jumped.

Rewrite the paragraph, and as you do so, include one or two pieces of backstory about Ingrid's past, the history of the lake, a memory of this spot, etc. The information you include should impact the emotion and direction of the paragraph.

Exercise 3.3: Analyzing Backstory

Choose a novel that you have read at least once before. Reread the first few chapters, looking for moments of backstory both in the exposition and after the inciting incident. Analyze the author's use of backstory:

- When is the backstory incorporated?
- What types of information does the backstory reveal?
- What techniques are used to convey the backstory?
- Is the backstory used to create emotional impact?

INCITING INCIDENTS

In *Technique of the Drama*, Gustav Freytag writes,

> The beginning of the impassioned action must arise, like the first notes of a melody from the introductory chords. This first stir of excitement, this stimulating impulse, is of great importance for the effect of the drama.[6]

The inciting incident—what Freytag calls the "stimulating impulse"—is a disruptive event that sets the story in motion, starting the character's internal journey of transformation and the external journey of the plot. For an inciting incident to work, it must be strong enough to make it so the characters cannot continue

---

6. Freytag, *Technique of the Drama*, 29.

living as they did before. An inciting incident cannot be ignored, brushed over, or forgotten about: It must be dealt with. The protagonist cannot stay on their prior path. In *Emma*, Miss Taylor has married and is no longer Emma's constant companion. Every single day will look different for Emma now that her home only contains her and her father. In *Pride and Prejudice*, the arrival of Mr. Bingley and his party completely changes the social dynamics of the town. Not only do the Bennets interact with these new community members, but their interactions with each other and the town are changed by this disruption. In *Persuasion*, the Elliots' decision to rent out their home not only forces Anne to live elsewhere, but also leads to the return of Captain Wentworth, for his brother-in-law becomes the Elliots' tenant.

In *Sense and Sensibility*, the inciting incident is the death of Mr. Dashwood. His estate is inherited by his eldest son, John Dashwood, the child of his first wife. John and his wife Fanny promptly move to the estate. Mr. Dashwood's second wife and his three daughters are left with only ten thousand pounds and no property. Despite Mr. Dashwood's death, Elinor, Marianne, Margaret, and Mrs. Dashwood continue to live at Norland, but now they are visitors in what had once been their home. This is uncomfortable for everyone, but especially for Fanny and Mrs. Dashwood.

When Fanny's brother Edward visits, he and Elinor Dashwood form an attachment. Fanny notices and rudely confronts Mrs. Dashwood on the subject. Mrs. Dashwood decides that they will withdraw from the estate:

> To quit the neighbourhood of Norland was no longer an evil; it was an object of desire; it was a blessing, in comparison of the misery of continuing her daughter-in-law's guest; and to remove for ever from that beloved place would be less painful than to inhabit or visit it while such a woman was its mistress.

An inciting incident can be negative or positive, a loss or an opportunity. In either case, the characters often resist change. Even though the world has shifted and can't return to what it once was, it is difficult to embrace and follow a new path. The Dashwoods stay at Norland for *months* after Mr. Dashwood's death, until doing so becomes intolerable.

In *Save the Cat! Writes a Novel,* Jessica Brody calls this period the "debate." The characters face difficult decisions on what their life will look like and what actions they want to take. Ultimately, the characters must actively begin their external journey, thus commencing the rising action. Brody describes this as breaking into the second act of the story; it's "the moment the hero decides to accept the call to action, leave their comfort zone, try something new, or venture into a new world or way of thinking."[7]

While Marianne and Elinor both mourn Norland, physically moving to a new location creates opportunities for new relationships and begins their internal journeys of transformation.

Sometimes a negative inciting incident—an event that creates a loss for the character—does not cause major sadness or regret. While Emma knows she will miss sharing constant interactions with Miss Taylor, she rejoices in Miss Taylor's marriage; she loves her friend and wants her to move forward with her life. As previously discussed, Emma credits herself for this marriage and chooses a want: She wants to be a matchmaker. She is excited to take this journey and commence the rising action. Yet there is still a moment of debate: Mr. Knightley attempts to dissuade her from matchmaking. She ignores him, running headlong into her quest.

In *Northanger Abbey*, the inciting incident is an opportunity: an invitation to visit Bath. Catherine Morland does not resist or question this opportunity (and neither do her family members or anyone else). We have a **positive inciting incident and a positive response.** When they arrive in Bath,

> Catherine was all eager delight—her eyes were here, there, everywhere, as they approached its fine and striking environs, and afterwards drove through those streets which conducted them to the hotel. She was come to be happy, and she felt happy already.

But shortly, Catherine realizes this opportunity is not as gilded as she supposed. They are late to the first ball, and Mrs. Allen does not know anyone. Catherine doesn't speak to anyone, she doesn't dance with anyone, and she's miserable as she's pressed among the crowd. After initially embracing this opportunity, she now questions it. Ultimately, she does not reverse her choice and ask to

---

7. Brody, *Save the Cat! Writes a Novel*, 25.

return home. After all, she overhears two gentlemen declare her to be "a pretty girl," and so she goes "to her chair in good humour with everybody, and perfectly satisfied with her share of public attention."

An inciting incident can be negative or positive or mixed, but it must be **an event that carries weight for the main character and creates the opportunity for change, both internally and externally.** The character may react negatively or positively to the inciting incident, but either way, **there must be some resistance or difficulty in dealing with it, whether that friction comes from the self, other characters, or other complications.** As humans, we are stationary beings. We do what we have been doing: We stay still, or, if we have a path, we stick to that path unless something changes. And a story is all about change, so we need a strong inciting incident.

Exercise 3.4: Four Approaches, Four Examples

Find four examples of stories that use different types of inciting incidents, with positive and negative disruptions, and positive and negative reactions. For example, a positive inciting incident could be an opportunity; a negative inciting incident might be a setback, loss, problem, or complication. A positive reaction might include optimism or excitement, while a negative reaction often includes resistance. Fill out the chart with details about each inciting incident.

	Title of the Book/ Movie/ Media	The Inciting Incident: What Occurs and Why It's Disruptive	The Character's Reaction
Positive Inciting Incident with a Positive Reaction			
Positive Inciting Incident with a Negative Reaction			
Negative Inciting Incident with a Positive Reaction			
Positive Inciting Incident with a Negative Reaction			

Exercise 3.5: Adding a Disruption

In the following paragraph, a character is pursuing something she wants: the opportunity to be the pianist for the high school musical. Yet this paragraph contains no story, no plot. Add an inciting incident, something that will disrupt and change things for Luciana. This could happen before, during, or after the audition. You can choose a genre (e.g., a coming-of-age story, a young adult romance, or a cozy mystery). For the purposes of this exercise, keep the inciting incident short—from a sentence to a full paragraph. Once you've written the inciting incident, consider how it would change the character's trajectory and what sort of story might result from it.

> Luciana ran her fingers up and down the keys of an imaginary piano. She had been preparing for this audition for months, and now the time had finally come. She closed the book and looked at her hands. They were warm, they were flexible, and they were ready. She would be chosen as the accompanist for the high school musical this year, surely. She waited impatiently for her turn on the grand piano, but she need not have worried. Luciana played the music flawlessly, and the music director gave her a reassuring smile as she left the room.

AN EARLY START

Most stories start not long before the inciting incident, providing a brief description, moment, scene, or chapter that encapsulates the period before everything changes for the characters. Yet occasionally, authors begin long before the inciting incident. For example, the first sentence of *Northanger Abbey* mentions Catherine Morland "in her infancy." In a single chapter, Austen covers seventeen years, showing Catherine's entire life trajectory. **This exposition establishes a shared set of reference points with the reader, reference points that help us understand the main character and who she is prior to the inciting incident.** Without this knowledge, it could be difficult to understand Catherine's choices—her life trajectory informs her naivety, her desire to be liked, her fascination with new people and places, and her habit of turning to books for an escape.

It's rather rare for modern writers to cover several decades in the exposition. In *Northanger Abbey*, it works because of the narrator's voice and because the entire story is a commentary on what it means to be a hero. If you decide to start at the character's birth in your own story, you should have a good reason to do so; otherwise, it can feel like too much exposition that doesn't move the story forward.

Austen also starts early in *Mansfield Park*. The narrator focuses on the weddings of the prior generation. Three sisters marry, taking on new names: Lady Bertram, Mrs. Norris, and Mrs. Price. Mrs. Price disappoints her family by marrying beneath her station. She loses contact and only reestablishes it when expecting her ninth child. At this point, her eldest daughter, nine-year-old Fanny, is about to experience a cosmic shift.

> Mrs. Norris was often observing to the others, that she could not get her poor sister and her family out of her head, and that, much as they had all done for her, she seemed to be wanting to do more; and at length she could not but own it to be her wish, that poor Mrs. Price should be relieved from the charge and expense of one child entirely out of her great number. "What if they were among them to undertake the care of her eldest daughter, a girl now nine years old, of an age to require more attention than her poor mother could possibly give? The trouble and expense of it to them, would be nothing, compared with the benevolence of the action." Lady Bertram agreed with her instantly. "I think we cannot do better," said she; "let us send for the child."

Sir Thomas initially resists the idea but is won over by his wife and sister-in-law. As the scene continues, we come to understand the character of these three adults, and without having met Fanny, we know intuitively that this will not be a warm and welcoming place.

We meet Fanny in the second chapter of *Mansfield Park*, as she begins her "long journey." We are with her throughout this epic change and feel her discomfort at her new home. Fanny feels inferior and unrefined compared to her cousins. In this exposition, we also come to know, in more depth, another key character, Edmund Bertram.

> [Fanny] was found one morning by her cousin Edmund, the youngest of the sons, sitting crying on the attic stairs.
>
> "My dear little cousin," said he, with all the gentleness of an excellent nature, "what can be the matter?"

Fanny as a child, after arriving at Mansfield Park.
Illustration by C. E. Brock, 1908.

A touching scene follows in which Edmund helps Fanny share her thoughts. He learns about her family and her relationships with her siblings, then helps her write and send a letter, promising she will not need to pay for it. This first real moment between Edmund and Fanny sets up their entire relationship and is better experienced in scene rather than through summary or flashback.

Then, in the third chapter, the novel jumps forward a number of years, introducing another pivotal, life-changing event:

> The first event of any importance in the family was the death of Mr. Norris, which happened when Fanny was about fifteen, and necessarily introduced alterations and novelties.

Mr. Norris's death and the arrival of a new set of extremely disruptive characters—Mr. and Mrs. Grant, Mr. Crawford, and Miss Crawford—disrupt not only Fanny's life, but the lives of the entire family, inciting much of the story's plot.

I've spent years internally debating about which event qualifies as the inciting incident of *Mansfield Park*. Is it Mr. Norris's death? After all, the narrator even points out that this is the "first event of any importance" to the family and that it "introduce[s] alterations and novelties." These alterations and novelties lead to many of the key events throughout the rising action of the story. And as a result, the climax is when Fanny rejects Henry's proposal and is forced to leave Mansfield Park. All of this is good evidence for Mr. Norris's death acting as the inciting incident. In this case, Fanny's move to Mansfield Park is just starting the story very early to give us adequate exposition.

But what if we considered the inciting incident to be Fanny's initial move to live at Mansfield Park? If so, the internal and external journey would be about Fanny adjusting to her new life—it would be about her trying to find a home where she can feel at home. Arguably, that is the entire point of the book. This comes to a climax when Fanny rejects Henry's proposal and as a result is forced to leave Mansfield Park. Fanny only achieves this sense of home during the denouement.

I would argue that *Mansfield Park* starts early so it can use a **double inciting incident**. It takes both inciting incidents to send Fanny on her internal and external journeys, and both of the external journeys reach the climax in the same chapter sequence.[8]

---

8. Using a double inciting incident is tricky, but following Austen's lead, I did so in my third published novel, *The Lady's Guide to Death and Deception*. The first inciting incident happens in the first chapter, when my characters hear that Napoléon Bonaparte

In *Mansfield Park*, Austen starts the story early in order to demonstrate a prior inciting incident that causes a drastic shift in the main character's life and creates a new (albeit unhappy) normal, which is then disrupted by the second inciting incident.

While starting the story early can be a powerful approach to exposition, it should not be the default. In *Persuasion*, there are several formative shifts and disruptions for Anne prior to the start of the novel, including her mother's death and her short-lived engagement. Yet Anne's experience of these moments is revealed effectively through backstory, and in fact, their placement later in the story serves to reveal Anne's character and her regrets at key moments.

We should start the story early only if readers will be particularly enlightened by experiencing these events in scene.

Exercise 3.6: Analyzing an Early Start

Find another story that starts early and analyze it. Does it paint a character trajectory? Does it show a prior disruptive moment? Or is it doing something else entirely?

Exercise 3.7: Life Sketch

Take one of your characters (or an idea you have for a character) and write a 500-word life sketch, that begins either before or at their birth. Once you're finished, analyze the results.

- What new things did you learn about your character?
- What were the biggest, most defining moments in your character's early life? What shaped them into who they are as they enter the story?
- Are there elements of your character's early life that should be woven into the story as backstory? Or is this a case where it would be useful to experience the character's early life as part of the exposition?

---

has escaped from the Isle of Elba. Then, my main character travels to Brussels, where everyone is gathering to prepare to fight Napoleon. This creates a new normal. Then, there's a second inciting incident: a murder. Unlike Austen, these journeys don't come to a climax at the same time; instead I used a double climax. First, there's the final battle in which Napoleon is defeated, and a few chapters later, my main character solves the murder. Like in *Mansfield Park*, the internal and external journeys caused by both inciting incidents are constantly woven together throughout the story. You could make the argument that the Napoleon plot is actually just a subplot that starts rather early and that the murder mystery is the main plot. In this sense, I just started the story and introduced subplots. However, in terms of process, I thought about it as a double inciting incident.

Even if none of the life sketch is incorporated into the story, writing a life sketch can be a useful practice for understanding your character, their personality, and their choices.

Exercise 3.8: Adding Details

Choose a classic story or a fairy tale that does not give many specific details about a character's younger years (for example, Elizabeth Bennet in **Pride and Prejudice**). Brainstorm specific events and incidents that could have occurred before the start of the story and would be in keeping with what we know of their character and the story world.

STARTING A STORY IN MEDIAS RES

Most of Austen's novels start with exposition. The world and its characters are established, and then we see the inciting incident and the main character's reaction. This is the case in *Northanger Abbey, Sense and Sensibility, Persuasion,* and *Mansfield Park.* Yet two of Austen's novels begin *in medias res.*

In medias res means, literally, "in the middle of things." It's a term originally used by Horace over two thousand years ago in his work *Ars Poetica* (Poetic Arts). While plot structure demands a beginning, a middle, and an end, sometimes a story does not actually need a beginning—or at least, it doesn't need to start at the beginning.

In *Emma,* the inciting incident occurs before the first page of the novel. Miss Taylor has been married. We don't spend time with Emma before this: We don't see her in scene, we don't see her immediate reaction to the engagement, and we don't sit with Emma at the wedding. While the novel starts after the inciting incident, we still linger, for a time, in the beginning stages of the story, as the narrator establishes the exposition: Emma's situation, her past, and her personality. It's a rather unusual and innovative approach to *in medias res*—using a narrator's exposition, followed by a brief summary of a previous inciting incident, followed by a scene that shows the main character dealing with the inciting incident.[9]

Pride and Prejudice uses a more classic approach to *in medias res*, throwing us into a scene after the inciting incident, and showing only very minimal exposition through brief moments of backstory. In many cases, we need exposition before we can understand or appreciate how the world has been changed and what incites the characters to action. Yet as we will see in *Pride and Prejudice*, there are benefits to jumping straight into the heart of the story.

CHAPTER 1 OF PRIDE AND PREJUDICE

The first two paragraphs (beginning with the famed "It is a truth universally acknowledged") are thematic and provide commentary on society and the characters. This is a sort of exposition: It establishes how this particular community treats marriage. Then, starting in the third paragraph we read,

> "My dear Mr. Bennet," said his lady to him one day, "have you heard that Netherfield Park is let at last?"
>
> Mr. Bennet replied that he had not.
>
> "But it is," returned she; "for Mrs. Long has just been here, and she told me all about it."
>
> Mr. Bennet made no answer.
>
> "Do you want to know who has taken it?" cried his wife, impatiently.
>
> "*You* want to tell me, and I have no objection to hearing it."
>
> That was invitation enough.

We are brought immediately into the action of the novel, as Mrs. Bennet attempts to use all of her powers of persuasion to convince Mr. Bennet to call on Mr. Bingley so their daughters can be introduced to this newly arrived, eligible bachelor.

Bits of exposition and backstory are woven naturally into the interaction. Characters are established, and so is Mrs. Bennet's want: to marry off her daughters.

---

9. While Jane Austen pulls off this approach perfectly, I'm tempted to say, "Don't try this at home." It seems like it would be very challenging to do well. However, if it fits your stance (which we will discuss in the next chapter), and you're up for a challenge, go for it!

"What is his name?"

"Bingley."

"Is he married or single?"

"Oh, single, my dear, to be sure! A single man of large fortune; four or five thousand a year. What a fine thing for our girls!"

"How so? how can it affect them?"

"My dear Mr. Bennet," replied his wife, "how can you be so tiresome! You must know that I am thinking of his marrying one of them."

"Is that his design in settling here?"

"Design? Nonsense, how can you talk so! But it is very likely that he *may* fall in love with one of them, and therefore you must visit him as soon as he comes."

The dialogue feels natural—it does not seem like the characters are making these statements in order to convey information to the reader. Instead, Mrs. Bennet is attempting to spur her husband to action, and Mr. Bennet is attempting to annoy her and feign ignorance of her matrimonial plans.

Interestingly, we don't actually see the main character, Elizabeth, in scene until the next chapter. Unlike in *Emma*, in which the narrator describes the main characters and gives information on their pasts, in *Pride and Prejudice*, we must learn of the characters on the way. In the first chapter, Mr. and Mrs. Bennet specifically reference only three of their daughters, and only briefly:

"I will send a few lines … to assure him of my hearty consent to his marrying which ever he chooses of the girls—though I must throw in a good word for my little Lizzy."

"I desire you will do no such thing. Lizzy is not a bit better than the others: and I am sure she is not half so handsome as Jane, nor half so good-humoured as Lydia. But you are always giving *her* the preference."

"They have none of them much to recommend them," replied he: "they are all silly and ignorant like other girls; but Lizzy has something more of quickness than her sisters."

From this chapter, it's clear that there are a number of benefits from starting a story *in medias res*:

- It immediately focuses the reader on the main stakes—what could be gained and what is at risk.
- There is inherent excitement, energy, and movement.
- We immediately see how the inciting incident has impacted the characters and the world, and we join them as they respond to this disruption.
- It avoids what could be slow or unnecessary exposition.
- It can create suspense to learn not just what will happen next, but also, what happened before.

If you're going to start *in medias res*, the opening scene must be understandable without in-depth exposition or explanation. It must still be very clear how the inciting incident has changed the story world and set the characters on their journey. And, perhaps most importantly, starting *in medias res* requires trusting the reader. You must avoid the temptation to infodump and instead slowly weave in the most relevant pieces of backstory and exposition. If you start *in medias res*, follow Austen's lead by focusing on a compelling, engaging scene that connects us to the characters.

Exercise 3.9: Skip the Beginning

Choose a novel that you've never read and start reading—but skip the first few chapters. As you read, how do you figure out what's going on? How do you orient yourself? How do you learn about the characters, and what can you conclude about what happened previously?

Write about your experience doing this and about what this teaches you about starting *in medias res*.

Exercise 3.10: Shifting the Start

Take a short story or a novel that you've written that begins with exposition. Spend a few minutes and experiment with reorganizing the story so it starts in the middle of things. How late could you start the story? What details can you weave in later?

CRAFTING A PROMISING BEGINNING

When Fanny arrives at Mansfield Park, she is distraught. She misses her home and her family. Lady Bertram tries to comfort her with a gooseberry tart, but Fanny "could scarcely swallow two mouthfuls before tears interrupted her."

Mrs. Norris does not approve of Fanny's behavior. She declares, "This is not a very promising beginning."

While it may not be a promising beginning for Fanny's time at Mansfield Park, it is a promising beginning for the book. Conflict, loss, wants, needs, disruption—all these are established and propel the story forward.

A lot of weight is placed on the beginning of a novel. Often, readers will decide whether or not to continue reading a story within the first few pages. Thus, it's essential to hook the reader, whether it's through a strong storytelling voice; captivating exposition; an important scene before, during, or after the inciting incident; an intriguing problem; a fascinating world; or a moment that connects us to character. Once the reader is hooked and engaged with the story, the writer can continue to establish the reader-writer contract. However expectations must be set and agreed upon before the main forward movement of the story. As a personal rule of thumb, I like to establish all the essential parts of my reader-writer contract, from point of view to genre to the character's want, in the first 10–25 percent of the story.

As we've seen in Austen's novels, there are many good ways to start a story. Regardless of how you approach exposition and backstory, or whether you start early, just before the inciting incident, or *in medias res*, the beginning must set the stage, and something must disrupt the main character's life, sending them on an external and internal journey. How we introduce our characters and their journeys is a strategic decision, and part of the overall stance adopted by the author, which we'll discuss in the next chapter.

CHAPTER FOUR

STANCE

"The History of England from the reign of Henry the 4th to the death of Charles the 1st. By a partial, prejudiced, & ignorant Historian.... N.B. There will be very few Dates in this History."
—Jane Austen, *The History of England*

At the age of fifteen, Jane Austen wrote a short work titled "The History of England."[1] The piece is a burlesque, a type of parody that employs absurd, often ridiculous exaggerations of a particular form, medium, or genre. In this case, she mocks the history books of her time—in particular, some of the books in her family's library.[2] I'm not British, I have no strong opinions on the Stuarts, and I'm not familiar with many of the historical events that Austen references, but even so, I find her history delightful and hilarious.

Instead of providing a traditional byline or author credit, the narrator defines herself as "a partial, prejudiced, & ignorant Historian." The commentary is clear—anyone who writes a history is partial, prejudiced, and ignorant, but at least this narrator admits it. The text continues in a similar manner:

1. Austen, *History of England*.
2. Byrne, *The Real Jane Austen*, 60–61.
According to Paula Byrne, Jane Austen's history makes direct mockery of Oliver Goldsmith's *History of England from the Earliest Times to the Death of George II*. This was a four-volume abridgement of a longer history, and later, Goldsmith abridged his own abridgement, which Jane clearly found amusing.

Henry the 4th ascended the throne of England much to his own satisfaction in the year 1399, after having prevailed on his cousin & predecessor Richard the 2d to resign it to him, & to retire for the rest of his Life to Pomfret Castle, where he happened to be murdered.[3]

Original illustrations for Jane's copy of The History of England: *Henry IV, Elizabeth I, Mary Queen of Scotts, and Edward IV. Illustrations by Cassandra Austen (Jane's sister), circa 1790.*

This history does not necessarily reflect Austen's views; in order to reach her narrative goals, she has adopted a narrator's voice, a point of view, a tone, and a persona. Like Austen, every writer must choose an **authorial stance**. A stance has been defined as "the way in which someone stands, esp. when deliberately adopted (as in baseball, golf, and other sports)."[4] We can think about stance similarly in writing: What **deliberate positioning** is being used in order to prepare for the narrative task at hand? This strategic

3. Austen, *History of England.*
4. *New Oxford American Dictionary,* "stance," 1698.

positioning includes where the author stands in relation to the story, the characters, and the reader.

While there is no specific point in the writing process in which you must choose a stance, many writers do so before writing the first chapter, because it impacts everything about how you tell the story. Other writers select a stance after exploring their characters through a few chapters or an entire first draft. Regardless of when the overall positioning choices occur, it's very common to shift or refine the stance during revisions. Some writers have even discovered they need to completely rewrite their stories in order to adopt an entirely new stance.

POINT OF VIEW

An essential component of the author's stance is the **point of view**. In her book *Steering the Craft*, Ursula K. Le Guin defines point of view as "the technical term for who is telling the story and what their relation to the story is."[5] In *The History of England*, the point of view is a third-person commentary from a biased historian. The historian is outside of the story and its events, looking in and adding insights such as "this unfortunate Prince lived so little a while that nobody had time to draw his picture."[6]

While there's no right or wrong point of view, certain genres and certain decades tend to favor particular points of view. Each presents different storytelling possibilities, with opportunities and constraints. Austen skillfully uses various points of view in her stories, and examining her usage can help us consider the implications of our own choices. While we often consider point of view as a static, rigid choice, Austen uses it in a dynamic way; analyzing her methods can expand our own narrative possibilities.

Most of Austen's works are written in **third person**—the narrator is not a character in the plot; the narrator is an outside voice. She generally uses **past tense**—the events occurred in the past and are now described to us.

---

5. Le Guin, *Steering the Craft*, 61.
6. Austen, *History of England*.

Austen's works tend to be **selectively omniscient**. Omniscient means all-knowing, and indeed, Austen's narrators know quite a lot. If *Emma* was written in **third-person limited**, we would see and know and experience only what Emma sees and knows and experiences, which could help us connect to her as a character and fully immerse us in her vision. Yet Austen's narrator knows much more than Emma's perspective: In the second chapter, the narrator provides a history of the Westons and the Churchills, their careers and marriages, and their relationships with each other and with Highbury. This particular history is not told through the lens of Emma's thoughts and experiences. The narrator shares insights into the minds of other community members, dipping us into their points of view. For instance, of Mr. Weston we read, "He had never been an unhappy man; his own temper had secured him from that, even in his first marriage; but his second must shew him how delightful a well-judging and truly amiable woman could be."

This ability to switch perspectives is a fundamental strength of omniscience. In the fifth chapter, the narrator jumps to a scene between just two characters: Mr. Knightley and Mrs. Weston. For most of the scene, we receive only dialogue and brief description. It reads like a **fly-on-the-wall point of view**. The narrator is an observer; there is no commentary or filter as Mr. Knightley and Mrs. Weston discuss Emma's virtues, her faults, and her interference in Harriet's life. Then Mr. Knightley raises Emma's intention to never marry, and Mrs. Weston states, "There does, indeed, seem as little to tempt her to break her resolution at present." Only in the final paragraph of the chapter do we receive thoughts from either of the characters. The narrator exerts her omniscience by dipping into Mrs. Weston's thoughts and motivations:

> Part of her meaning was to conceal some favourite thoughts of her own and Mr. Weston's on the subject, as much as possible. There were wishes at Randalls respecting Emma's destiny, but it was not desirable to have them suspected.

While the narrator knows much, I would argue that *Emma* is not written from a fully omniscient point of view. **The omniscience is selective**. We never see inside the perspectives of Frank Churchill or Jane Fairfax. We largely access Harriet through Emma's lens and interpretations. The narrator focuses on using a **deep point of view**, immersing us as deeply and richly as possible into a single charac-ter's perspective (this approach is common in third-person limited, but can clearly be used in omniscient). For instance, when Mrs. Elton joins the community, Emma is not impressed; after their first meeting, Emma's "mind returned to Mrs. Elton's offences, and long, very long, did they occupy her."

"Mrs. Elton was first seen at church."
Illustration by Chris (Christiana) Hammond, 1898.

In the next chapter, we see how Mrs. Elton dotes on Jane Fairfax. The narrator uses **free indirect speech** (which we will discuss in Chapter 7) to slide smoothly into Emma's thoughts and emotions:

> Emma's only surprize was that Jane Fairfax should accept those attentions and tolerate Mrs. Elton as she seemed to do. She heard of her walking with the Eltons, sitting with the Eltons, spending a day with the Eltons! This was astonishing!—She could not have believed it possible that the taste or the pride of Miss Fairfax could endure such society and friendship as the Vicarage had to offer.

As we see in this passage, even with a particular point of view—this paragraph is in third-person limited—we can be brought closer or further from the character, their thoughts, and their emotions. Writer John Gardner talks about this as **psychic distance**, or the "distance that the reader feels between himself and the events of the story."[7] This distance does not need to be fixed, and there are advantages to modulating it even within a chosen stance and point of view.

Throughout the novel, Emma frequently makes poor judgments. We recognize some of these judgments from the start; for instance, we can sense the narrator's irony as she describes how Emma provides "services towards her friend" by convincing Harriet to reject Mr. Martin's proposal. Yet at other times, the narrator aligns herself so closely to Emma's viewpoint that the narrator also becomes an **unreliable** reporter of events. Like Emma, the narrator does not see or reveal Frank Churchill's actual motivations, intentions, and relationships. Emma interprets Frank Churchill entirely incorrectly, and the narrator allows the reader to also reach the wrong conclusions until the grand reveal, when Emma learns everything.

This approach to selective omniscience differs from that used in *Northanger Abbey*. While in *Emma*, the narrator often aligns with Emma's perspective, in *Northanger Abbey*, the narrator consistently points out Catherine's limitations. We never become so entrenched in Catherine's perspective that we don't see the bigger picture. Yet the omniscience is still selective; we don't learn why General Tilney wants his son to marry Catherine until she learns it.

This selectivity is a common approach for the omniscient point of view. Instead of using the term "omniscient", Ursula K. Le Guin prefers to call it the "involved author": a **storytelling voice** where the storyteller can draw on a wealth of material but must still choose where to focus.[8]

Some of Austen's works are written in first person, including her novella, *Lady Susan*, which went unpublished during her lifetime. *Lady Susan* is an **epistolary work**: It consists of letters written between characters. As such we receive a **first-person** perspective from each letter-writing individual; they each tell their own stories and experiences, and they attempt to change and influence each

---

7. Gardner, *The Art of Fiction*, 111.
8. Le Guin, *Steering the Craft*, 65–6.

other through their writing. Besides the final few paragraphs, there is no outside narrative commentary; instead, we receive insight through the juxtaposition of different perspectives. For instance, in one letter, Catherine Vernon warns her mother that Lady Susan might be trying to lead Catherine's brother Reginald astray:

> Lady Susan's intentions are of course those of absolute coquetry, or a desire of universal admiration; I cannot for a moment imagine that she has anything more serious in view; but it mortifies me to see a young man of Reginald's sense duped by her at all.[9]

This is followed by a letter from Lady Susan's friend, who attempts to convince her to marry Reginald; Lady Susan writes back that "I cannot easily resolve on anything so serious as marriage; especially as I am not at present in want of money." Catherine writes again to her mother of her fears about Reginald, and then Catherine's father writes a strongly worded letter to Reginald, warning him that "everything [is] at stake—your own happiness, that of your parents, and the credit of your name." Next, Catherine's mother writes her, apologizing that Catherine's father has learned about the whole affair. Finally, Reginald becomes involved, sending a letter to his father in which he defends Lady Susan and states,

> I can have no other view in remaining with Lady Susan, than to enjoy for a short time (as you have yourself expressed it) the conversation of a woman of high intellectual powers.

This is first-person **multiple points of view** with a very **natural rhetorical situation**: people communicating with each other in the common long-distance method of the time. For contemporary first-person novels, at times the narrator tells their own story with a similar rhetorical situation or with a storytelling voice and implied audience. More often, however, a **constructed situation** is used, in which the character recounts their story with a more ambiguous reason, audience, or justification for doing so. When an author writes in **first-person present**, it creates a strong sense of immediacy and moves us even further from a traditional storytelling voice, narrowing and focusing the vision of the narrator, which

---

9. Austen, *Lady Susan*.

creates new opportunities (such as greater emotional depth) and different limitations (such as difficulty in describing the big picture).

Today, most authors write in **first person** (past or present), in **third-person limited** (normally past tense, but sometimes present, and generally with a deep perspective), or in **third-person limited with multiple viewpoints** (in which case the story generally switches from one viewpoint to another at either scene or chapter breaks). Austen's primary point of view, **selective omniscience**, has become less common, and many modern writers struggle to write omniscience without jarring the reader or sounding unnatural, though there does seem to be a small resurgence of this point of view.[10]

When we choose a point of view for the narrator, it is essential to decide who should tell the story, how this person relates to the story, and how this point of view will impact the telling. Is the narrator a conscious storyteller? Will the narrator add commentary or acknowledge the reader? Is there an implied audience? Is the narrator a character in the story? If a part of the story, are they a main character, a side character, or an observer? How objective is the narrator? Is the narrator reliable? What knowledge can the narrator access? Does the narrator feel present or invisible?

Often, it's best to stick with a point of view that is currently common in your genre. But even within the norms, flexibility and opportunities to experiment and push boundaries exist. In *Emma*, we saw how the omniscient narrator moved closer and further from Emma's perspective, jumping into some heads and not others, and at times acting as a silent observer. If you decide to do something experimental with the point of view, it's generally a good practice to start doing so within the first 10–25 percent of the book, so readers expect and buy into it and aren't jolted by it later. This is actually a good practice regardless of your chosen point of view—make it a part of the reader-writer contract. If your story is omniscient, either adopt a storytelling voice or dip into multiple perspectives in the first few chapters. If you're including multiple points of view, whether in third or first person, don't wait until halfway through the book to include a second perspective. If, within third-person limited, you intend to shift closer to

---

10. This resurgence may be small, but I find it glorious. There are certain things that can only be done in omniscience, and it's exciting to see new works discover and use new possibilities for this very old point of view.

and further from your character's emotions, consider how you might begin doing so in the opening scenes or the rising action of the story. As always, there are exceptions, when a point of view change can be introduced later, but it's challenging to make a late shift work well.

The narrator's point of view may match the author's overall stance, or it may intentionally diverge. Yet this point of view is a key part of the author's conscious, deliberate positioning for the story. It controls the way in which the reader accesses the tale and much of the attitude they will feel toward the story.

Exercise 4.1: Library Quest

Go to the library and look through recent releases in your genre, or visit the main section for your genre. For at least five to ten books, spend a minute or two determining the point of view (first, third, omniscient, storyteller, limited, fly-on-the-wall, multiple, objective, unreliable, past tense, present tense, etc.). Make a log of the point of view for each book. What is the norm in your genre? Make sure to find at least one or two books that use a different point of view or that use the standard point of view but in innovative ways. (It's possible to do this with your home library, but you may gravitate to reading and purchasing only certain points of view, so it may not be as representative.)

After doing this exercise, consider where your own writing falls in comparison to these samples. When reading, which points of view do you prefer? Is there a new point of view that you would like to try for a story?

Exercise 4.2: One Incident, Three Points of View

Write a paragraph or two about something terrible happening in a work or a school setting. The catch? You need to write the passage three times, each using a different point of view. If you'd like, you can create a point of view by combining several elements from the list below. (For example, first-person past with an implied audience; omniscient yet largely distant; third person with multiple narrators.)

· First person	· Fly on the wall	· Reliable
· Third person	· Deep	· Unreliable
· Past tense	· More distant	· Single narrator
· Present tense	· Connected to the	· Multiple narrators
· Omniscient	story/narrator as a	· Implied audience
· Selective	character	· No implied
omniscience/	· Not connected to	audience
storytelling voice	the story	
· Limited/focused	· Invisible narrator	

Once you've written the passage three times, consider what story-telling opportunities and limitations were provided by these points of view.

Exercise 4.3: Rewriting from a New Perspective

Take a scene that you have written and rewrite it from the perspective of a different character. (For example, in *Emma*, a scene focused on Emma's perspective could be rewritten to focus on Harriet's perspective.) Afterward, reflect: How did this change the story?

TONE AND DICTION

Another essential element in positioning the story is the tone. In *Sense and Sensibility*, Mrs. Dashwood chooses to move to Barton Cottage in large part because of Sir John's tone:

> He seemed really anxious to accommodate them and the whole of his letter was written in so friendly a style as could not fail of giving pleasure to his cousin; more especially at a moment when she was suffering under the cold and unfeeling behaviour of her nearer connections.

The tone of a work is the mood or overall feeling that is conveyed to the reader. The tone generally conveys the narrator's perspective or attitude on the reader, the subject, the characters, and/or the events in the plot.

Austen's novels do not all share the same tone. For instance, *Mansfield Park* has a heavier, less optimistic tone than *Pride and Prejudice*. While the tone of *Pride and Prejudice* feels light, with sparkling humor and witty commentary, the tone of *Mansfield Park* allows Austen to explore the dark situations and relationships that Fanny faces on a regular basis.

As an example, let's consider cases from each novel where the main characters feel apart from the other characters in a scene. In

Pride and Prejudice, Elizabeth is slighted during a walk: Mrs. Hurst and Miss Bingley stand next to Mr. Darcy, forcing her to walk alone. Mr. Darcy senses the rudeness and proposes that they find a wider path. Instead of acknowledging the rudeness by accepting Mr. Darcy's kindness, Elizabeth laughs, makes a clever quip ("You are charmingly grouped, and appear to uncommon advantage. The picturesque would be spoilt by admitting a fourth"), and then runs "gaily off, rejoicing, as she rambled about, in the hope of being at home again in a day or two."

Elizabeth leaves the others to their walk.
Illustration by Hugh Thomson, 1894.

In contrast, note the different tone in *Mansfield Park* when Fanny feels separate from the other characters because she has chosen not to participate in the play because of moral concerns:

> She was safe; but peace and safety were unconnected here. Her mind had been never farther from peace…. Everybody around her was gay and busy, prosperous and important; each had their object of interest, their part, their dress, their favourite scene, their friends and confederates…. She alone was sad and insignificant: she had no share in anything; she might go or stay; she might be in the midst of their noise, or retreat from it to the solitude of the East room, without being seen or missed. She could almost think anything would have been preferable to this.

These scenes both occur early in their novels, and while they include parallel situations, they employ strikingly different tones.

There are dozens of possible tones that a narrator may adopt: formal, casual, serious, lighthearted, playful, optimistic, pointed, persuasive, skeptical, humorous, analytical, etc. While a work often uses an overall tone, variations can be included. For instance, while we still have some humor in *Pride and Prejudice* after Elizabeth learns of Wickham and Lydia's behavior, the tone becomes heavier and weightier. And the tone of *Mansfield Park* lifts a little as Fanny gains freedoms, develops friendships, and finds her voice. While her situation improves, the tone of the final chapter is still darker than that of *Pride and Prejudice*. Gustav Freytag presents a useful analogy in *The Technique of the Drama*: "Every piece … has a ground mood, which may be compared to a musical chord or a color. From this controlling color, there is necessary a wealth of shadings, as well as of contrasts."[11]

For one of my novels, the biggest editorial note that I received was to lighten the tone for the first half.[12] At the midpoint, something devastating happens, leaving the main character wracked by guilt and anxiety. But up until that point, my agent wanted the tone to be lighter. She wanted it to feel more optimistic and hopeful; even though the main character had some self-doubts at the start of

---

11. Freytag, *Technique of the Drama*, 80.
12. The book in question is *The True Confessions of a London Spy*. I was working on this book during the 2020 pandemic, so it is little wonder that I needed to lighten the tone for the first half.

the story, she needed to see her choices and options as opportunities. This would engage the reader more from the beginning of the book and give my main character further to fall at the midpoint.

It took weeks to revise the tone. I added a few mini-scenes, including a playful game between the characters in the first chapter. I changed how my character reacted to other characters' comments and to setbacks. I also shifted the narrator's focus and perspective, particularly through my word choice.

One of the biggest ways to control tone is through **diction— word choice**. Choosing a different verb, adjective, or noun can shift the tone of a sentence, and the overall choices of words in a scene, a chapter, or a book, will shift the larger tone. Let's compare *Mansfield Park* and *Pride and Prejudice* once again, this time focusing on diction.

When Fanny first arrives at Mansfield Park, her female cousins spend time getting to know her, but it "produce[s] little union." They give her "a generous present of some of their least valued toys, and leave her to herself, while they [adjourn] to whatever might be the favourite holiday sport of the moment, making artificial flowers or wasting gold paper." The diction creates humor and witty narrative commentary—is a present really generous if it's a least valued item? Yet the humor feels dark; through the word choice, we, like Fanny, feel trapped, watching the cousins with their *artificial* flowers as they *waste* gold paper. In the word choice, even the beautiful has negative connotations. The chapter ends a bit more positively, as Fanny becomes friends with Edmund, but the overall tone has been established, for both the narration and Fanny's experience at Mansfield Park.

In *Pride and Prejudice*, when Mr. Bennet reveals that he has called upon Mr. Bingley, he is not forthcoming on the details of the visit—and he's especially silent on details about Mr. Bingley. Mrs. Bennet and her daughters attempt to draw him out:

> They attacked him in various ways, with barefaced questions, ingenious suppositions, and distant surmises; but he eluded the skill of them all; and they were at last obliged to accept the second-hand intelligence of their neighbour, Lady Lucas.

Throughout this sentence, the narrator plays with words. "Attack" is often used in a true conflict, with high stakes, such as personal injury. Yet their attack is simply an attempt to gain information on a neighbor. They use barefaced questions, ingenious suppositions, and distant surmises—elevated rhetorical techniques are employed simply to gain a brief character description. But, as the narrator describes grandiosely, Mr. Bennet "eluded the skill of them all." By using these words in unexpected ways, it creates a humorous, playful tone.

The Bennet family. Illustration by Hugh Thomson, 1894.

In both *Mansfield Park* and *Pride and Prejudice*, words are used ironically, in ways that contrast with their traditional usage, meaning, and associations. We'll discuss irony more in Chapter 15, but it's important to note the same tool can be used for various effects—in this case, to create a different tone.

The tone doesn't have to match the perspective of the main character. As previously discussed, in *Northanger Abbey*, the narrator stands apart, commenting on the characters as heroines and heroes in the story. On a stormy night, we read that Catherine "felt for the first time that she was really in an abbey." The diction that follows reflects her internal experience. Here are a few of the overly dramatic words and phrases used in the scene:

- tempest
- horrid scenes
- solemn
- midnight assassins

- drunken gallants
- suffer
- violence of the wind
- died away
- struck
- whimsical
- the effect of gold
- strange fancy
- so very odd
- torrents
- yielded
- flushed
- snuffed and extinguished
- trembled
- affrighted ear

"Good God! How came you up that staircase?"

Catherine sees everything at the abbey in the light of her Gothic novels. Here, she is startled by Henry Tilney's appearance on the staircase. Illustration by C. E. Brock, 1907.

While the diction gives us a window into Catherine's experience, the overall tone remains light. We do not actually worry about something terrible happening to Catherine. We stand with the narrator, looking from the outside in, with more knowledge than the character. We're able to appreciate Catherine's fear because of the diction, yet her utter terror only serves to further the narrator's amused mood.

The tone of a story is a crucial component of both its stance and its style (which we'll discuss in a later chapter), an overarching choice that impacts hundreds—even thousands—of smaller choices in the story, from diction to sentence structure to the types of metaphors used.

Exercise 4.4: A New Tone

Choose a paragraph from one of your favorite books. Shift the tone by rewriting the paragraph with a new approach to diction. You might replace adjectives, verbs, nouns, or other words. Once you're finished, read both the original version and the new version aloud. Reflect on how this new tone would change the story.

Exercise 4.5: Revising for Tone

After finishing the first draft of a short story or a novel, analyze the tone. What sort of tone is established in the first chapter or opening scene? When does the tone shift in the story? With what tone does the story close?

Choose several ways in which you can revise for tone. (A few possibilities: revising a scene so the diction matches the overall tone; shifting the tone for a scene or chapter; making the tone match or diverge from the character's perspective; making a larger change in the tone of the story.)

SHOWING AND TELLING THE STORY

The choice of when to show and when to tell is also an important part of the author's stance. Showing and telling are two seemingly opposite storytelling approaches.

When something is shown, we see it before us—we see actions performed, in detail, and we receive direct dialogue, straight from the characters. For example, at the Netherfield ball in *Pride and Prejudice*, as Mr. Darcy and Elizabeth dance, Sir William speaks to them, and as he does so, he implies that Jane and Mr. Bingley might soon become engaged. Austen **shows** Darcy's reaction to Sir William's comments, and then **shows** the conversation between Darcy and Elizabeth:

> The latter part of this address was scarcely heard by Darcy; but Sir William's allusion to his friend seemed to strike him forcibly, and his eyes were directed, with a very serious expression, towards Bingley and Jane, who were dancing together. Recovering himself, however, shortly, he turned to his partner, and said,—
>
> "Sir William's interruption has made me forget what we were talking of."
>
> "I do not think we were speaking at all. Sir William could not have interrupted any two people in the room who had less to say for themselves. We have tried two or three subjects already without success, and what we are to talk of next I cannot imagine."
>
> "What think you of books?" said he, smiling.
>
> "Books—oh no!—I am sure we never read the same, or not with the same feelings."

We see the turn of Mr. Darcy's head and the focus of his eyes. We see his smile. We hear his words, and those of Elizabeth. It's an engaging scene, and as readers, we enjoy watching as it is shown before us.

In contrast, **telling** is when the narrator tells the reader about things, often by summarizing events, actions, dialogue, exposition, character traits, emotions, and more. For instance, after Mr.

Collins and Charlotte become engaged in *Pride and Prejudice*, the narrator tells us about what happens over the coming week, condensing and interpreting it:

> After a week spent in professions of love and schemes of felicity, Mr. Collins was called from his amiable Charlotte by the arrival of Saturday. The pain of separation, however, might be alleviated on his side by preparations for the reception of his bride, as he had reason to hope, that shortly after his next return into Hertfordshire, the day would be fixed that was to make him the happiest of men. He took leave of his relations at Longbourn with as much solemnity as before; wished his fair cousins health and happiness again, and promised their father another letter of thanks.

None of the situations, dialogue, or facial expressions are shown to us. Instead, the summarized events move the story forward quickly, giving us the essence of Mr. Collins without forcing us to experience the extended version of his happiness.

A common piece of contemporary writing advice is "show, don't tell." The phrase was rarely used before 1980, but since then it has become an increasingly prolific instruction—and in some cases, authors and writing instructors treat it as a commandment.[13] While showing is a powerful, immersive storytelling method, it's not the only good approach to storytelling, and the advice "show, don't tell" is often overused. Austen frequently uses both showing and telling, and she also writes scenes that mix the two. In the coming pages, we'll discuss both techniques in greater detail by looking at when, how, and why Austen uses them, and we'll consider how we should use both in our own stories.

First, let's consider how to **show** a story. The idea is that instead of having someone tell us what happened, we want to feel like we are there, watching the dialogue and the action as if it were happening live before us, like in a film or a theatrical performance. This is often called experiencing the story **in scene**, as if we are

---

13. There are lots of fun debates about who coined the term, with credit being given in various directions and Anton Chekhov almost always being seen as a key influence. While the term gained greater usage after 1980, William Noble's 1991 book on writing, *Show, Don't Tell: A Writer's Guide*, likely contributed to the continued growth of the term. For a useful chart showing an increase in the term's usage, you can visit Google Book's Ngram viewer and search for the phrase "show don't tell" (don't use a comma in the search).

present in the scene with the characters.

While this is not an exhaustive list, here are a few specific techniques that can be used to show something in scene:

- Provide full lines of dialogue, directly as they are spoken by the characters.
- Show the actions taken by the characters with details, steps, and components.
- Incorporate facial expressions and descriptions of how a character speaks.
- Give descriptions only as they are relevant in the moment. (We'll talk about this more in Chapter 10, on setting.)
- Use free indirect speech and incorporate character thoughts. (We'll talk about this more in Chapter 7, on emotion.)
- Decrease the psychic distance. For first-person narrators, focus only on what is happening in the moment; for third-person and omniscient narrators, focus in on a character's perspective with little or no commentary.

A great example of showing through use of these techniques is found in *Emma*. One of the characters, Jane Fairfax, acts as both a rival and a foil to Emma. Jane Fairfax receives an incredibly generous gift from an anonymous benefactor: a pianoforte.[14]

Everyone in the community debates who could have sent such an expensive item. Could it be friends of Jane who do not live in Highbury, like the Campbells or Mr. Dixon? Yet one character, Mrs. Weston, believes the gift giver is a local—in fact, she believes it to be Mr. Knightley. Emma does not like this idea—she cannot believe that Mr. Knightley secretly loves Jane. But at the same time, she wonders if Mrs. Weston is right.

The pianoforte is still on everyone's minds when the Cole family holds a gathering. At events such as this, it was common for guests to provide part of the entertainment. Emma is asked to perform, and she plays the pianoforte, even though she knows her talents at the instrument are much less than Jane Fairfax's. Then, it's Jane's turn to play. The narrator **shows** us the scene as Jane plays and Emma watches. In the following passage, we see, moment by

---

14. I feel like a surprise anonymous piano would be just as shocking today as it was hundreds of years ago, especially if the piano is new. Please note: I already own a piano, and I don't actually need any additional pianos.

moment, the dialogue, actions, and expressions of the characters, as well as Emma's immediate thoughts.

> Presently Mr. Knightley looked back, and came and sat down by [Emma]. They talked at first only of [Jane's] performance. His admiration was certainly very warm; yet she thought, but for Mrs. Weston, it would not have struck her....
>
> "This present from the Campbells," said she—"this pianoforte is very kindly given."
>
> "Yes," he replied, and without the smallest apparent embarrassment.—"But they would have done better had they given her notice of it. Surprizes are foolish things. The pleasure is not enhanced, and the inconvenience is often considerable. I should have expected better judgment in Colonel Campbell."
>
> From that moment, Emma could have taken her oath that Mr. Knightley had had no concern in giving the instrument. But whether he were entirely free from peculiar attachment—whether there were no actual preference—remained a little longer doubtful. Towards the end of Jane's second song, her voice grew thick.
>
> "That will do," said he, when it was finished, thinking aloud—"you have sung quite enough for one evening—now be quiet."
>
> Another song, however, was soon begged for. "One more;—they would not fatigue Miss Fairfax on any account, and would only ask for one more." And Frank Churchill was heard to say, "I think you could manage this without effort; the first part is so very trifling. The strength of the song falls on the second."
>
> Mr. Knightley grew angry.
>
> "That fellow," said he, indignantly, "thinks of nothing but shewing off his own voice. This must not be." And touching Miss Bates, who at that moment passed near—"Miss Bates, are you mad, to let your niece sing herself hoarse in this manner? Go, and interfere. They have no mercy on her."

It's a beautiful scene, as we sit with Emma, watching her prod Mr. Knightley in an attempt to discover whether or not he gifted the pianoforte. At the moment her certainty appears, we experience it, and then, immediately, we experience her doubt—even if he did not give Jane the pianoforte, he still might be romantically interested in her. We hear Jane's voice grow thick and see Mr.

Knightley's worried reaction. Many voices make requests of Jane, and Mr. Knightley grows angry—we see this in his speech. And then he touches Miss Bates and asks for her assistance. It's a powerful scene; it progresses in front of us like a play.

Mrs. Cole is surprised when she sees
Jane Fairfax's anonymously-gifted pianoforte.
Illustration by Chris (Christiana) Hammond, 1898.

REASONS TO SHOW THE STORY, BY PUTTING IT IN SCENE:
1. Showing can provide an immersive experience, making the reader feel present.
2. We most readily believe and feel that which we experience, and showing something in scene allows us to personally gain an experience with the characters. If we're told a character is selfish, it has less impact than seeing the character behave selfishly.
3. Key turning points in the plot—big, crucial moments in which everything shifts for the character—are generally

best shown in scene, to both give more detail to the reader and increase the weight of these moments. (We see this with Austen's key turning points, which will be discussed in Chapters 6 and 10.)

4. To truly establish a relationship, we must see the characters together in scene. It's also important to show major relationship shifts. (See Chapter 8.)

5. Actions and dialogue are inherently present for the characters and thus are often shown in scene, so we can hear the dialogue in the characters' own words or see the characters' actions as if with our own eyes.

6. Showing is a powerful way to convey emotions, both of the viewpoint character and of other characters.

7. Showing often brings us deeper into a point of view, closer to the thoughts and impressions of the viewpoint character.

While Austen is skilled at showing and uses it in every one of her novels, she does not write everything in scene. A complete reliance on showing erases the narrator, creating a cinematic point of view. The narrator is, after all, a **story*teller***, a person who **tells** us a story. As previously stated, how much of the story is shown and how much is told is an essential part of the author's stance. The chosen point of view also influences the ratio of show vs. tell; an omniscient or involved narrator will naturally use a higher ratio of telling than other points of view, though even a story told in first-person present must use telling at times, if only to skip past the nonessentials.

Here are some of the major techniques of telling:

- Summarize events, conversations, and thoughts.
- Condense time and events.
- Use fewer details.
- Provide commentary from the narrator's point of view.
- Rely more heavily on the narrator's voice and focus us on the act of telling.

A great example of effective **telling** is found in *Persuasion*, when Anne visits Lyme. On a particular evening, she befriends the heartbroken, depressed Captain Benwick. They talk extensively of poetry, yet the entire conversation is summarized, which allows the narrator to demonstrate how Anne gauges Benwick's character. This condenses the conversation—if the hours-long conversation was shown, it could take several full chapters. The summary gives a stronger overall *feel* for the conversation, without needing to watch it unfold, line by line. We also see Anne's reflections on how this conversation might apply to herself:

> It fell to Anne's lot to be placed rather apart with Captain Benwick; and a very good impulse of her nature obliged her to begin an acquaintance with him. He was shy, and disposed to abstraction; but the engaging mildness of her countenance, and gentleness of her manners, soon took their effect; and Anne was well repaid the first trouble of exertion.... [They] talked of poetry, the richness of the present age, and ... [made] a brief comparison of opinion as to first-rate poets, trying to ascertain whether *Marmion* or *The Lady of the Lake* were to be preferred, and how ranked the *Giaour* and *The Bride of Abydos*.... She ventured to hope he did not always read only poetry, and to say, that she thought it was the misfortune of poetry to be seldom safely enjoyed by those who enjoyed it completely; and that the strong feelings which alone could estimate it truly were the very feelings which ought to taste it but sparingly.

This is followed by another two paragraphs of summary in which Anne recommends that Benwick also read prose; Benwick listens attentively to her rather lengthy list of recommendations, which is summarized by stating that she "mentioned such works of our best moralists, such collections of the finest letters, such memoirs of characters of worth and suffering, as occurred to her at the moment as calculated to rouse and fortify the mind by the highest precepts." After the conversation concludes, the narrator summarizes Anne's reflections:

> When the evening was over, Anne could not but be amused at the idea of her coming to Lyme, to preach patience and resignation to a young man whom she had never seen before; nor could she help fearing, on more serious reflection, that, like many other great moralists and preachers, she had been eloquent on a point in which her own conduct would ill bear examination.

These insights are told—we don't experience a single grand moment of revelation. Rather, her entire reflections on the evening are distilled in a poignant way.

Reasons to tell rather than show the story:

1. Telling is a strong way to present exposition and backstory. (As we saw in Chapter 3, while exposition and backstory are sometimes presented in scene, small pieces are often interwoven into the story through telling.)
2. By telling, the narrator can compress time, show the passage of time, or transition quickly between scenes.
3. Summary can condense less important dialogue and actions.
4. Telling allows the narrator to group repetitive or reoccurring actions or dialogue.
5. Using telling in a scene can focus the reader on the most important dialogue and actions, which are shown in scene.
6. Interpretation and commentary, which often come from the narrator as part of a storytelling voice, are generally best told.
7. Further, telling can draw us into the perspective of the narrator or draw us into the perspective of a character.
8. Telling can be useful when there is a mismatch between a character's views/thoughts and their outer behavior/words.
9. Finally, telling can create humor or irony.

While in the conversation between Anne and Captain Benwick, summary takes less time than showing the events in scene, at times telling or summarizing can take the same amount of page time as showing the dialogue or events—or it can even take more time.

For example, in *Pride and Prejudice*, when the Bingleys leave to go to London, Caroline Bingley writes a letter to Jane. In scene, the narrator gives us Jane's exact dialogue, in which she summarizes the news—the Bingleys have left Netherfield. Then Jane says, "You shall hear what she says." However, even though Jane is reading the letter aloud to Elizabeth, the narrator summarizes it for the reader:

> She then read the first sentence aloud, which comprised the information of their having just resolved to follow their brother

to town directly, and of their meaning to dine that day in Grosve-
nor Street, where Mr. Hurst had a house.

By summarizing the sentence but not omitting any details, this
statement is the same length as the original sentence in Caroline's
letter. Yet summarizing this line actually serves to put more focus
on the next lines, which are directly quoted:

> "I do not pretend to regret any thing I shall leave in Hertford-
> shire except your society, my dearest friend; but we will hope,
> at some future period, to enjoy many returns of that delightful
> intercourse we have known, and in the mean while may lessen
> the pain of separation by a very frequent and most unreserved
> correspondence. I depend on you for that."

We need these sentences in Caroline's own words—it would not
be enough for the narrator to summarize Caroline as speaking with
"high-flown expressions" that mask an emptiness and insincerity.
This particular part of the letter must be in scene. The narrator
then summarizes Elizabeth's analysis during and after the letter.

Austen's narrators often use a mixture of telling and showing,
alternating between them from one sentence or clause to the next.

Near the end of *Northanger Abbey*, Catherine Morland is uncer-
emoniously thrown out of Northanger Abbey by an angry General
Tilney. When she arrives home, she tells her family what happened.
Soon, they meet up with her friends, the Allens, and they too must
hear the story. Rather than showing the full scene, Austen intermixes telling and showing. Notice how she begins with telling, by
summarizing the overall reactions and emotions, and then shifts
to showing a particular passage of dialogue in full:

> [Catherine] was received by the Allens with all the kindness
> which her unlooked-for appearance, acting on a steady affection,
> would naturally call forth; and great was their surprise, and warm
> their displeasure, on hearing how she had been treated—though
> Mrs. Morland's account of it was no inflated representation, no
> studied appeal to their passions. "Catherine took us quite by sur-
> prise yesterday evening," said she. "She travelled all the way post
> by herself, and knew nothing of coming till Saturday night; for
> General Tilney, from some odd fancy or other, all of a sudden

> grew tired of having her there, and almost turned her out of
> the house. Very unfriendly, certainly; and he must be a very odd
> man; but we are so glad to have her amongst us again! And it is
> a great comfort to find that she is not a poor helpless creature,
> but can shift very well for herself."

The summary frames the conversation, giving a bird's-eye view of the interactions and offering insight into the Allens' responses. Then we see, in scene, the exact four sentences of dialogue that Mrs. Morland uses to tell the story, which puts great emphasis on both her own feelings and her interpretation of the events and people.

This paragraph is followed by another paragraph that interweaves summary and direct quotes. Yet note that the quotes are not single pieces of dialogue; instead, they are statements that the characters say multiple times. Their inclusion represents the type of response that Mr. and Mrs. Allen make.

> Mr. Allen expressed himself on the occasion with the reason-
> able resentment of a sensible friend; and Mrs. Allen thought his
> expressions quite good enough to be immediately made use of
> again by herself. His wonder, his conjectures, and his explana-
> tions became in succession hers, with the addition of this single
> remark—"I really have not patience with the general"—to fill up
> every accidental pause. And, "I really have not patience with the
> general," was uttered twice after Mr. Allen left the room, without
> any relaxation of anger, or any material digression of thought.

Later in the scene, showing and telling are once again mixed. The following passage begins with dialogue that is spoken by Mrs. Allen:

> "It was very agreeable, was not it? Mr. Tilney drank tea with us,
> and I always thought him a great addition, he is so very agree-
> able. I have a notion you danced with him, but am not quite
> sure. I remember I had my favourite gown on."
>
> Catherine could not answer; and, after a short trial of other
> subjects, Mrs. Allen again returned to—"I really have not
> patience with the general! Such an agreeable, worthy man as
> he seemed to be!"

The summarized phrases—"Catherine could not answer" and "after a short trial of other subjects"—emphasize how Catherine struggles to participate in this conversation, because everything connects back to the Tilneys. While Mrs. Allen introduces other subjects, the exact subjects aren't included because they aren't truly relevant to the story. What is relevant is Catherine's inability to engage with the topics.

There are moments in Austen's novels where the modern author would likely show more than Austen does. For instance, in *Sense and Sensibility*, we never see Elinor and Edward Ferrars in scene at Norland. The development of their relationship is summarized, and we are shown Elinor and Marianne's conversation about Edward. While at Norland, we do see a very brief conversation in scene between Edward and Mrs. Dashwood. However, we never actually see Elinor and Edward together until Edward visits the family at Barton Cottage. That's in the sixteenth chapter. Film adaptations often add at least one scene showing them together at Norland.

In some ways, it seems that in *Sense and Sensibility*, the romantic relationships are actually less important than the relationship between Elinor and Marianne. Scholars at UCD's Centre for Cultural Analytics created visualizations of the social networks in Austen's novels. Each main character becomes a point on their chart, so Marianne is a point, and so is Elinor, and so are Edward Ferrars and Willoughby and Colonel Brandon. Then lines are drawn between characters for each interaction between them, and for each line of dialogue they speak to each other. The visual results are striking: There's a dark, thick line between Elinor and Marianne. Marianne and Willoughby have a very solid line, though it's much smaller than the line between Marianne and Elinor. Willoughby and Elinor's line is also distinct. The lines between Elinor and Edward, and between Marianne and Colonel Brandon, are rather insignificant; you have to look for them. When the novel is visualized using a social network analysis, Elinor and Marianne's relationship is clearly the focal point of the story.[15] Of course, the novel was originally titled *Elinor and Marianne*. In practical terms, throughout the story, a huge portion of Elinor and Marianne's interactions are shown in scene rather than summarized.

15. Wade, "Jane Austen's Social Networks."
I highly recommend looking at their visualizations of all of Austen's novels.

Both showing and telling can be difficult storytelling techniques—especially if we want to show and tell well. When I was a developing writer, I struggled to effectively write in scene and create an immersive, immediate experience. I think many early writers experience this same struggle, and so they are often given the advice to "show, don't tell." And it can be useful advice—a novel *should* include immersive moments filled with snappy dialogue, compelling action, and only brief description. Even as a published author, I still receive the advice to "show, don't tell" from my writing group or critique partners when I've not fully developed a moment of emotional importance, when I've moved the story too quickly, or when my summary is clunky and uninteresting.

At times, I also find telling difficult—yet so essential. Sometimes I'll get so focused on writing in scene that I include unnecessary details or make a dialogue long and boring because I forget that I can summarize parts of it. Reading Austen reminds me how effective telling can be at condensing and compressing, providing backstory, making commentary, and giving the narrator a stronger storytelling voice.

There are stories that use only showing (though scenes are still generally shown selectively, and with carefully chosen starts and stops). And there are stories that use only telling, with nothing shown in scene.[16] Yet it is more likely that we will treat showing and telling as Austen does, interweaving both together to forward our narrative goals.

Exercise 4.6: Dialogue and Summary

Write a short scene that consists largely of dialogue between two characters. However, there's a catch. For one of the characters, you can include their exact words, but for the second character, you can only summarize. Try to give a feel for the second character's dialogue and its effect even though you are not directly quoting the dialogue.

Exercise 4.7: Examples of Showing and Telling

Choose a novel by an author other than Jane Austen. Find the following:

---

16. I don't believe I've ever seen this done in a full-length novel, though I have read several short stories that use only telling, and many fairy tales and legends use solely this technique.

1. A passage that focuses on showing the events in scene
2. A passage that largely summarizes or tells
3. A passage that intermixes showing and telling

If you can't find one of these types of passages in a particular book, choose a different author or genre. Once you've found the three techniques, consider what techniques the author uses to show, tell, or show and tell. What type of content (e.g., relationship development, exposition, character showcase, key turning point, etc.) is presented in each scene? How does the point of view impact the way in which showing and telling are used?

THE IMPACT OF STANCE

Jane Austen originally drafted *Pride and Prejudice* at the age of twenty, using the title *First Impressions*. Austen's father tried to find a publisher for it but failed; however, family and friends loved the book. In fact, Jane wrote to her sister Cassandra,

> I would not let Martha read First Impressions again upon any account, and am very glad that I did not leave it in your power.— She is very cunning, but I saw through her design; she means to publish it from memory, and one more perusal must enable her to do it.[17]

The original manuscript no longer exists, but several scholars believe that it was written as an epistolary novel, similar to *Lady Susan*.[18] If these scholars are correct, then we see many traces of

---

17. Jane Austen to Cassandra Austen, June 11, 1799. *Letters of Jane Austen.*
18. Southam, *Jane Austen's Literary Manuscripts*, 58–62.
One of the main proponents of this theory is B. C. Southam. Other scholars push back against it, arguing that there is not enough historical and textual evidence to support it. Still others argue that the more interesting question is not whether or not the novel was originally epistolary, but the role the epistolary form plays within the text. Unfortunately, this footnote is coming to a close, so if you'd like to dive into this subset of scholarship,

the original epistolary form in the *Pride and Prejudice* we read and love today. The story contains numerous letters of import, including Mr. Collins's letter to Mr. Bennet, informing him that he'll visit with an olive branch; Caroline Bingley's letter to Jane, which we discussed earlier in this chapter; Mr. Darcy's lengthy letter to Elizabeth after his failed proposal; and Jane's two letters to Elizabeth, informing her that Lydia has run away with Mr. Wickham.

If epistolary, *First Impressions* took a very different stance than *Pride and Prejudice*. Everything would be told in first person, and these first-person accounts would be impacted by the perceived recipient of the letter and the letter writer's rhetorical goals. The book would rely heavily on summary; perhaps some of the letter writers would attempt to paint a scene, but it is likely that we would receive much less detail for many of our favorite moments, like Mr. Collins's and Mr. Darcy's proposals, the Meryton assembly, and the Netherfield ball. The tone, which in *Pride and Prejudice* is largely established by the witty narrator, who regularly incorporates humor and irony, would likely be very different. Humor would still be present but would rely primarily on the humor of individual characters and the juxtaposition of letters, rather than humor created by the narrator. The narrator's ironic commentary on people and events would be entirely absent.

Even if all the major plot points, relationship arcs, and character transformations in *First Impressions* were exactly the same as those in *Pride and Prejudice*, the different stance would make it an entirely different story.

The author's stance is a series of fundamental choices, all of which impact the type of story, how it is told, and how it is received by the audience. Throughout the rest of this book, we'll see how the stance impacts storytelling choices, from conveying key turning points to planting emotional clues to establishing the setting. As we've seen, the stance should be established at the beginning of the novel and should continue to impact the narrative. When choosing a stance, even if you choose the stance that comes naturally to you or that is most common for your genre, it's important to consider the impact your stance will have on the story and your readers.

CHAPTER FIVE

ANTAGONISM

"Lady Russell felt obliged to oppose her dear Anne's known wishes."
—Persuasion

In *Persuasion*, when the family decides to rent out Kellynch Hall in order to stay financially solvent, they can choose between three places to live: "London, Bath, or another house in the country." Anne dislikes Bath and is not interested in London, but she loves the idea of "a small house in their own neighborhood, where they still might have Lady Russell's society, still be near Mary, and still have the pleasure of sometimes seeing the lawns and groves of Kellynch." Anne makes her desires known. She is opposed not only by her father and her sister Elizabeth—after all, they never value her or her thoughts—but also by one of her closest friends, Lady Russell.

Long before the novel began, it was also Lady Russell who provided the strongest arguments against Anne's engagement. "She deprecated the connexion in every light," providing continual opposition.

> Young and gentle as [Anne] was, it might yet have been possible to withstand her father's ill-will, though unsoftened by one kind word or look on the part of her sister; but Lady Russell, whom she had always loved and relied on, could not, with such steadiness of opinion, and such tenderness of manner, be continually advising her in vain. She was persuaded to believe the engagement a wrong thing: indiscreet, improper, hardly capable of success, and not deserving it.

Many writing resources discuss creating a single main antagonist or villain, who actively works in opposition to the protagonist over the course of the story. At times Austen does create a single constant antagonist; for instance, in the novella *Lady Susan*, Lady Susan herself is an active, incessant antagonist in the lives of a number of characters. She constantly coerces and denigrates her daughter, she attempts to entangle multiple men, and she actively breaks marriages and families. Some of the characters in the story would see Lady Susan as not just an antagonist, but a villain.

Yet Austen does not always use antagonists in this way. In *Persuasion*, Anne Elliot faces much antagonism, from friends, family, acquaintances, and even potential suitors. While much of the opposition she faces comes from other people, she also faces other obstacles that interfere with her path: war, financial hardship, and a lack of independence. And we're going to consider antagonism from this broader lens: constant antagonists and villains like Lady Susan, but also self-antagonism, antagonism from friends, and antagonism in the form of life obstacles.

Antagonism is important because it is not enough to begin a story, to craft engaging, nuanced characters, or to establish the perfect tone and point of view. In a novel, when a character begins a journey—an internal journey of transformation, and an external journey toward a want—they should not quickly succeed. If a character immediately or easily gets what they want, there is no real journey, there is no *story*, and there is no opportunity for character growth. Without struggle, opposition, or interference—in other words, without antagonism—a character has no reason to change or become.

DEFINING THE TERMS OF ANTAGONISM

While many of my favorite writing craft books use "antagonist" as an umbrella term that applies to anyone or anything that stands in opposition to a character, I find it useful to follow Freytag's lead and apply narrower definitions. For the purposes of this book, I'm going to use the term "antagonist" to focus largely on opposition a character might face from other humans and the term "obstacle" for other sorts of opposition. There is, of course, overlap, but breaking antagonism into these subcategories enables us to focus on the different techniques that are used when writing about human and non-human opposition.[1]

An **obstacle** is anything that gets in the way of the character as they go on their journey. An obstacle may be a challenge, a physical or emotional impediment, or anything that must be overcome in order for the character's wants and needs to be met.

In *Mansfield Park*, Fanny faces many challenges as she strives to maintain a basic level of well-being and happiness. Fanny is rather sickly; while Austen never specifies her condition, she struggles to walk long (or even medium) distances and becomes ill easily. Early in the story, Fanny's horse dies. Suddenly she has no way to exercise, which negatively impacts her health while also robbing her of the small amount of autonomy she possessed.

After some physical suffering on Fanny's part and great debate among the rest of the family over whether Fanny even deserves to own a horse, Edmund solves the problem by trading one of his three horses—a road horse—for an animal more suited for riding. Yet this solution is not a permanent one: When Edmund develops interest in Mary Crawford, he starts lending Mary the horse allotted for Fanny, once again leaving Fanny without exercise or agency.

Throughout the story, Fanny faces **active obstacles**—obstacles that actively apply negative force to a character. These can be one-time events or circumstances that occur multiple times. In addition

---

1. You are welcome, of course, to speak about opposition using any terms you like! I wouldn't dare oppose you.

Fanny picks roses. Illustration by C. E. Brock, 1908.

to the loss of her horse, another active obstacle is the choice of her cousins and their friends to perform the play *Lovers' Vows*. She finds the content of the play objectionable, and the others apply constant pressure by requesting that she participate.

Fanny also faces **inactive obstacles**—present and existing obstacles that create challenges for the character but do not apply new or active force and pressure.

One of Fanny's sources of inactive opposition is her poverty, which makes her beholden to her uncle and aunts, robbing her of power and decision-making. This poverty is not something that has changed over time, and there seems to be no way that it could change. No one actively makes her poor, no single event has created this poverty—it's just the way things are.

In addition to situations and circumstances that make Fanny's life difficult, a number of characters also provide opposition. These are the antagonists of the story.

An **antagonist** is a person who actively opposes the main character and tries to interfere with them achieving their wants and needs, typically over multiple scenes or a large portion of the story.

An example of this is Fanny's aunt, Mrs. Norris. As we saw previously, it was Mrs. Norris who originally proposed that the Bertrams care for one of their nieces. Yet despite this outward appearance of charity, Mrs. Norris does not love Fanny or show her affection.

For four days in a row, Edmund lends the riding horse to Mary Crawford, leaving Fanny with no ability to exercise, and "without any excuse for avoiding whatever her unreasonable aunts might require." On the fourth day, Mrs. Norris and Lady Bertram task Fanny with rose picking, which involves walking back and forth, back and forth, in the hot sun, heeding their every whim, and fetching items like a servant.

As the day progresses, Fanny develops a severe headache and feels ill. She rests for a few minutes on a sofa, only to be berated by Mrs. Norris:

> "That is a very foolish trick, Fanny, to be idling away all the evening upon a sofa. Why cannot you come and sit here, and employ yourself as *we* do? If you have no work of your own, I can supply you from the poor basket. There is all the new calico, that was bought last week, not touched yet. I am sure I almost broke my back by cutting it out. You should learn to think of

other people; and, take my word for it, it is a shocking trick for a young person to be always lolling upon a sofa."

Mrs. Norris never varies from her role as antagonist. She constantly belittles, disregards, and threatens Fanny. Not only does she make Fanny's life miserable, but she also encourages others to mistreat Fanny. She displays classic **antagonism**—active opposition to a character, often **with hostility**.

Mrs. Norris supervises Fanny's needlework.
Illustration by C. E. Brock, 1908.

According to the *New Oxford American Dictionary*, in the field of biochemistry, antagonism is "inhibition of or interference with the action of one substance or organism by another."[2] This is a useful definition to apply to stories, particularly because it focuses on the "inhibition or interference" of someone's actions. Whenever one character opposes another character, or whenever a character inhibits or interferes with another character's actions, they show antagonism. Like Mrs. Norris, many antagonists possess an underlying hostility toward the character, and they directly or indirectly express their negative, angry, hateful, or unfriendly emotions.

Yet not all antagonism comes from antagonists or from those who have negative feelings toward the protagonist. **Antagonism without hostility** is active opposition by a character, yet without any hostility or ill will.

Fanny's cousin Edmund is her closest friend and confidante. He feels no ill will toward her, yet his actions inhibit and oppose her and her well-being. After Fanny's headache, due to four days without the horse and her aunts' incessant demands, Edmund recognizes that he is largely responsible for her suffering:

> Vexed as Edmund was with his mother and aunt, he was still more angry with himself. His own forgetfulness of her was worse than anything which they had done. Nothing of this would have happened had she been properly considered.... He was ashamed to think that for four days together she had not had the power of riding, and very seriously resolved, however unwilling he must be to check a pleasure of Miss Crawford's, that it should never happen again.

While Edmund regrets this instance of antagonism, he continues to interfere with Fanny's wants and needs, often unknowingly or with what he sees as good intent. His pursuit of Mary Crawford gives Fanny constant pain, and he encourages Fanny to marry Henry Crawford without listening to her reasons against doing so.

At times in *Mansfield Park*, it is not only people who act as antagonists. **The setting itself can be an antagonist** when it acts as a character in the story and provides active opposition and character-like antagonism. Throughout *Mansfield Park*, settings are

---

2. *New Oxford American Dictionary*, "antagonism," 65.

extremely important to Fanny. What she *needs* is a home that is safe and reassuring and allows her to feel like herself. And yet what she has is an opulent, vast estate, Mansfield Park, where she is not even allowed a fire in the winter. In the book, Mansfield Park feels like more than just an obstacle: It is an entity, a concept, a place that she feels a connection to even when it hurts her. When she's forced from Mansfield Park, her parents' house also acts as more than an obstacle in her mind, taking on the role of an active antagonist with an intent that feels malevolent to her:

> The sun's rays falling strongly into the parlour, instead of cheering, made her still more melancholy, for sunshine appeared to her a totally different thing in a town and in the country. Here, its power was only a glare: a stifling, sickly glare, serving but to bring forward stains and dirt that might otherwise have slept. There was neither health nor gaiety in sunshine in a town. She sat in a blaze of oppressive heat, in a cloud of moving dust, and her eyes could only wander from the walls, marked by her father's head, to the table cut and notched by her brothers, where stood the tea-board never thoroughly cleaned, the cups and saucers wiped in streaks, the milk a mixture of motes floating in thin blue, and the bread and butter growing every minute more greasy than even Rebecca's hands had first produced it.

The milk has a blueish tint and has motes floating in it—clearly it's low quality and probably going bad.[3] The dishes are not washed, just partially wiped. The bread is disgusting. The dust moves as a cloud. And as a result of living in this setting, Fanny's health deteriorates. Using the setting as an antagonist rather than an obstacle is common in survival stories and other *man vs. nature* stories, but it can also be used in novels like *Mansfield Park*, when places are intrinsically connected to a character's internal and external journeys.

While *Mansfield Park* contains numerous antagonists, there's some debate about whether this novel includes any true villains. A **villain** is an antagonist who causes significant, lasting, and often irreversible harm in the main character's life or in the lives of those the main character cares deeply about. Villains often have truly

---

3. I have a new life goal: to never drink blue milk.

wicked or evil motives and act as an opposite force to the protagonist. In my personal opinion, Mrs. Norris plays too small a role
in the story to qualify as a villain, and other characters, like Henry
Crawford, are complicated candidates.

"No, no, no!, she cried,
hiding her face.

Fanny Price refuses Henry Crawford's proposal.
Illustration by C. E. Brock, 1908.

In the initial rising action of the story, Henry Crawford breaks
the hearts of Fanny's cousins, Maria and Julia Bertram. Once they
are out of the picture, Henry decides to pursue Fanny's affections.
His sister Mary protests,

"I do desire that you will not be making her really unhappy; a *little* love, perhaps, may animate and do her good, but I will not have you plunge her deep, for she is as good a little creature as ever lived, and has a great deal of feeling."

"It can be but for a fortnight," said Henry; "and if a fortnight can kill her, she must have a constitution which nothing could save. No, I will not do her any harm, dear little soul! I only want her to look kindly on me, to give me smiles as well as blushes, to keep a chair for me by herself wherever we are, and be all animation when I take it and talk to her; to think as I think, be interested in all my possessions and pleasures, try to keep me longer at Mansfield, and feel when I go away that she shall be never happy again. I want nothing more."

His goals are selfish: He sees Fanny only as a conquest to be made. He simply wants her to feel that she will never be happy again. When Fanny refuses his proposal, she loses everything—her uncle sends her away from Mansfield Park with no specific date of return. Henry Crawford continues to pursue Fanny, and at this point, he might actually love her, yet the affections he has developed for Fanny do not prevent him from seducing her now-married cousin Maria. Running off with Henry Crawford ruins Maria's marriage and brings shame to the entire family.

Some readers classify Henry Crawford as only an antagonist, but not a villain. Others find him to be the most interesting character in the novel, and some authors have even written fan fiction in which he does marry Fanny, bringing both of them happiness. Yet regardless of whether we find him villain or antagonist or redeemable bad boy, the opposition he provides is essential to the plot and to Fanny's growth as a character.

Exercise 5.1: An Antagonist List

Make a list of your favorite antagonists and villains from books, movies, or any other stories. Which ones are antagonists? Which ones are villains? Why do you like them? Include other sources of antagonism, including active and inactive obstacles and friends who may be antagonistic.

Exercise 5.2: Hobby Trouble

Choose a character name and give your new character a hobby (such as knitting, fencing, stamp collecting, or competitive cheese making). Write a scene in which antagonism or opposition is shown toward the character and their hobby. For an extra challenge, include both antagonism from an enemy or adversary *and* from a friend or loved one. As you write this scene, consider how your character will react differently depending on who provides the antagonism.

Exercise 5.3: From Antagonist to Villain

Take a story you have written and choose one of your antagonists. Brainstorm what you could do to shift this character from an antagonist to a villain. (As an alternative, do the reverse: Choose a villain and brainstorm how you could shift this character from a villain to an antagonist.)

GIVING ANTAGONISTS UNDERSTANDABLE MOTIVES

Austen's antagonists are largely effective because of their motives. As readers, we don't always initially know the reasons for their behavior, but by the end of the story their motives become explainable and understandable.

In her novels, Austen gives her antagonist four primary types of motives, which can be categorized as self-interested, outwardly negative, positive, and neutral.

SELF-INTERESTED MOTIVES

Antagonists are often driven by self-interest.

All characters, antagonists and protagonists, act with a certain amount of self-interest. It's the only way, as people, we can survive—it's the only way to achieve our own wants and desires. As we saw in Chapter 2, we generally support characters who strive for their wants and needs. Self-interest becomes antagonism when:

- A character's self-interest interrupts the protagonist's journey
- A character's self-interest harms other characters or is done with a regard *only* for oneself

Self-interest often includes selfishness; an emphasis on bodily passions; a focus on gaining power, wealth, or material objects; and a disregard for societal norms. Ultimately, self-interest is a prioritization of one's own needs and wants over the needs and wants of others.

In *Sense and Sensibility*, Fanny Dashwood is an antagonist with self-interested motives. Fanny does not want to see any of her husband's inheritance go to his half sisters or stepmother because she would like it for herself.

> "It was my father's last request to me," replied her husband, "that I should assist his widow and daughters."
>
> "He did not know what he was talking of, I dare say; ten to one but he was light-headed at the time. Had he been in his right senses, he could not have thought of such a thing as begging you to give away half your fortune from your own child."

Slowly Fanny wears her husband down, appealing to *their* son's supposed needs and other self-focused arguments. Ultimately, her husband decides not to give his half sisters any money.

> [Her] argument was irresistible. It gave to his intentions whatever of decision was wanting before; and he finally resolved, that it would be absolutely unnecessary, if not highly indecorous, to do more for the widow and children of his father, than such kind of neighbourly acts as his own wife pointed out.

Another character who acts with self-interest in *Sense and Sensibility* is Lucy Steele, who has been secretly engaged to Edward Ferrars for four years. Now he has fallen in love with Elinor Dashwood, and it's understandable that Lucy would act in her own self-interest and attempt to maintain her engagement. She obviously has (or at least, had) feelings for Edward, and this is her chance for a better life.

OUTWARDLY NEGATIVE MOTIVES
Antagonists often possess outwardly negative motives, including:

- Spite
- Bitterness
- Jealousy
- Anger
- Revenge

- Cruelty
- A desire to control others
- Intentional breaking of social rules, laws, and expectations

Mrs. Ferrars. Illustration by Chris Hammond (Christiana Hammond), 1899.

Outwardly negative motives manifest natural human emotions and inclinations. It's natural for humans to feel ill will toward others, and most people act on these feelings at some point. Some characters are fixed in these sorts of motives, embracing them; others resist these motives or turn to them only in moments of extreme pressure, struggle, or pain.

In *Sense and Sensibility*, Mrs. Ferrars is generally cruel, controlling, and unpleasant to those around her. Lucy describes Mrs. Ferrars as a "very headstrong proud woman," likely to act in a "first fit of anger." And indeed, when Edward and Lucy's secret engagement is revealed, Mrs. Ferrars lashes out, disinheriting Edward.

Mrs. Ferrars and Fanny Dashwood are both characters who use and maintain power in a society where women often lack power and autonomy. While they can be unlikable, their anger, desire for money or control, and in Mrs. Ferrars's case, quick retribution, serve to sustain their power. Despite their cruelty, readers can understand their motives and at times even sympathize with them.

Often, characters act on negative motives in the heat of the moment. At other times, their behaviors are planned and premeditated. While Lucy Steele is self-interested, she also has negative feelings toward Elinor: She cannot like the woman who holds Edward's affection. Lucy intentionally manipulates Elinor by sharing knowledge of her secret engagement after extracting a promise that Elinor will not tell a soul. Lucy continues to be intentionally cruel and manipulative, manifesting a fair amount of spite toward Elinor.

Positive Motives for Antagonism

Sometimes good people, trying to do good things, unintentionally make life more difficult for others. Positive motives can be antagonistic when:

- A character helps or assists others in a way that they don't want to be helped
- A character helps someone at an inconvenient time or place
- Helping someone creates an unwanted sense of obligation to the helper
- Kind, understanding, or sensitive actions cause additional problems for the protagonist

In *Sense and Sensibility*, kind individuals attempt to help the Dashwood family but in the process are unintentionally antagonistic.

Sir John Middleton's generosity toward the Dashwoods seems to have no bounds. He allows them to use his cottage for a reasonable rate, brings them gifts, pays for their mail, and routinely invites them to dinner. This creates a strong sense of obligation to him, even though his wife's "cold insipidity ... was so particularly repulsive." Sir Middleton insists that at any point, the Dashwoods can borrow his carriage, but Mrs. Dashwood refuses to do so, to the point of only interacting with those who live in walking distance: "The independence of Mrs. Dashwood's spirit overcame the wish of society for her children." She wants to maintain her sense of self, which requires independence, and she does not want to feel over-reliant on Sir John.

Marianne Dashwood also finds antagonism in their new relationships with the Middletons. She feels beset by Sir John, Lady Middleton, Mrs. Jennings, and Mrs. Palmer. They constantly interfere with Marianne's need for both solitude and time with company that *she* chooses. They also try to force a relationship between Marianne and Colonel Brandon. They do this because of good motives—Marianne and Colonel Brandon seem like a good match, and marrying Colonel Brandon would allow Marianne to escape poverty. But it's not what Marianne wants.

Another antagonistic character in *Sense and Sensibility* is Mrs. Dashwood herself. At the beginning of the novel, she does not want to economize, which makes finding a new home difficult. She also overprioritizes her love for Marianne, to the point where she refuses to act as a parent figure and talk to Marianne about the pitfalls of her behavior. She's so afraid of damaging their relationship that she won't even ask Marianne if she is engaged. Ultimately, this hurts rather than helps Marianne. Mrs. Dashwood is a likable character—good and kind and yet so very flawed.

Neutral Motives for Antagonism

While many antagonistic motives are clearly either negative or positive, some motives are neutral. Often this occurs when a character:

- Is forced to choose between their wants and needs
- Is faced with no good paths or options; any choices they make will negatively impact themselves and others

- Believes they know better than other characters and imposes their will on others
- Believes that a greater good is worth some negative actions to achieve
- Lacks the perspective to see the impact of their choices

A sometimes-antagonistic character with neutral motives is Edward Ferrars. Elinor falls in love with Edward, and while at Norland Park he seems to return her affections. But for years, he has been secretly engaged to Lucy Steele. Because he is a man of his word, he won't break off his engagement to Lucy. Yet in being honorable to Lucy, he breaks Elinor's heart, and it wasn't fair to give his attention to Elinor in the first place if he couldn't actively create a relationship.

Neutral motives that create antagonism are often some of the most interesting because they allow writers to explore the nuances and complexities of relationships and morality.

Bringing Together All Four Types of Antagonism

In *Sense and Sensibility*, John Willoughby is an interesting case study because he demonstrates all four types of motives for antagonism.

- Selfish motives: Sleeping with an easily influenced teenage girl.
- Negative motives: Disregarding propriety and societal expectations; playing with Marianne's affections.
- Positive motives: Showing genuine interest in Marianne and trying to make a relationship possible, even when he knows it's unlikely he will succeed because of outside pressures and obligations.
- Neutral motive: Seeking financial stability/security. (In and of itself, the need for financial security is not negative; many of Austen's characters seek financial security for themselves or others, including Elinor Dashwood and her mother, and in other novels, Mrs. Bennet, Charlotte Collins, Anne Elliot, Jane Fairfax, and Fanny Price.)

Interestingly, Willoughby doesn't begin as an antagonist—he is Marianne's friend and romantic interest, the hero who saves her when she falls down a hill (a "save the cat" moment that makes him a sympathetic character). He demonstrates many positive qualities that Marianne prizes: He's friendly, handsome, and generous with his time and means, and he possesses a poetic sensibility.

Cover of Sense and Sensibility.
Published by George Routledge and Sons, 1884.

Yet despite his positive qualities, Elinor never quite trusts Willoughby. She finds some of his behaviors problematic, such as when he takes Marianne on a private, unsupervised tour of his aunt's estate, or when he offers to give Marianne a horse, which seems to be too big of a gift. (It's also impractical; they have no way to care for a horse.)

While everyone believes Marianne and Willoughby must be engaged, he never proposes to her or solidifies their connection.

When he suddenly leaves, Marianne is heartbroken. During Marianne's visit to London, he avoids and snubs her. Later on, he marries Miss Grey for financial reasons. We learn that he had previously impregnated a teenage girl and has no intention of helping her or her child.

Over the course of the story, Willoughby shifts from the person to whom Marianne feels closest to an unsympathetic man who has broken her heart.

Willoughby requests that Elinor listen to his story.
Illustration by C. E. Brock, 1908.

Yet Austen does not stop there: She once again complicates his character and our connection to him. When Marianne is deathly ill—at the moment when the reader should despise Willoughby the most—the narrator gives him a chance to explain himself. He arrives in the middle of the night and insists on speaking to Elinor.

> "I mean," said he, with serious energy, "if I can, to make you hate me one degree less than you do *now*. I mean to offer some kind of explanation, some kind of apology, for the past; to open my whole heart to you, and by convincing you, that though I have always been a blockhead, I have not been always a rascal, to obtain something like forgiveness from Ma—from your sister."

Austen then gives Willoughby page after page after page to explain himself. He admits all his terrible motives, stating,

> "Careless of her happiness, thinking only of my own amusement, giving way to feelings which I had always been too much in the habit of indulging, I endeavoured, by every means in my power, to make myself pleasing to her, without any design of returning her affection."

We see his angst, his attempts to justify himself, his pride and selfishness, his arguments good and bad. And we catch glimpses of redemption:

> "The happiest hours of my life were what I spent with her when I felt my intentions were strictly honourable, and my feelings blameless."

Ultimately, Elinor comes to understand him a little, and to truly understand a person is a token of forgiveness, a gift of humanity for them and for the reader.

> [Elinor's] thoughts were silently fixed on the irreparable injury which too early an independence and its consequent habits of idleness, dissipation, and luxury, had made in the mind, the character, the happiness, of a man who, to every advantage of person and talents, united a disposition naturally open and honest, and a feeling, affectionate temper. The world had made

him extravagant and vain—Extravagance and vanity had made him cold-hearted and selfish. Vanity, while seeking its own guilty triumph at the expense of another, had involved him in a real attachment, which extravagance, or at least its offspring, necessity, had required to be sacrificed. Each faulty propensity in leading him to evil, had led him likewise to punishment.

It is John Willoughby's motives that make him an antagonist, but it is also his motives that make him understandable. We don't have to like him or offer him a measure of forgiveness (as Elinor does) in order to accept that he is a true portrait of a certain type of person. Austen's antagonists are some of her most memorable characters because they are full of depth, complexity, and nuance. For example, as I read *Pride and Prejudice*, I find myself condemning Mr. Wickham's behavior—but I also find myself fascinated by him. He is a compelling character who does much to move the plot forward.

In Austen's novels, we often come to understand the motives and characters of the antagonists, but in *Sense and Sensibility*, Austen takes this one step further. She gives Willoughby a gift not often given to non-viewpoint antagonists: the opportunity to fully tell his own story. While we may not ever give our antagonists this same opportunity, it's important for us as writers to understand the motives of our antagonists, because these motives will influence how we write these characters.

Exercise 5.4: Examples of Antagonistic Motives

Find examples of four antagonists from published works (by authors other than Jane Austen). Each should be driven by one of the following types of motives for antagonism (though they may display other motives as well):

- Self-interested
- Outwardly negative
- Positive
- Neutral

Write down a few notes on how the motives are manifest in the character's actions and decisions.

Exercise 5.5: The Unexpected Motive for Antagonism

Write a short scene in which a character has a small, everyday want, like arriving on time for a meeting, trying to buy a pie, or convincing someone to see a movie. In the scene, an antagonist should interfere or place obstacles in their way. The scene should be written from the point of view of the character with the want.

Afterward, reflect:

· What would be the most obvious motives for antagonism in this scene?
· What would be an unusual or unexpected motive for antagonism in this situation?

Make minor revisions to your scene with this unexpected motive in mind.

Exercise 5.6: Let the Antagonist Explain

Take an antagonist that you plan to write in a future story or that you have included in an early story draft. Give them the opportunity to explain themselves, whether through the form of an internal monologue, a journal entry, a letter to a close friend, or a conversation. This self-explanation should not necessarily be included in the story, but it will inform how you write the character.

THE PURPOSE OF ANTAGONISM

The word "journey" includes the implication that the process of travel—whether physical or metaphorical—requires struggle. In a physical journey, difficult land must be traversed in order to reach a destination. In a more metaphorical plot journey, Elizabeth Bennet cannot simply meet and then immediately marry a man of ten thousand pounds a year, solving her family's financial troubles without any effort or difficulty along the way.

In *The Technique of the Drama*, Freytag writes, "What the drama presents is always a struggle, which, with strong perturbations of soul, the hero wages against opposing forces." These "strong perturbations of the soul" are part of the internal journey, an arc of self-transformation. Internal change would be unlikely to occur in a vacuum, without outside forces, and Freytag explains that "the opposing power must be made visible in a human representative."[4] It is not enough for a protagonist to recognize weakness in themselves and make a change or correction. In a story, we need to see their opposition embodied in a physical form.

In *Pride and Prejudice*, Mr. Darcy is Elizabeth's primary antagonist, and they are the greatest stimulus for each other's change. Elizabeth faces numerous other antagonists—her mother, Mr. Collins, Caroline Bingley, Mr. Wickham, and Lady Catherine—each who highlight different aspects of her character and apply pressure, creating the strong perturbations of her soul.

In the next chapter we'll consider how to make antagonists and protagonists fit within the larger structure of the story by discussing the rising action and how to make scenes build on each other in a manner both logical and satisfying. Ultimately, the antagonists and the rising action serve as a test of character and a refining power. We come to better know a protagonist through their responses to obstacles and antagonism, such as when, while playing the pianoforte at Rosings, Elizabeth tells Mr. Darcy,

> "You mean to frighten me, Mr. Darcy, by coming in all this state to hear me.... There is a stubbornness about me that never can bear to be frightened at the will of others. My courage always rises with every attempt to intimidate me."

---

4. Freytag, *Technique of the Drama*, 104–105.

CHAPTER SIX

RISING ACTION

"The progress of the friendship between Catherine and Isabella was quick as its beginning had been warm.... If a rainy morning deprived them of other enjoyments, they were still resolute in meeting in defiance of wet and dirt, and shut themselves up, to read novels together."
—*Northanger Abbey*

In *Northanger Abbey*, Catherine Morland takes three physical journeys: to Bath, to Northanger Abbey, and then back home. As she takes these physical journeys, the primary external journey—in other words, the plot—focuses on her relationship with Henry Tilney. She meets him shortly after her arrival in Bath, finds him attractive, experiences disappointment when he disappears, et cetera, et cetera. Their relationship builds, with plenty of setbacks, until the Tilneys invite her to stay with them at Northanger Abbey. Meanwhile, Catherine's internal journey, as we discussed in Chapter 1, is one of transformation, as she learns to read the people around her, pass useful judgments, and act decisively.

In addition to the external romance and Catherine's internal transformation, *Northanger Abbey* also includes multiple subplots that interact with each of her journeys and help carry the story.

One of the primary subplots is her friendship with Isabella Thorpe; quickly, the two young women become inseparable. This subplot connects to a second subplot, John Thorpe's romantic interest in Catherine, which leads both Thorpe siblings to interfere with Catherine's relationship with Henry Tilney.

Catherine Morland and Isabella Thorpe in Bath.
Illustration by C. E. Brock, 1907.

Another important subplot is Catherine's love of books. She reads with Isabella and discusses novels with multiple characters. These Gothic novels often contain fantastical situations that inform how Catherine sees the world. As a result, she pictures herself as the heroine of her own story, and at times she misinterprets the intentions of others—going so far as to believe that General Tilney might have harmed his wife—based off of her readings.

All of these components of the story are explored and developed in the rising action.

The rising action is the movement of the story from the inciting incident until the climax. This is the core of the story, the middle, in which the reader spends most of their time. This is what Aristotle calls the **complication**. This is also the section that many writers struggle to write. Some call it the "murky middle"; author Maria V. Snyder describes it as "the cold hard slog."[1]

The rising action contains dozens of scenes. But how do we choose what scenes to include? How do we build from inciting incident to climax? How do we keep readers engaged in the story? How do we keep ourselves engaged as writers?

In *Novelist's Essential Guide to Crafting Scenes*, Raymond Obstfeld explains that a scene "usually focuses on a specific purpose," including:

- "giv[ing] the reader information necessary to further plot"
- "show[ing] the conflict between characters"
- "develop[ing] a particular character by highlighting a specific trait or action"
- "creat[ing] suspense"

Obstfeld goes on to write that

> The best scenes do a combination of the above, sometimes all of the above. What's important is that the writer (1) knows why that scene exists and (2) justifies its existence by making it memorable.[2]

---

1. Snyder, "Writing Through the Middle."
2. Obstfeld, *Novelist's Essential Guide to Crafting Scenes*, 2–3.

Every scene must have a purpose, and every scene must fulfill its purpose in an engaging way. And the rising action must contain multiple scenes, distributed somewhat evenly throughout the story, that:

- Address the progress of the main plot
- Show the character figuring out who they are
- Show the character developing and practicing new skills
- Set up and develop subplots
- Show key relationships

Often, before writing a second or third draft, I create a massive Excel spreadsheet in which I track my characters, relationships, plot, and subplots throughout the book. Not every component can or should be present in each scene, but if a scene doesn't make substantive contributions, then I cut it. If a scene performs only a single purpose, I rewrite it to make it do more—a scene can include an important discovery *and* complicate a relationship; a character can discover something about themselves *while* engaging with a subplot; an antagonist can reveal some of their motives *while* interfering with the protagonist's journey.

It's often easy to think of what the big, flashy scenes contribute to a story. For instance, in an Austen novel, a proposal scene acts as a catalyst for the characters, sometimes even serving as a key turning point or the midpoint, which we'll talk about later in this chapter. Yet most books are not filled with only big moments, and the "smaller" scenes are essential for the rising action. After all, key moments of change only matter because of all the other building blocks.

Let's consider the sequence of scenes in Chapter 10 of *Northanger Abbey* and what each scene contributes to the story in terms of character, relationships, plot, structure, and suspense.

CHAPTER 10 SCENE 1		
Location: The theatre	**Characters:** Catherine and her brother James; Isabella and John Thorpe; the Allens	
What occurs: Isabella speaks at great length to Catherine; Catherine gives only short answers. Isabella discusses how much John Thorpe likes Catherine and that Mr. Tilney clearly also likes Catherine. Isabella wishes she could meet Mr. Tilney. Isabella expresses how perfectly she and James get along. Isabella and Catherine argue about how Catherine would have behaved in a situation.		
Plot forwarding: Isabella tries to solidify relationships both between herself and James and between Catherine and John. Despite Isabella's efforts, Catherine leaves the scene hoping to spend more time with Miss Tilney and strengthen her other relationships.	**Character:** Catherine attempts to express her opinions and thoughts but is unable to get Isabella to listen to her.	**Relationship development:** We begin to see a divide between Isabella and Catherine, especially in Catherine's short reactions and Isabella's insistence that "I know you better than you know yourself."

CHAPTER 10 SCENE 2

Location:	Characters:
The pump-room	Catherine, James, Isabella, Miss Tilney

What occurs:
Catherine feels unhappy to be the third wheel, as Isabella and James spend all their time together and rarely allow her to contribute to the conversation. Eventually, Miss Tilney arrives and Catherine finds an opportunity to speak to her. Catherine compliments Miss Tilney's brother Henry, and explains why she wasn't able to spend time with Henry the last time they saw each other. They confirm that they will see each other at the next ball.

Relationship development #1:	Relationship development #2:
Catherine feels trapped by her relationship with the Thorpes and fears they will make it impossible for her to spend time with anyone else.	Catherine strengthens her relationship with Miss Tilney, and by extension, with her brother. As the narrator states, "They parted—on Miss Tilney's side with some knowledge of her new acquaintance's feelings, and on Catherine's, without the smallest consciousness of having explained them."

Plot forwarding:	Suspense:
Isabella and James grow closer, which takes us one step closer to the midpoint of the novel (when they become engaged).	We learn that both Catherine and Henry Tilney will be at the next ball, which builds anticipation.

CHAPTER 10 SCENE 3 (MINI-SCENE)

Location:	Characters:
Catherine's room	Catherine

What occurs:
Catherine prepares for the ball.

Structural purpose:	Character insight:
This is a transitional scene, which connects scenes 2 and 4 without a scene break.	We see how much Catherine cares and worries about the ball and the possible interactions she may have with Henry Tilney.

CHAPTER 10 SCENE 4

Location: The ball	**Characters:** Catherine, Isabella, John Thorpe, Henry Tilney, background characters

What occurs:

Catherine attempts to hide from John Thorpe because she does not want to be forced to dance with him and miss the opportunity to dance with Henry Tilney. Henry notices Catherine and asks her to dance. As they head to the dance floor, John Thorpe interrupts their progress by speaking to Catherine. He insists that they were supposed to dance, and she says that he never actually asked her. John Thorpe finds out who Henry Tilney is and becomes distracted by the idea of selling Henry a horse. The dance begins. Henry expresses his frustrations with John's interruption. Henry and Catherine discuss obligations in dance partners vs. in marriage. They flirt, speak about other topics, and enjoy the dance. Afterward, Catherine sees Henry's father for the first time; Henry informs her, "That gentleman knows your name, and you have a right to know his." Catherine speaks to Miss Tilney, and they make plans for the next day.

Relationship insight: We see the contrast between Catherine's relationship with John Thorpe (who dominates the conversation and hardly allows Catherine to speak) and her relationship with Henry Tilney (who values what Catherine has to say; their conversation is much more even and equal). Jealousy is clear between both gentlemen, which sets up later plot events.	**Relationship shifts:** Her friendship with Miss Tilney has an extra conversation to help it develop, while "of her other, her older, her more established friend, Isabella, of whose fidelity and worth she had enjoyed a fortnight's experience, she scarcely saw anything during the evening."
Relationship development: Catherine is able to make it clear to Henry that despite not always having spent time with him in the past, due to other obligations, she values him and prefers his company over that of others.	**Character development:** Catherine verbally disagrees with John Thorpe. Even though he doesn't really listen to her, this is progress.
Character introduction: We see General Tilney for the first time. This is important because he plays a key role in the second half of the story.	**Structural:** We learn that Catherine and Miss Tilney will meet in the next chapter. This creates anticipation and a hook for the next chapter.

Each of these scenes serves multiple purposes in forwarding the story. Relationships shift and develop, and Catherine takes small steps toward finding her voice and figuring out how she relates to others.

Ultimately, the scenes in the middle of the novel do much of the heavy lifting, especially in terms of the internal journey. After all, **the key purpose of the rising action is to take the main character from where they are as a person at the inciting incident to who they need to be by the climax**.

Exercise 6.1: Analyzing Rising Action

Select a portion of the rising action from a novel by one of your favorite authors. Choose either a chapter with multiple scenes or a sequence of chapters; the selected portion should occur after the inciting incident but before the climax. Ideally, these scenes should not include any huge turning points or major life-changing events— they should consist of smaller building blocks of the rising action.

Now analyze the scenes by creating a chart. What characters are present? How does the plot develop? What do we see of character development and the main character's progress on their journey? Are there any changes or shifts in relationships? What key subplots are included/developed? What is the purpose of each scene, and how does each scene forward the story?

TRY-FAIL CYCLES, DISTRACTIONS, INTERRUPTIONS, AND RED HERRINGS

If Catherine Morland were easily able to shift from naivete to being a perceptive judge of character, it would not create a satisfying story. In fiction, the internal journey is often about answering the fundamental questions of self. Yet it is difficult to "know thyself." It is difficult to change and progress and become. As such, this transformation should be difficult for characters—characters should have failures on their way to success.

Some authors talk about this as constructing **try-fail cycles** for your characters. Novelist Dan Wells explains, "Before the heroes succeed at anything important, they should try and fail at least twice. Victory should be earned. A problem that can be solved on the first try is not big enough for your readers to care about."[3]

For instance, in *Pride and Prejudice*, we see a number of try-fail cycles in Elizabeth and Darcy's relationship, even before Elizabeth is interested in a relationship:

- At the Meryton assembly, Mr. Darcy verbally snubs Elizabeth.
- At the Lucases' gathering, Elizabeth refuses to dance with Mr. Darcy.
- At Mr. Bingley's ball, they argue about Mr. Wickham and pride.
- Elizabeth rejects Mr. Darcy's proposal.
- When Lydia runs away with Wickham, Elizabeth assumes that any chance of connection between her and Mr. Darcy is lost forever.

As part of these try-fail cycles, we often see pressure applied by obstacles and antagonists, which we discussed in the previous chapter. In addition, try-fail cycles often include distractions,

---

3. Presentation slide from Wells, "Dan Wells on Story Structure, part 4 of 5."

interruptions, and red herrings. These can interfere with the character's internal journey, with the external journey of the plot, or with the subplots.

A **distraction** draws the attention of the main character away from their core want—it's a side path on the external journey.

In *Persuasion*, Anne wants to rebuild a relationship with Captain Wentworth, but she is distracted by other men (Captain Benwick and Mr. Elliot) who show interest in her. She takes genuine pleasure in their company.

Mr. Elliot steps back, and as he does so, he admires Anne.
Illustration by C. E. Brock, 1909.

For instance, while in Lyme,

> Anne found Captain Benwick again drawing near her. Lord
> Byron's "dark blue seas" could not fail of being brought forward
> by their present view, and she gladly gave him all her attention
> as long as attention was possible.

On the surface, the time and attention she pays to Captain Benwick and Mr. Elliot distract her from her relationship with Captain Wentworth. Yet these distractions force Anne to consider what she wants. She visualizes different possible futures and takes more initiative. She realizes how much she still loves Wentworth. And finally, these interactions stir jealousy in Captain Wentworth—he realizes he could lose Anne.

Good distractions—like those employed by Austen—help the character learn and ultimately bring them closer to their goals.

An **interruption** halts the forward movement of the internal and external journey.

When Anne and Mr. Elliot see each other for the first time, Mr. Elliot seems to admire her. This causes a moment between Captain Wentworth and Anne:

> Captain Wentworth looked round at her instantly in a way which
> shewed his noticing of it. He gave her a momentary glance, a glance
> of brightness, which seemed to say, "That man is struck with you,
> and even I, at this moment, see something like Anne Elliot again."

This is progress for Anne and Captain Wentworth's relationship. At this point, it seems likely that they will now interact in more positive ways, speak to each other, and resolve their differences. In other words, the external journey could wrap up quickly.

But then a colossal interruption occurs: Louisa falls and experiences a head injury. As a result, Anne returns to her family. Worse, Captain Wentworth is placed in a position of obligation to Louisa. Because he romantically pursued her, now he feels he must assist her in her sickness and possibly even marry her.

Yet this interruption has several positive effects. When Anne begins to live with her father and older sister in Bath, she shifts from being in a group that appreciates and understands her to being largely unappreciated and misunderstood, which seems like a setback. Yet she does not wallow in inactivity. She makes conscious efforts to assert herself, for instance, by spending time with her friend Mrs. Smith even though her family disapproves of it.

This event also gives Wentworth clarity on his feelings and the consequences of his actions. When Louisa becomes engaged to someone else, he is free to choose anew what he wants, and he more actively attempts to create a relationship with Anne.

Interruptions create hardships or difficulties for characters, often in ways that help them grow internally.

A **red herring** is a conclusion that is false or misleading or causes the protagonist to pursue the wrong path.

Throughout *Persuasion*, Anne follows multiple red herrings. Early in the novel, when Captain Wentworth pursues Louisa, Anne concludes that he has completely moved on from their relationship. This leads her to avoid spending time with him. After the accident, Anne learns that Louisa is engaged and falsely concludes that she is to marry Captain Wentworth. Both of these false conclusions cause setbacks, not only in Anne's relationship with Captain Wentworth, but also in her internal journey to discover her place in the world, her voice, and possibilities for happiness.

Red herrings make it more difficult to find the truth, creating internal and external obstacles that the character must overcome in order to continue the path of discovery.

Try-fail cycles, with their accompanying distractions, interruptions, and red herrings are essential elements of the rising action. They don't exist simply to make the story longer. **Try-fail cycles exist because struggle is essential for refining character.** If the things that characters most want and need are truly worth seeking, then they *should* be initially outside of the characters' grasp.

Exercise 6.2: Personal Try-Fail Cycles

Consider some of the things in life that you have achieved, skills you have gained, or relationships you have forged.

What try-fail cycles did you experience on the way to success? What distractions, interruptions, and red herrings interfered with your goals? Reflect on this by writing a brief passage.

Exercise 6.3: Adding Difficulty

Take a scene that you have written and add at least one distraction, interruption, or red herring. This difficulty can be small and localized (and could potentially be overcome by the end of the scene), or it could be larger, with implications for later in the story.

Exercise 6.4: Slowing Down Red Riding Hood

Picture the classic character of Little Red Riding Hood, who desires to visit her grandmother in the woods. Set a timer for five minutes and create a list of as many possible distractions, interruptions, and red herrings as you can think of that she could encounter on her journey. This can include those in the original tale but should not be limited to them. Circle the three ideas that interest you most.

Bonus: Write a new version of the Little Red Riding Hood story using your chosen distractions, interruptions, and red herrings.

INFORMATION GAPS AND DISCOVERIES

Sometimes it is very clear that a particular event or scene belongs before another event or scene. Yet at other times, it is more difficult to decide on sequencing and scene order within the rising action. During the revision process, I often reorganize the scenes and chapters in the middle of the book. Once, I took a chapter with four scenes—scene A, scene B, scene C, and scene D—and put them in the reverse order—D, C, B, A. This made the chapter build toward a revelation or discovery at its end, which propelled the reader forward through the coming chapters. In my third published novel, I examined six chapters between the midpoint of the novel and the climax and ended up completely switching their order.[4] The original chapter order was A, B (with scenes B1 and B2), C, D, E, F. Rearranging the chapters resulted in the final sequence: A, B1, D, B2, E, F, C. This created a better sense of building, progression, and tension for the characters and the reader.

Austen's novels are a masterclass in scene order. Much of what makes her sequences work is the way in which Austen **sets up information gaps and then unveils discoveries** for her readers.

An article by Jonah Lehrer, "The Itch of Curiosity," provides a good explanation of the information gap:

> The information gap theory of curiosity ... was first developed by George Loewenstein of Carnegie-Mellon in the early 90s. According to Loewenstein, curiosity is rather simple: It comes when we feel a gap "between what we know and what we want to know". This gap has emotional consequences: it feels like a mental itch, a mosquito bite on the brain. We seek out new knowledge because that's how we scratch the itch.[5]

In *Made to Stick: Why Some Ideas Survive and Others Die*, it says, "*Curiosity* is the intellectual need to answer questions and close open patterns. *Story* plays to this universal desire by doing the opposite, posing questions and opening situations."[6] Austen constantly poses questions and opens up situations and then builds scenes to explore and ultimately answer these questions. She uses five core techniques to create information gaps or heighten their importance in the story.

1. ESTABLISH AN INFORMATION GAP BY USING CHARACTER ANTICIPATION

One of the simplest ways to establish an information gap is to show the characters anticipating something, through their thoughts and words and actions. If the characters desire to know something, readers also develop this desire.

---

4. The novel in question is *The Lady's Guide to Death and Deception*. It required the least revision of the books in the Mary Bennet trilogy, though as you can see, it did require structural work.
5. Lehrer, "The Itch of Curiosity."
6. Heath and Heath, *Made to Stick*, 83.

In *Emma*, almost all the characters anticipate meeting Frank Churchill. Getting to know his personality and character is established as intrinsically interesting:

> Mr. Frank Churchill was one of the boasts of Highbury, and a lively curiosity to see him prevailed, though the compliment was so little returned that he had never been there in his life. His coming to visit his father had been often talked of but never achieved.

2. Establish an Information Gap by Breaking a Pattern

The human brain relies on patterns to make sense of the world. The book *Made to Stick* explains that our attention is drawn when a pattern is broken.[7]

Many of the patterns established in *Emma* relate to societal expectations. For instance, individuals are expected to meet their verbal and written commitments and to pay obligations to family members. In the story, Mr. Churchill commits to visit his father, Mr. Weston, in Highbury. This is both a commitment and a family obligation, yet Mr. Churchill does not visit. This breaks a pattern:

> "Where is the young man?" said John Knightley. "Has he been here on this occasion—or has he not?"
>
> "He has not been here yet," replied Emma. "There was a strong expectation of his coming soon after the marriage, but it ended in nothing; and I have not heard him mentioned lately."

Whenever a pattern is broken in a story, it creates an information gap: We want to know why this pattern has been broken. This is especially true for behavioral patterns. In *Emma*, a behavioral pattern is broken when Jane Fairfax receives an anonymous gift: a pianoforte. As previously discussed, people simply do not receive pianofortes from mysterious benefactors, then or today. This break from societal norms immediately creates an information gap, a mystery that Emma is compelled to unravel.

---

7. Heath and Heath, *Made to Stick*, 64.

*Frank Churchill breaks the expectations of Highbury
by traveling all the way to London for a haircut.
Illustration by Hugh Thomson, 1896.*

3. Establish That an Information Gap Has Important Consequences

As readers, we care most about information gaps when consequences are involved. Characters need a reason for a discovery. Consequences, whether good or bad, can provide that reason. If an information gap has no stakes, then the character has no reason to close this gap, and the reader will not care whether or not they do.

In *Emma*, we like the characters of Mr. and Mrs. Weston; they are good people who matter to Emma and others in the community. Because we like them, we care that Frank Churchill refuses to visit.

Yet the stakes are not just for the Westons. Emma's desire to know Mr. Churchill relates to her overarching want. She is a matchmaker, and she has envisioned a match for herself:

> Now, it so happened that in spite of Emma's resolution of never marrying, there was something in the name, in the idea of Mr. Frank Churchill, which always interested her. She had frequently thought—especially since his father's marriage with Miss Taylor—that if she *were* to marry, he was the very person to suit her in age, character and condition. He seemed by this connexion between the families, quite to belong to her. She could not but suppose it to be a match that every body who knew them must think of. That Mr. and Mrs. Weston did think of it, she was very strongly persuaded; and though not meaning to be induced by him, or by any body else, to give up a situation which she believed more replete with good than any she could change it for, she had a great curiosity to see him, a decided intention of finding him pleasant, of being liked by him to a certain degree, and a sort of pleasure in the idea of their being coupled in their friends' imaginations.

Filling this information gap—coming to know Mr. Churchill and his character—has personal consequences for Emma and her future happiness.

4. Establish an Information Gap by Raising New Questions When Questions are Answered

While obstacles, setbacks, and opposition inevitably occur, eventually characters should make discoveries, filling their information gaps. Yet if a question is resolved or answered, then why should the reader keep reading? Often, the characters have more than one information gap. And often, when a question is answered, a new question is raised. Author Mary Robinette Kowal talks about this as writing with a "yes-but, no-and" mindset.[8] Let's start with the

---

8. *Writing Excuses*, season 17, episode 32, "Everything is About Conflict."

second half of her formula: *no-and*. When a character reaches for something, they often face internal and external obstacles that keep them from achieving their goals or finding answers and also reveal new obstacles. The characters face a *no*. They have failed, or things have gotten worse. However, they don't stop striving; they keep going and attempting. That's the *and*. They reach a *no, and* then they keep going. *No-and*. The other option is *yes-but*. In this case, a character does make a discovery or achieve their goals. This is a *yes*. But then something complicates their situation: There might be unintended consequences or a new information gap. This is the *but*, an interference or new setback. There is a victory, a *yes, but* it's not final or complete. *Yes-but*.

In *Emma*, Frank Churchill does ultimately visit Highbury. We meet him, we see him in front of us. Yet new questions are raised: Is he the sort of man Emma expected? Will he treat his father and new stepmother with the consideration they deserve? Will he fall in love with Emma? Will there be a ball, and who will he dance with at the ball?

Each time a question about Frank Churchill is answered, we find a new, compelling question. In a sense, the larger question established before his arrival—what is Frank Churchill's character?—is never clearly answered during the rising action. It takes the entire novel to explore this question, and each discovery is just one piece of the puzzle.

5. Establish an Information Gap by Revealing Key Information

While information gaps are often created by concealing information, the reverse can also be done. Revealing key information can create an information gap as we become curious about the consequences of this information. This is especially true when what is revealed has the potential to disrupt the forward path of the protagonist.

While Austen's novel *Emma* relies on concealing information about Frank Churchill and others, in *Mansfield Park,* information is revealed in order to create a need for discovery.

In *Mansfield Park*, Fanny Price has watched with disapproval as Henry Crawford flirts shamelessly with her cousins Maria and Julia, even though Maria is engaged. When Maria weds, both she and Julia leave Mansfield Park, and Henry Crawford turns his attentions to Fanny.

At this point, Austen could have created an information gap by simply continuing to show Fanny's viewpoint. Through Fanny's eyes, we would see Henry's attentions and wonder at their cause. We would want to know first, if he has changed on a fundamental level, and second, how Fanny will act in response.

Yet Austen does not follow this storytelling path. Instead, she shows a scene from the Crawfords' perspectives. We read part of it in the previous chapter, but let's look at another passage, when Henry first reveals his plans.

Henry and Mary discuss his plans to break Fanny's heart.
Illustration by Hugh Thomson, 1896.

"And how do you think I mean to amuse myself, Mary, on the days that I do not hunt? I am grown too old to go out more than three times a week; but I have a plan for the intermediate days, and what do you think it is?"

"To walk and ride with me, to be sure."

"Not exactly, though I shall be happy to do both, but *that* would be exercise only to my body, and I must take care of my mind. Besides, *that* would be all recreation and indulgence, without the wholesome alloy of labour, and I do not like to eat the bread of idleness. No, my plan is to make Fanny Price in love with me."

"Fanny Price! Nonsense! No, no. You ought to be satisfied with her two cousins."

"But I cannot be satisfied without Fanny Price, without making a small hole in Fanny Price's heart."

Showing this scene to the reader raises both the stakes and our curiosity. We know that Mr. Crawford only intends to gain Fanny's affections because he wants to amuse himself. This immediately establishes two information gaps: Will Fanny discover the motives behind his behavior? And could his motives change?

In this particular case, key information is revealed to the reader but not to the protagonist, yet at times key information is revealed to both the reader and the protagonist in order to create an information gap.

ENDING CHAPTERS WITH INFORMATION GAPS

Information gaps can be established at any point in a plot—the beginning, the middle, or the end. On a more granular level, an information gap can be established or developed at any point in a scene or chapter. Yet because information gaps keep us turning the pages—because we thirst for answers—chapters often end with a clear gap. This acts as a sort of hook to keep the reader reading. The gap can be new, or it can be already established and raised again or developed in some way. It can be large or small, as long as it matters to the reader and the characters.

Let's look at the first six chapter endings of *Emma* with an eye for information gaps.

Chapter	Exact Location	Information Gap
1	Last three paragraphs	Emma decides to make a match for Mr. Elton. Both her father and Mr. Knightley push against this idea. We know she won't listen to them, so we want to see what actions she will take.
2	No strong information gap.	
3	Midway through chapter and final paragraph	Halfway through the chapter, Emma makes Harriet's acquaintance and decides that "she would improve her; she would detach her from her bad acquaintance, and introduce her into good society; she would form her opinions and her manners." In the final paragraph, we learn that Harriet is gratified by Emma's attention. We want to know how their relationship will develop next.
4	Last four paragraphs	Emma spends much of the chapter convincing Harriet to reject Mr. Martin's proposal. At the end of the chapter, Emma talks of Mr. Elton to Harriet, and in the final paragraph, Emma decides that Mr. Elton and Harriet would make a good match. The information gap is clear: Will she manage to bring them together? And how will she do so?
5	Final paragraph	After Mrs. Weston and Mr. Knightley discuss Emma's declaration that she does not plan to marry, we receive access to Mrs. Weston's thoughts: "There were wishes ... respecting Emma's destiny, but it was not desirable to have them suspected." We want to know what Mrs. Weston hopes for Emma, and we sense that she—Emma's close friend—believes that Emma will indeed marry someday, which creates another information gap.
6	Final paragraph	Emma reflects on the nature of Mr. Elton's love, and whether it is too gallant (and full of sighs) to be considered love. This creates an information gap: can Emma actually recognize love when she sees it?

Sometimes an information gap that propels us to the next chapter is the mention of an upcoming ball or other event. Sometimes it's an insight into character that makes us more invested in their wants or their relationships. And not all chapters need information gaps or a clear hook for the next chapter. Yet incorporating information gaps throughout a story can help create structure and audience interest, as well as a sense of building and progression. We have things we want to learn and discover, and so do the characters. We'll look in more detail at discoveries—and how to unveil big discoveries—in Chapter 11.

Exercise 6.5: Analyzing Information Gaps

Choose a story in which a character actively tries to discover something. Analyze the author's techniques: When is the primary information gap set up? What techniques are used to establish the information gap? Are there multiple information gaps? When the character discovers or learns something, what new questions are raised?

Exercise 6.6: Revising Chapter Endings

For a novel that you've drafted, consider the end of each chapter. How does the chapter resolve? What makes the reader want to keep reading? Is there a hook or an information gap, either within the chapter or at the end of the chapter, that will help propel the reader forward?

Choose at least one chapter that seems to have a weaker ending and revise.

KEY TURNING POINTS

Of the dozens of scenes in a novel, a few typically stand out for their importance in the story. Obviously, the inciting incident, the climax, and the final suspense are three such moments. But most novels contain several additional moments: in other words, **key turning points**. These turning points may occur in a single scene or in a sequence of scenes.

While every scene in a novel should be compelling and serve a purpose, turning points change everything. These moments are hinges for the story, major shifts or catalysts. They often include a large triumph or a large failure. They create change that feels irreversible. This does not mean that change cannot happen later—Mr. Darcy's first failed proposal to Elizabeth is such a moment, and yet ultimately they wed—but it does mean that the characters cannot simply forget about this moment, brush it aside, or easily move past it. Author Dan Wells talks about these as **pinch points** that apply pressure to the characters and the plot.[9] These moments raise the stakes and put a lens on the characters' behavior and choices, for we see how they react and who they are at these key turning points.

In modern novels and films, we often see a key turning point at the midpoint of the story. Three of Austen's novels contain a strong turning point at the story's midpoint:

- *Northanger Abbey*: Isabella Thorpe becomes engaged to Catherine Morland's brother. This creates a closer connection between the Thorpes and the Morlands, leading the Thorpes to take larger actions to secure the supposed Morland fortune.
- *Pride and Prejudice*: Mr. Darcy proposes to Elizabeth; she rejects him; he writes a letter explaining everything. In Chapter 1, we discussed how this becomes a major transformative moment for both Elizabeth and Mr. Darcy.
- *Persuasion*: Louisa falls on rock stairs at Lyme; Anne is the only one to take decisive action. As we saw earlier in this chapter, this moment seems to guarantee that Captain Wentworth will marry Louisa. Anne is also forced to travel to Bath to stay with her family.

Austen's novels were originally released in volumes. For instance, *Persuasion* was published in two volumes; the first half of the story was printed in the first physical book, and the second half of the story was printed in the second book. Thus, we have a strong turning point at the midpoint, right before the final pages. This increases the chances that a reader will purchase and read the second volume. *Northanger Abbey* was also printed in two volumes and uses the

---

9. Wells, "Dan Wells on Story Structure, part 2 of 5."

same structure.[10] (As a note, we have a chicken-and-egg problem. We don't know whether Austen or her publisher chose the volume breaks, if Austen wrote with volume breaks in mind, or if the publisher selected volume breaks based on the text.)

Austen's other four published novels were printed in three volumes. In the following chart, you'll see how in three of the novels, there is either a key turning point or a strong hook/large information gap directly before the end of each volume. It's important to note that there is frequent overlap between these two categories. Key turning points often create information gaps both large and small, resolve information gaps, or increase the importance of resolving an information gap.

THE END OF VOLUME 1:

Novel	Type of Ending	What Occurs	Story Impact
Sense and Sensibility	Key turning point and large information gap	Lucy informs Elinor that she is secretly engaged to Edward, the man Elinor loves.	Elinor is devastated. We want to learn more about Lucy and Edward and how their relationship will play out.
Pride and Prejudice	Key turning point	Elizabeth rejects Mr. Collins's proposal. Mr. Collins and Charlotte Lucas become engaged.	Elizabeth is shaken, and her relationship with Charlotte is damaged.[11]
Emma	Key turning point	Mr. Elton proposes to Emma instead of to Harriet.	Emma learns she was wrong but doesn't try to change herself.

---

10. Both *Persuasion* and *Northanger Abbey* were published not long after Austen's death, and they were actually published together, as a four-volume set, with *Northanger Abbey* as the first and second volumes, and *Persuasion* as the third and fourth volumes.

11. We'll discuss this situation in more detail in Chapter 8, on relationships.

The End of Volume 2:

Novel	Type of Ending	What Occurs	Story Impact
Sense and Sensibility	Key turning point	Lucy and Edward visit Elinor. In the next chapter, Lucy is invited to stay with Edward's family.	Elinor sees this as a sure sign that the marriage is moving forward.
Pride and Prejudice	Strong hook/large information gap	Travel plans change: Elizabeth will be visiting Pemberley!	We wonder what will happen. This leads to a key turning point near the beginning of Volume 3, when Elizabeth begins to think of Darcy more positively.
Emma	Strong hook/large information gap	Emma learns that Frank Churchill will return; Emma is no longer certain that she's in love with him.	We want to know what will happen to Emma and Frank Churchill.

Some modern editions of Austen's novels use continuous chapter numbering and don't mark the volume breaks. Yet even without a visual or physical marker, the reader still feels the importance of these key turning points. The locations of the turning points are less important than the fact that these moments are spread throughout the rising action in a way that builds tension and compels the reader forward. In addition to using turning points at midpoints and volume breaks, Austen includes other turning points that create crucial moments of struggle for her characters. For instance, in *Sense and Sensibility*, two other key turning points are when Willoughby leaves Marianne (a scene we'll discuss in detail in Chapter 7) and when Willoughby slights Marianne at a large London gathering and subsequently returns her letters and her lock of hair.

In *Mansfield Park*, a major sequence in the rising action is the characters' preparations for the play *Lovers' Vows*. Fanny and

Edmund do not see the play as appropriate, and we see several try-fail cycles as the characters attempt to convince both Fanny and Edmund to participate. Edmund is convinced more readily; Fanny resists but helps everyone in their preparations. In the final hours, she agrees to participate in the play. Yet before they can perform, a key turning point occurs: Fanny's uncle returns from his extended trip overseas.

Maria Bertram and Henry Crawford upon hearing the news that Sir Thomas has returned. Illustration by Hugh Thomson, 1897.

Almost all of the characters know that this will cause terrible consequences:

> Mr. Yates might consider it only as a vexatious interruption for the evening, and Mr. Rushworth might imagine it a blessing; but every other heart was sinking under some degree of self-condemnation or undefined alarm, every other heart was suggesting, "What will become of us? what is to be done now?"

The "infamously tyrannical" Sir Thomas destroys the carefully constructed sets and once again takes control of the household:

> Sir Thomas was in hopes that another day or two would suffice to wipe away every outward memento of what had been, even to the destruction of every unbound copy of Lovers' Vows in the house, for he was burning all that met his eye.

No one dares to face the wrath of Sir Thomas; no one stands up to him and insists that the play be performed. His word is law. The narrator explains, "Under his government, Mansfield was an altered place." Edmund laments that they have lost all possibilities of joy and freedom:

> "How strong the impression that only a few weeks will give! I have been feeling as if we had never lived so before."

In *Mansfield Park*, Fanny is the character with the least power. Yet this turning point shows that none of them have any real power compared to Sir Thomas. This becomes important later in the novel when Fanny does attempt to stand up to him. She does so knowing that no one has succeeded in resisting her uncle's will.

Another crucial part of the theatrical-destruction turning point is Sir Thomas's shifted treatment of Fanny. His expansive anger includes not only his children and their friends, but also his sister-in-law Mrs. Norris. Yet he is not upset at Fanny: He does not see her as part of the problem, and she has grown prettier in his absence. For perhaps the first time, he pays her positive attention. This engenders a greater sense of obligation in Fanny toward her uncle, which makes it harder for her to stand up to him later.

When we craft key turning points, they should impact both plot and character. These pivot or pinch points often influence the subplots as well. Turning points can be good or bad, exhilarating or terrifying. By creating large shifts that feel irreversible and have lasting consequences, these turning points raise the stakes for the characters and the reader, propelling us toward the climax and final crisis.

Exercise 6.7: Remembering Key Turning Points

Choose one of your favorite books. *Without looking at the text*, make a list of the story's key turning points. These are big enough moments that they likely stand out to you, even if it's been a while since you've read the book. Now reflect on these turning points: How do they impact the characters and the plot? What makes them memorable?

Exercise 6.8: Create a Speed Outline

Create a speed outline for a novel. This doesn't need to be a novel you actually plan to write—in fact, this activity can sometimes be easier if you don't plan to write the story, because it can free you from worrying too much about choosing the perfect plot events.

Set a timer for fifteen minutes. In that time, create an outline for a novel. First, choose the main character's want and need and the focus of their internal and external journeys. Then use these to help you choose an inciting incident, two to four turning points, a climax, and a moment of final crisis.

Note: Even if you are a discovery writer and don't outline your novels, this is a useful exercise to help you better internalize turning points and how they fit in the rising action of the story.

- Want:
- Need:
- Focus of the external journey:
- Focus of the internal journey:
- Inciting incident:
- Turning point 1:
- Turning point 2:
- (Optional) Turning point 3:
- (Optional) Turning point 4:
- Climax:
- The final suspense:

RAISING THE STAKES

In Austen's novella *Lady Susan*, one of the other characters argues that Lady Susan "has no real love for her daughter." And indeed, Lady Susan does not seem particularly fond of Frederica. She hides sixteen-year-old Frederica away in boarding school, and then informs Frederica, via letter, that she must marry a wealthy man whom she detests. In response, Frederica runs away. Later, Lady Susan recounts,

> "The prospect of it frightened [Frederica] so thoroughly, that, with a mixture of true girlish perverseness and folly, she resolved on getting out of the house and proceeding directly by the stage to her friends, the Clarkes; and had really got as far as the length of two streets in her journey when she was fortunately missed, pursued, and overtaken."[12]

How quickly is Frederica's journey interrupted—she only travels two streets before being missed, pursued, and overtaken. And so it

---

12. Austen, *Lady Susan*.

is with our characters during the rising action: They each pursue their wants and needs. Inevitably, their journeys are interrupted. Change occurs. They fail again and again. Positive results come with a price. Negative results lead to continued striving.

Frederica's capture leads to her ejection from boarding school, forcing her to live with her mother, a negative turning point for both of them. More is now at risk in their personal journeys and in their relationship.

We've spoken briefly about stakes—what the characters have to lose or gain in a story. This meaning of the word stakes comes from gambling. According to the *Online Etymology Dictionary*, by the 1530s the word "stake" was used to signify "that which is placed at hazard as a wager, the sum of money or other valuable consideration which is deposited as a pledge or wager to be lost or won according to the issue of a contest or contingency."[13] As a character strives for a want, they make deposits of energy, time, and emotions to achieve their goals. Throughout the rising action, each attempt pushes more chips onto the poker table: More has been invested into this goal, and as a result, the prize could be higher, but more could also be lost. For instance, as Jane Bennet becomes closer to Mr. Bingley—as their relationship develops and she imagines marrying him—she has more that she could lose. The stakes are also raised by losses and failures, as we see the devastating effects of not achieving our wants. For instance, when Mr. Elton proposes to Emma instead of to Harriet, Harriet is heartbroken. Emma's failure at matchmaking enables the reader to see how much could be lost if she continues down this path.

The character's internal journey, along with their needs and their weaknesses and their strengths, becomes irrevocably interwoven with the results of their story gambles. The stakes are also raised for the reader, who becomes more and more attached to the characters through the rising action. At risk are the reader's and the character's emotions—which we'll discuss in the next chapter. Also at risk are the character's relationships, their identity, and their place in the world.

---

13. *Etymonline: Online Etymology Dictionary*, "stake (n.2)."

CHAPTER SEVEN

EMOTION

"Fanny walked back to the breakfast-room with a very saddened heart to grieve over the melancholy change; and there her uncle kindly left her to cry in peace, conceiving, perhaps, that the deserted chair of each young man might exercise her tender enthusiasm, and that the remaining cold pork bones and mustard in William's plate might but divide her feelings with the broken egg-shells in Mr. Crawford's. She sat and cried *con amore* as her uncle intended, but it was *con amore* fraternal and no other. William was gone, and she now felt as if she had wasted half his visit in idle cares and selfish solicitudes unconnected with him."

—*Mansfield Park*

When Fanny's brother William departs after visiting Mansfield Park, Austen leaves us with a compelling image: Fanny crying among the breakfast dishes and deserted chairs. Fanny's uncle, Sir Thomas, likes that Fanny feels strongly for her brother, but he also wants her to feel for Mr. Crawford, her prospective suitor. Sir Thomas hopes that the physical setting will create emotions of tenderness—if Fanny longs for her brother while sitting next to his cold pork bones and mustard, will she not long for Mr. Crawford while sitting next to his broken eggshells?

Yet Sir Thomas doesn't truly understand her, and his attempt at stimulating emotion for Mr. Crawford is in vain; the eggshells make Fanny regret the time and emotional energy consumed by Mr. Crawford.

Emotion can be difficult to convey. Like Sir Thomas, as writers we often hope that the characters and the readers will feel what we want them to feel. But sometimes, like Sir Thomas, we're off the mark. What we set up to be a deeply emotional scene with a particular meaning might not come across properly to the reader. The reader notices a different emotion or no emotion at all. Or the reader interprets the correct character emotion but doesn't feel the way we would like them to in response.

In this passage, while Sir Thomas doesn't understand Fanny's emotions, we as readers do, due to the **emotional clues** planted by Austen. These clues—details that hint at feeling—are layered and built around characters and situations, immersing the reader in the perspectives, thoughts, and sentiments of both viewpoint characters and characters whom we only know through their words and behaviors.[1]

EMOTIONAL CLUES

As I've studied Austen's works, I've categorized the emotional clues she uses into **seventeen different types**. We'll look at examples from multiple novels to see how and why she uses each technique. As you'll see, these clues are closely related to point of view, so if needed, review the section on point of view in Chapter 4. Some of these clues are surely ones that we've mastered, yet examining them with focused attention can help us discover new insights and applications.

First, let's consider a passage rife with emotion from *Sense and Sensibility*. At this point in the novel, most characters assume that

---

1. Patterson, "Reaching for Beats."
Some writers, including Janci Patterson, talk about using emotion beats—if you want to convey an emotion, you have to include an emotion beat or multiple beats. While I've shifted to thinking about the process of planting emotional clues, much of my thinking and part of my taxonomy was influenced by Patterson.

Marianne Dashwood and John Willoughby are engaged. The other Dashwood family members leave the house, knowing that Willoughby will likely call upon Marianne. They return to witness a flurry of unexpected emotions.

> They were no sooner in the passage than Marianne came hastily out of the parlour apparently in violent affliction, with her handkerchief at her eyes; and without noticing them ran up stairs.

Marianne's emotional exit. Illustration by Hugh Thomson, 1896.

Several phrases help plant emotional clues:

- Marianne came hastily out of the parlour
- apparently in violent affliction
- with her handkerchief at her eyes
- without noticing them
- ran up stairs

From these components, we can extract the first four types of emotional clues:

Emotional Clue #1: Concrete Actions and Behavior

Concrete actions and behavior are the results of choices made by a character, and choices are *always* influenced by a character's emotions. Different characters react to different situations in different ways. As we'll discuss at the end of this chapter, not everyone expresses strong emotions with strong outward displays. But even if a character suppresses, hides, or attempts to ignore their emotions, it still impacts their actions and behavior.

In the sentence from *Sense and Sensibility*, we see a number of concrete actions and behaviors: Marianne moves with speed; she presses her handkerchief to her eyes (which leads us to assume she is crying); she runs up the stairs.

Actions and behaviors are important emotional clues that can be used for both viewpoint and non-viewpoint characters.

Emotional Clue #2: Awareness/Lack of Awareness

Certain types of emotions point a character outward and make them more aware of others, such as pity or a feeling of responsibility. Other emotions point a character inward, narrowing their focus and creating a smaller sense of awareness.

In the sample sentence, Marianne does not notice or acknowledge her family members, even as she rushes past them.

Austen uses this clue less frequently, but to great effect. It's often something the narrator or viewpoint character recognizes in a non-viewpoint character. Viewpoint characters may not always realize how aware they are of others and their surroundings, but their level of awareness will still impact the description and focus of a scene. For example, in *Pride and Prejudice*, while at the Bingley's ball, Elizabeth's embarrassment at her family's behavior makes her more aware of not just her family, but also of how everyone else at the ball responds to her family. She worries about their thoughts and perceptions. Later, after Elizabeth rejects Mr. Collins's proposal, she becomes less aware of others and their thoughts and behaviors. She does not notice the clues about Charlotte and Mr. Collins's burgeoning relationship, which she might have noticed if she were in a different emotional state.[2]

EMOTIONAL CLUE #3: GENERAL IMPRESSIONS

Characters often create impressions of other characters' emotions—they see someone else's behavior, and they interpret it in a particular way. This interpretation can be provided to the reader.

Returning to the passage from *Sense and Sensibility*, the narrator explains that Marianne is "apparently in violent affliction." Marianne is not a viewpoint character in this chapter—the scene is from Elinor's perspective, and the narrator doesn't give us access to Marianne's mind. Therefore, Elinor and her mother cannot *actually*, with any certainty, know how Marianne feels.

Yet they interpret their general impressions—their sense of the situation. This is likely influenced by dozens of tiny details that Austen does not describe. Maybe Marianne's face is pale; maybe her arms hang a little limply; maybe she's sniffling. We constantly interpret dozens of tiny details—sometimes subconsciously—and come to conclusions. Rather than including every possible detail, the narrator provides Elinor and Mrs. Dashwood's most likely interpretation of the details.

When a character interprets someone's emotions, it's often useful to include a qualifier that signifies that the point-of-view character is making an interpretation. Without a signal, readers may feel that the narrator is proclaiming this emotion as fact, which in first-person or third-person limited can create a jolting point of view shift; in omniscient, without a signal, the reader assumes that the narrator is dipping into a character's mind. In this instance, Austen uses the word "apparently"; writers also use "likely," "probably," "it seemed that," and a number of other words and phrases.

Providing an interpretation of an emotion reminds the reader of the viewpoint character's involvement; not only are we meant

---

2. To make sure we as readers notice the clues, at this point in the story the narrator pulls back from Elizabeth's point of view and provides a more omniscient lens, even dipping into Charlotte's perspective for a chapter.

to understand the emotive character's feelings, but we're also given insight into how the viewpoint character processes events and sees the world.

EMOTIONAL CLUE #4: SETTING

The setting can be used to convey emotion by how the character interacts with the setting or by using the details of the setting to complement or contrast with a character's emotions.

In this sentence, Marianne rushes past her mother and sister, not noticing them or the setting, and rushes up the stairs. The stairs act as an avenue of escape—a way to seclude herself from everyone in the house. Marianne wants to be separate, and the stairs create physical separation by placing her on a different floor of the cottage.

While at times emotions are conveyed by how the characters navigate existing, recurring settings within a story, settings can also be constructed particularly to convey or create emotions. We'll discuss this in Chapter 10, when we see how Austen uses distinctive settings for key turning points. When creating distinctive settings for emotional resonance, the setting can parallel the emotion (e.g., a storm for a stormy or sad mood) or contrast with the emotion (e.g., a storm that cannot disrupt a character's utter happiness).

As we saw in the example with Fanny at the breakfast table, setting can be used to add nuance, subvert expectations, and express complicated emotions.

ⅎↃ

After Marianne rushes up the stairs, Austen plants more emotional clues, both to further hint at Marianne's emotions and to convey the emotions of Elinor, Mrs. Dashwood, and Willoughby:

> Surprised and alarmed they proceeded directly into the room [Marianne] had just quitted, where they found only Willoughby, who was leaning against the mantel-piece with his back towards them. He turned round on their coming in, and his countenance showed that he strongly partook of the emotion which over-powered Marianne.
>
> "Is anything the matter with her?" cried Mrs. Dashwood as she entered—"is she ill?"
>
> "I hope not," he replied, trying to look cheerful; and with a forced smile presently added, "It is I who may rather expect to be

ill—for I am now suffering under a very heavy disappointment!"

"Disappointment?"

"Yes, for I am unable to keep my engagement with you. Mrs. Smith has this morning exercised the privilege of riches upon a poor dependent cousin, by sending me on business to London. I have just received my dispatches, and taken my farewell of Allenham; and by way of exhilaration I am now come to take my farewell of you."

"To London!—and are you going this morning?"

"Almost this moment."

"This is very unfortunate. But Mrs. Smith must be obliged;— and her business will not detain you from us long I hope."

He coloured as he replied, "You are very kind, but I have no idea of returning into Devonshire immediately. My visits to Mrs. Smith are never repeated within the twelvemonth."

"And is Mrs. Smith your only friend? Is Allenham the only house in the neighbourhood to which you will be welcome? For shame, Willoughby, can you wait for an invitation here?"

His colour increased; and with his eyes fixed on the ground he only replied, "You are too good."

EMOTIONAL CLUE #5: STATING THE EMOTION

The emotion of the viewpoint character can be stated, as Austen does in the above passage: We learn that Elinor and Mrs. Dashwood are "startled and alarmed." It's rare for Austen to directly state the emotion. If used improperly, this emotional clue can feel like cheating—unearned and unbelievable. When Austen states the emotion, it's almost always in moments like this, where the situation and our past knowledge of the characters make it obvious that the viewpoint character feels this emotion. Of course Elinor and Mrs. Dashwood are going to be startled and alarmed by Marianne's extreme emotional reaction. Stating it allows Austen to quickly solidify the reaction and move on to more important parts of the scene. Sometimes, Austen states emotions in order to establish a baseline before diving deeper into the emotions, how they're expressed, or their implications.

Most of the time, you can only state the emotion if you are writing about the viewpoint character's emotion or if you're using an omniscient point of view. (In this scene, the omniscient narrator dips into both Mrs. Dashwood's and Elinor's perspectives.)

Willoughby looks at the ground as he speaks.
Illustration by Chris (Christiana) Hammond, 1899.

EMOTIONAL CLUE #6: BODY LANGUAGE

Body language is a powerful indicator of a character's emotions. For instance, if a character feels confident, upset, flustered, or distracted, it often impacts their body language. Some characters have little control over their body language, while other characters attempt to control it to mask emotions.

In this scene, Willoughby leans against the mantelpiece with his back toward them. He is preoccupied and turned into his own emotions, despite the fact that a distraught Marianne has just rushed from the room. This also uses our second type of emotional clue, in this case showing his lack of awareness.

EMOTIONAL CLUE #7: FACIAL EXPRESSIONS

Facial expressions can provide clues to a character's emotions. Austen typically uses this type of clue when capturing the emotions of a non-viewpoint character. Viewpoint characters are less likely to think about their own facial expressions (though some characters do, to great effect).

In this passage, we read that Willoughby's "countenance showed that he strongly partook of the emotion which over-powered Marianne." Elinor and Mrs. Dashwood read Willoughby's facial expression and can tell that something is wrong.

EMOTIONAL CLUE #8: CAREFULLY CHOSEN VERBS AND ADJECTIVES

This technique often overlaps with other techniques, yet it is powerful and is useful to consider on its own. Verbs and adjectives can express and enlighten the emotions of a scene. If well chosen, a specific, more expressive word can carry great emotional weight, such as the following words and phrases from the above passage:

- Cried Mrs. Dashwood
- With a forced smile
- He coloured

Mrs. Dashwood does not just ask what is wrong with her daughter—she cries it. Willoughby's smile is forced rather than genuine. Willoughby's face colors, and we sense his shame or embarrassment.

It's important not to overindulge in this technique. Note that most of the scene's dialogue doesn't include adjectives or verbs describing the characters or how they say their lines. By using this technique sparingly, it focuses the reader on the key emotional details.

EMOTIONAL CLUE #9: DIALOGUE

What a character says can reveal or conceal their emotions. Ultimately, dialogue is an action taken by a character, and what they choose to say and how they say it is influenced by their emotional state.

Mrs. Dashwood asks Willoughby a question about Marianne, but his response focuses on himself and his troubles. Mrs. Dashwood's continuing questions indicate her constant surprise and changing understanding of the situation. Willoughby keeps most of his statements formal and factual. At this point in the novel, we as readers—like Mrs. Dashwood—cannot come to conclusions about Willoughby's motivations or the deeper layers behind his dialogue.

We'll discuss more ways in which dialogue can convey emotion in Chapter 9.

Emotional Clue #10: Shifts of Emotion

Emotions—whether large or small—are not static. They can change or shift within a sentence or scene, or they can be joined by other emotions. As characters react to each other's emotions, their own emotions may shift. Conveying shifts of emotion helps readers better understand the characters and the situation.

As the conversation in *Sense and Sensibility* continues, we see a shift in Willoughby's emotions. Not only does he feel whatever emotions were incited by his conversation with Marianne, but a new emotion arrives: a discomfort and a desire to escape the situation.

As the scene continues, Mrs. Dashwood tells Willoughby that he is *always* welcome at their cottage, and then we read,

> "My engagements at present," replied Willoughby, confusedly, "are of such a nature—that—I dare not flatter myself—"
>
> He stopped. Mrs. Dashwood was too much astonished to speak, and another pause succeeded. This was broken by Willoughby, who said with a faint smile, "It is folly to linger in this manner. I will not torment myself any longer by remaining among friends whose society it is impossible for me now to enjoy."
>
> He then hastily took leave of them all and left the room. They saw him step into his carriage, and in a minute it was out of sight.

Viewing emotions as fluid rather than fixed and static can help a scene move forward; the story can shift and move with the character's feelings.

Emotional Clue #11: Silence/Pauses

Silences and pauses can be powerful tools to reveal emotions. Sometimes emotions can be too strong for action or dialogue. At these moments, inaction reveals an inability to process an emotion.

Pauses may also occur because an emotion makes it difficult to see a way forward. Who breaks the pause and how can also be revelatory.

In the most recent passage, we saw that "Mrs. Dashwood was too astonished to speak." Then there's another pause as the characters remain quiet. In fact, Elinor has not spoken yet during this scene, perhaps because she feels it is not her place. We'll talk more about pauses and silence in the chapter on dialogue.

⁎⁎⁎

As mentioned in the previous chapter, this emotional scene involving Marianne, her family, and Willoughby is a turning point in the novel: Everything changes for the characters. Because of their impact on characters' internal and external journeys, turning points are often filled with emotions. It makes sense that in this scene alone, Austen uses eleven different techniques to provide clues to the reader.

For more emotional clues, let's return to *Mansfield Park*. At this point in the story, Fanny's female cousins have left home, and her uncle, Sir Thomas, pays Fanny more attention. Sir Thomas decides to throw a ball, and as it begins, he surprises her by telling her that "*she* was to lead the way and open the ball." Fanny protests, for this "idea … had never occurred to her before," but he insists. Then we read,

> She could hardly believe it. To be placed above so many elegant young women! The distinction was too great. It was treating her like her cousins! And her thoughts flew to those absent cousins with most unfeigned and truly tender regret, that they were not at home to take their own place in the room, and have their share of a pleasure which would have been so very delightful to them. So often as she had heard them wish for a ball at home as the greatest of all felicities! And to have them away when it was given—and for *her* to be opening the ball—and with Mr. Crawford too! She hoped they would not envy her that distinction *now*; but when she looked back to the state of things in the autumn, to what they had all been to each other when once dancing in that house before, the present arrangement was almost more than she could understand herself.
>
> The ball began. It was rather honour than happiness to Fanny, for the first dance at least: her partner was in excellent spirits,

and tried to impart them to her; but she was a great deal too much frightened to have any enjoyment till she could suppose herself no longer looked at.

In these paragraphs, we feel as if we are with Fanny on the dance floor. We are fully immersed in her perspective and experience because of Austen's use of two additional types of emotional clues.

Fanny and Henry Crawford open the ball.
Illustration by C. E. Brock, 1908.

EMOTIONAL CLUE #12: REVEALING CHARACTER THOUGHTS

Several emotional clues are *only* available if expressing the emotions of a viewpoint character. The first of these is character thoughts. While the author can know all of the characters' perspectives and emotions, only for a viewpoint character can the narrator be seen to know, fully and completely, what that individual is thinking. This is especially true in first-person and third-person limited, but as we've seen in Austen's omniscient novels, she often focuses on a single viewpoint character and only dips into the minds of a limited number of characters in any given scene.

Throughout this passage in *Mansfield Park*, the omniscient third-person narrator sticks close to Fanny's perspective. This provides an opportunity to describe Fanny's thoughts and reflections, her reactions and her emotions.

When a narrator provides a character's thoughts, it is typically through one of the following:

- **Summarizing** the character's thoughts. Example: "It was rather honour than happiness to Fanny, for the first dance at least. ... She was a great deal too much frightened to have any enjoyment." Note that we don't receive the details of her specific thoughts, but we are given, through summary, a sense of the whole.
- **Stating** the character's thoughts. Example: "Her thoughts flew to those absent cousins with most unfeigned and truly tender regret, that they were not at home to take their own place in the room, and have their share of a pleasure which would have been so very delightful to them." In this case, the narrator states Fanny's precise thoughts in the sequence she experiences them.
- **Connecting** the character's thoughts to other things, people, or events. Example: "She hoped they would not envy her that distinction now; but when she looked back to the state of things in the autumn ... the present arrangement was almost more than she could understand herself." These connections lead to greater understanding for Fanny as she considers the implications of her treatment, and we are better able to understand her emotions because of the connections she makes.

In each of the above examples, we access Fanny's thoughts **through the filter of the narrator**. These thoughts are summarized, they are stated, they are made beautiful through connection and analysis. And these thoughts certainly give the reader a lens clearly into Fanny's emotions, in a way that's only possible because she is the viewpoint character.

EMOTIONAL CLUE #13: FREE INDIRECT SPEECH

Free indirect speech is another method of revealing character thoughts. Free indirect speech (also known as free indirect discourse) was not invented by Austen, but she was one of the first writers to use it extensively. In **free indirect speech**, the narrative shifts from the slightly more distant perspective of the narrator to placing the reader directly and fully into the character's perspective, thoughts, and visceral experience. In other words, the psychic distance diminishes to the point where it is nonexistent.

While much of the passage is written in close or deep third point of view (as part of the book's selective omniscience), at a few points, the narration slips into free indirect speech, completely immersing us in Fanny's perspective. Let's look again at a portion of the same passage. The sentences in which the narrator summarizes, states, or connects Fanny's thoughts are written normally; sentences that use free indirect speech are in bold.

> She could hardly believe it. **To be placed above so many elegant young women! The distinction was too great. It was treating her like her cousins!** And her thoughts flew to those absent cousins with most unfeigned and truly tender regret, that they were not at home to take their own place in the room, and have their share of a pleasure which would have been so very delightful to them. **So often as she had heard them wish for a ball at home as the greatest of all felicities! And to have them away when it was given—and for *her* to be opening the ball—and with Mr. Crawford too!** She hoped they would not envy her that distinction *now*; but when she looked back to the state of things in the autumn, to what they had all been to each other when once dancing in that house before, the present arrangement was almost more than she could understand herself.

In the bolded lines, the narrator's filter—even though it is close to Fanny—is removed. We are completely in her thoughts, with no summary or big-picture perspective. We are immersed with her in the moment. At times, we want and need a distance between us as readers and the character, or we want the context, connections, and commentary that are best provided by a narrator. But at other times, slipping completely into a character's mind is revelatory:

To be placed above so many elegant young women! The distinction was too great. It was treating her like her cousins!

These are Fanny's actual thoughts—this is her emphasis, her
internal exclamations. And then, a few lines later we read,

> So often as she had heard them wish for a ball at home as the
> greatest of all felicities! And to have them away when it was
> given—and for her to be opening the ball—and with Mr. Craw-
> ford too!

For a few brief moments, we become one with Fanny and her
perspective.

In this final sentence of free indirect speech, note how the syntax
changes. Three clauses, each starting with "and," are stacked on
each other using em dashes. For this sentence, it creates almost a
miniature use of **stream of consciousness**—the natural, continuous, not always sequential direction of thoughts. (Authors who
are famous for their use of stream of consciousness, like Virginia
Woolf, often use it for much longer passages. In this passage by
Austen, this sentence leans toward stream of consciousness but
may not have the length to truly be a full *stream*—a flowing body
of water that meanders through hill and vale.)

Instead of using free indirect speech, some modern stories will
italicize the character's direct thoughts. This draws attention to it
as a thought, separate from the main narrative, but has many of
the same effects as using free indirect speech.

Texts written in first person rather than third person or omniscient are, by definition, entirely in the thoughts and viewpoint of
the first-person narrator. However, there is still often a sense of the
narrator as the storyteller—a first-person narrator can still act as a
filter. This is especially true with first-person past tense: The story
is told later, sometimes with accompanying reflection. At times,
the descriptions and thoughts will feel even closer, more immediate, and more immersive, and this can create an effect similar to
using free indirect speech.

First-person present tense feels even more immediate than
first-person past tense, as everything is unfolding before the character (and the reader) in the present. Yet as with first-person past

tense, the author can control the psychic distance—how close and how far we are from the character's thoughts and emotions.

ॐ◌ल

There are four more types of emotional clues that are largely used for viewpoint characters. To analyze these clues, we'll consider passages from *Northanger Abbey*. Throughout the novel, Catherine Morland is filled with emotions, so much so that she is sometimes carried away in flights of fancy. As discussed in Chapter 4, on stance, Austen keeps the reader at a bit of a distance from Catherine—we are meant to understand her emotions while seeing them from an objective, outside perspective.

As Catherine falls for Henry Tilney, she also becomes friends with Henry's sister, Eleanor. Eleanor wants a companion, so she and her father, General Tilney, invite Catherine to stay with them at their home, Northanger Abbey. The narrator captures Catherine's reaction:

> Northanger Abbey! These were thrilling words, and wound up Catherine's feelings to the highest point of ecstasy. Her grateful and gratified heart could hardly restrain its expressions within the language of tolerable calmness. To receive so flattering an invitation! To have her company so warmly solicited! Everything honourable and soothing, every present enjoyment, and every future hope was contained in it; and her acceptance, with only the saving clause of Papa and Mamma's approbation, was eagerly given. "I will write home directly," said she, "and if they do not object, as I dare say they will not—"

Emotional Clue #14: Punctuation, Syntax, and Rhythm

Punctuation, syntax, and rhythm can be powerful tools for conveying emotion, especially when the punctuation, syntax, and rhythm are markedly different from other sentences, passages, or scenes. This technique is used primarily for viewpoint characters but can also be used in the dialogue of non-viewpoint characters.

In the above passage, note the heavy use of exclamation marks, the short sentences and other phrases that build with rapid commas, and the way that the rhythm builds to match her excitement.

Exclamation marks and commas aren't the only punctuation marks Austen employs to convey emotion—at other points in her novels she uses em dashes, question marks, and periods in revelatory ways. Long and short sentences, sentences with broken or smooth rhythm, sentences that feel like poetry—all of these tools impact the reader's experience of the character's lives.

We'll talk more about punctuation, syntax, and rhythm in Chapter 13.

EMOTIONAL CLUE #15: POINTING TO THE PAST AND/OR TO THE FUTURE

Another effective way to reveal emotion is to have a character think of something that happened in the past or in the future. Once again, this is almost always used for viewpoint characters.

Past events can be ones that the character experienced earlier in the novel. Pointing again to them creates emotional resonance between those events and the new passage. It can show the character creating meaning or connection, for good or for bad. It can recall prior emotions or reinterpret past emotions into something new.

The narrator can also point to past events that happened before the start of the story. This provides backstory, paints a fuller picture of the characters' lives, and can also illuminate why something might impact a character in a certain way.

After receiving the invitation to visit Northanger Abbey, Catherine's experiences create a sudden emotional shift—her day goes from poor to wonderful.

> The circumstances of the morning had led Catherine's feelings through the varieties of suspense, security, and disappointment; but they were now safely lodged in perfect bliss; and with spirits elated to rapture, with Henry at her heart, and Northanger Abbey on her lips, she hurried home to write her letter.

As she writes her parents to tell them of the invitation, Catherine looks back on all her experiences in Bath, even the negative ones, in a rosy light, as if each of them led to this moment.

> By the kindness of her first friends, the Allens, she had been introduced into scenes where pleasures of every kind had met her. Her feelings, her preferences, had each known the happiness of a return. Wherever she felt attachment, she had been able to create it.

While recalling the past often serves to return the character and the reader to previously felt emotions, in this case, recalling the past is an opportunity for her to rewrite her emotions on her past experiences.

As the scene continues, Catherine shifts to thinking about the future and the time she will spend with the Tilneys at Northanger Abbey. Her vision of the future serves to further demonstrate her present emotional state:

> She was to be their chosen visitor, she was to be for weeks under the same roof with the person whose society she mostly prized—and, in addition to all the rest, this roof was to be the roof of an abbey!

As the paragraph continues, Catherine's thoughts on the Abbey are bounteous, and the sheer quantity of time spent on enthusiastic, detailed envisioning **shows** Catherine's excitement in a way that other sorts of description and summary would be unlikely to do as effectively.

> Her passion for ancient edifices was next in degree to her passion for Henry Tilney—and castles and abbeys made usually the charm of those reveries which his image did not fill. To see and explore either the ramparts and keep of the one, or the cloisters of the other, had been for many weeks a darling wish, though to be more than the visitor of an hour had seemed too nearly impossible for desire. And yet, this was to happen. With all the chances against her of house, hall, place, park, court, and cottage, Northanger turned up an abbey, and she was to be its inhabitant. Its long, damp passages, its narrow cells and ruined chapel, were to be within her daily reach, and she could not entirely subdue the hope of some traditional legends, some awful memorials of an injured and ill-fated nun.

Pointing to the future is a powerful tool to convey emotion because it can reveal what a character expects, what they hope for or fear, whether they are high-strung or analytical or relaxed. A character has no way of knowing what the future will actually hold, but how they think about the future reveals their current state.

EMOTIONAL CLUE #16: REPETITION

Repetition is a powerful tool that shows a character's focus, often hinting at their driving emotion for a scene. Repetition makes connections between the objects, people, or ideas that receive the repetitive treatment. Repetition shows what the character focuses on, what their thoughts can't avoid, what they keep coming back to. It can create rhythm, it can call back to something from earlier, or it can further develop an emotion or thought.

While at Northanger Abbey, Catherine spends a frightening night in her bedroom, largely because the Gothic novels she loves have convinced her that terrible things must have happened in such a place. Part of what troubles and fascinates her is an old-fashioned cabinet. Throughout the scene, she tries to open it again and again—a repetition of action. She also repeatedly experiences the wind. The wind could've been mentioned once, with phrasing that indicates that it's continuous, but instead, it's mentioned again and again, each time showing the building of her emotions.

> The window curtains seemed in motion. It could be nothing but the violence of the wind penetrating through the divisions of the shutters; and she stepped boldly forward, carelessly humming a tune, to assure herself of its being so, peeped courageously behind each curtain, saw nothing on either low window seat to scare her, and on placing a hand against the shutter, felt the strongest conviction of the wind's force.

A little later in the scene we read, "The wind roared down the chimney, the rain beat in torrents against the windows, and everything seemed to speak the awfulness of her situation." And again: "A violent gust of wind, rising with sudden fury, added fresh horror to the moment." Later still: "She had not been used to feel alarm from wind, but now every blast seemed fraught with awful intelligence." One final reference is made to the wind: "The storm still raged, and various were the noises, more terrific even than the wind, which struck at intervals on her startled ear."

For viewpoint characters, repetition can convey emotion in a myriad of ways. For non-viewpoint characters, repetition can convey emotion through dialogue or repeated external actions. We'll discuss repetition in more depth in Chapter 14.

EMOTIONAL CLUE #17: PHYSICAL SENSATIONS

Physical sensations are things the body perceives through the senses, particularly those things that impact the body in either an external or internal way. Physical sensations can also include ways in which the body's behavior changes based on emotions. Often these sensations are known only to the character experiencing them.

When Catherine finally opens the cabinet, she searches drawer after empty drawer until she finds a piece of paper:

> Her feelings at that moment were indescribable. Her heart fluttered, her knees trembled, and her cheeks grew pale. She seized, with an unsteady hand, the precious manuscript, for half a glance sufficed to ascertain written characters.

She can't describe her emotions, and apparently neither can the narrator. But the narrator can give the reader Catherine's physical sensations: Her heart flutters, her knees tremble, her cheeks grow pale, and her hand is unsteady. Each of these physical sensations is her body's manifestation of her emotions. Some of these sensations are internal, like her heart fluttering, while others have an external component, such as her knees trembling or her cheeks growing pale. Completely internal physical sensations can only be used for viewpoint characters, while some sensations with an external component can be used for other characters.[3]

While some authors rely heavily on physical sensations to convey emotions, Austen does so sparingly but to great effect.

THE SEVENTEEN EMOTIONAL CLUES

Later in this chapter, we'll discuss the size or degree of emotions, as well as how different characters feel and express emotion. Both will impact which emotional clues to use and how many to layer in a given scene. But before we move on, let's look again at the seventeen emotional clues, now in list form:

1. Concrete Actions and Behavior
2. Awareness/Lack of Awareness
3. General Impressions
4. Setting

---

3. If you want a resource on how to write about internal and external physical sensations, as well as body language and actions that might reflect certain emotions, I highly recommend *The Emotion Thesaurus* by Angela Ackerman and Becca Puglisi.

5. Stating the Emotion
6. Body Language
7. Facial Expressions
8. Carefully Chosen Verbs and Adjectives
9. Dialogue
10. Shifts of Emotion
11. Silences/Pauses
12. Revealing Character Thoughts
13. Free Indirect Speech
14. Punctuation, Syntax, and Rhythm
15. Pointing to the Past and/or to the Future
16. Repetition
17. Physical Sensations

There is actually an eighteenth clue that Austen regularly uses: objective correlative. This involves using objects and sequences to build an emotional response. Discussing objective correlative is beyond the scope of this chapter; however, you can read about objective correlative in Appendix A.

Exercise 7.1: Incorporating Emotional Clues

Step 1: Choose an everyday task (going to the grocery store, attending school, working out, etc.).

Step 2: Choose a predominant emotion (happiness, anger, frustration, fatigue, despair, etc.).

Step 3: From the list of emotional clues, choose the three to five that you are *most* comfortable using to convey emotions. Write a paragraph or brief scene about a character performing the everyday task, and use these emotional clues.

Step 4: Now return to the list and choose the three to five clues that you are *least* comfortable using to convey emotions. Rewrite the paragraph or brief scene using these emotional clues instead.

Exercise 7.2: Emotion Analysis

Analyze a scene from an author you love (who is not Jane Austen). What emotional clues are used to convey the characters' emotions?

Does the author use the same emotional clues as Austen or different ones? How are the clues incorporated into scenes? How does the point of view impact the emotional clues? Does the narrator shift how close or far we are from the characters' emotions?

Exercise 7.3: Summary/Statement, Italics, and Free Indirect Speech

Using third-person limited, write three versions of a paragraph in which a character experiences emotion. In the first version, summarize or state the character's thoughts. In the second version, express the character's thoughts in italics. In the third version, incorporate these same thoughts, but this time use free indirect speech. Which approach works better for your particular passage and writing style?

Exercise 7.4: Chart Your Own Physical Sensations

Over the course of several hours or a day, record your own external and internal physical sensations. Did you touch something scratchy? Did something taste sour? Did the chair feel hard? Did your knee itch? Did your eyes feel unfocused? Did your back hurt? Did you lose your balance?

If relevant, jot down a word or two that captures your emotional state at the time. Did your physical sensation reflect or contrast with your emotions? How did your physical sensations influence your emotions?

Consider what you learned about physical sensations and emotions that you can incorporate into your writing.

Exercise 7.5: Emotion Revision

Take a scene that you have written. Which emotional clues did you use? Could any of the existing clues be strengthened? Would other clues be more powerful? Are more emotional clues needed? After analyzing, revise the scene.

THE SIZE OR DEGREE OF CHARACTER EMOTIONS

When we talk about emotions in writing, we often think of large emotions. Yet while some emotional states are strong or overwhelming, others are fleeting and less consequential.

When considering the size of the emotion, it's useful to ask some questions:

- To what degree does your character experience this emotion?
- How important is this emotion to the story?
- How many emotional clues need to be planted to convey this emotion?

In *Pride and Prejudice*, Austen conveys Elizabeth's small, mid-size, and large emotions using different techniques, which we can incorporate into our own writing.

SMALL EMOTIONS

Small emotions are experienced either for a short time or only to a small degree. For instance, small emotions could include a minor annoyance, a temporary flush of joy, or a fleeting reaction to a character or event.

While attending the Meryton assembly, Elizabeth overhears Mr. Bingley trying to convince Mr. Darcy to dance, and Bingley points out that Elizabeth could be a good partner. Mr. Darcy replies, "She is tolerable: but not handsome enough to tempt me."

While this is a rather weighty insult, Elizabeth has only a small emotional response:

> Mr. Darcy walked off; and Elizabeth remained with no very cordial feelings towards him. She told the story, however, with great spirit among her friends; for she had a lively, playful disposition, which delighted in anything ridiculous.

Throughout *Pride and Prejudice*, Elizabeth often uses humor as a lens to deal with small emotions. Clearly she's not happy with

Darcy, but rather than wallowing in the emotion, she turns the experience into a funny story.

Mr. Darcy declares that Elizabeth is tolerable.
Illustration by Hugh Thomson, 1894.

For some characters, this circumstance could create a much larger emotional response, but for Elizabeth it remains small, and she moves on. This is a memorable moment for readers because it sets up Elizabeth and Mr. Darcy's antagonism and begins their relationship arc. Yet it doesn't require much space on the page.

At other times emotions are implied, suggested, or only briefly mentioned. The emotion is important enough to be included but doesn't need to be dwelt upon.

After Mr. Collins's arrival, he showers compliments on the family:

He had not been long seated before he complimented Mrs. Bennet on having so fine a family of daughters, said he had heard much of their beauty, but that, in this instance, fame had fallen short of the truth; and added, that he did not doubt her seeing them all in due time well disposed of in marriage.

Austen immediately provides the emotional response of Elizabeth and her sisters and contrasts it with Mrs. Bennet's response:

This gallantry was not much to the taste of some of his hearers; but Mrs. Bennet, who quarrelled with no compliments, answered most readily.

It's a simple phrase—"not much to the taste of some of his hearers"—but it establishes Elizabeth's sentiments toward her cousin.

*The five Bennet sisters. Jane is "not for sale," but
Mr. Collins is welcome to choose any of the other daughters.
Illustration by Hugh Thomson, 1894.*

MIDSIZE EMOTIONS

Midsize emotions occupy more of the character's heart and mind—they linger or are not as quickly resolved. They generally have a weightier impact and often require more sentences on the page—more emotional clues.

In *Pride and Prejudice*, Elizabeth witnesses Mr. Darcy and Mr. Wickham seeing each other for the first time in Meryton:

[Mr. Darcy's eyes] were suddenly arrested by the sight of the stranger; and Elizabeth happening to see the countenance of

> both as they looked at each other, was all astonishment at the effect of the meeting. Both changed colour, one looked white, the other red. Mr. Wickham, after a few moments, touched his hat—a salutation which Mr. Darcy just deigned to return. What could be the meaning of it? It was impossible to imagine; it was impossible not to long to know.

Darcy and Wickham experience strong emotions, which piques Elizabeth's own emotions, particularly her curiosity. She wants to know the cause of their feelings. Later on in the scene, Elizabeth returns to her emotion, re-experiencing her puzzlement and curiosity as she expresses it to Jane:

> As they walked home, Elizabeth related to Jane what she had seen pass between the two gentlemen; but though Jane would have defended either or both, had they appeared to be in the wrong, she could no more explain such behaviour than her sister.

Midsize emotions often either need more emotional clues or need to recur again at some point in the scene.

Later, at a gathering held by the Phillipses, Mr. Wickham confides in Elizabeth, telling the story of how Mr. Darcy wronged him. This revelation produces emotions in Elizabeth that are larger than her initial curiosity but still midsize. A number of emotional clues are layered on each other, giving a sense of her feelings.

Elizabeth declares, "This is quite shocking! He deserves to be publicly disgraced." She asks follow-up questions. She pauses when speaking. She reflects. She remembers things Mr. Darcy has previously said that seem to corroborate Wickham's claims. She also uses stronger word choice and more exclamation marks than in her normal dialogue:

> "How strange!" cried Elizabeth. "How abominable!—I wonder that the very pride of this Mr. Darcy has not made him just to you!—If from no better motive, that he should not have been too proud to be dishonest,—for dishonesty I must call it."[4]

---

4. For this quotation I use the punctuation from the first edition of *Pride and Prejudice*. Some later editions (including the Project Gutenberg) remove some of Elizabeth's exclamation marks, which is quite intolerable.

Mr. Wickham and the other officers arrive at the Phillipses' home.
Illustration by C. E. Brock, 1895.

Even once she concludes her conversation with Mr. Wickham, she returns to it in her mind. Her emotions and her thoughts of him become her entire focus:

> There could be no conversation in the noise of Mrs. Phillips's supper party, but his manners recommended him to everybody. Whatever he said, was said well; and whatever he did, done gracefully. Elizabeth went away with her head full of him. She could think of nothing but of Mr. Wickham, and of what he had told her, all the way home.

Her emotions don't end in this scene. The next chapter begins, "Elizabeth related to Jane, the next day, what had passed between Mr. Wickham and herself."

Note how much more page time is given to this emotion than to when Mr. Darcy insulted her at the ball. She is engrossed by her emotions, and Austen employs a larger variety of emotional clues.

Large Emotions

Large emotions are generally more personal and with even larger consequences. They often occur at the key turning points and at moments of grand discoveries and revelations about either the internal or external journey. These emotions are large because the circumstances require the character to develop a new understanding of the world and their place in it.

As with midsize emotions, large emotions require more page time, a layering of emotional clues, and a return, multiple times, to the emotion. Large emotions also provoke stronger reactions, create stronger or more extreme physical sensations, and lead the character to engage in behavior that is outside of their norms.

In a pivotal scene in *Pride and Prejudice*, Colonel Fitzwilliam reveals that Mr. Darcy separated Mr. Bingley and her sister Jane. Elizabeth asks why, and in reply he states that "there were some very strong objections against the lady."

Paragraphs follow in which Elizabeth deals with her emotions, thinking about what she has learned. She considers the possible merits of Mr. Darcy's objections, but then she counters her own thoughts by remembering how much Jane has been wronged.

> The agitation and tears which the subject occasioned brought on a headache; and it grew so much worse towards the evening that, added to her unwillingness to see Mr. Darcy, it determined her not to attend her cousins to Rosings, where they were engaged to drink tea.

For most of her smaller negative emotions, Elizabeth uses humor. For midsize negative emotions, she grapples with the problem, considering it from many sides—which she also does here. But she experiences this emotion to a new degree, which causes tears and a headache. And while Elizabeth normally meets basic societal expectations, she decides not to visit Rosings.

In the next chapter she examines all of Jane's letters, trying to see how Mr. Bingley's absence has impacted her sister.

It's only a few pages later that Mr. Darcy proposes to her. In part because of her multi-chapter feelings, she angrily turns him down. After he leaves, the narrator shows her thoughts, and then we experience a longer shift into free indirect speech than at other points in the novel.

> The tumult of her mind, was now painfully great. She knew not how to support herself, and, from actual weakness, sat down and cried for half an hour. Her astonishment, as she reflected on what had passed, was increased by every review of it. That she should receive an offer of marriage from Mr. Darcy! That he should have been in love with her for so many months! So much in love as to wish to marry her in spite of all the objections which had made him prevent his friend's marrying her sister, and which must appear at least with equal force in his own case, was almost incredible! It was gratifying to have inspired unconsciously so strong an affection. But his pride, his abominable pride, his shameless avowal of what he had done with respect to Jane, his unpardonable assurance in acknowledging, though he could not justify it, and the unfeeling manner in which he had mentioned Mr. Wickham, his cruelty towards whom he had not attempted to deny, soon overcame the pity which the consideration of his attachment had for a moment excited.
>
> She continued in very agitating reflections till the sound of Lady Catherine's carriage made her feel how unequal she was to encounter Charlotte's observation, and hurried her away to her room.

Later, she receives Mr. Darcy's letter full of explanations. We read the letter with Elizabeth—the entire letter is included with no interruptions, no character actions or thoughts. We experience our own emotions as readers and can guess at Elizabeth's. Then after the letter, the narrator provides lengthy passages in which Elizabeth walks, rereads, analyzes specific phrases, and reflects. Her emotions undergo multiple shifts—and we experience these shifts with her.

Large emotions are often not as clear-cut as smaller emotions—anger, joy, frustration, and forgiveness can be complicated and filled with nuance, requiring exploration by the character and the

Mr. Darcy asks Elizabeth to read his letter.
Illustration by C. E. Brock, 1895.

reader. The emotions shift, grow, lessen, and increase, and as we ride the character's emotional roller coaster, we empathize and at times experience catharsis.

In a symphony, the orchestra does not play at full volume the entire time. That would make rather poor music. Instead, some movements are performed quietly, while others swell to fortissimo; some passages highlight the violins, while others may feature brass instruments, and others use a soloist. The cymbal might be crashed only a handful of times, but it will surely be at key moments.

We should do the same when we write character emotions: include a range of emotions that receive focus at different times. Sometimes we touch on an emotion for only a moment; at other times we explore the emotion for an extended period or bring back an emotional theme later in the story. Including varying degrees of emotions—small, midsize, and large—creates contrast and emphasis, directs the readers' attention, and serves to better illustrate character as we see how they react and change in moments big and small.

Exercise 7.6: Emotion Chart

As you read a book or watch a film, create a chart of the main character's emotions. Track the types of emotions, the size of the emotions, and what emotional clues are used.

How does the character experience and express different sizes of emotions? Are some types of emotional clues employed more than others? Do the largest emotions align with the key turning points of the story?

Exercise 7.7: Emotion Reversal

Write about a small emotion you experienced, but use the techniques normally reserved for writing large emotions. Use several paragraphs and layer emotional clues. For example, you could spend a significant amount of time writing about the mild irritation of finding no ripe avocados, or the quotidian joy of completing a crossword puzzle.

Now, write about a large emotion you experienced by using the techniques normally reserved for small emotions. Write only a single phrase or a few sentences. For example, you might dismiss the loss of a job or use brief humor to make light of a major betrayal.

Reflect on both passages. While often it's useful to write about large emotions in a large way and small emotions in a small way, in what circumstances would it be useful to do the reverse?

DIFFERENT CHARACTER APPROACHES TO EMOTION

When writing emotions, it's important to consider that they are an extension of character. As such, different characters will deal with and express the same emotions in different ways.

In *Sense and Sensibility*, not only are Elinor and Marianne sisters, but they experience a similar loss: They are both separated from and hurt by the men they love. Yet they express their emotions in drastically different ways. As we saw earlier in the chapter, when Willoughby leaves Marianne, she suffers "violent affliction." As the story continues, everyone sees her pining and despair. When Elinor learns that Edward Ferrars is secretly engaged to Lucy Steele, she suffers intense pain but does not show it outwardly, even masking her emotions from her family. When it becomes public knowledge that Edward is engaged to Lucy Steele, Marianne notices that her sister is not surprised.

> "How long has this been known to you, Elinor? Has he written to you?"
>
> "I have known it these four months. When Lucy first came to Barton Park last November, she told me in confidence of her engagement."

At these words, Marianne's eyes expressed the astonishment which her lips could not utter. After a pause of wonder, she exclaimed—

"Four months!—Have you known of this four months?"

Elinor confirmed it.

"What! while attending me in all my misery, has this been on your heart? And I have reproached you for being happy!"

"It was not fit that you should then know how much I was the reverse!"

"Four months!" cried Marianne again. "So calm! So cheerful! How have you been supported?"

Marianne struggles to understand how Elinor's outward reality could be in such contrast to her inward reality, because Marianne's inward and outward realities generally align. She accuses Elinor of not truly loving Edward—for if she actually loved him, would she not express her loss? Elinor explains her promise of secrecy, describes her misery, and rebukes Marianne for assuming Elinor did not experience great depths of emotion.

"If you can think me capable of ever feeling, surely you may suppose that I have suffered *now*. The composure of mind with which I have brought myself at present to consider the matter, the consolation that I have been willing to admit, have been the effect of constant and painful exertion; they did not spring up of themselves; they did not occur to relieve my spirits at first. No, Marianne. *Then*, if I had not been bound to silence, perhaps nothing could have kept me entirely—not even what I owed to my dearest friends—from openly showing that I was *very* unhappy."

Marianne is convinced of the depths of Elinor's emotions and exclaims, "How barbarous have I been to you!" Ultimately, they reconcile—they heal their relationship and come to better understand each other's emotive approaches.

"Emotional" characters, like Marianne, do not necessarily have more emotions—they simply express them more strongly. It is important to note, however, that **the way a character chooses to express their emotions does have consequences**. Because Elinor does not share her emotions, she receives no support in her struggles; because Marianne overindulges her emotions, she neglects her well-being and becomes deathly ill. There are a multitude of ways in which your own characters might experience and express emotions. Their approaches should reflect or be influenced by their inner being, their history, and their relationships with other characters and society, which we'll talk about more specifically in the next chapter.

"Mrs Dashwood would sit up with her all night"

Mrs. Dashwood sits through the night
with Marianne during her illness.
Illustration by Chris (Christiana) Hammond, 1899.

CHAPTER EIGHT

RELATIONSHIPS AND CONNECTION

"In vain have I struggled. It will not do. My feelings will not be repressed. You must allow me to tell you how ardently I admire and love you."
—*Pride and Prejudice*

Elizabeth Bennet and Mr. Darcy share what is arguably the most famous relationship in Austen's works. By the end of *Pride and Prejudice*, they develop a deep connection and love, yet it is the long, twisty journey to this point that makes their relationship compelling.

When Mr. Darcy first proposes to Elizabeth, "He spoke well; but there were feelings besides those of the heart to be detailed, and he was not more eloquent on the subject of tenderness than of pride." He mentions "her inferiority," uses the term "degradation," insults her family, and assumes that Elizabeth will agree to marry him without any hesitation. This proposal comes not long after Elizabeth learns that Mr. Darcy was responsible for separating

Jane and Mr. Bingley, and she immediately rejects him. They argue, throwing barbs and pointed rhetorical questions with reckless abandon. Ultimately, Elizabeth declares, "I had not known you a month before I felt that you were the last man in the world whom I could ever be prevailed upon to marry."

Mr. Darcy's first proposal to Elizabeth.
Illustration by C. E. Brock, 1895.

Elizabeth and Mr. Darcy's relationship is a fundamental building block of *Pride and Prejudice*—without it, the plot would crumble. Throughout most of the novel, they struggle to understand each other and see their relationship in different ways. This proposal occurs at the midpoint of the story, and as discussed in the first chapter, it's a key turning point in both Elizabeth's and Mr. Darcy's internal journeys of transformation and discovery.

Relationships are crucial, not only in our stories, but also in our lives. For thousands of years, philosophers, religious leaders, and social scientists have argued that humans are inherently social beings, and that we need connection, relationships, and community. The Dalai Lama explains this eloquently:

> We human beings are social beings. We come into the world as the result of others' actions. We survive here in dependence on others. Whether we like it or not, there is hardly a moment of our lives when we do not benefit from others' activities. For this reason, it is hardly surprising that most of our happiness arises in the context of our relationships with others.[1]

While it's possible to find novels, short stories, films, and plays that include only a single character, these works are rare. Our relationships and feelings of connectedness influence everything about our lives, as does any lack in this area.

The first definition for the word *relationship* in the *Oxford English Dictionary* (*OED*) is "the state or fact of being related; the way in which two things are connected; a connection, an association."[2] Examining the relationship between two things means considering why they are associated or what connects them. Family members, friends, neighbors, enemies, rivals, peers, work associates—there are endless points of connection. Relationships can be defined by similarities or contrasts. They can be deep or passing, static or evolving, and in them we find a treasure trove of storytelling possibilities.

---

1. Satici et al., "Linking social connectedness to loneliness," 306.
2. *Oxford English Dictionary*, "relationship (n.), sense 1."

ESTABLISHING RELATIONSHIPS, NEW AND OLD

In *Pride and Prejudice*, Elizabeth Bennet is aware of Miss Caroline Bingley before they meet. Elizabeth sees Caroline and her sister at the Meryton assembly, and we learn that they are "fine women, with an air of decided fashion." Elizabeth also reads the letter in which Caroline invites Jane to dine at Netherfield. Yet Elizabeth's first true interaction with Caroline occurs after Elizabeth walks to Netherfield to visit her sister Jane, who is ill:

> [Elizabeth] was shown into the breakfast parlour, where all but Jane were assembled, and where her appearance created a great deal of surprise. That she should have walked three miles so early in the day in such dirty weather, and by herself, was almost incredible to Mrs. Hurst and Miss Bingley; and Elizabeth was convinced that they held her in contempt for it. She was received, however, very politely by them.

Elizabeth immediately senses a difference between Caroline Bingley's exterior politeness and her true emotions. Their next full interaction occurs when Elizabeth joins the group after caring for Jane. The entire party is playing cards, but Elizabeth declines in favor of a book because she suspects they are "playing high."

> "Miss Eliza Bennet," said Miss Bingley, "despises cards. She is a great reader, and has no pleasure in anything else."
> "I deserve neither such praise nor such censure," cried Elizabeth; "I am *not* a great reader, and I have pleasure in many things."

Elizabeth and Caroline's relationship is defined by tension and word slinging, politely packaged with a polished veneer. Caroline sees Elizabeth as a threat to her own relationship with Mr. Darcy and constantly tries to maneuver around her. Elizabeth sees

Caroline as an outsider who thinks herself superior to those in Meryton. This relationship is established quickly, in just a few words. Each time we see Elizabeth and Caroline together, we sense their underlying animosity. Yet they continue to spend time with each other because they are of the same social class and because Caroline's brother likes Elizabeth's sister.

Caroline Bingley attempts to flirt with Mr. Darcy
by telling him that he writes "uncommonly fast."
Illustration by C. E. Brock, 1895.

Any time that we write an interaction between two characters, we must consider **how and why they are connected**. What links them? What is their history? What is the nature of their relationship? How do they interact, how often do they interact, and why do they interact? What are the consequences of their relationship on each other and on the plot?

Whether you consider these questions in advance of writing, discover the answers as you write, or craft and refine the relationships during the revision process—or do a combination of all three—it's important to consider *how* to establish these relationships on the page.

Austen often establishes connections between characters quickly, with an **interesting and memorable interaction that helps define the relationship for the reader**. In *Pride and Prejudice*, Mr. Collins's relationship with the Bennet family is established by how Mr. Bennet introduces him. Mr. Bennet teases his family about having a dinner guest, leaving them guessing as to the guest's identity, and then reveals,

> "About a month ago I received this letter ... from my cousin, Mr. Collins, who, when I am dead, may turn you all out of this house as soon as he pleases."

Even before we see Mr. Collins in scene, Austen has established tension between him and the family, as well as the stakes for this relationship. Mrs. Bennet expresses anger with the entailment and Mr. Collins, and then Mr. Bennet reads a letter from Mr. Collins in which he expresses a desire to "heal the breach" between them.

Each of the family members reacts to the letter in a different way, which foreshadows the different relationships each family member will form with him.

Mrs. Bennet:
> "If he is disposed to make [the girls] any amends, I shall not be the person to discourage him."

Jane:
> "Though it is difficult," said Jane, "to guess in what way he can mean to make us the atonement he thinks our due, the wish is certainly to his credit."

Elizabeth and Mr. Bennet:
> Elizabeth was chiefly struck with his extraordinary deference for Lady Catherine, and his kind intention of christening, marrying, and burying his parishioners whenever it were required.

"He must be an oddity, I think," said she. "I cannot make him out. There is something very pompous in his style. And what can he mean by apologizing for being next in the entail? We cannot suppose he would help it, if he could. Can he be a sensible man, sir?"

"No, my dear; I think not. I have great hopes of finding him quite the reverse. There is a mixture of servility and self-importance in his letter which promises well. I am impatient to see him."

Mary:

"In point of composition," said Mary, "his letter does not seem defective. The idea of the olive branch perhaps is not wholly new, yet I think it is well expressed."

Kitty and Lydia:

To Catherine and Lydia neither the letter nor its writer were in any degree interesting. It was next to impossible that their cousin should come in a scarlet coat, and it was now some weeks since they had received pleasure from the society of a man in any other colour.

Of these relationships, the most important is between Mr. Collins and Elizabeth. This is due in part to the fact that the semi-omniscient narrator focuses largely on Elizabeth's perspective and story, which means her relationships naturally take center stage. Their relationship also plays a prominent role in the plot: Mr. Collins proposes to Elizabeth, Elizabeth rejects him, and he marries her friend Charlotte Lucas.

New relationships, like those between Elizabeth and Caroline Bingley, or Elizabeth and Mr. Collins, act as a plot propellant, introducing energy and new possibilities for the story. Yet old, established relationships are just as essential, for they often define the main character, illuminate their past, and provide constraints. Like new relationships, old relationships can also shift the direction of the plot.

Writing an old relationship on the page requires a delicate balancing act; the relationship is old, familiar, and normal to the characters, and yet it is new to the readers. The audience must understand enough about the characters and their relationship to not be disoriented, and yet, as we discussed in Chapter 3, it's important not to be heavy-handed in the exposition and use of backstory.

In *Emma*, Mr. Knightley has known Emma for *her* entire life, and he has spent *his* entire life interacting with Emma's father, Mr. Woodhouse. Mr. Knightley visits them in the first chapter, and the narrator provides a brief introduction to him (his age, where he lives, his demeanor, and the fact that his younger brother is married to Emma's older sister). This telling is useful, but what truly establishes this old relationship is the conversation that unfolds in scene. First, we hear Mr. Woodhouse and Mr. Knightley speak:

> "It is very kind of you, Mr. Knightley, to come out at this late hour to call upon us. I am afraid you must have had a shocking walk."
>
> "Not at all, sir. It is a beautiful moonlight night; and so mild that I must draw back from your great fire."
>
> "But you must have found it very damp and dirty. I wish you may not catch cold."
>
> "Dirty, sir! Look at my shoes. Not a speck on them."
>
> "Well! That is quite surprising, for we have had a vast deal of rain here. It rained dreadfully hard for half an hour while we were at breakfast. I wanted them to put off the wedding."

Mr. Woodhouse assumes that Mr. Knightley must feel the same way he does about walking, dirt, and cold—he cannot recognize that even an old friend might experience life differently than himself. Yet he seems to genuinely care about Mr. Knightley. Mr. Knightley is kind and considerate in his reply yet is not afraid to express disagreement, though he does so in a lively, amused manner. This feels like an established conversational pattern between these two gentlemen, and it teaches the reader about their relationship.

As the conversation continues, Mr. Knightley offers congratulations on the wedding of Emma's former governess, Miss Taylor, and Mr. Woodhouse laments that Miss Taylor has left him. Mr. Knightley can only see the benefits of the marriage, and he says,

> "At any rate, it must be better to have only one to please than two."
>
> "Especially when *one* of those two is such a fanciful, troublesome creature!" said Emma playfully. "That is what you have

in your head, I know—and what you would certainly say if my father were not by."

"I believe it is very true, my dear, indeed," said Mr. Woodhouse, with a sigh. "I am afraid I am sometimes very fanciful and troublesome."

"My dearest papa! You do not think I could mean *you*, or suppose Mr. Knightley to mean *you*. What a horrible idea! Oh no! I meant only myself. Mr. Knightley loves to find fault with me, you know—in a joke—it is all a joke. We always say what we like to one another."

It is clear that Emma and Mr. Knightley also have a comfortable relationship. She teases him and knows she will receive his criticism, whether or not she likes it. Even though she enjoys Mr. Knightley's company, when her father is present, she prioritizes his emotions and needs.

Emma caring for her father. Illustration by Hugh Thomson, 1896.

As the conversation continues, Emma declares that she is fully responsible for Miss Taylor's wedding and makes plans to continue matchmaking. Mr. Knightley argues that she can't take credit for the match and that she shouldn't meddle with others' lives. The narrator had previously declared that "Mr. Knightley … was one of the few people who could see faults in Emma Woodhouse, and the only one who ever told her of them," but now we have seen this in action.

In each of these many relationships—Mr. Knightley and the Woodhouses, Mr. Collins and the Bennets, Elizabeth and Caroline Bingley—there is distance between the characters. Each individual is their own person, with different personalities, their own wants and needs, and different levels of power, privilege, and voice (which we'll discuss in Chapter 9). Certain relationships bridge some of the distance between characters: Close friends or family members can often see and understand each other's perspectives or try to help each other reach their goals. Other relationships, especially those that include antagonism, may lack the desire or ability to bridge that distance, even if some factor continues to tie the characters together.

Ultimately, a story is like a visit to a theme park. Each character is in a bumper car, banging into strangers and friends, intentionally and unintentionally. Sometimes two characters decide to share the same car or work together; sometimes two characters avoid each other or continuously ram each other. These moments of tension, friction, and impact move the plot forward and influence the characters' internal journeys. Yet the stakes are high, because relationships impact our characters' emotions and determine the ways in which they are able to interact with the world around them.

Exercise 8.1: Relationship Self-Analysis

Take ten or fifteen minutes to write about your own relationships. What are your oldest relationships, and what defines them? How did your newest relationships start, and what connections—positive or negative—do you share with these people? How do your interactions differ between your old and new relationships?

Exercise 8.2: Old and New

Write a short scene involving three characters: a viewpoint character, someone they have an old relationship with, and someone they have a new relationship with. In the scene, include some sort of problem that must be resolved. Remember that this scene must introduce the characters and their relationships to the reader.

MINOR/INSIGNIFICANT CHARACTERS AND RELATIONSHIPS

While a rich story should include well-rounded characters with developed relationships, it's often necessary to briefly include characters and relationships that play a minor yet important role in a scene, but aren't significant for the story as a whole. In *Pride and Prejudice*, after the Meryton assembly, Elizabeth and her family discuss Mr. Darcy's pride with Charlotte and Maria Lucas. The scene ends in a delightful way:

> "If I were as rich as Mr. Darcy," cried a young Lucas, who came with his sisters, "I should not care how proud I was. I would keep a pack of foxhounds, and drink a bottle of wine every day."
>
> "Then you would drink a great deal more than you ought," said Mrs. Bennet; "and if I were to see you at it, I should take away your bottle directly."
>
> The boy protested that she should not; she continued to declare that she would; and the argument ended only with the visit.

The interaction is humorous and emphasizes the fact that the Bennets cannot reach a firm conclusion on whether or not Darcy's pride is merited. Instead, they become distracted by the threat of winebibbing. The boy's comment wouldn't make sense from any of the more important characters. His presence also reminds us of the large size of Charlotte's family (which is partially why she decides to marry Mr. Collins). Even though the boy has a line of dialogue, Austen does not allow him to develop into a full-fledged character; he doesn't even have a name. We know his relationship role (younger brother) and we see a hint of his relationship with Mrs. Bennet, but their argument reveals more about her character than about their relationship.

The unnamed Lucas boy telling Mrs. Bennet how much wine he would drink daily if he had Mr. Darcy's wealth. Illustration by C. E. Brock, 1895.

Human beings have the capacity for a large number of relationships. The anthropologist Robin Dunbar has argued that humans can maintain 150 social relationships. (Other researchers use lower or higher numbers, but it's a useful approximation.) When interviewed by *The Guardian*, Dunbar explained, "This is the number of people you can have a relationship with involving trust and obligation—there's some personal history, not just names and faces."[3]

Yet in a standard novel of approximately 70,000 to 100,000 words, including 150 relationships would cause the reader to lose sight of the story and make a book nigh incomprehensible (even most epic fantasies don't contain nearly that many developed relationships). Thus, any relationships that are fully developed on the page *must* be important to the plot or the character.

The Centre for Cultural Analytics at University College Dublin analyzed each of Austen's published novels to understand the relationships between characters. They categorized characters as either major or minor and ran their previously mentioned social network analysis on only the relationships between the major characters. In *Emma*, they found reference to 198 characters in total, including shopkeepers, parishioners, and Emma's five nieces and nephews. Yet of the 198 characters, they only categorized fourteen as main characters: Emma, Mr. Woodhouse, Mr. Knightley, Harriet Smith, Mr. Elton, Frank Churchill, Jane Fairfax, Mr. Weston, Mrs. Weston, Mrs. Elton, Miss Bates, Mrs. Bates, Isabella Knightley, and Mr. John Knightley.[4]

The relationships between these characters are shown in more depth. Even among these characters, some relationships receive greater priority and space on the page than others. We see much more of Emma's relationship with Harriet Smith than her relationship with her sister Isabella, in part because Isabella lives elsewhere, but also because Emma's relationship with Harriet is the primary method by which Emma enacts her desire to be a matchmaker. Minor relationships in the novel are shown in shorthand, if they are shown at all. For instance, we understand that Emma is a good aunt because she is shown holding her eight-month-old niece, who is "very happy to be danced about in her aunt's arms." Relationships help create the sense of the world of the characters, and they provide points of interaction, but even if the main character of a novel finds a relationship important, it should only be fully developed on the page if it's important to the story at hand.

---

3. Krotoski, "Robin Dunbar."
4. Wade, "Jane Austen's Social Networks."

Mr. Knightley and Emma playing with their young nephews.[5]
Illustration by Hugh Thomson, 1896.

Exercise 8.3: A Minor Character

Write a paragraph or a short scene in which a protagonist interacts with a minor character. The interaction should feel important or significant in some way, but at the same time, don't allow the minor character to feel too big or important.

---

5. Even before their marriage, Emma and Mr. Knightley share the same nieces and nephews, because Emma's sister is married to Mr. Knightley's brother.

RELATIONSHIP ARCS

Regardless of the type of relationship—a close family member, a tenuous work connection, an archenemy at the dog park, a best friend, a stranger your character runs into on the bus every week— there can be moments of friction and misunderstanding, as well as moments of unity and resolution. These positive and negative moments can create a shift or change in the relationship. The application of pressure can cause a connection to evolve, buckle, or strengthen. This pressure can come from the characters themselves, from other members of the community, or from outside plot events.

A **relationship arc** is the manner in which a relationship transforms throughout a story. One of my favorite relationship arcs is between Elizabeth Bennet and Charlotte Lucas in *Pride and Prejudice*. The narrator explains that Charlotte is "a sensible, intelligent young woman, about twenty-seven, [and] Elizabeth's intimate friend." The first time we hear Charlotte speak, she is upset by Mr. Darcy's treatment of Elizabeth at the Meryton assembly:

> "Mr. Darcy is not so well worth listening to as his friend, is he?
> Poor Eliza! To be only just *tolerable*."

While close emotionally, Charlotte and Elizabeth are not always of one mind; Charlotte defends Mr. Darcy's pride and argues with Elizabeth about the nature of love and marriage, and she disagrees with Elizabeth about how Jane should show her regard to Mr. Bingley. At several points, Elizabeth hears her mother insult Charlotte to others, yet Elizabeth says nothing to defend her friend.[6] While nuanced, Elizabeth and Charlotte's relationship feels strong and durable. They tease each other, share their personal grievances, and seek out each other's company.

---

6. I discussed this scene with my sister, Sarah Knapp, and she pointed out what I see as two crucial insights. First, Elizabeth doesn't even defend *herself* when she hears her mother disparaging her. Second, if Elizabeth had defended Charlotte, Mrs. Bennet likely would have doubled down on the insults or escalated the situation, making it worse for everyone.

As soon as Elizabeth turns down Mr. Collins's proposal, Elizabeth and Charlotte's relationship begins to fracture, without Elizabeth even realizing it. Charlotte helps the Bennets by listening to Mr. Collins for extended periods of time. Elizabeth thanks her:

> "It keeps him in good humour," said she, "and I am more obliged to you than I can express."
> Charlotte assured her friend of her satisfaction in being useful, and that it amply repaid her for the little sacrifice of her time.

In her reply, Charlotte conceals her true motivations. She not only wants to be a useful friend; she wants to marry Mr. Collins herself. Hiding this from Elizabeth jeopardizes their friendship, which is based in part on honesty and openness, yet if she shared her goals, she would invite derision and judgment. Elizabeth might attempt to persuade her to take a different course. And sharing her goals with Elizabeth would likely also damage the friendship they have built.

Charlotte desires a new category of relationship—a marital relationship that would lead to independence and financial stability—and she prioritizes this new relationship over her existing ones. Once Charlotte receives and accepts Mr. Collins's proposal, she dreads

> the surprise it must occasion to Elizabeth Bennet, whose friendship she valued beyond that of any other person. Elizabeth would wonder, and probably would blame her; and though her resolution was not to be shaken, her feelings must be hurt by such a disapprobation.

Charlotte's dread is justified. When she shares her news with Elizabeth, Elizabeth exclaims in disbelief and struggles to wish Charlotte happiness. As the story progresses, we see how much their relationship has fractured:

> Between Elizabeth and Charlotte there was a restraint which kept them mutually silent on the subject; and Elizabeth felt persuaded that no real confidence could ever subsist between them again.

This fracturing leads Elizabeth to rely more heavily on her friendship with her sister Jane, and it serves to isolate Charlotte. By the time Elizabeth and Charlotte experience a physical separation (Charlotte moves to her new home, fifty miles away), they already have an equally large emotional separation.

"Will you come and see me"

Charlotte asks Elizabeth to visit her.
Illustration by Hugh Thomson, 1894.

While their relationship has shifted, Elizabeth continues to feel the lingering echoes—and obligations—of their prior closeness. Charlotte extracts a commitment from Elizabeth to both write and visit. Their letters are regular but without intimacy. Elizabeth is initially reluctant to visit Charlotte, but months pass and Jane takes a trip to London.

> Absence had increased [Elizabeth's] desire of seeing Charlotte again, and weakened her disgust of Mr. Collins. There was novelty

in the scheme; and as, with such a mother and such uncompanionable sisters, home could not be faultless, a little change was not unwelcome for its own sake.

Elizabeth stays with Charlotte for over a month. While Elizabeth still finds Mr. Collins ridiculous and worries about Charlotte's long-term happiness, she's also impressed by her friend. Charlotte skillfully ignores Mr. Collins's faults, she has created a private space for herself in the house, and she finds ways to occupy her husband and thus give herself more independence.

Soon their party is invited to Rosings to meet Mr. Collins's esteemed patroness, Lady Catherine de Bourgh. When they return to the parsonage, "Elizabeth was called on by her cousin to give her opinion of all that she had seen at Rosings, which, for Charlotte's sake, she made more favourable than it really was." This brief moment is a positive step for Elizabeth and Charlotte—a point of healing.

During Elizabeth's prolonged visit, her friendship with Charlotte moves into a new stage. It can't return to its state before their rift, but it becomes comfortable and meaningful for both of them. While Elizabeth is not as open with Charlotte as before—for instance, she doesn't mention Mr. Darcy's proposal—they regain each other's trust. Their relationship reaches a new level of stability, and it remains in this state for the rest of the novel.

Once Elizabeth leaves Hunsford, the relationship becomes less important to the story. This doesn't mean that the friendship is less important to Elizabeth—she still values Charlotte. However, their relationship has played its role in Elizabeth's internal journey, and it is no longer essential to move the external events of the plot forward. In the rest of the book, Charlotte is mentioned only a handful of additional times.

As we consider this relationship, we can see a number of overarching principles that can guide us as we create relationship arcs in our own stories.

1. Relationship arcs should move the plot forward and intersect with the main character's internal journey.

Relationships are inseparable from character: They are formed because of the natural ways in which characters express themselves and interact with each other. As a character experiences an internal journey of change and growth, this impacts their relationships with those around them. The reverse is also true: A change in a relationship, caused by conflict or outside forces, can force introspection and character transformation. Plot events (such as a change in financial status) can either strengthen or strain a relationship. Similarly, relationship arcs help move the plot forward, often causing the key turning points.

Charlotte's relationship with Elizabeth is crucial to the plot at multiple levels. First, there's the issue of inheritance: When Elizabeth's father dies, Mr. Collins will inherit the Bennet family home. When Charlotte marries Mr. Collins, she becomes a co-beneficiary. While Elizabeth heals her relationship with Charlotte and is not troubled by the future loss of her home, Mrs. Bennet is quite bothered by this, and it damages not only Mrs. Bennet's relationship with Charlotte, but also her relationship with one of her oldest friends, Charlotte's mother. This provides extra motivation for Mrs. Bennet to marry off her daughters and create future stability for the family.

Charlotte's marriage to Mr. Collins is also a key plot catalyst because it creates an opportunity for Elizabeth to interact with Mr. Darcy in a new location, away from her family. In Hunsford, Elizabeth and Mr. Darcy's relationship develops and fractures in ways that would have been impossible in Meryton.

Finally, Charlotte and Elizabeth's friendship is crucial to Elizabeth's internal journey. Charlotte's choices shake Elizabeth largely because of how close they once were—if a mere acquaintance married Mr. Collins, it would not bother her so, but Elizabeth respected Charlotte and saw her as sensible. This forces Elizabeth to reconsider her preconceived notions and prejudices. The healing of their friendship foreshadows Elizabeth's ability to move from conflict with Mr. Darcy to a mutually meaningful relationship.

2. A RELATIONSHIP BETWEEN TWO CHARACTERS WILL STAY RELATIVELY CONSTANT, WITH ONLY GRADUAL UPS AND DOWNS, UNLESS A MAJOR EVENT OR FORCE CAUSES A LARGE SHIFT IN ONE DIRECTION OR ANOTHER.

There are numerous relationships in a novel that don't change or have arcs. For instance, Elizabeth's relationship with her sister Mary remains constant and unchanging, as does her relationship with Caroline Bingley. Yet in most important relationships, tension or force causes some level of change.

We can find a useful corollary for understanding relationship arcs in physics, particularly in Newton's Laws of Motion. NASA defines Newton's First Law of Motion as follows:

> An object at rest remains at rest, and an object in motion remains in motion at constant speed and in a straight line unless acted on by an unbalanced force.[7]

In terms of relationships, we could define our own First Law of Relationship Arcs:

> Fixed and stable relationships will remain fixed and stable, and dynamic relationships will continue moving forward in the same pathway throughout a story, unless acted upon by something that creates imbalance in the relationship.

In *Pride and Prejudice*, Mr. Collins disrupts the balance and stability of Elizabeth and Charlotte's relationship. Now let's consider Newton's Second Law of Motion, as defined by NASA:

> The acceleration of an object depends on the mass of the object and the amount of force applied.[8]

We could create a corollary Second Law of Relationship Arcs:

> The amount of shift in a relationship depends on the stability and the importance of the relationship, the characteristics of the individuals within the relationship, and the amount of force applied.

Elizabeth's relationship with her mother, Mrs. Bennet, remains relatively stable throughout the novel. However, Mrs. Bennet is quite upset when Elizabeth rejects Mr. Collins's proposal. She's insistent that Elizabeth change her mind, so much so that Mr. Bennet declares,

---

7. "Newton's Laws of Motion."
8. "Newton's Laws of Motion."

"Your mother will never see you again if you do *not* marry Mr. Collins, and I will never see you again if you *do*."

Elizabeth does not change her mind, which angers her mother. While this event causes a shift, it is not a strong shift, and Elizabeth and her mother soon return to their normal relationship. In part, it's because of the stability of their mother-daughter relationship and the fact that Elizabeth ultimately matters more to Mrs. Bennet than what happens to the family house. But it's also because of Mrs. Bennet's character: She may bluster and complain about others' choices, but she's unlikely to turn bluster into action. Thus, even a large event like Mr. Collins's failed proposal does not cause a significant change in their relationship.

On the other hand, Charlotte's marriage to Mr. Collins is a much greater force. It hits Charlotte and Elizabeth's relationship like a bowling ball. Large shifts in a relationship—especially when these shifts are sudden—typically require large plot events that exert a huge amount of force. As we discussed in Chapter 6, these key turning points are not reversible or forgettable. They create permanent change.

Charlotte and Mr. Collins. Illustration by Hugh Thomson, 1894.

As we consider what causes relationships to shift or change, we must not only focus on the size or quality of a relationship. It's a crude simplification to state that Elizabeth and Charlotte started as great friends, then moved to not-great friends, and finally settled on just friends, somewhere in the middle. Charlotte begins as Elizabeth's confidant and close friend. They see each other weekly and are a key part of each other's social lives. When Charlotte moves, they become correspondents with a large shared history but with less openness. At this point, maintaining the relationship is more important to Charlotte (who needs friends in her new situation) than it is to Elizabeth (who has turned to Jane and her other social connections). When Elizabeth visits Charlotte, the relationship becomes one of guest and host, which creates a different set of expectations for their roles. Charlotte has also become part of a larger unit, the Collinses, and Elizabeth develops a relationship with them as a couple. Ultimately Elizabeth and Charlotte find stability in the new version of their friendship, which they can positively maintain without much effort.

3. RELATIONSHIP ARCS THAT ARE IMPORTANT TO THE STORY NEED SIGNIFICANT TIME WITHIN THE PLOT AND/OR SIGNIFICANT PAGE SPACE.

Earlier in the chapter, we discussed how to quickly establish both old and new relationships. While a relationship can be established quickly, important relationship arcs require more time both within the plot and on the page. In *Pride and Prejudice*, Charlotte is mentioned or present in twenty-nine of the sixty chapters. In ten chapters she appears *in scene*—we see her in conversation or interacting with Elizabeth and other characters. (In one of these chapters, Charlotte even becomes the viewpoint character.) In two additional chapters she is present, yet in the background, not fully in the scene. In two chapters, other characters discuss her choice to marry Mr. Collins in great detail—while Charlotte is not present, she is the focus. And finally, in fifteen other chapters she is referenced in either small or large ways.

Chapter #	Use of Charlotte
3	Referenced
5	In Scene
6	In Scene
9	Referenced
13	Referenced
18	In Scene
20	In Scene
21	Referenced
22	In Scene; Viewpoint Character
23	*Discussed in detail*
24	*Discussed in detail*
25	Referenced
26	In Scene
27	Referenced
28	In Scene
29	*Present in Background*
30	In Scene
32	In Scene
33	Referenced
34	Referenced
36	Referenced
37	*Present in Background*
38	Referenced
40	Referenced
47	Referenced
48	Referenced
56	Referenced
57	Referenced
60	In Scene

For readers to **believe** that a large relationship shift has occurred, it needs enough page time. Often, it is useful to see a relationship play out in different contexts, whether in different physical settings or with different groups of people. A sentence or paragraph can be included that summarizes days, weeks, or months of a relationship; however, we also need to see some crucial interactions in scene—as we discussed in Chapter 4, some interactions must be shown. Essentially, in order for readers to **feel** the emotional weight of a relationship shift, we must experience the emotions and their causes with the characters. For a writer, it's less about making a scene longer in an attempt to create emotional weight—a short, punchy scene can often hold more weight than a longer, less focused scene. However, moments of significance must appear before us on the page.

Some important relationship arcs aren't shown on the page, especially if they don't involve a viewpoint character. For example, we don't see the large shifts in Lydia and Wickham's relationship. Yet we've seen Elizabeth and Lydia's relationship, we've seen Lydia throwing herself at all the officers, we've seen Elizabeth and Wickham's relationship arc, and we've learned about Darcy and Wickham's relationship arc. These moments act as foreshadowing. We don't need to see Lydia and Wickham at Brighton to believe it, or, like Elizabeth, to feel the emotional consequences.

Exercise 8.4: Categorizing Your Relationships

Make a list of people you have interacted with in the last week, either in person or otherwise (phone call, letter, digitally, etc.). Put these people into categories (friends, family, work, school, mortal enemies, acquaintances, salespeople, etc.).

Draw a star next to the three people whose relationships with you have changed or developed the most within the last month or year. What caused these shifts, and how have they impacted your life?

Exercise 8.5: Pressure and a Shift

Write a short scene in which pressure causes a work relationship to shift in a positive or negative direction.

Exercise 8.6: Track a Relationship

Choose a relationship that is important in a story you have drafted. This can be between two main characters, or between a main character and a supporting character. Create a chart that tracks their relationship in the story. Use the search function in your word processing program to find each mention of the second character (though note that they may also be referred to by pronouns, other names/nicknames, or roundabout references). Log each time the character does the following:

· Appears in scene
· Is present in the background
· Is referenced by another character

If needed, add other categories.

ROMANTIC RELATIONSHIP ARCS

In the *Oxford English Dictionary*, only a subdefinition of the word "relationship" addresses romantic connections: "An emotional and sexual association or partnership between two people."[9] This definition makes romantic relationships seem very clinical; Marianne Dashwood would be appalled.

Romantic relationship arcs do not always result in a partnership, or, in a Jane Austen novel, in marriage. When writing romantic relationship arcs, it's just as important to consider the false starts and failed relationships—like Marianne Dashwood and John Willoughby. Failed relationships are brimming with drama, angst, and struggle, or in other words, plot.

All of the techniques we've already discussed in this chapter can be applied to writing romantic relationships. There are a few additional principles worth considering. While these principles aren't exclusive to romance and can often be applied to other types of connections, they are especially important in romantic relationships, whether these relationships are successful or unsuccessful.

---

9. *Oxford English Dictionary*, "relationship (n.), sense 2.b."

Willoughby cuts a lock of Marianne's hair.
Illustration by Hugh Thomson, 1896.

1. RECIPROCATION AND LACK OF RECIPROCATION OF INTEREST

Not all relationships are mutually agreed upon or chosen—Elizabeth Bennet didn't choose Mr. Collins as a cousin. Yet in both Jane Austen's time and today, in order for romantic interest to culminate in a partnership or a marriage, both individuals must accept the relationship.[10]

Because of the agency involved in this sort of relationship, the characters' reciprocation of interest, or lack of reciprocation, plays a key role. Sometimes, from an initial meeting, **two characters reciprocate romantic interest.** We see this in *Northanger Abbey*, when Catherine Morland and Henry Tilney bond while discussing muslin at a ball. In other stories, **characters feel interest toward each other at different rates or different times.** In *Sense and Sensibility*, Colonel Brandon feels romantically inclined toward Marianne even as she invests her energy and attention in John Willoughby. Only after Marianne's heart is broken does Marianne turn to Colonel Brandon, and even once they marry, their sentiments for each other are not equal. In other stories, **one character never reciprocates the sentiments of another character.** In *Mansfield Park*, Fanny cannot be convinced to marry Henry Crawford, either by Henry or by her uncle. She doesn't respect him as a person or consider him the sort of man she wants to marry.

2. PHYSICALITY AND PHYSICAL AWARENESS

In romantic relationships, physicality is often much more present than in other relationships. In the Regency period, cultural customs meant this manifested in much smaller ways than today, though characters are given opportunities for physical touch in Austen's dance scenes. In *Sense and Sensibility*, Willoughby cuts a lock of Marianne's hair so he may keep it with him.

In *Persuasion*, after a long group walk, Anne is exhausted, both physically and emotionally. The Crofts pass by in their carriage.

> Captain Wentworth, without saying a word, turned to her, and quietly obliged her to be assisted into the carriage.

---

10. There are many modern cultures that use arranged marriages, and so this principle may not apply to a story within such a setting. Two amazing texts that transpose *Pride and Prejudice* to cultures with different marital expectations and norms are Soniah Kamal's novel *Unmarriageable*, which retells Austen's story in modern-day Pakistan, and the Bollywood film *Bride and Prejudice*.

> Yes; he had done it. She was in the carriage, and felt that he
> had placed her there, that his will and his hands had done it.

Anne reacts strongly to the fact that she has been touched and helped by Captain Wentworth's hands. Grammatically (and likely in Anne's mind), his will and his hands are given equal weight—in fact, the action of his hands may be considered a manifestation of his will.

Physical awareness is also important. When a character feels romantic interest, they are often more sensitive to the other person's physical location, demeanor, body language, and proximity to one's self.

At an evening gathering, when the dancing begins, Anne offers to play the pianoforte, which allows her to observe without truly participating in the events. As she plays, Anne maintains a constant awareness of Captain Wentworth—where he stands, who he speaks and dances with, and who seems to be in love with him.

> *Once* she felt that he was looking at herself, observing her altered
> features, perhaps, trying to trace in them the ruins of the face
> which had once charmed him; and *once* she knew that he must
> have spoken of her; she was hardly aware of it, till she heard the
> answer; but then she was sure of his having asked his partner
> whether Miss Elliot never danced?

3. WOOING AND ACTIVE CULTIVATION

We leave many of our relationships to chance. Some deteriorate as a result, while others become stronger. Yet romantic relationships are often marked by one of the characters wooing the other character, or both wooing each other. Some persuasion may be involved; a character may attempt to highlight their affections toward the other person and showcase their own positive attributes (or the positive results of a possible relationship). Many characters understand that actively cultivating a relationship can help it grow. This active cultivation might come in the form of compliments, kind actions, planning activities together, listening and talking, or sharing personal information that is not shared with everyone.

In *Persuasion*, both Musgrove sisters attempt to woo Captain Wentworth, but Anne notices that "Louisa certainly put more forward for his notice than her sister." At one point, Wentworth mentions that his sister always accompanies Admiral Croft on carriage rides, even though he is a poor driver and his sister risks being "tossed out" of the carriage. Immediately, we see Louisa's response; she uses his comment as an opportunity:

> "Ah! You make the most of it, I know," cried Louisa, "but if it were really so, I should do just the same in her place. If I loved a man, as she loves the Admiral, I would always be with him, nothing should ever separate us, and I would rather be overturned by him, than driven safely by anybody else."
>
> It was spoken with enthusiasm.
>
> "Had you?" cried he, catching the same tone; "I honour you!"

In Austen's novels, at times we see wooing and active cultivation of a relationship in non-romantic connections. Mr. Collins and Charlotte woo Lady Catherine de Bourgh, attempting to strengthen their relationship. Elizabeth recognizes that they likely sacrifice so many hours toward this relationship because not only did Lady Catherine give Mr. Collins his position as a clergyman, but "there might [also] be other family livings to be disposed of." In other words, she might be able to give Mr. Collins an even better job.

4. DIFFICULTIES AND INTERFERENCE

Challenges or difficulties are at the heart of story; without them, there is no plot. Relationship journeys are not interesting to a reader if they're too easy or nothing happens of note. As you write relationships, don't be afraid to add difficult choices, conversations, and conflicts, or outside interference.

If one character's romantic inclinations are not reciprocated, or if two characters feel different levels of interest, it creates automatic difficulties for a relationship. In *Sense and Sensibility*, when Mrs. Jennings attempts to play matchmaker for Marianne and Colonel Brandon, Marianne is bewildered. Marianne considers Colonel Brandon old and infirm, for he is thirty-five and "he talked of flannel waistcoats ... and with me a flannel waistcoat is invariably connected with aches, cramps, rheumatisms, and every species of ailment that can afflict the old and the feeble."

In Austen's novels, when romantic feelings are evenly reciprocated on both sides, the relationship arc is generally complicated by the interference of others. In *Northanger Abbey*, John Thorpe actively interferes in the development of Catherine and Tilney's relationship by canceling Catherine's plans. Later, when Catherine stays with Henry Tilney's family at Northanger Abbey, his father, General Tilney, becomes the primary source of interference. Yet their relationship is not only complicated by outside forces; Catherine upsets Henry when she sneaks around the abbey and speculates that General Tilney might have harmed his wife.

5. Tension, Mishaps, and Humor

One of the pleasures of writing a romantic relationship arc is creating tensions and mishaps between the involved parties. Romantic tension can arise when characters—like Darcy and Elizabeth— feel animosity toward each other and attempt to resist attraction. When characters admit and pursue feelings of attraction, mishaps still happen. After all, a romantic relationship involves two people who don't truly know or understand each other, and often they make false assumptions about the other person, causing all sorts of misadventures. Sometimes these moments are humorous for the characters, or at the very least, they're humorous for the reader.

In *Pride and Prejudice*, there are frequent mishaps as Mr. Collins attempts to woo Elizabeth. At the Bingley ball, he secures Elizabeth's hand for two dances, but

> they were dances of mortification. Mr. Collins, awkward and solemn, apologizing instead of attending, and often moving wrong without being aware of it, gave her all the shame and misery which a disagreeable partner for a couple of dances can give. The moment of her release from him was ecstasy.

This is humorous for the reader, but not for the characters.

Sometimes, something can start as a mishap but become humorous. In *Northanger Abbey*, when Catherine first meets Henry Tilney at a ball, he asks her a series of questions in an attempt to know her better. Because she does not know him well, Catherine is unsure of whether Henry is being intentionally or unintentionally humorous, and as a result, she is unsure as to how she should respond:

> "Have you been to the theatre?"
> "Yes, sir, I was at the play on Tuesday."
> "To the concert?"

"Yes, sir, on Wednesday."

"And are you altogether pleased with Bath?"

"Yes—I like it very well."

"Now I must give one smirk, and then we may be rational again." Catherine turned away her head, not knowing whether she might venture to laugh.

This momentary mishap—this bit of tension and uncertainty— is sensed by Henry, and as he continues the conversation, he refers directly to her uncertainty, and by so doing moves the conversation in a direction that is playful and humorous for both of them:

"I see what you think of me," said he gravely—"I shall make but a poor figure in your journal to-morrow."

"My journal!"

"Yes, I know exactly what you will say: Friday, went to the Lower Rooms; wore my sprigged muslin robe with blue trimmings—plain black shoes—appeared to much advantage; but was strangely harassed by a queer, half-witted man, who would make me dance with him, and distressed me by his nonsense."

"Indeed I shall say no such thing."

"Shall I tell you what you ought to say?"

"If you please."

"I danced with a very agreeable young man, introduced by Mr. King; had a great deal of conversation with him—seems a most extraordinary genius—hope I may know more of him. *That*, madam, is what I *wish* you to say."

"But, perhaps, I keep no journal."

"Perhaps you are not sitting in this room, and I am not sitting by you. These are points in which a doubt is equally possible. Not keep a journal! How are your absent cousins to understand the tenor of your life in Bath without one?"

Romance novels and films often contain comedy, because the mishaps and tensions of relationships lead naturally to humor. Yet even in stories with less humor—like *Mansfield Park*—developing relationships will be marked by these sorts of challenges.

6. BELIEF SYSTEMS

The attitudes that characters feel toward romance and relationships reflect their belief systems. These belief systems include how the characters define romance, what they see as an ideal relationship, how important or unimportant they find marriage, the role of money and position in relationships, and the importance of family tradition. These belief systems influence characters' behavior within all stages of relationships.

For Marianne Dashwood, marriage is about passion, youth, and wit. As she discusses Colonel Brandon's supposed infirmities with Elinor, Elinor takes a different position on his age:

> "Perhaps," said Elinor, "thirty-five and seventeen had better not have any thing to do with matrimony together. But if there should by any chance happen to be a woman who is single at seven and twenty, I should not think Colonel Brandon's being thirty-five any objection to his marrying *her*."

To this, Marianne replies, revealing her current belief system (which will shift throughout the novel):

> "A woman of seven and twenty," said Marianne, after pausing a moment, "can never hope to feel or inspire affection again, and if her home be uncomfortable, or her fortune small, I can suppose that she might bring herself to submit to the offices of a nurse, for the sake of the provision and security of a wife. In his marrying such a woman therefore there would be nothing unsuitable. It would be a compact of convenience, and the world would be satisfied. In my eyes it would be no marriage at all, but that would be nothing. To me it would seem only a commercial exchange, in which each wished to be benefited at the expense of the other."

7. OTHER PEOPLE'S INVESTMENT IN RELATIONSHIPS

Whenever there is a romantic relationship or the possibility of such, other characters like to invest interest, time, gossip, and action into discussing or trying to influence it. This investment can result from personal amusement, caring about one or both people involved, or attempting to advance one's own motives.

In *Sense and Sensibility*, Mrs. Jennings loves to tease and joke and gossip. Elinor tries to avoid becoming Mrs. Jennings's subject but is not helped by her youngest sister Margaret:

> When Mrs. Jennings attacked [Margaret] one evening at the park, to give the name of the young man who was Elinor's particular favourite, which had been long a matter of great curiosity to her, Margaret answered by looking at her sister, and saying, "I must not tell, may I, Elinor?"
>
> This of course made every body laugh; and Elinor tried to laugh too. But the effort was painful. She was convinced that Margaret had fixed on a person whose name she could not bear with composure to become a standing joke with Mrs. Jennings.

Marianne tries to discourage Margaret from revealing Elinor's love interest, but she partially fails:

> "Margaret," said Marianne with great warmth, "you know that all this is an invention of your own, and that there is no such person in existence."
>
> "Well, then, he is lately dead, Marianne, for I am sure there was such a man once, and his name begins with an F."

A more extreme case of other characters' investment in a relationship is when Lucy Steele reveals that she is secretly engaged to Edward Ferrars. As a result, Edward's family is outraged and disinherits him.

8. Personal and Deep Nature of Romance

Different relationships hold different weight for the characters. For instance, if a relationship is severed with a minor work acquaintance, it might have little personal or emotional consequence, while being disowned by one's parents will carry huge emotional weight. Romantic relationships tend to be deeply personal and important. Roadblocks, stop signs, and detours in the relationship greatly impact the characters, as do green lights, clear roads, and arriving at the destination.

We discussed Elinor's and Marianne's heartbreaks in Chapter 7. While they express their emotions differently, they're both devastated by the romantic turns in their lives. Even in moments that could be seen as positive for a romance, characters can experience deep and conflicted emotions. In *Persuasion*, after Captain Went-worth helps Anne into the carriage, she reflects on the experience:

> She understood him. He could not forgive her, but he could not be unfeeling. Though condemning her for the past, and consider-ing it with high and unjust resentment, though perfectly careless of her, and though becoming attached to another, still he could not see her suffer, without the desire of giving her relief. It … was a proof of his own warm and amiable heart, which she could not contemplate without emotions so compounded of pleasure and pain, that she knew not which prevailed.

Romance is personal because it often impacts every area of a character's life: their financial situation, their communities, their societal roles, their ability to pursue their wants and needs, and their personal well-being.

Exercise 8.7: First Meeting

Write a short scene in which two characters meet and begin what could become a romantic relationship. Consider what stimulates one or both of the characters' interest in each other, and what factors distinguish this relationship as different than their other, non-roman-tic relationships. Choose one to three of the principles discussed in this section that play a significant role in this scene (such as recip-rocation and lack of reciprocation of interest, physicality, wooing, difficulties/interference, etc.).

Exercise 8.8: Failed Romantic Relationships

Make a list of ten failed romantic relationships in literature or film. (For instance, Elizabeth and Mr. Collins, Elizabeth and Mr. Wickham, etc.) For three of the relationships, record the following:

· A one- or two-sentence summary of the relationship
· Why this relationship had potential
· Why this relationship failed, ended, or shifted to a non-roman-tic relationship

RELATIONSHIP ECOSYSTEMS

One way that we can think about character connections is in terms of larger relationship ecosystems. Every community has an ecosystem, different individuals that interact with each other and play particular roles within the group. For instance, in *Emma*, Mr. Woodhouse is a rich old man whose wishes are often catered to; Jane Fairfax is the talented but poor young woman whom everyone loves—except for Emma.

Often, a few individuals hold more power in a particular community, influencing not only their own relationships, but the relationships of others. For instance, in *Pride and Prejudice*, two of the newcomers, Mr. Bingley and Mr. Darcy, both hold extra influence on the ecosystem. Mr. Bingley is wealthy and has rented a long-empty estate in Meryton. Immediately, the town is interested in him, and his presence changes the ecosystem of the town. He holds weight not just in the town, but also in his own party. Mr. Darcy has come to Meryton only because of Bingley. And Mr. Bingley's sister, Caroline, is cordial and friendly to Jane Bennet because of her brother's influence and his interest in Jane. Because of his off-putting mannerisms, Mr. Darcy has less influence in Meryton than Bingley, despite his greater wealth. However, he holds a strong influence over Mr. Bingley and is able to halt the relationship between Bingley and Jane.

In most of Austen's novels, characters move between ecosystems. They often play different roles and wield different amounts of power and influence in new ecosystems. In *Persuasion*, Anne inhabits four distinct ecosystems:

1. Kellynch Hall, where she is unwanted.
2. Uppercross, where the Musgroves and Wentworth play a key role, and where Anne attempts to withdraw.
3. Lyme, a place where Anne shines and plays a larger part.
4. Bath, a place that she initially despises. However, she ultimately finds happiness here as she experiences internal growth and becomes more active in her life and her communities. Bath is also unique in that characters from all

areas and time periods of Anne's life come together in a single ecosystem.

Emma is Austen's only novel in which the main character stays in the same relationship ecosystem for the entire story. Yet this ecosystem experiences disruption and change by the insertion of a returning member—Jane Fairfax—and new members—Mrs. Elton and Frank Churchill. Other existing members of the community, like Harriet Smith, Mr. Martin, the Coles, and even Mr. Knightley, experience shifts in their roles within their community and in their relationships with Emma.

"The sight of Harriet's tears"

Harriet cries upon learning that Mr. Elton favors Emma, not her.
Illustration by Chris (Christiana) Hammond), 1898.

A change in a single connection or relationship can have ripple effects on other relationships. In *Northanger Abbey*, Isabella Thorpe's flirtations with Henry Tilney's brother weaken her relationship with her fiancé, James Morland, and fracture her relationship with Catherine. Relationships impact individuals and communities, and they play an essential role in characters' internal and external journeys.

In the next chapter, we'll continue to look at relationships and connections between characters as we focus on dialogue, the way characters talk to each other, the power and influence they have when they speak, and the impact this has on the story.

CHAPTER NINE

DIALOGUE

"She spoke, and seemed only to offend."

—Persuasion

In *Persuasion*, Anne Elliot attempts to warn her sister Elizabeth that Elizabeth's friend, the widowed Mrs. Clay, may have designs on their father. Anne knows that Elizabeth is unlikely to listen, but she speaks anyway. When the conversation is over, we read,

> Anne had done; glad that it was over, and not absolutely hope-less of doing good. Elizabeth, though resenting the suspicion, might yet be made observant by it.

Characters speak because of the belief that doing so is "not abso-lutely hopeless"—characters believe that their words matter and can create change. They use dialogue to express themselves and to interact with other individuals and with the broader community. Different characters speak in different ways, for different reasons, and with a wide range of results.

When writing dialogue, four key components should be considered:

1. What the characters say
2. How the characters say it
3. What the characters don't say
4. What the characters do

Marianne sends a letter to Willoughby.
Illustration by Chris (Christiana) Hammond, 1899.

Each of these components is present in a short scene in *Sense and Sensibility*. When Elinor and Marianne first arrive in London, Marianne sends a letter to Willoughby to let him know that they are visiting. In the next chapter, a letter arrives and is set on the table.

"For me?" cried Marianne, stepping hastily forward.

"No, ma'am, for my mistress."

But Marianne, not convinced, took it instantly up.

"It is indeed for Mrs. Jennings, how provoking!"

"You are expecting a letter, then?" said Elinor, unable to be longer silent.

"Yes; a little—not much."

After a short pause, "you have no confidence in me, Marianne."

"Nay, Elinor, this reproach from *you*—you who have confidence in no one!"

"Me!" returned Elinor in some confusion; "indeed, Marianne, I have nothing to tell."

"Nor I," answered Marianne with energy, "our situations then are alike. We have neither of us any thing to tell; you, because you do not communicate, and I, because I conceal nothing."

Elinor, distressed by this charge of reserve in herself, which she was not at liberty to do away, knew not how, under such circumstances, to press for greater openness in Marianne.[1]

1. WHAT THE CHARACTERS SAY

What the characters choose to say is influenced by who they are as individuals and by their goals for the conversation. Sometimes two characters share the same goal or objective for a conversation, but often, they have different goals.

In this scene, Elinor's primary goal is to discover the truth from Marianne so she can better help her very depressed sister. For quite some time, she has wondered how to talk to Marianne about Willoughby, and so she takes the opportunity to ask Marianne a single question, hoping her sister will then confide in her. When Marianne doesn't give a clear answer, Elinor expresses her emotions, stating, "You have no confidence in me," which makes Marianne defensive.

Marianne's original goal is to conceal her anxieties about her relationship with Willoughby; she does not want her older sister's judgment or advice. To this is added the goal of pointing out Elinor's hypocrisy. She knows that Elinor often fails to communicate her thoughts, desires, and problems, keeping them to herself. Stating that Elinor has "confidence in no one!" does not lead Elinor

---

1. For this quotation, I use the punctuation from the first edition of *Sense and Sensibility*.

to change her ways, but it does achieve Marianne's goal of ending the conversation quickly.

When characters have different goals for a conversation, it creates organic and compelling dialogue with forward movement and momentum. (This is true even if the characters have similar goals. Characters' goals will never entirely overlap, and this will be reflected in what they say.)

2. HOW THE CHARACTERS SAY IT

In this scene, most of how the characters speak, such as their tone and their volume, is implied by the dialogue itself. For instance, in the following sentence, the exclamation mark and the sentence structure indicate how Marianne makes her statement:

> "It is indeed for Mrs. Jennings, how provoking!"

Skilled writers like Austen reveal most of how the characters speak by the speech itself, without relying heavily on description or dialogue tags. In Austen's novels, most of the time if she includes a dialogue tag, she uses the word "said" (e.g., "she said" or "said Elinor").[2] In some lines of this passage, Austen does use more descriptive dialogue tags, such as "cried Marianne," which gives us a deeper insight into Marianne's expression. However, if these sorts of qualifiers were used on every line, it would clutter, distract, and dilute their expression.

In this dialogue, Austen provides two additional descriptions of how the characters speak: "returned Elinor in some confusion" and "answered Marianne with energy." These descriptions occur in brief succession and paint a contrasting portrait of the two sisters, demonstrating how even in this short moment, the sisters act as foils to each other.

Pauses are also an important part of how a character speaks. Note the power in Elinor's pause before she makes her accusation:

---

2. The author Elliott Slaughter performed a study of Jane Austen's use of dialogue tags in *Pride and Prejudice*. He found that often, Austen does not include dialogue tags; when she does, she uses the dialogue tag "said" 50 percent of the time. She also uses "functional dialogue tags" like *replied, added,* and *repeated;* "descriptive dialogue tags" such as *exclaimed* and *whispered;* and the very occasional adverb, such as *warmly* and *resentfully.* To read the entire study, see Slaughter, "Dialogue Tags: An Empirical Study."

> "You are expecting a letter, then?" said Elinor, unable to be longer silent.
>
> "Yes; a little—not much."
>
> After a short pause, "you have no confidence in me, Marianne."

This pause provides a space for Elinor to decide to push the subject, and it provides a space for the reader as we watch the characters struggle through this interaction. A different sort of pause comes at the end of the scene when Elinor does not know what to say and we glimpse her internal thoughts.

Including how the characters speak can offer insight into their motives, their emotions, and who they are as individuals.

3. What the Characters Don't Say

In any conversation, a multitude of things are left unsaid: motivations and emotions, backstory and baggage. Very few people are entirely open in conversation, even to those who are closest to them. (When characters are finally open with each other, it can create huge emotional resonance for readers.)

What the characters choose not to say should greatly impact the dialogue. In this scene from *Sense and Sensibility*, the very subject of the conversation is what they refuse to tell each other. In addition to not talking about their secrets, they do not talk about how irritated they are with each other. This is fueled by their frustration with their situations and a latent sense of hopelessness, especially for Marianne, but also for Elinor.

Often we see characters' biggest desires and anxieties in what the characters choose not to say or find themselves unable to say, and this can help create dynamic interactions.

What characters do not say is a type of **subtext**—something that is not stated in the text or by the characters but that influences the story and can be observed or sensed by the reader.

4. What the Characters Do

Generally, actions are peppered throughout dialogue scenes and are just as important as the words that people say.

In this scene, Marianne's actions betray how much she hopes for a letter from Willoughby. Her haste in stepping forward underlines her impatience and longing, and she cannot trust the word of the servant—she must pick the letter up herself to see that it is truly not for her.

At times, a character action or behavior can be used instead of a dialogue tag. For example, in *Mansfield Park*, we read,

> Lady Bertram soon brought the matter to a certainty by carelessly observing to Mrs. Norris—
>
> "I think, sister, we need not keep Miss Lee any longer, when Fanny goes to live with you."
>
> Mrs. Norris almost started. "Live with me, dear Lady Bertram! what do you mean?"

The first line of dialogue has a dialogue tag—in simplified form, we could write it as "Lady Bertram carelessly observed." But the second line, Mrs. Norris's dialogue, has no direct dialogue tag. Instead of a tag like "With surprise, Mrs. Norris replied," an action is included: "Mrs. Norris almost started." We see her physical response, and because this is coupled with a line of dialogue, it sets up the dialogue as belonging to her.

It's not necessary to have characters do things as they speak; in her novels, Austen includes dialogues in which no actions are taken. But she often uses small actions (such as Marianne picking up a letter or a character gesturing at something) and large actions (like moving through a space) to add weight and physicality to the conversation and to show how the dialogue fits in the larger story.

Exercise 9.1: Random Dialogue

Take a book off your shelf and open it to a random page. Find the first sentence of dialogue on the page and use it as the first line of a conversation you write for brand-new characters. Make sure to consider what the characters say, how the characters say it, what the characters don't say, and the actions of the characters. Omit dialogue tags when they are unnecessary. (Note: An alternative is to use an online random dialogue generator to create your first line of dialogue.)

Exercise 9.2: Three Versions

Write a short passage of dialogue (approximately three to five lines/paragraphs), featuring two characters: a girl who wants to buy a lollipop she sees in a shop and a guardian who does not want to buy the lollipop.

You will write this passage three different times:

- Version 1: Have both characters say exactly what they want.
- Version 2: Have one of the characters say what they want, while the other character does not say what they want but nevertheless tries to achieve their goal.
- Version 3: Neither character should say exactly what they want, yet both should attempt to achieve their goals.

In each version of the dialogue, consider how the characters speak and what actions they might take.

Exercise 9.3: Trimming Dialogue

It's easy to overwrite dialogue and include more than is necessary. Take a scene of dialogue that you have drafted and cut out at least 25 percent of the dialogue by eliminating words, phrases, and entire sentences.

DIALOGUE AS COMMUNICATION

One of the major ways in which we use dialogue in real life is to communicate. We give and receive information. We make plans. We learn about events that have happened. We ask someone to buy something at the store, summarize what we read in the news, schedule meetups, tell people we're running late, repeat what someone says to us, and give background information and context. Because this sort of communication makes up such a large part of how we speak in real life, it's tempting to give it a lot of page time.

Yet these sorts of conversations risk feeling dull and uninteresting to the reader. It might take multiple conversations to schedule a work meeting, but that doesn't mean we want to read them. At other times, the dialogue can feel stilted or unnatural, particularly if the information is filled with backstory and exposition, meant more for the reader than for the characters.

Austen often avoids these pitfalls by summarizing dialogue (using the techniques we discussed in Chapter 4). In the following passage from *Pride and Prejudice*, she takes multiple information-heavy conversations and condenses them, giving us only the outlines and results of what was said:

> As no objection was made to the young people's engagement with their aunt, and all Mr. Collins's scruples of leaving Mr. and Mrs. Bennet for a single evening during his visit were most steadily resisted, the coach conveyed him and his five cousins at a suitable hour to Meryton.

At other times Austen includes information-heavy dialogue. For instance, near the beginning of Volume 2 of *Pride and Prejudice*, Mrs. Gardiner visits the Bennets. Three important pieces of information must be communicated to her: Elizabeth rejected an offer of marriage from Mr. Collins; Mr. Collins is marrying Charlotte Lucas; and Mr. Bingley has left Meryton and in so doing, he has broken Jane's heart. As readers, we have seen all of these events occur in scene. We know exactly what has happened and don't personally need this information. It would be easy for Austen to summarize, but instead, the narrator summarizes only a few of Mrs. Bennet's words and then includes the rest of the communication in full:

> "I do not blame Jane," she continued, "for Jane would have got Mr. Bingley if she could. But, Lizzy! Oh, sister! it is very hard to think that she might have been Mr. Collins's wife by this time, had not it been for her own perverseness. He made her an offer in this very room, and she refused him. The consequence of it is, that Lady Lucas will have a daughter married before I have, and that Longbourn estate is just as much entailed as ever. The Lucases are very artful people, indeed, sister. They are all for what they can get. I am sorry to say it of them, but so it is. It makes me very nervous and poorly, to be thwarted so in my own family, and to have neighbours who think of themselves before anybody else. However, your coming just at this time is the greatest of comforts, and I am very glad to hear what you tell us of long sleeves."

Elizabeth, of course, is sitting in the same room, listening as her mother berates her to her beloved aunt. Jane is also present and must listen to a summary of her heartbreak. And then the narrator reveals that this information was not new to Mrs. Gardiner—"the chief of this news had been given [to her] before," in Jane's and Elizabeth's letters.

Yet even though we, as readers, don't need to learn of these events, the dialogue is fascinating. We receive insights into Mrs. Bennet's character. We better understand her relationship with her sister-in-law as we see her heartily complain and then immediately thank Mrs. Gardiner for telling them about the latest London fashion. We feel the pressure of expectations placed on Jane and Elizabeth, and we see the consequences of their choices and the choices of others. This is more than just communication: It is a tangled web of relationships and an insightful social commentary on the part of the narrator.

And then we read that Mrs. Gardiner "made her sister a slight answer, and, in compassion to her nieces, turned the conversation." By including Mrs. Bennet's dialogue, and a summary of Mrs. Gardiner's response, we see the contrast between them and better appreciate Mrs. Gardiner's role in the family.

Later, when she and Elizabeth are alone, Mrs. Gardiner brings up the subject again, and at this point, we've moved past conveying information. Their communication becomes about trying to make sense of events. Mrs. Gardiner states, "It seems likely to have been a desirable match for Jane. … I am sorry it went off. But these things happen so often!" Elizabeth counters that this is not simply the normal inconstancies of men and that "we do not suffer by accident." She explains that Bingley was "violently in love" with Jane. Mrs. Gardiner replies, "That expression of 'violently in love' is so hackneyed, so doubtful, so indefinite, that it gives me very little idea." They discuss what love looks like and Mrs. Gardiner says,

> "Poor Jane! I am sorry for her, because, with her disposition, she may not get over it immediately. It had better have happened to *you*, Lizzy; you would have laughed yourself out of it sooner. But do you think she would be prevailed on to go back with us? Change of scene might be of service—and perhaps a little relief from home may be as useful as anything."

Mrs. Gardiner's words foreshadow Lizzy's future romantic troubles—though she is wrong, for Elizabeth is not able to simply laugh herself out of it after Mr. Darcy's proposal. The conversation allows Elizabeth to explore how she defines love and the importance she sees in it. This conversation is not only a chance for the characters and the reader to continue to react and respond to momentous events; as a direct result of this dialogue, Mrs. Gardiner decides to ask Jane to join her in London, which sets off another series of events.

Whenever Austen includes a dialogue that conveys information to the reader and/or to a character, the dialogue is always layered, revealing character and relationships, causing shifts in emotion, demonstrating subtext, creating tension, and making a tangible impact on the plot. When we use dialogue as communication in our own stories, we must avoid imitating the banality of many conversations in our actual lives, focus on the essential parts of the conversation, and use it to enlighten the reader and forward the story.

Exercise 9.4: Dialogue Tracking

Spend a portion of a day tracking the times you speak with other people, whether in person, on the phone, or via text or other digital forms. How many of your conversations were focused on giving and receiving information? Did any of these times have more at play, in terms of relationships, emotions, tension, or subtext?

Exercise 9.5: Making Information Compelling

Choose a basic set of information that two characters might need to communicate, such as a shopping list, a homework assignment, or a plan for meeting up. Write a dialogue that conveys this information but in a way that is interesting and compelling because of what it reveals about the characters or their relationship.

DIALOGUE AS ACTION, CONFLICT, AND PERSUASION

Dialogue often acts as a tool of the plot, moving the story forward. In large part, this is because **dialogue is an action: The act of speaking is a manifestation of thought and will.**

Sir Walter and Mr. Shepherd. Illustration by C. E. Brock, 1898.

In *Persuasion*, a single paragraph of dialogue irreversibly changes the course of the story. After Sir Walter decides to rent out Kellynch Hall, his friend says the following:

> "I must take leave to observe, Sir Walter," said Mr. Shepherd one morning at Kellynch Hall, as he laid down the newspaper, "that the present juncture is much in our favour. This peace will be turning all our rich naval officers ashore. They will all be wanting a home. Could not be a better time, Sir Walter, for having a choice of tenants, very responsible tenants. Many a noble fortune has been made during the war. If a rich admiral were to come in our way ..."

At first Sir Walter resists the idea of renting the house to an officer, but ultimately, he is won over. He rents the house to Admiral Croft, which brings Croft's brother-in-law, Captain Wentworth, back into Anne's life. Austen frequently uses dialogue as an action, a vehicle for change, and we can do so in our own stories.

Dialogue can also be a vehicle for conflict. Any tensions in a relationship will manifest in their dialogue. Characters frequently misinterpret each other or take offense at words, which can also create conflict.

In *Persuasion*, Mary and her husband, Mr. Musgrove, happily discuss the prospect of Captain Wentworth marrying one of Mr. Musgrove's sisters, Louisa or Henrietta. All is well in their conversation until Mary raises the idea that Henrietta's other suitor, Charles Hayter, is not good enough for Henrietta:

> "You know," said she, "I cannot think him at all a fit match for Henrietta; and considering the alliances which the Musgroves have made, she has not right to throw herself away.... And, pray, who is Charles Hayter? Nothing but a country curate. A most improper match for Miss Musgrove of Uppercross."

This instantly creates conflict with her husband:

> Her husband, however, would not agree with her here; for besides having a regard for his cousin, Charles Hayter was an eldest son, and he saw things as an eldest son himself.
> "Now you are talking nonsense, Mary," was therefore his answer.

And then, he begins a lengthy argument on the merits of Charles Hayter.

When characters argue with each other, it is generally in an attempt to persuade, for words can create change. Characters often unknowingly or knowingly draw upon different appeals, or types of persuasive arguments. Aristotle created three overarching categories to describe the appeals commonly used in persuasion: ethos, pathos, and logos.[3]

Ethos: appeals to the authority of the speaker, or to other sources that the listener would find authoritative

Pathos: appeals to emotion

Logos: appeals to logic and reason

Throughout *Persuasion*, Lady Russell draws upon ethos, pathos, and logos, especially when she attempts to persuade Anne to consider Mr. Elliot as a possible marriage partner. She says,

> "I only mean that if Mr. Elliot should some time hence pay his addresses to you, and if you should be disposed to accept him, I think there would be every possibility of your being happy together. A most suitable connection everybody must consider it, but I think it might be a very happy one."

Here, she draws upon pathos, appealing to emotion as she encourages Anne to consider her future happiness. She also draws upon ethos—*everyone*, including herself, would consider this a "most suitable connection." As we discussed in the chapter on antagonism, it was Lady Russell who originally encouraged Anne to break off her engagement with Captain Wentworth, and Lady Russell knows that she is an authority figure in Anne's life. Her opinion and blessing matter to Anne.

Yet Anne is not convinced. She says, "Mr. Elliot is an exceedingly agreeable man, and in many respects I think highly of him … but we should not suit."

Lady Russell is not persuasive because she assumes that Anne and Mr. Elliot are well-suited, but Anne does not feel the same. In other words, Lady Russell and Anne do not share an implicit assumption.

---

3. Herrick, *History and Theory of Rhetoric*, 87–90.

Implicit assumptions are the assumptions that undergird an argument and its appeals. These assumptions must be accepted as true for the argument to work. Often, implicit assumptions tap into the way a character views the world, their philosophy toward life and people, and what matters to them. In order for an argument to be successful, the speaker and the listener must share at least one implicit assumption.

Lady Russell sees that her argument is not working, so she shifts her approach. Instead of making an argument about Mr. Elliot, which would be harder to win, she makes an argument that taps into Anne's priorities for herself. She uses an implicit assumption that both she and Anne share: Anne wants to be like her mother.

> "I own that to be able to regard you as the future mistress of Kellynch, the future Lady Elliot, to look forward and see you occupying your dear mother's place, succeeding to all her rights, and all her popularity, as well as to all her virtues, would be the highest possible gratification to me. You are your mother's self in countenance and disposition; and if I might be allowed to fancy you as she was, in situation and name, and home, presiding and blessing in the same spot, and only superior to her in being more highly valued! My dearest Anne, it would give me more delight than is often felt at my time of life!"

She uses logos—logic and reasoning—when she states that Anne can have her lifelong home back if she marries Mr. Elliot. She uses pathos—emotion—by conjuring memories of Anne's mother. She uses ethos—appeal to authority—as she talks about the joy that this sort of decision would bring her. And because the implicit assumption underneath these appeals is shared, it's quite an effective argument:

> Anne was obliged to turn away, to rise, to walk to a distant table, and, leaning there in pretended employment, try to subdue the feelings this picture excited. For a few moments her imagination and her heart were bewitched. The idea of becoming what her mother had been; of having the precious name of "Lady Elliot" first revived in herself; of being restored to Kellynch, calling it her home again, her home for ever, was a charm which she could

not immediately resist. Lady Russell said not another word, willing to leave the matter to its own operation.

Many characters are not nearly as persuasive as Lady Russell—
for example, Mr. Collins also uses appeals to ethos, pathos, and
logos when he proposes to Elizabeth.

Mr. Collins proposes to Elizabeth.
Illustration by Hugh Thomson, 1894.

He attempts to establish ethos by appealing to Lady Catherine as an authority figure—but Elizabeth does not see her as an
authority. He appeals to pathos by assuring her "in the most animated language of the violence of my affection," but Elizabeth does

not share these emotions. He uses logos as he presents his long list of reasons for marrying and then later when he argues that "in spite of your manifold attractions, it is by no means certain that another offer of marriage may ever be made you." Spoiler: Elizabeth immediately rejects him, not only because of his misguided use of ethos, pathos, and logos, but because they have different implicit assumptions on the meaning and purpose of marriage. Yet whether or not these tools are used effectively, characters frequently use dialogue to persuade, to create or to resolve conflict, and as an action.

Exercise 9.6: Dialogue as Conflict

Find three examples in books or movies in which dialogue is a vehicle for conflict. For each example, record the following:

- The subject and purpose of the dialogue
- The source of conflict
- Whether the conflict was present before the dialogue or if it arose during the dialogue
- The specific tools used by the writer to express or create tension
- What makes this scene compelling

Exercise 9.7: Ethos, Pathos, and Logos

Write a short scene in which a character attempts to convince another character to change their plans by using appeals to ethos, pathos, and logos. Their argument can be successful or unsuccessful. If their argument is successful, they should at least encounter resistance; there must be a reason that persuasion is necessary. As you write the scene, consider who the characters are and their relationship to each other, and how this will affect the dialogue.

DIALOGUE AS VOICE, POWER, AND PRIVILEGE

Near the end of *Persuasion*, there is a famous conversation in which Anne Elliot and Captain Harville debate whether or not women are inconstant and whether men or women feel the loss of love more deeply. Captain Harville says,

> "I do not think I ever opened a book in my life which had not something to say upon woman's inconstancy. Songs and proverbs, all talk of woman's fickleness. But perhaps you will say, these were all written by men."

Anne immediately replies,

> "Perhaps I shall. Yes, yes, if you please, no reference to examples in books. Men have had every advantage of us in telling their own story. Education has been theirs in so much higher a degree; the pen has been in their hands."

Anne's argument rests on voice, power, and privilege. **Voice:** Who has been given an opportunity to tell their story? **Power:** Who has control and influence in a situation? **Privilege:** Who has been given unfair advantages in a situation?

In this particular matter, primarily men's stories have been voiced; men have owned the power of the pen and publication; and men have more generally had the privilege of education, which allows them greater opportunities to use their voice. Anne is well-educated, well-read, and well-able to express herself—all marks of privilege— yet she has often possessed little power or influence.

Considering the ways in which voice, power, and privilege impact conversations can help you craft compelling dialogue that reflects dynamic relationships and creates a sense of movement. In the coming pages, we will explore several key questions that can help you write better dialogue, both within individual scenes and in your stories as a whole.

WHAT VOICES DO WE HEAR FROM? WHO IS GIVEN LINES OF DIALOGUE?

Throughout Austen's novels, almost all the lines of dialogue belong to upper-class characters. With a few exceptions, such as Mr. Darcy's housekeeper in *Pride and Prejudice*, servants are not given any voice, if they are even seen at all. In *Persuasion*, voice is given almost entirely to upper-class adults. Minimal voice is given to children, though we see Anne's young nephew misbehaving and hear the rowdiness of the children at Christmastime.

Only two characters in *Persuasion* receive a voice despite not being part of the upper class. One is Mrs. Smith. However, she did have greater wealth years before, but then she was widowed, lost most of her fortune, and suffered from health challenges. She is Anne's friend, and Anne values her voice, which is why it is present in the narrative.

The other non-upper-class character who receives a voice is the nurse, Mrs. Rooke. Yet we never hear her directly—she is quoted by Mrs. Smith, thus giving her a voice only through the filter of someone else's voice:

> "It was my friend, Mrs. Rooke; Nurse Rooke.... She it was who told me you were to marry Mr. Elliot. She had had it from Mrs. Wallis herself, which did not seem bad authority. She sat an hour with me on Monday evening, and gave me the whole history."

The voices Austen prioritizes in part reflect the story that she has chosen to tell, but they also reflect her own position within society. Some modern adaptations of Austen prioritize the voices of servants, such as the novel *Longbourn* by Jo Baker, the play *Pride and Prejudice* (*sort of)* by Isobel McArthur, and the play *The Wickhams: Christmas at Pemberley* by Lauren Gunderson and Margot Melcon. By giving voices to the voiceless, these adaptations create new possibilities for the sorts of stories that can be told and the interactions that can be had. When you are writing your own stories, regardless of the genre, it is important to ask yourself questions about the choices you make regarding dialogue.

Whose voices am I including? Who am I leaving out? Do the choices I make about voicing characters reflect the biases of myself or of society?

In *Persuasion*, a large part of Anne's internal journey is about gaining a voice. At the beginning of the novel, she often self-silences and does not contribute to conversations because she feels that her voice is not valued. She also feels self-conscious around Captain Wentworth because of their broken engagement, and so she is less likely to speak if he is present.

The eighth chapter of *Persuasion* features a dinner party filled with interesting conversations about service in the military, whether women should go to sea, and news and insights about family and friends. There are thirty-nine units of voiced dialogue (dialogue that is written out in full, rather than summarized); some are only a sentence in length, but many are full paragraphs. Of these thirty-nine units, not a single line of dialogue belongs to Anne. Throughout the chapter, we receive her internal reflections on the conversation—after Captain Wentworth tells of a near-death experience, we read "Anne's shudderings were to herself alone"—but never once does she voice her thoughts.

The only time in the chapter that Anne speaks, it is not voiced but instead is summarized. She unintentionally nears Captain Wentworth, and as a result, he stands.

> "I beg your pardon, madam, this is your seat;" and though she immediately drew back with a decided negative, he was not to be induced to sit down again.

We know Anne spoke. She gave a "decided negative," likely something along the lines of "No, that is not my seat." Austen's choice of summarizing Anne's sole line of dialogue rather than voicing it is clearly intentional. Anne does not feel like she has a voice in the chapter, so the one time she speaks, it is not directly quoted.

Who has power and influence in a conversation?

Not every character is aware of the power dynamics of a situation, and when a character is unaware of or insensitive to power dynamics, it creates immediate tension. Yet often, characters are aware of who holds power, and they adjust what they say accordingly.

In *Persuasion,* we watch as Mary Musgrove argues with her husband. He plans to dine with his parents, leaving her at home with their sick child, and she attempts to convince him that he should stay at home as well. He gives a firm rebuttal, and then we read,

> Husbands and wives generally understand when opposition will be vain. Mary knew, from Charles's manner of speaking, that he was quite determined on going, and that it would be of no use to teaze him. She said nothing, therefore, till he was out of the room, but as soon as there was only Anne to hear—
>
> "So you and I are to be left to shift by ourselves, with this poor sick child; and not a creature coming near us all the evening! I knew how it would be. This is always my luck.... I did not think Charles would have been so unfeeling. So here he is to go away and enjoy himself, and because I am the poor mother, I am not to be allowed to stir.... My being the mother is the very reason why my feelings should not be tried. I am not at all equal to it. You saw how hysterical I was yesterday."

While Mary wins some arguments with her husband, in this situation she realizes she does not have the power to influence him, so she stops trying. But she feels that her arguments—or at least her complaints—will have more sway on her sister Anne.

Anne also feels like she has more power in this situation than she does with her other family members. She attempts to convince her younger sister to shift her perspective:

> "But that was only the effect of the suddenness of your alarm— of the shock. You will not be hysterical again. I dare say we shall have nothing to distress us."

Mary explains that she is no use to a sick child and that it is no good for her to be here with her son, to which Anne replies:

> "But, could you be comfortable yourself, to be spending the whole evening away from the poor boy?"
> "Yes; you see his papa can, and why should not I?"

Anne feels she has more power—she is more willing to engage in an argument or discussion with her sister—yet she still does not manage to convince her. Ultimately Anne offers to stay with Charles while Mary goes to dine. Mary is immediately persuaded—how easily we are persuaded to that which we want!

At times, a character with power can shift the power dynamics of a conversation simply by who they pay attention to and whose opinion they seem to value. Later, when Anne is in Bath, she finds that, like at home, her father Sir Walter and her sister Elizabeth have no interest in her words. Then their cousin Mr. Elliot comes to call. Despite Sir Walter and Elizabeth's attempts to draw the conversation to other subjects, Mr. Elliot wants to hear more about Anne's experiences in Lyme.

> [Mr. Elliot's] enquiries, however, produced at length an account of the scene [Anne] had been engaged in there.... Having alluded to "an accident," he must hear the whole. When he questioned, Sir Walter and Elizabeth began to question also, but the difference in their manner of doing it could not be unfelt. She could only compare Mr. Elliot to Lady Russell, in the wish of really comprehending what had passed, and in the degree of concern for what she must have suffered in witnessing it.

Mr. Elliot's interest in Anne's account leads Sir Walter and Elizabeth to feel interest, yet Anne can still sense that they are less engaged than Mr. Elliot.

WHAT SORTS OF POWER DO THESE CHARACTERS HAVE? WHICH CHARACTERS CHOOSE TO EXERT POWER, AND WHICH CHARACTERS CHOOSE TO GIVE POWER TO OTHERS? HOW DOES AN AWARENESS OF POWER IMPACT THE CONVERSATION?

By the end of the story, Anne has gained more power, and she is more willing to resist her father's influence. He informs her that she must join him in visiting Lady Dalrymple, who has a high place in society. Anne declines because she is already "engaged to spend the evening with an old schoolfellow."

> They were not much interested in anything relative to Anne; but still there were questions enough asked, to make it understood what this old schoolfellow was; and Elizabeth was disdainful, and Sir Walter severe....

"A Mrs. Smith. A widow Mrs. Smith; and who was her husband? One of five thousand Mr. Smiths whose names are to be met with everywhere. And what is her attraction? That she is old and sickly. Upon my word, Miss Anne Elliot, you have the most extraordinary taste! Everything that revolts other people, low company, paltry rooms, foul air, disgusting associations are inviting to you."

Sir Walter carries on, recommending that she put off the engagement. Despite the ferocity of his disapproval and the strong verbiage of his arguments, Anne maintains power by responding rationally and civilly, as if he had not spoken so critically of her taste and her friend:

"I do not think I can put off my engagement, because it is the only evening for some time which will at once suit her and myself. She goes into the warm bath to-morrow, and for the rest of the week, you know, we are engaged."

Their attempts at persuasion continue, but Sir Walter's view of Mrs. Smith does not change, and neither does Anne's decision to visit her. While he is disappointed, he does not force her to change her plans, which brings us back to the idea of privilege.

HOW DOES PRIVILEGE IMPACT WHAT A CHARACTER SAYS AND HOW THEY ARE ABLE TO SAY IT?

According to the *Oxford English Dictionary*, the word privilege comes from the Latin word *privilēgium*, which meant a bill or law related to individuals or groups having special rights or claims.[4] Historically, these laws intentionally *gave* individuals or groups special rights not granted to others; at other times these laws *prevented* groups from having special rights that others did not share.

In *Persuasion*, we see that certain groups have privilege while others do not, and this constantly impacts both what they say and how they speak. While Anne lacks certain privileges in comparison to her older sister and her father, and she lacks certain privileges by virtue of being a woman, she still is in a position of privilege: She still possesses a number of rights, abilities, and advantages.

---

4. *Oxford English Dictionary,* "privilege (n.), Etymology."

Mrs. Smith, on the other hand, is a widow of no consequence. She has lost her fortune and can barely make ends meet. The person assigned to execute her husband's estate, Mr. Elliot, refuses to do so. She has no family or anyone else to give her advice. She has severe health problems that limit her mobility and her ability to act in her own interest. Most of her opportunities for conversation and her knowledge of the outside world come from Nurse Rooke, and Mrs. Smith cannot go to her; she must wait for Mrs. Rooke. The only other advantage or right she has—her only privilege—is her friendship with Anne Elliot, and she is afraid to lose that as well.

We see Mrs. Smith's awareness of her lack of privilege when Anne must leave a visit early so she can attend a concert with her family and her cousin Mr. Elliot:

> [Anne] had once partly promised Mrs. Smith to spend the evening with her; but in a short hurried call she excused herself and put it off, with the more decided promise of a longer visit on the morrow. Mrs. Smith gave a most good-humoured acquiescence.
>
> "By all means," said she; "only tell me all about it, when you do come. Who is your party?"
>
> Anne named them all. Mrs. Smith made no reply; but when she was leaving her said, and with an expression half serious, half arch, "Well, I heartily wish your concert may answer; and do not fail me to-morrow if you can come; for I begin to have a foreboding that I may not have many more visits from you."
>
> Anne was startled and confused; but after standing in a moment's suspense, was obliged, and not sorry to be obliged, to hurry away.

Mrs. Smith believes that Anne is falling in love with Mr. Elliot—the very same Mr. Elliot who has wronged her and is partially responsible for her dreadful situation. Because of her lack of privilege, she dares not speak against Mr. Elliot, though she cannot help but allude to the situation in a way that makes Anne uncomfortable.

Anne attends the concert and receives the attentions of both Mr. Elliot and Captain Wentworth (who is jealous of Mr. Elliot's relationship with Anne). Then, in the morning, Anne returns to visit Mrs. Smith.

Mrs. Smith alludes to what she thinks was a pleasurable night for Anne with Mr. Elliot, speaking of how her countenance reveals her emotions. Anne blushes, remembering Captain Wentworth. Then Mrs. Smith mentions Mr. Elliot, asking if he knows that she is in Bath. Anne is surprised that Mrs. Smith and Mr. Elliot know each other. She says,

> "Had I known it, I would have had the pleasure of talking to him about you."
>
> "To confess the truth," said Mrs. Smith, assuming her usual air of cheerfulness, "that is exactly the pleasure I want you to have. I want you to talk about me to Mr. Elliot. I want your interest with him. He can be of essential service to me; and if you would have the goodness, my dear Miss Elliot, to make it an object to yourself, of course it is done."

Mrs. Smith hopes that her friendship with Anne, and the privileges Anne holds in her relationship with Mr. Elliot, will lead to Mrs. Smith receiving the assistance she is owed. Anne disabuses Mrs. Smith of the notion that she is about to become engaged— she explains that she does not want to marry Mr. Elliot at any point. Then she says,

> "Though there is no truth in my having this claim on Mr. Elliot, I should be extremely happy to be of use to you in any way that I could. Shall I mention to him your being in Bath? Shall I take any message?"
>
> "No, I thank you: no, certainly not. In the warmth of the moment, and under a mistaken impression, I might, perhaps, have endeavoured to interest you in some circumstances; but not now. No, I thank you, I have nothing to trouble you with."

Anne presses Mrs. Smith for more details—she wants to know more of Mr. Elliot's acquaintance with Mrs. Smith, she wants to know what he was like as a younger man. Only when Mrs. Smith feels secure, only when she does not feel at a complete disadvantage due to her situation, does she tell the truth of her story:

> "Mr. Elliot is a man without heart or conscience; a designing, wary, cold-blooded being, who thinks only of himself.... Oh! he is black at heart, hollow and black!"

Then, for the rest of the chapter, she gives details—supported by correspondence—of Mr. Elliot's character and their history.

Mrs. Smith shares one of Mr. Elliot's letters with Anne Elliot. Illustration by C. E. Brock, 1909.

Anne is not aware of her privilege until it is raised by Mrs. Smith, in large part because in many situations, especially early in the story, she has not had a voice or true power.

In some stories, the characters with voice, power, and privilege stay consistent throughout the story. But more often, as characters and relationships change, this creates shifts in who speaks and whose dialogue has weight and influence.

Exercise 9.8: Personal Reflection

Reflect on situations in your own life in which you've had a voice and felt able to use it, and reflect on other situations in which you haven't had a voice or your voice has been ignored, belittled, or silenced. What about the context led to how much voice you had in the situation? What can you learn that can be applied to your own writing?

Exercise 9.9: Without Power/Privilege

Write a short scene featuring a character who normally has power and privilege in their interactions yet does not in this particular situation. Make sure to incorporate dialogue. Consider how (or if) your character will use their voice in this situation and how others will react to them.

Exercise 9.10: Revising for Power Dynamics

Choose a scene you have drafted in which there is dialogue and one character has more power than another. Revise the scene, considering how you can make the power disparity have a greater impact on the characters. Think about how this could increase the tension or raise the stakes for the story.

DISTINCTIVE CHARACTER VOICES AND WHAT DIALOGUE REVEALS ABOUT CHARACTER

As we've seen throughout this chapter, dialogue is one of the primary ways in which relationships are expressed. Dialogue is also an extension of character—a result of who they are, their backgrounds, their wants, and their needs.

In *Persuasion*, Mary speaks in a distinctive way, often focusing on herself. She doesn't have very much dialogue, but her words, sentence patterns, and topics are recognizable. Stripped of dialogue tags and actions, a reader could likely still recognize her lines as belonging to her. Some of her frequent phrases, like "Bless me!," are used by other characters. The phrase "Dear me!" is used exclusively by Mary. She often uses the word "I" and regularly uses exclamations, such as "There! you see!" When Louisa falls off the stairs in Lyme, it is Mary who screams, "She is dead! she is dead!"

Miss Bates, a character from *Emma*, has a distinctive way of speaking, unlike that of any other Austen character. When Emma asks if she has heard from Jane Fairfax, Miss Bates hunts for the most recent letter and says,

> "Oh! here it is. I was sure it could not be far off; but I had put my huswife upon it, you see, without being aware, and so it was quite hid, but I had it in my hand so very lately that I was almost sure it must be on the table. I was reading it to Mrs. Cole, and since she went away, I was reading it again to my mother, for it is such a pleasure to her—a letter from Jane—that she can never hear it often enough; so I knew it could not be far off, and here it is, only just under my huswife—and since you are so kind as to wish to hear what she says;—but, first of all, I really must, in justice to Jane, apologise for her writing so short a letter—only two pages you see—hardly two—and in general she fills the whole paper and crosses half. My mother often wonders that I can make it out so well. She often says, when the letter is first opened, 'Well, Hetty, now I think you will be put to it to make out all that checker-work'—don't you, ma'am?—And then I tell her, I am sure she would contrive to make it out herself, if she had nobody to do it for her—every word of it—I am sure she would pore over it till she had made out every word. And, indeed, though my mother's eyes are not so good as they were, she can see amazingly well still, thank God! with the help of spectacles. It is such a blessing! My mother's are really very good indeed. Jane often says, when she is here, 'I am sure, grandmama, you must have had very strong eyes to see as you do—and so much fine work as you have done too!—I only wish my eyes may last me as well.'"

We know so much about Miss Bates just by the way she speaks. Emma describes her as "so silly—so satisfied—so smiling—so prosing—so undistinguishing and unfastidious—and so apt to tell every thing relative to every body." In her critique, Emma is not completely fair to Miss Bates, and she certainly isn't charitable, but she does capture the manner and effect of Miss Bates's dialogue.

Miss Bates speaking to Emma.
Illustration by Hugh Thomson, 1896.

Sometimes, when I am revising, I copy all the dialogue from a single character into a document and analyze it, asking myself, What characterizes their speech? How does the way in which they speak differ based on the context and their relationships? Could the same dialogue be said by another character, and if so, how can I change it so it truly belongs to this character?[5]

Dialogue becomes one of the most powerful tools to express character and one of the most powerful tools used by characters as they seek to achieve their ends. As we'll see in the next chapter, Austen often combines dialogue with other techniques, like setting, to create powerful effects.

---

5. Bonus writing exercise: Do this for your own work! Or take another author besides Jane Austen and analyze the dialogue and what make each character's speech distinctive.

CHAPTER TEN

SETTING

"Emma had never been to Box Hill; she wished to see what every body found so well worth seeing."

—*Emma*

One of the most famous scenes from the book *Emma* occurs at Box Hill, a hill popular as a sightseeing attraction both in Austen's time and today. At seven miles away, Box Hill is the farthest Emma goes from home over the course of the novel, and this is a significant event for the characters, a trip planned well in advance.

In this scene, Emma's flaws are brought to the forefront: In an attempt to be clever, Emma is cruel to Miss Bates. Frank Churchill sets the stage by proposing a verbal game:

> "Ladies and gentlemen—I am ordered by Miss Woodhouse to say, that she ... requires something very entertaining from each of you.... [She] demands from each of you either one thing very clever, ... two things moderately clever[,] or three things very dull indeed, and she engages to laugh heartily at them all."

"Oh! very well," exclaimed Miss Bates, "then I need not be uneasy. 'Three things very dull indeed.' That will just do for me, you know. I shall be sure to say three dull things as soon as ever I open my mouth, shan't I? (looking round with the most good-humoured dependence on every body's assent)—Do not you all think I shall?"

Emma could not resist.

"Ah! ma'am, but there may be difficulty. Pardon me—but you will be limited as to number—only three at once."

Miss Bates, deceived by the mock ceremony of her manner, did not immediately catch her meaning; but, when it burst on her, it could not anger, though a slight brush shewed that it could pain her.

"Ah!—well—to be sure. Yes, I see what she means, (turning to Mr. Knightley,) and I will try to hold my tongue. I must make myself very disagreeable, or she would not have said such a thing to an old friend."

While the dialogue is brilliant and this passage employs many of the techniques discussed in Chapter 9, this scene's effectiveness also relies on the setting:

1. The setting has brought these characters together.
2. The setting has created a set of trying circumstances for the characters.

Much of the scene's tension is caused by the contrast between the high expectations for Box Hill and the lack of enjoyment and feeling. Earlier in the chapter, the narrator describes it as a "very fine day for Box Hill," and everyone commences the seven-mile journey in good spirits:

Seven miles were travelled in expectation of enjoyment, and every body had a burst of admiration on first arriving; but in the general amount of the day there was deficiency. There was a languor, a want of spirits, a want of union, which could not be got over.

Two hours are spent walking around the hill and seeing the sights, yet throughout the entire time, they are plagued by division and separation. In Emma's opinion, people behave in a manner that is "dull" and "insufferable."

Those gathered at Box Hill play a rather disastrous word game.
Illustration by Chris (Christiana) Hammond, 1898.

Perhaps it is this struggle with the setting that brings Emma to an internal lowness that invites her to act in an outwardly low manner to Miss Bates. After her rudeness, the group continues the conversation for a few more minutes before breaking apart:

Even Emma grew tired at last of flattery and merriment, and wished herself rather walking quietly about with any of the others, or sitting almost alone, and quite unattended to, in tranquil observation of the beautiful views beneath her.

Box Hill, Surrey, with Dorking in the distance.
Painting by George Lambert, 1733.

Yet she cannot enjoy the beauty in solitude: In the next sentence, the carriages arrive. In a private moment, Mr. Knightley reproaches Emma, asking, "How could you be so unfeeling to Miss Bates?" They argue until Emma can no longer hide behind her excuses.

After this confrontation, which once again occurs in stark contrast to the beautiful surroundings, Emma feels the full weight of guilt. The chapter ends with the following line:

> Emma felt the tears running down her cheeks almost all the way home, without being at any trouble to check them, extraordinary as they were.

In fiction, the setting of a scene should always be an intentional choice. A well-chosen setting greatly influences the plot and the characters, and the way in which the setting is described provides a lens into the viewpoint character's thoughts and emotions.

Exercise 10.1: Same Argument, Two Settings

Write a short scene that includes two characters arguing about a subject of your choice—but write it twice, with two different settings. Consider how the two settings will influence not only the description of the setting but also the dialogue and actions of the characters.

Exercise 10.2: Brainstorming Settings

Take a scene that you plan to write in a story. Brainstorm three possible settings that could help fulfill the purposes of the scene. For each setting, list the key attributes of the setting, the advantages of using the setting, and the disadvantages of using the setting.

	Setting 1	Setting 2	Setting 3
Key attributes of the setting			
Advantages of using this setting			
Disadvantages of using this setting			

INTRODUCING THE SETTING THROUGH DESCRIPTION

During graduate school, I wrote an essay about the Latin term *descriptio*, or what today we would call *description*. According to *Silva Rhetoricae*, description "bring[s] the subject clearly before the eyes."[1] Words, phrases, and sentences are used to enable the reader to visualize people, places, and objects.

Greek and Roman rhetoricians considered *descriptio* (description) to be the opposite of *narratio* (narrative). Narrative is about forward movement: Events occur, actions are taken, and the story progresses. Any time an author includes description, it halts the forward movement: The reader watches as something is painted before their eyes. And word paintings take time.

This is not to say that all description should be avoided, but it is essential to remember that description competes with narrative. Austen masterfully uses description, including enough detail to portray the setting without truly disrupting the forward movement of the story. She employs five key techniques to do so.

1. PROVIDE A FEW KEY DETAILS THAT GIVE A SENSE OF THE WHOLE.

One of Austen's primary techniques in establishing setting is to use a few pertinent details. Unlike a production designer in a film, who must physically choose, create, acquire, and place *every single item* that we see, a novelist is generally best served by focusing on a few points that give a taste, a feel, or a sense of the whole.

In *Pride and Prejudice*, Elizabeth's first trip away from home is to visit her friend Charlotte, after Charlotte's marriage to Mr. Collins. As discussed in Chapter 8, Charlotte's marriage created a rift between her and Elizabeth, but time has softened Elizabeth's emotions.

In the following passages, Elizabeth arrives at the parsonage. Note how the narrator gives only a smattering of concrete descriptive

---

1. "Description (The Progymnasmata)," in Burton, *Silva Rhetoricae*.

details, yet from this we understand not just the setting, but the people who are part of it. (Emphasis has been added to draw attention to the description.)

> Elizabeth was prepared to see [Mr. Collins] in his glory; and she could not help fancying that in displaying **the good proportion of the room, its aspect, and its furniture,** he addressed himself particularly to her, as if wishing to make her feel what she had lost in refusing him.... After sitting long enough to admire **every article of furniture in the room, from the sideboard to the fender,** ... Mr. Collins invited them to take a stroll in **the garden, which was large and well laid out,** and to the cultivation of which he attended himself.

The sideboard and the fender stand in for all of the furniture, the rest of which we are meant to conjecture. For the garden we learn only two details: It is large, and it is well laid out. More concrete particulars are not relevant. The next passage appears later in the scene and includes additional brief description.

> Charlotte took her sister and [Elizabeth] over the house, extremely well pleased, probably, to have the opportunity of showing it without her husband's help. It was **rather small, but well built and convenient;** and everything was fitted up and arranged with **a neatness and consistency, of which Elizabeth gave Charlotte all the credit.** When Mr. Collins could be forgotten, there was really **a great air of comfort throughout,** and by Charlotte's evident enjoyment of it, Elizabeth supposed he must be often forgotten.

In this passage, Austen swiftly paints a picture of the house, interweaving concrete details with value judgments (the neatness and consistency reflect positively on Charlotte). The narrator also includes a more general, abstract sense of the feel ("a great air of comfort throughout").

Some writers struggle to write description or don't include it in early drafts. If that's the case for you, I recommend considering what details you could add that would evoke a sense of place and give the reader an understanding of how the characters feel about the setting and interact with it.

2. USE THE DESCRIPTION OF THE SETTING TO REVEAL THINGS ABOUT THE CHARACTERS AND THEIR STATES OF MIND.

On its most basic level, describing a setting orients the reader—we feel grounded when we know where we are and what's going on. Yet Austen never just uses description solely for orientation; she always makes it serve double duty. After all, a good description reveals as much about characters and their states of mind as it reveals about the setting itself.

Mr. Collins's parsonage abuts Rosings, the grand estate belonging to Lady Catherine de Bourgh. She invites him and his guests to dinner, and they walk together to Rosings. In the following description of the setting, notice what is revealed about Elizabeth, Mr. Collins, Charlotte's sister Maria, and Charlotte's father, Sir William.

> Every park has its beauty and its prospects; and Elizabeth saw much to be pleased with, though she could not be in such raptures as Mr. Collins expected the scene to inspire, and was but slightly affected by his enumeration of the windows in front of the house, and his relation of what the glazing altogether had originally cost Sir Lewis De Bourgh.
>
> When they ascended the steps to the hall, Maria's alarm was every moment increasing, and even Sir William did not look perfectly calm. Elizabeth's courage did not fail her. She had heard nothing of Lady Catherine that spoke her awful from any extraordinary talents or miraculous virtue, and the mere stateliness of money and rank she thought she could witness without trepidation.

It is clear that while Elizabeth sees the beauty and wealth of Rosings and its park, she does not let it intimidate or overly influence her, unlike Mr. Collins (who expects raptures), Maria (who feels alarm), and Sir William (who feels overwhelmed even though his rank means he should theoretically be the most comfortable with this level of wealth).

3. COUPLE THE DESCRIPTION OF THE SETTING WITH ACTION WITHIN OR IN RELATION TO THE SETTING.

While description often slows or halts the plot, at times description and narrative can be paired together. Rather than completely describing a setting and then including character actions, Austen often provides details of the setting as an action occurs. As Elizabeth encounters Rosings, the characters move, both physically and emotionally, to meet the great Lady Catherine.

> From the entrance hall, of which Mr. Collins pointed out, with a rapturous air, the fine proportion and finished ornaments, they followed the servants through an antechamber, to the room where Lady Catherine, her daughter, and Mrs. Jenkinson were sitting.

Mr. Collins's rapturous descriptions draw aspects of the setting to our attention and provide characterization of both him and Lady Catherine. A few pages later, Austen introduces other objects as they are used.

> When the gentlemen had joined them, and tea was over, the card tables were placed. Lady Catherine, Sir William, and Mr. and Mrs. Collins sat down to quadrille; and as Miss De Bourgh chose to play at cassino, the two girls had the honour of assisting Mrs. Jenkinson to make up her party.

We don't need to know about the card tables or the games until they are used. Often, saving description until it is relevant helps create a faster pace and avoids disrupting the narrative.

4. USE MINIMAL DESCRIPTION OF THE SETTING (OR OMIT IT ENTIRELY) WHEN THE SETTING IS NOT NECESSARY TO THE STORY.

For some writers, it is tempting to describe, in full detail, fascinating places, buildings, and objects, even when doing so is not absolutely necessary to the story. Austen avoids this indulgence. (Some writing styles and genres like to linger on setting for setting's sake, and doing so can be effective, but moderation should still be applied.[2])

Later in *Pride and Prejudice*, Elizabeth travels with her aunt and uncle to Derbyshire. Despite this being a sightseeing trip for Elizabeth, full of interesting towns, landscapes, and historic sights, Austen does not provide any description of the setting, a fact that her narrator comments on:

---

2. I'm looking at you, epic fantasy.

> It is not the object of this work to give a description of Derbyshire, nor of any of the remarkable places through which their route thither lay—Oxford, Blenheim, Warwick, Kenilworth, Birmingham, etc., are sufficiently known. A small part of Derbyshire is all the present concern.

The small part of Derbyshire the narrator focuses on is Lambton, which Mrs. Gardiner has a personal connection to, and which happens to be near Mr. Darcy's home, Pemberley.

5. Give more detailed setting descriptions when the setting can strengthen a key component of the narrative.

While at many points in a story description is unnecessary or is useful only in small portions, at other times, detailed description of a setting can add depth, highlight a character's deep emotions or internal transformation, and prepare the reader for what is to come.

In contrast to the minimal description of the parsonage and Rosings, and the complete lack of description of the "remarkable places" during the journey to Lambton, Austen provides pages of description about the grounds and interior of Pemberley. Here are the first few paragraphs:

> Elizabeth, as they drove along, watched for the first appearance of Pemberley Woods with some perturbation; and when at length they turned in at the lodge, her spirits were in a high flutter.
>
> The park was very large, and contained great variety of ground. They entered it in one of its lowest points, and drove for some time through a beautiful wood stretching over a wide extent.
>
> Elizabeth's mind was too full for conversation, but she saw and admired every remarkable spot and point of view. They gradually ascended for half a mile, and then found themselves at the top of a considerable eminence, where the wood ceased, and the eye was instantly caught by Pemberley House, situated on the opposite side of the valley, into which the road with some abruptness wound. It was a large, handsome stone building, standing well on rising ground, and backed by a ridge of high woody hills; and in front a stream of some natural importance was swelled into greater, but without any artificial appearance. Its banks were neither formal nor falsely adorned. Elizabeth

was delighted. She had never seen a place for which nature had done more, or where natural beauty had been so little counteracted by an awkward taste. They were all of them warm in their admiration; and at that moment she felt that to be mistress of Pemberley might be something!

This level of description is more powerful for having been saved for this moment. Elizabeth's high engagement with the setting, as demonstrated by the copious description, shows her attentiveness not just to Pemberley but to its owner, Mr. Darcy. Elizabeth not only notices the setting, she interacts and engages with it, and as she does so, she realizes, for the first time, that maybe she should have accepted Mr. Darcy's proposal.

Exercise 10.3: Analyzing a Favorite Author

Choose one of your favorite authors and examine how they use description to establish setting in a scene. (Your chosen scene could be the first time the setting is used in the novel, or it could be a later instance of the setting when the setting is important for the story.) What techniques does the author use? Are they the same as those used by Austen or different? What is the effect of the description on the scene?

Exercise 10.4: States of Mind

Write a short scene involving three people walking through a graveyard. Include details about the setting, but do so in a way that reveals things about all three characters and their states of mind.

Exercise 10.5: Revising for Description

Find at least two of the following in a draft that you have written:

- A passage that needs more description
- A passage where you could reduce or eliminate description
- A passage where you could use different details that might give a better overall sense of the setting
- A passage where setting could be revealed through action

- A scene in which the description of the setting could reveal more about the characters and their states of mind
- A key scene in which more description of the setting could be added to increase the impact

If these changes match your writing style and your vision for the story, revise.

SETTING AND POINT OF VIEW

Setting is intrinsically connected to point of view. We see and experience the setting with the narrator. If the narrator and the characters are not aware of the setting, then it should not be described in detail. When the narrator and the characters engage deeply with the setting, this is manifest on the page.

One way we see this is through **familiar** and **unfamiliar settings**. **Familiar settings** are places where characters have spent much time and often feel comfortable. Generally, characters don't pay much attention to familiar settings, and so neither does the narrator, especially if the story is written in first person or close third (though this also holds true for Austen's approach to omniscient).

An important setting in *Pride and Prejudice* is the Meryton assembly, which is a public gathering and dance for the town of Meryton. It is in this setting, after all, that Jane and Elizabeth meet Mr. Bingley and Mr. Darcy. Throughout the scene, the omniscient viewpoint sticks close to the minds of the Bennet family, occasionally peeking into the viewpoint of the town as a whole. The narrator never shows us the thoughts and emotions of the newcomers, relying instead on the perspectives of those for whom the setting is familiar. Thus, the descriptions we receive of the physical location and how people interact are brief. We learn that "within five minutes after [Mr. Darcy's] entrance," everyone knows that he has ten thousand pounds a year. Clearly, there is gossip; people mingle together. We learn that "Mr. Bingley had soon made himself acquainted with all the principal people in the room," which implies that not everyone present is "principal," or of high class. Later in the chapter, we find that "Elizabeth Bennet had been obliged, by the scarcity of gentlemen, to sit down for two dances; and during part of that time, Mr. Darcy had been standing near enough for her to overhear a conversation between him and Mr. Bingley." We now know that the numbers of men and women are uneven and have a vague feel for the space.

Austen—and, by extension, her narrator—assumes that her reader understands the setting of a public ball. Because Elizabeth and the others pay little attention to the setting, the narrator pays little attention to it. Our focus is placed instead on the character interactions.

At times, characters pay more marked attention to a familiar setting. For instance, Lydia and Wickham visit Longbourn after their elopement, and suddenly Elizabeth's home feels less comfortable. Entryways, hallways, and rooms that have never received the narrator's attention are now mentioned:

> They came. The family were assembled in the breakfast-room to receive them. Smiles decked the face of Mrs. Bennet, as the carriage drove up to the door; her husband looked impenetrably grave; her daughters, alarmed, anxious, uneasy.
>
> Lydia's voice was heard in the vestibule; the door was thrown open, and she ran into the room.

Later in the scene we read,

> Elizabeth could bear it no longer. She got up and ran out of the room; and returned no more, till she heard them passing through the hall to the dining-parlour. She then joined them soon enough to see Lydia, with anxious parade, walk up to her mother's right hand, and hear her say to her eldest sister,—
>
> "Ah, Jane, I take your place now, and you must go lower, because I am a married woman."

For Elizabeth—and for her sister Jane—the order of their home has been turned upside down. Incorporating extra awareness of familiar settings is a powerful way to show changes in characters or relationships.

Unfamiliar settings are new to a character and possess unknown physical characteristics. These settings often contain new characters, new social expectations, and new modes of behavior. Unfamiliar settings can be described with either abundant or minimal description, but they often do require more description than familiar settings. When a character encounters a setting for the first time, they must learn to navigate it. They give the setting their attention, and so the narrator gives the setting attention as well.

In *Northanger Abbey*, Catherine's first experience of an unfamiliar setting, Bath, is marked by excitement—Bath is everything she hoped for!—and then struggle—she doesn't know anyone at the ball! During her weeks in Bath, sometimes the city meets or exceeds her expectations, and at other times it disappoints. The next time she travels to an unfamiliar setting is when she visits Northanger Abbey. Now, she has more experience with unfamiliar settings; she is more world-wise and better able to read people and places. Because of her growth, while she approaches the abbey she observes, evaluates, and reflects:

> As they drew near the end of their journey, her impatience for a sight of the abbey ... returned in full force, and every bend in the road was expected with solemn awe to afford a glimpse of its massy walls of grey stone, rising amidst a grove of ancient oaks, with the last beams of the sun playing in beautiful splendour on its high Gothic windows. But so low did the building stand, that she found herself passing through the great gates of the lodge into the very grounds of Northanger, without having discerned even an antique chimney.
>
> She knew not that she had any right to be surprised, but there was a something in this mode of approach which she certainly had not expected.

The character's perspective on a setting can be shown in scene or it can be summarized, but as long as the narration matches the main character's perspective, we stay close to their viewpoint. In order to present details about the setting that don't align with the main character's experience, the narrator must step further away from the character's perspective, which works best with a storytelling or omniscient voice, though it is possible to do in other viewpoints. We see this in *Mansfield Park* when the characters tour the Rushworth home. One of the locations they visit is the chapel. For much of the scene, we stick close to Fanny's perspective. She hears Mrs. Rushworth's description of the chapel:

> "This chapel was fitted up as you see it, in James the Second's time. Before that period, as I understand, the pews were only wainscot; and there is some reason to think that the linings and cushions of the pulpit and family seat were only purple cloth."

We see the chapel through Fanny's eyes, and the narrator follows her attention, thoughts, and emotions:

> Fanny's imagination had prepared her for something grander than a mere spacious, oblong room, fitted up for the purpose of devotion: with nothing more striking or more solemn than the profusion of mahogany, and the crimson velvet cushions appearing over the ledge of the family gallery above.

But then, as the scene concludes, the narrator steps back from Fanny's perspective in order to give the reader more details about the place (and provide ironic commentary):

> The chapel was soon afterwards left to the silence and stillness which reigned in it, with few interruptions, throughout the year.

The viewpoint that is taken on a setting—whose lens is used, how close we are to the setting, and how much it is described—can be likened to film. In film, a cinematographer can use many different shots: many angles and placements of the camera in order to capture characters and setting. Different types of shots change how close we are to characters or a place.[3]

What follows is a visual representation and then a description of a few common cinematography shots.[4]

---

3. For my minor in college, I studied film and media arts, which means I am highly qualified to severely oversimplify everything related to this amazing medium.

4. Some of the original images have been cropped in ways never intended by their original artists. Alas, the risk of dying and having your works enter the public domain!

Extreme long shot/establishing shot

Bath pump room and baths.
Engraving by unknown artist, 1864.

Long shot

John Thorpe and Catherine Moreland in a carriage.
Illustration by Hugh Thomson, 1897.

Medium long shot

Miss Bates helps someone less fortunate than herself.
Illustration by Chris (Christiana) Hammond, 1898.

Medium shot

Mrs. Jennings and Sir John speak to Elinor through her window.
Illustration by Chris (Christiana) Hammond, 1899.

Medium close-up shot

Mr. Darcy during his first proposal to Elizabeth.
Illustration by C. E. Brock, 1895.

Close-up shot

Mr. Wickham is "surprised, displeased, alarmed."
Illustration by C. E. Brock, 1895.

Extreme close-up shot
Rose pencil drawing.
Artist unknown, from the Wellcome Library collection

- **Extreme long shot/establishing shot:** a look at the big picture, often showing—or establishing—the entire area, such as a city, a farm, a house in a landscape, etc.
- **Long shot:** still a distant shot, but giving a better sense of people in their surroundings
- **Medium long shot:** showing some of the setting around the characters, but placing the viewer physically closer to the characters, their actions, and their perspective
- **Medium shot:** often including two or three characters, with little of the setting
- **Medium close-up shot:** focusing on a single character, often from the chest up
- **Close-up shot:** showing a single character's face, or alternately, a focused look at a single object in a setting
- **Extreme close-up shot:** emphasizing a single portion of a person, such as an eye, or a zoomed-in look at part of an object in the setting

In a film, different shots are used for different purposes. In college I took a number of film editing classes and learned how to combine different shots to create a cohesive story. Often, an extreme long shot is used at the beginning of a scene to orient the reader and provide context. A dialogue between characters might use a combination of medium long shots, to show them in their surroundings; medium shots, to focus us on the characters; and medium close-ups, to focus us on the emotion of a single character. When a character interacts with a setting, filmmakers often use long shots and medium shots, unless specific attention is meant to be drawn to details, in which case close-ups or extreme close-ups are used.

A character's awareness of a setting can move between a broad awareness of the larger setting, to no awareness, to a focused awareness on a single object or aspect of the setting. In *Mansfield Park*, after visiting the chapel, the characters head out of doors. At first, we are given a long shot:

> All were attracted at first by the plants or the pheasants.

Then the characters' attention is drawn by the broader scenery, and we receive a wider, establishing shot:

> The lawn, bounded on each side by a high wall, contained beyond the first planted area a bowling-green, and beyond the bowling-green a long terrace walk, backed by iron palisades, and commanding a view over them into the tops of the trees of the wilderness immediately adjoining.

We then switch to medium shots, with a focus on a group of characters who experience the setting together (Edmund, Miss Crawford, and Fanny).

Miss Crawford wants to enter the wood, but she worries that the door is locked, which creates a close-up on the door, which is followed by extreme long shots, long shots, and medium long shots.

> The door, however, proved not to be locked, and they were all agreed in turning joyfully through it, and leaving the unmitigated glare of day behind. A considerable flight of steps landed them in the wilderness, which was a planted wood of about two

acres, and though chiefly of larch and laurel, and beech cut down, and though laid out with too much regularity, was darkness and shade, and natural beauty, compared with the bowling-green and the terrace. They all felt the refreshment of it, and for some time could only walk and admire.

Then Mary Crawford begins to argue with Edmund about careers. The setting is forgotten as medium shots and medium close-ups focus us entirely on the characters, their dialogue, and their relationships. It is only when Fanny mentions her fatigue that an awareness is brought back to the setting, how far they have walked through it, and where they are now.

Thinking about setting in terms of point of view can help us, as writers, choose the focus that matches the story and perspective. At times we need more or less description of the setting, and at times we need an establishing shot or a focused look at a single aspect of the characters' surroundings. The way in which a character interacts with the setting is an outward manifestation of how they interact with their society and other characters, as well as their character traits, their emotions, and how they feel about themselves.

Exercise 10.6: Making the Familiar Unfamiliar

Choose a setting that you are very familiar with, or that matches your expertise and interests. For example, if you love creating arts and crafts, choose an arts and crafts store. If you know hundreds of types of plants, choose a nursery or an arboretum. Or choose your home, your neighborhood, your school, or your town.

Write a brief scene in the setting from the point of view of a character who does not share your expertise and is unfamiliar with the setting. Make sure to only incorporate details about the setting that reflect the character's perspective, experience, and knowledge.

Exercise 10.7: Create a Storyboard

Create a storyboard either for a scene you have written or for a classic fairy tale. Think about what visuals are needed to tell the story and include at least three types of shots (for example, establishing shots, medium shots, and close-ups).

What did you learn? How are settings used differently in film and in written texts? What are the benefits of both mediums?

Note: There are many free, printable storyboard templates available online. You don't have to be good at drawing to complete this exercise—you are welcome to use stick figures.

USING DISTINCTIVE SETTINGS FOR MAJOR PLOT TURNS

Many of the scenes in Austen's novels occur in what, for her characters, would be ordinary settings—drawing rooms and gardens and family parties. Yet sometimes Austen uses very distinctive settings for her scenes, especially for key turning points.

As discussed in Chapter 6, a key turning point is when both the story and the characters undergo a large shift. Something happens that irrevocably changes the future direction of the plot and has a profound impact on character and relationship arcs.

In *Persuasion*, a distinctive setting is the town of Lyme, which is visited by a number of characters, including the protagonist, Anne Elliot; her former love, Captain Wentworth; and his current romantic interest, Louisa Musgrove.

As we saw previously, this new, distinctive setting allows Anne to meet other important characters, including Captain Benwick and Mr. Elliot. This distinctive location also heightens the awareness of setting for both the characters and the reader. Distinctive settings are often unfamiliar to characters. Whether familiar or unfamiliar, these settings force characters to consciously navigate the space— its physical characteristics and the objects within it. Emotions are often higher, and actions have greater consequences. **Distinctive settings often draw out people's strengths and weaknesses, demonstrate who they really are, and provide opportunities**

for characters to transform in either a positive or a negative direction.

At Lyme, a number of the characters take a walk along the Cobb, which is a wall near the harbor. There is a heightened awareness of the setting, which is distinctive enough to evoke Byron's poetry as Anne walks with Captain Benwick:

> Lord Byron's 'dark blue seas' could not fail of being brought forward by their present view, and she gladly gave him all her attention as long as attention was possible.

Steps on the Cobb. These may have been the steps Austen describes. Photograph by Chris Talbot, 2009.

While walking along the Cobb, one of the most dramatic events in *Persuasion* occurs, in large part because the setting draws out Louisa's firmness of character and the way she resists persuasion. Previously, Captain Wentworth has seen this characteristic as a virtue—he's attracted to the way Louisa does not yield to influence. But now, the negative side of this character trait is made clear.

There was too much wind to make the high part of the new Cobb pleasant for the ladies, and they agreed to get down the steps to the lower, and all were contented to pass quietly and carefully down the steep flight, excepting Louisa; she must be jumped down them by Captain Wentworth. In all their walks, he had had to jump her from the stiles; the sensation was delightful to her. The hardness of the pavement for her feet, made him less willing upon the present occasion; he did it, however; she was safely down, and instantly, to show her enjoyment, ran up the steps to be jumped down again. He advised her against it, thought the jar too great; but no, he reasoned and talked in vain, she smiled and said, 'I am determined I will:' he put out his hands; she was too precipitate by half a second, she fell on the pavement on the Lower Cobb, and was taken up lifeless!

Almost all of the characters panic and freeze. Except for Anne. We see her kindness, her rational and perceptive nature, and her ability to act in the face of challenge. First, she instructs Captain Benwick to go and help Captain Wentworth as he attempts to care for Louisa, and then she continues to give guidance:

"Go to him, go to him," cried Anne, "for heaven's sake go to him…. Rub her hands, rub her temples; here are salts; take them, take them."

Captain Benwick obeyed, and Charles at the same moment, disengaging himself from his wife, they were both with him; and Louisa was raised up and supported more firmly between them, and everything was done that Anne had prompted, but in vain; while Captain Wentworth, staggering against the wall for his support, exclaimed in the bitterest agony—

"Oh God! her father and mother!"

"A surgeon!" said Anne.

He caught the word; it seemed to rouse him at once, and saying only—"True, true, a surgeon this instant," was darting away, when Anne eagerly suggested—

"Captain Benwick, would not it be better for Captain Benwick? He knows where a surgeon is to be found."

Every one capable of thinking felt the advantage of the idea.

Emotional clues are layered to create an intensity of feeling. After Louisa's fall, actions and descriptions are expressed in a short and concise manner. Short snippets of dialogue are stacked on each other with almost no interruption. Most of the paragraphs are only a single sentence, and two of the paragraphs do not end with a full stop before we leap to the next paragraph. And in this scene, everything changes for Anne, Captain Wentworth, and Louisa.

Everyone is shocked at Louisa's injury.
Illustration by C. E. Brock, 1909.

A distinctive setting, like the Cobb at Lyme, seems a fitting backdrop for such a pivotal event that impacts the entire trajectory of the novel.

MAKING AN ORDINARY SETTING DISTINCTIVE

Sometimes distinctive settings are unfamiliar, and sometimes they are picturesque, grand, or unusual. Yet at other times, Austen takes an ordinary setting and makes it distinctive in some way in order to use it as a location for a key turning point.

An example of this is the setting for Mr. Elton's proposal to Emma, in the book *Emma*. This proposal is important not only because she rejects him, but also because it marks the beginning of Emma's awareness that her judgment can be faulty (she thought Mr. Elton was in love with her friend Harriet, but he is actually in love with her).

The proposal occurs in a carriage, an ordinary setting for an Austen character. Yet this setting is made distinctive. First, Emma, John Knightley, and Mr. Elton travel via carriage to the Weston home for a dinner party—a Christmas dinner party, which can be held but once a year. As they sit in the carriage, Mr. Elton speaks of its supreme comfort and security:

> "What an excellent device," said he, "the use of a sheepskin for carriages. How very comfortable they make it;—impossible to feel cold with such precautions. The contrivances of modern days indeed have rendered a gentleman's carriage perfectly complete. One is so fenced and guarded from the weather, that not a breath of air can find its way unpermitted. Weather becomes absolutely of no consequence. It is a very cold afternoon—but in this carriage we know nothing of the matter."

Attention is drawn to the minute details of this carriage. We are forced to pay attention to its features, and to Mr. Elton's symbolic interpretation of them. In a carriage such as this, he feels safe from outside troubles.

Then, while at the dinner, catastrophe strikes: It begins to snow. This causes a panic for several characters. John Knightley tells Mr. Woodhouse,

"This will prove a spirited beginning of your winter engagements, sir. Something new for your coachman and horses to be making their way through a storm of snow."

But John Knightley says they should not worry, for "if one [of the carriages] is blown over in the bleak part of the common field," then they can climb into the other carriage. John Knightley has introduced a counterpoint to Mr. Elton's vision of the security of a carriage—for John, riding a carriage in the winter means danger.

At this point, two separate theories have been put forward on carriages, making this ordinary setting the object of practical and philosophical attention.

A carriage in "Christmas weather."
Illustration by Chris (Christiana) Hammond, 1898.

The characters decide to end the dinner early and travel home before more snow falls. Due to a seating mix-up, Emma and Mr. Elton end up together in a carriage. Alone. At the time, it was uncommon for an unmarried man and woman to share a carriage—yet another distinctive element. Mr. Elton seizes the opportunity and proposes:

> Scarcely had they passed the sweep-gate and joined the other carriage, than she found her subject cut up—her hand seized—her attention demanded, and Mr. Elton actually making violent love to her: availing himself of the precious opportunity, declaring sentiments which must be already well known, hoping—fearing—adoring—ready to die if she refused him; but flattering himself that his ardent attachment and unequalled love and unexampled passion could not fail of having some effect, and in short, very much resolved on being seriously accepted as soon as possible. It really was so. Without scruple—without apology—without much apparent diffidence, Mr. Elton, the lover of Harriet, was professing himself *her* lover. She tried to stop him; but vainly; he would go on, and say it all.

The carriage traps the characters: They are stuck in a moving box together, which adds to the pressure that Emma feels. After she denies his offer of marriage, Mr. Elton's view on carriages has been overturned (a parallel to John's fear that the carriages themselves would overturn). The danger, in the end, was not the snow, but relationships.

> He was too angry to say another word; her manner too decided to invite supplication; and in this state of swelling resentment, and mutually deep mortification, they had to continue together a few minutes longer.

A distinctive setting—whether it is grand and full of danger, like the Cobb, or a familiar place made distinctive, like Emma's carriage—is a powerful location for a major plot turn. It can create plot opportunities, heighten awareness and tension, and draw out characters' strengths and weaknesses.

Exercise 10.8: Making the Ordinary Distinctive

Consider the following list of ordinary places. Add a description to each that could make it distinctive and open up storytelling possibilities.

- A grocery store
- A school bus
- A bar
- A movie theater
- A kitchen
- A place of worship

Exercise 10.9: Setting Analysis

Choose a book or a film, and find a scene with a distinctive setting in terms of landscape, architecture, cultural/historical significance, etc.

How does the use of this setting impact the plot and the character? What strengths and weaknesses of the characters are manifest because of the setting? How does this setting fit within the context of the other settings used in the story?

Exercise 10.10: Revising for Distinctiveness

Choose a key turning point from a story you have written. Revise the scene by doing one of the following:

1. Editing the setting to make it more distinctive. This should impact your description as well as how your characters interact with and within the setting.
2. Rewriting the scene with a new, more distinctive setting. In choosing the setting, consider how it will function for both the plot and the character's internal journey.

ESTABLISH THE CHARACTER OF A SETTING

As we write settings, we should remember that, like people, places can also have character. The **character of a setting** is its essence, its overall nature that is experienced by those who interact with it (both the characters within a story and the readers of the story).

In *Emma,* a shop called Ford's is the setting for several key scenes: It is here that Harriet runs into her first love, Robert Martin, and Emma and Frank Churchill also share a key interaction in this location. The essence of the shop is described by the narrator:

> Ford's was the principal woollen-draper, linen-draper, and haberdasher's shop united; the shop first in size and fashion in the place.

We see this essence again when Frank Churchill proposes that he and Emma visit it:

> "If it be not inconvenient to you, pray let us go in, that I may prove myself to belong to the place, to be a true citizen of Highbury. I must buy something at Ford's. It will be taking out my freedom.—I dare say they sell gloves."

To belong to Highbury, one must shop at Ford's. The shop's essence—its role and relationship to the town—is clear.

In Austen's uncompleted novel *Sanditon,* Mr. Parker attempts to transform Sanditon into the ultimate destination town. We read that "Sanditon was a second Wife & 4 children to him—hardly less Dear—& certainly more engrossing."[5] Mr. Parker wants to mold Sanditon, but it has a life of its own. Not only does Sanditon have character—it *is* a character in the story.

---

5. Austen, *Fragment of a Novel.*

From Jane Austen, we learn that while setting is the backdrop for a story, it should be more. Place is integral to the characters' experiences—it creates substance and materiality for both external and internal journeys, and it often creates opportunities for discovery, for both the characters and the reader.

CHAPTER ELEVEN

DISCOVERY

"Marianne Dashwood was born to an extraordinary fate. She was born to discover the falsehood of her own opinions, and to counteract, by her conduct, her most favourite maxims."

—*Sense and Sensibility*

It truly is "an extraordinary fate" for a character to discover that what they thought and believed was false, and that they must change. And Austen excels at this sort of discovery. In Chapter 6, we discussed information gaps and discoveries as a way to structure the rising action and to create a sense of progression and forward movement. These discoveries can be about anything—wants, needs, plot, characters, relationships, the world, truth—but as we near the end of our characters' internal journeys, it's especially important to include discoveries of self.

Not all characters change in positive ways by the end of a novel. In the final chapter of *Persuasion*, Sir Walter and his daughter Elizabeth discover that Mrs. Clay has befriended them in an attempt to get gain.

> It cannot be doubted that Sir Walter and Elizabeth were shocked and mortified by the loss of their companion, and the discovery of their deception in her. They had their great cousins, to be sure, to resort to for comfort; but they must long feel that to flatter and follow others, without being flattered and followed in turn, is but a state of half enjoyment.

Their discovery helps them learn something about themselves: They enjoy flattery. They experience a loss in happiness but do not change their ways or how they relate to others.

In *Mansfield Park*, when Henry Crawford plans to propose to Fanny Price, his sister expresses her happiness for him but then wonders what the effect will be on Fanny's two cousins, the women with whom Henry originally flirted. Henry states,

> "I care neither what they say nor what they feel. They will now see what sort of woman it is that can attach me, that can attach a man of sense. I wish the discovery may do them any good. And they will now see their cousin treated as she ought to be, and I wish they may be heartily ashamed of their own abominable neglect and unkindness."

Henry Crawford recognizes that Fanny has been mistreated by her family, and he wants them to recognize their own negative behavior. Yet in his statement "I wish the discovery may do them any good," he seems almost doubtful that it will. Can they experience change? And can he? While Fanny has changed him, ultimately, he reverts back to his original behavior. Yet at the end of the story, some of Fanny's family members do change how they interact with her—for example, Sir Thomas recognizes that she "was indeed the daughter that he wanted" and treats her with "perfect approbation and increased regard." However, Lady Bertram still sees Fanny through a selfish lens, as someone who can serve her. She is only willing to allow Fanny to pursue happiness because Fanny's sister, Susan, becomes "her substitute"—Susan assumes the role of the uncomplaining, helpful companion who does whatever Lady Bertram asks.

Henry Crawford helps Fanny with her shawl.
Illustration by Hugh Thomson, 1897.

In *Pride and Prejudice*, Elizabeth's biggest moment of self-discovery actually comes near the midpoint of the book, after she rejects Mr. Darcy's first proposal and then reads his letter of explanation:

> She grew absolutely ashamed of herself. Of neither Darcy nor Wickham could she think, without feeling that she had been blind, partial, prejudiced, absurd.
>
> "How despicably have I acted!" she cried. "I, who have prided myself on my discernment! I, who have valued myself on my abilities! who have often disdained the generous candour of my sister, and gratified my vanity in useless or blameless distrust. How humiliating is this discovery! Yet, how just a humiliation! Had I been in love, I could not have been more wretchedly blind.

But vanity, not love, has been my folly. Pleased with the preference of one, and offended by the neglect of the other, on the very beginning of our acquaintance, I have courted preposession and ignorance, and driven reason away where either were concerned. Till this moment, I never knew myself."

While in *Sense and Sensibility*, Marianne's self-discovery and change comes at the end of the novel, by placing it earlier in *Pride and Prejudice*, the question of the story shifts from:

Will Elizabeth make discoveries about herself?

to:

How will Elizabeth act now that she knows herself better?
Or, in other words, how will her discoveries change her?

As readers, we have almost half of the novel to explore what Elizabeth's life will look like now that she knows herself, while in *Sense and Sensibility*, we receive a short summary on the impact of Marianne's discovery on her life. Both are good storytelling techniques that engage the reader.

Throughout this chapter, we'll go into greater depth on the writing techniques Austen uses for discoveries, particularly in regard to foreshadowing and unveiling major discoveries. However, it's important to remember that the point of discovery is not just to create a compelling plot or external journey—even though discovery is a good way to do that. The most meaningful discoveries help our characters along their internal journeys of growth and change.

Exercise 11.1: Moments of Self-Discovery

Think about a moment of self-discovery in your own life, when you learned something positive or negative about yourself. Write a reflection about this moment. What led to the self-discovery? Describe the moment itself. Reflect on if and how this moment changed your future actions, behaviors, or thoughts about yourself.

FORESHADOWING

Mr. Darcy's first proposal may be a surprise to Elizabeth, but it is foreshadowed by his glances, his attention, and his conversation, as well as by Charlotte's observation that "he must be in love with you, or he would never have called on us in this familiar way." The truth about Mr. Wickham is also hinted at by his words, his behaviors, and his interactions, but through the first half of the novel, Elizabeth ignores these hints because those individuals who oppose Wickham (Mr. Darcy and Caroline Bingley) are people she dislikes.

Austen is an expert at foreshadowing. In each of her books, she leaves a trail of breadcrumbs for readers that lead up to her larger discoveries and reveals, like Mr. Darcy's feelings and Mr. Wickham's true nature. On a second read, it's much easier to see these breadcrumbs, yet even if a reader does not notice these clues, foreshadowing creates a better reading experience. And foreshadowing is essential to set up key plot turns, the midpoint, and any grand reveals or transformations in the climax and falling action.

It's easy, as a writer, to throw in something shocking or unexpected or create a huge twist. Yet readers feel cheated—the experience feels lacking and hollow—if these elements are not set up or foreshadowed properly. Discoveries, especially major discoveries, must be earned. This applies to any type of discovery, whether it's a reveal, a plot twist, a deeper understanding of someone's character, or the moment when a character obtains a missing piece of information. In the podcast *Writing Excuses*, the hosts talk about the importance of making these sorts of discoveries "surprising yet inevitable."[1] They must follow from what is established in the narrative.

In *Persuasion*, one such discovery is the knowledge of Mr. Elliot's true character. This knowledge is not personally learned by Anne; it is imparted by her old school friend, Mrs. Smith. Because Anne learns about Mr. Elliot through another's experiences, it could easily feel like a contrived moment, inserted to move the story forward to a particular conclusion. It could feel unearned or unbelievable.

---

1. *Writing Excuses*, season 17, episode 3, "Chekov's Surprising Yet Inevitable Inverted Gun."

When Mrs. Smith mentions Mr. Elliot near the end of the book, Anne is surprised, exclaiming,

> "Are you acquainted with Mr. Elliot?"
>
> "I have been a good deal acquainted with him," replied Mrs. Smith, gravely, "but it seems worn out now. It is a great while since we met."
>
> "I was not at all aware of this. You never mentioned it before."

Anne finds this strange and surprising, just as the reader does. And if it had truly not been set up, this revelation would be unsatisfying. But the very chapter before, Mr. Elliot's connection to Mrs. Smith was set up by Mr. Elliot himself. At a concert, Anne had asked Mr. Elliot to stop flattering her:

> "Perhaps," said Mr. Elliot, speaking low, "I have had a longer acquaintance with your character than you are aware of."
>
> "Indeed! How so? You can have been acquainted with it only since I came to Bath, excepting as you might hear me previously spoken of in my own family."
>
> "I knew you by report long before you came to Bath. I had heard you described by those who knew you intimately. I have been acquainted with you by character many years. Your person, your disposition, accomplishments, manner; they were all present to me."

Anne questions Mr. Elliot, trying to learn who had spoken of her, but Mr. Elliot refuses to tell her. Then, in the next chapter, as Mrs. Smith reveals her deceased husband's intimate friendship with Mr. Elliot, Anne wonders if the person who had described her might, in fact, have been her teenage friend, Mrs. Smith. Suddenly, everything makes sense.

Other foreshadowing is also used:

- Mr. Elliot's prior rift with Sir Walter Elliot
- Gaps in Mr. Elliot's story, particularly around the years of his marriage
- Anne's sense that Mr. Elliot, despite his charms, might have outside motives

These other foreshadowing moments help support Mrs. Smith's revelations, yet they would not be enough without the foreshadowing that Mrs. Smith and Mr. Elliot are intimately acquainted. Mrs. Smith could have stated or hinted at her relationship with Mr. Elliot beforehand, yet this would lessen the surprise. And Mrs. Smith's revelations are made more powerful by having *Mr. Elliot himself* allude to the relationship.

The word foreshadowing literally means "before-shadow": a shadow coming before. According to the *Online Etymology Dictionary*, "the notion seems to be a shadow thrown before an advancing material object as an image of something suggestive of what is to come."[2] Readers expect a narrative world to feel fair and logical. Even surprises cannot come from nowhere—they must have roots. Further, if something big is going to happen—or has happened and we don't know about it—it's going to impact other things in the story. This impact is like a stone thrown in a pond—ripples spread in all directions, not just forward, but also backward in the plot. Thus, foreshadowing.

Exercise 11.2: Setting Up a Side Character

Side characters are useful, and sometimes they provide our main characters with knowledge, skills, connections, or possessions that are needed later on in the story. Yet if a side character owns a boat that the main character can borrow, knows the head zookeeper, or can run ten miles without stopping, we should not find this out in a crucial scene when this skill is needed. This must be foreshadowed in a natural way that sets it up without being over-the-top or out of place.

Choose a random piece of knowledge, a skill, a connection, or a possession that a side character could possess (like being able to run ten miles without stopping).

Write down how this side character could use this skill, knowledge, etc., in a story to help a main character.

2. *Etymonline: Online Etymology Dictionary*, "foreshadow."

Now write a few sentences or paragraphs that could appear earlier in the story to provide foreshadowing. (For instance, if the side character can run ten miles, maybe they are always wearing their race t-shirts. Or maybe they arrive late to a meeting because of a running event, or maybe the main character likes to tease them about their running obsession. Or perhaps it could be something more subtle—the main character or reader may not realize that the side character is always checking their phone to look at their running stats.)

FORESHADOWING TECHNIQUES

Sense and Sensibility is a novel filled with discoveries. As a recap on a few of the main storylines, after her father's death, Elinor Dashwood falls in love with Edward Ferrars, though it is clear that Edward's family opposes their interest in each other. When Elinor moves to a cottage in Devonshire, she does not hear from Edward, and when he finally visits, he seems cold and reserved, though he comes to enjoy himself. Not long after he leaves, Lucy Steele arrives. She extracts a promise from Elinor to keep a secret, and then Lucy reveals that *she* has been secretly engaged to Edward for years.

This is a grand, wrenching discovery for Elinor.

A few other key discoveries in *Sense and Sensibility*:

- We learn of Colonel Brandon's past and why he never married his love.
- We learn that Willoughby has seduced a teenager named Eliza Williams; once she becomes pregnant, he abandons her. Eliza Williams, it turns out, is Colonel Brandon's ward (a girl who he financially supports; some of the characters believe Eliza is the Colonel's illegitimate child, but she is actually the illegitimate daughter of the woman he loved).
- We learn that despite appearances, Marianne and Willoughby never became engaged.

Colonel Brandon tells Eliza's story to Elinor.
Illustration by C. E. Brock, 1908.

That's a *lot* of big discoveries—and some of them act as key turn-ing points in the novel. And yet each of these discoveries is set up ahead of time by Austen, using five key foreshadowing techniques.

1. INTRODUCE EVENTS THAT WILL HAVE RENEWED IMPORTANCE LATER ON.

In *Sense and Sensibility*, Colonel Brandon organizes a large party to visit Whitehall. It's a location of interest that he has a connec-tion to—they could not visit it without him. Elinor and Marianne are invited, as are Sir John, Willoughby, and others.

A few minutes before they are to leave for Whitehall, Colonel Brandon receives a letter and announces that they must cancel the visit, for he must travel to London immediately. He refuses to tell them the nature of his business or delay his trip.

"We must go [to Whitehall]," said Sir John.—"It shall not be put off when we are so near it. You cannot go to town till tomorrow, Brandon, that is all."

"I wish it could be so easily settled. But it is not in my power to delay my journey for one day!" ...

"You would not be six hours later," said Willoughby, "if you were to defer your journey till our return."

"I cannot afford to lose *one* hour."

This event becomes important later on. Much later in the book, we discover *why* Colonel Brandon has gone to London: His ward, Eliza Williams, is pregnant. Colonel Brandon reveals this fact after Willoughby breaks Marianne's heart and becomes engaged to another.

Clearly, this event has renewed importance thematically, for the plot, and for the characters later in the story. Yet it's also an important event in the moment. Directly after Colonel Brandon's statement that he cannot delay a single hour, we read,

Elinor then heard Willoughby say in a low voice to Marianne, "There are some people who cannot bear a party of pleasure. Brandon is one of them. He was afraid of catching cold I dare say, and invented this trick for getting out of it. I would lay fifty guineas the letter was of his own writing."

"I have no doubt of it," replied Marianne.

Marianne mentally compares Colonel Brandon and Willoughby. She sees Brandon's abandoning of their party in a negative light and sees Willoughby only in a positive light. (Ironically, Willoughby is the actual person at fault—it was his behavior that caused this crisis.)

When Colonel Brandon leaves, everyone decides to drive carriages together for pleasure. Marianne joins Willoughby in his carriage, and they soon separate from the rest of the party—for many hours. This could be scandalous in and of itself, but then he gives her a private tour of the home he is to inherit, which is certainly outside the bounds of respectability. This action leads many to assume that Marianne and Willoughby are secretly engaged.

Colonel Brandon's decision to leave London could've happened off the page instead of in a scene and then been mentioned by another character. ("Where is Colonel Brandon?" "He had to leave for London on urgent business.") Yet this sort of foreshadowing tends to be most effective if shown on the page, in scene, with character dialogue and reactions. We experience it with the characters, which gives it more weight when it becomes important later.

2. GIVE HINTS OF AN INDIVIDUAL'S TRUE CHARACTER.

As discussed at the beginning of the chapter, many of the most interesting discoveries that a character can make in a novel are those that reveal the true nature or character of both others and themselves. In his *Poetics*, Aristotle writes that "character is that which reveals moral purpose, showing what kinds of things a man chooses or avoids."[3] Someone's true character is shown through their choices and tendencies. Everyone has a mixture of positive and negative attributes, but certain attributes are more defining and essential than others. Someone's essence or true character may be hidden from the reader or other characters at first, but it should still be foreshadowed.

For example, in *Sense and Sensibility*, Willoughby is truly dashing. He's charming and romantic, and his attention thrills Marianne.

Willoughby carries Marianne down the hill after her injury.
Illustration by C. E. Brock, 1908.

3. Aristotle, *Poetics*.

At one point, Mrs. Dashwood makes comments on the improvements she would like to make to the cottage, in order to make it more comfortable for their family. Willoughby passionately insists that their home is "faultless. ... I consider it as the only form of building in which happiness is attainable." He flatters them and their home and earnestly tries to convince Mrs. Dashwood to not make any changes:

> "Tell me that not only your house will remain the same, but that I shall ever find you and yours as unchanged as your dwelling; and that you will always consider me with the kindness which has made everything belonging to you so dear to me."

The entire conversation makes Marianne feel all aflutter. It's incredibly romantic—he speaks with the passion of her favorite poets and writers. Yet it hints at his character, foreshadowing his flaws and later choices. He wants to fix the Dashwoods and their home, as if they are a museum exhibit for him to enjoy, rather than living, changing human beings. He wants them for his own purposes and pleasures, without considering their needs and desires. This foreshadows his true character and how he later abandons Marianne.

3. HIDE OR "SANDWICH" KEY DETAILS BETWEEN OTHER INFORMATION THAT SEEMS MORE SALIENT.

As soon as Elinor leaves Norland, she nurses her heartache for both her old home and for Edward Ferrars. One day as Elinor and Marianne take a walk, they see a man approaching on horseback. Marianne longingly hopes it is Willoughby, but it is not Willoughby: Edward has come to visit. Elinor is lost for words, but Marianne is excited for her sister. Yet all does not seem well:

> He was confused, seemed scarcely sensible of pleasure in seeing them, looked neither rapturous nor gay, said little but what was forced from him by questions, and distinguished Elinor by no mark of affection.

A little later we read,

After a short silence which succeeded the first surprise and inqui-
ries of meeting, Marianne asked Edward if he came directly from
London. No, he had been in Devonshire a fortnight.

"A fortnight!" she repeated, surprised at his being so long in
the same country with Elinor without seeing her before.

He looked rather distressed as he added, that he had been
staying with some friends near Plymouth.

"Have you been lately in Sussex?" said Elinor.

"I was at Norland about a month ago."

"And how does dear, dear Norland look?" cried Marianne.

"Dear, dear Norland," said Elinor, "probably looks much as it
always does at this time of the year. The woods and walks thickly
covered with dead leaves."

"Oh," cried Marianne, "with what transporting sensation have
I formerly seen them fall! How have I delighted, as I walked, to
see them driven in showers about me by the wind! What feelings
have they, the season, the air altogether inspired! Now there is
no one to regard them. They are seen only as a nuisance, swept
hastily off, and driven as much as possible from the sight."

"It is not every one," said Elinor, "who has your passion for
dead leaves."

This passage has a number of salient moments that draw our
attention. First we have Edward's reticence and the fact that he
has been in the area for an entire fortnight—two weeks!—without calling on them. And then we learn that he has visited their
old home, Norland, which invites Elinor and Marianne to reflect
on what they have lost. We can see how both sisters deal with loss
and emotions differently by how they each talk about dead leaves.

Yet sandwiched in between the two weeks of Edward not calling
on them and the leaves of Norland is a seemingly small, unimportant detail: "He had been staying with some friends near Plymouth."

This small detail becomes essential later on, for it turns out that
Lucy Steele is one of the friends from Plymouth.

This sort of foreshadowing technique is often used in mystery
novels—a small detail is given that does not seem relevant at the
time but later holds the key to unlocking greater truths. Yet this
technique is just as useful in other genres.

"Hiding" key details between things that seem more important provides the information without drawing our attention to

it—we are meant to notice the information without focusing on it. In order for a big reveal or a plot twist to surprise readers, we can't expect it. If too much attention was drawn to a detail such as the friends at Plymouth, we would know this foretold a large revelation. Yet if the detail was not included, the twist would feel inorganic to the story. Thus, details such as this can be sandwiched or hidden in other things to strike the right balance of foreshadowing without lessening later surprises.

4. INTENTIONALLY DRAW ATTENTION TO KEY MOMENTS.

While at times it is important to distract or draw attention away from important details, at other times Austen draws attention to key moments.

After Edward, Elinor, and Marianne discuss dead leaves, they drink tea with Mrs. Dashwood. As Edward picks up a teacup, Marianne notices that he wears a ring on one of his fingers, and in that ring is a plait of hair.[4] Marianne immediately comments on the ring, asking if it is his sister's hair:

> "I never saw you wear a ring before, Edward," she cried. "Is that Fanny's hair? I remember her promising to give you some. But I should have thought her hair had been darker."

Edward's embarrassment is obvious.

> He coloured very deeply, and giving a momentary glance at Elinor, replied, "Yes; it is my sister's hair. The setting always casts a different shade on it, you know."
>
> Elinor had met his eye, and looked conscious likewise. That the hair was her own, she instantaneously felt as well satisfied as Marianne; the only difference in their conclusions was, that what Marianne considered as a free gift from her sister, Elinor was conscious must have been procured by some theft or contrivance unknown to herself.

---

4. During the eighteenth and nineteenth centuries, it was relatively common to include hair of both living and deceased loved ones in rings. If you have the opportunity to see these sorts of rings in person, I highly recommend it. A great online collection of mourning rings with hair is found at Hayden Peters's website, *Art of Mourning*.

The ring could have been mentioned in a simple way or sandwiched between other details, but in this case a flag is placed above it, drawing the reader's attention. At this moment, we *know* the ring is important.

Not all foreshadowing can be subtle and invisible, or the setup will feel inadequate. We should draw attention to foreshadowing that creates emotional resonance for the characters. Here, we see Elinor's complicated emotions for Edward: She is flattered but conflicted because he has taken her hair without her knowledge and permission. Focusing on the ring and exploring Elinor's reaction sets up her new emotions the next time the ring is mentioned. Which leads us to the final foreshadowing technique.

5. USE A LACK OF KNOWLEDGE TO ALLOW FOR NEW MEANINGS AND UNDERSTANDING LATER.

While some foreshadowing is very direct and clear—Colonel Brandon has left for an unknown reason, and later we learn the reason—at other times it is effective for the characters to misinterpret or misunderstand these moments of foreshadowing. When characters and the reader misinterpret information or events, it sets up later discoveries while creating greater surprise (and other strong emotions) because we expected a different result.

As previously mentioned, Lucy Steele arrives shortly after Edward leaves. Based on the comments of other characters, Lucy suspects that Elinor is in love with Edward, and so she makes a rather manipulative play to keep him for herself (as we saw in Chapter 5, she acts with self-interested motives). She makes Elinor promise not to tell anyone of her secret and then confides in her, telling her of her engagement to Edward. It takes some convincing and a fair amount of explanation on Lucy's part to achieve her ends. Yet Elinor remembers that Edward has stayed in Plymouth with friends, she remembers that he was "sadly out of spirits," and she begins to believe Lucy. And then Elinor learns the truth of the ring:

> "Writing to each other," said Lucy, returning the letter into her pocket, "is the only comfort we have in such long separations. Yes, *I* have one other comfort in his picture, but poor Edward has not even *that*. If he had but my picture, he says he should be easy. I gave him a lock of my hair set in a ring when he was at Longstaple last, and that was some comfort to him, he said,

but not equal to a picture. Perhaps you might notice the ring when you saw him?"

"I did," said Elinor, with a composure of voice, under which was concealed an emotion and distress beyond any thing she had ever felt before. She was mortified, shocked, confounded.

Lucy and Elinor, moments before Lucy reveals her secret.
Illustration by Hugh Thomson, 1896.

This scene is full of emotion for both Elinor and the reader. It is a grand, unexpected twist, yet it has been properly foreshadowed, which makes it more powerful, for it feels more true and more terrible as a result. It hearkens back to "hidden" or "sandwiched" details, yet it also draws upon an emotionally powerful object that received focus and misinterpretation in a previous scene. An incredibly effective use of foreshadowing built to this moment.

We can use Austen's same foreshadowing techniques to set up key turning points, revelations, and discoveries in a way that creates emotion and resonance for readers.

Exercise 11.3: Setting Up the Surprise

Write a scene in which the main character and the reader are surprised by a discovery at the end of the scene. This could be any sort of discovery, such as a surprise birthday party, a surprise proposal, or a surprise award at work. Use several different foreshadowing techniques in the scene to hint at the upcoming revelation without giving it away.

Exercise 11.4: Revising for Foreshadowing

Take a draft you have written of a short story, novella, or novel. Choose a key moment of discovery, a twist, or a reveal, and then look back to see what moments of foreshadowing you used to set it up. Could the foreshadowing be refined or enhanced? Are there any points where it would be more effective to use a different foreshadowing technique? Do you need to add more foreshadowing or use less?

LARGE DISCOVERIES

It is not enough to foreshadow a major discovery: We must write the discoveries themselves, and write them well. In this section, we'll consider how Austen conveys her discoveries with enough weight.

Near the end of *Emma*, there are four large discoveries and plot twists:

Discovery 1: Frank Churchill and Jane Fairfax have been secretly engaged for months.

Discovery 2: Harriet is not in love with Frank Churchill; she is in love with Mr. Knightley. Further, Mr. Knightley might be in love with her.

Discovery 3: Emma is in love with Mr. Knightley. For Emma, this is a startling self-discovery.

Discovery 4: Mr. Knightley loves Emma.

When I read *Emma* for the first time, I was completely surprised by the first discovery, of Frank Churchill and Jane Fairfax's secret engagement. I did not expect it in the slightest, and yet it was beautiful and horrifying and compelling and perfect and made me reconsider everything I'd read. I was also surprised that Harriet Smith had fallen in love with Mr. Knightley. Like Emma, I interpreted events falsely, because of how closely the point of view sticks to Emma's perspective. I suspected the third and the fourth discoveries (Emma and Mr. Knightley's feelings for each other), but that did not lessen the impact of these scenes, because they surprised Emma and meant so much to her.

For each of the four discoveries, Austen includes five core components—essential elements that help convey the discoveries and their effects. These elements are not always included in the same order. Sometimes these components occur more than once within the same scene, or they may occur across several scenes. Not every component *must* be included with a discovery, but they each serve a purpose and can enhance the story.

1. Advance Signaling

Austen likes to build up anticipation right before a large discovery or twist.

Before Emma finds out about Frank and Jane's engagement, Mr. Weston requests that Emma visit his house for news that only his wife can tell her, which sets off all sorts of warning signals in Emma's head (she even worries that something has happened to her sister, her brother-in-law, or her nieces and nephews).

Before Harriet's revelation that she loves Mr. Knightley, Emma notices that Harriet's speech and mannerisms are not what she would expect:

> It was, indeed, so odd; Harriet's behaviour was so extremely odd, that Emma did not know how to understand it. Her character appeared absolutely changed.

The advance signaling can be obvious or subtle, but it indicates to the character and to the reader that something is about to happen.

2. The Discovery Itself

The discovery itself is always expressed in a compelling way, whether it's through events, dialogue, or action.

When Emma discovers her own true nature by recognizing her feelings toward Mr. Knightley, we read,

> Why was it so much worse that Harriet should be in love with Mr. Knightley, than with Frank Churchill? Why was the evil so dreadfully increased by Harriet's having some hope of a return? It darted through her, with the speed of an arrow, that Mr. Knightley must marry no one but herself!

When Mr. Knightley expresses his love for Emma, he uses some of the most romantic lines in the novel:

> "I cannot make speeches, Emma.... If I loved you less, I might be able to talk about it more.... At present, I ask only to hear, once to hear your voice."

The discoveries themselves are generally best shown in scene, and are often lingered on by the narrator.

Mr. Knightley proposes to Emma.
Illustration by Hugh Thomson, 1896.

3. PHYSICAL REACTION

Whether positive or negative, a large discovery or twist marks a huge shift of knowledge and understanding for a character. In cases like this, there is always some sort of physical reaction. Sometimes this is an internal reaction for the character (for example, a headache, stomach pain, etc.), and sometimes this is expressed in outward physical behavior (for example, speech, body language, movement, etc.).

After Mrs. Weston gives news of Frank and Jane's engagement, we read,

> Emma even jumped with surprize;—and, horror-struck, exclaimed, "Jane Fairfax!—Good God! You are not serious? You do not mean it?"

Later, as Emma learns of Harriet's true affections, we read,

> [Emma] could not speak another word.—Her voice was lost; and she sat down, waiting in great terror till Harriet should answer.

A physical reaction makes the discovery feel more tangible for the character and reader—like an item of great physical weight.

4. EMOTIONAL REACTION

Important discoveries almost always create an emotional reaction within the character, and as such, emotional clues must be provided to the reader. Oftentimes, the emotional reaction is partially manifested in a physical way—after all, as we discussed in Chapter 7, this is a tool for expressing emotion. However, for a major discovery, a physical reaction is not enough: Austen *always* couples the physical reaction with additional emotional clues, often including the clues that help demonstrate the interior thoughts and experiences of viewpoint characters.

Here's a passage that occurs after Emma's discoveries of Harriet's affections and of her own affections, which relies heavily on punctuation, syntax, character thoughts, and free indirect speech.

> The rest of the day, the following night, were hardly enough for her thoughts.—She was bewildered amidst the confusion of all that had rushed on her within the last few hours. Every moment had brought a fresh surprise; and every surprise must be matter of humiliation to her.—How to understand it all! How to understand the deceptions she had been thus practising on herself, and living under!—The blunders, the blindness of her own head and heart!—she sat still, she walked about, she tried her own room, she tried the shrubbery—in every place,

every posture, she perceived that she had acted most weakly; that she had been imposed on by others in a most mortifying degree; that she had been imposing on herself in a degree yet more mortifying; that she was wretched, and should probably find this day but the beginning of wretchedness.

A significant discovery or plot twist will impact the character's soul, forcing it out of repose. Stacking other sorts of emotional clues on top of a physical reaction helps convey this to the reader.

5. REFLECTION

Finally, large discoveries and twists demand further reflection from the character (which allows for reflection by the reader). During this reflection, the character considers the discovery in context, often thinking about what it means for the future. This reflection can occur in the same scene as the discovery or in a later scene.

A few minutes after she learns of the secret engagement, Emma reflects verbally on the discovery as she speaks to the Westons:

> "Well," said Emma, "I suppose we shall gradually grow reconciled to the idea, and I wish them very happy. But I shall always think it a very abominable sort of proceeding. What has it been but a system of hypocrisy and deceit,—espionage, and treachery?— To come among us with professions of openness and simplicity; and such a league in secret to judge us all!—Here have we been, the whole winter and spring, completely duped, fancying our-selves all on equal footing of truth and honour, with two people in the midst of us who may have been carrying round, com-paring and sitting in judgment on sentiments and words that were never meant for both to hear.—They must take the con-sequence, if they have heard each other spoken of in a way not perfectly agreeable!"

After the final revelation—of Mr. Knightley's love for Emma— we once again see Emma's reflections:

> What totally different feelings did Emma take back into the house from what she had brought out!—she had then been only daring to hope for a little respite of suffering;—she was

now in an exquisite flutter of happiness, and such happiness moreover as she believed must still be greater when the flutter should have passed away.

Often, it is the moments of reflection that allow us to see how the discovery has changed the character.

*Mr. Knightley and Emma, when he
realizes that Emma returns his affections.
Illustration by Chris (Christiana) Hammond, 1898.*

Exercise 11.5: The Five Elements of Discovery

Choose a character from a story you're already writing, or a brand-new character you create particularly for this exercise. Now consider a large discovery, twist, or change for this character, something that would have a significant impact on them. (For instance, you could choose a high school student, and she could discover that her best friend has betrayed her in some way.)

First, write this discovery in a single paragraph, but still include all five elements: advance signaling, the discovery itself, physical reaction, emotional reaction, and reflection. Next, write a longer scene with this discovery, again using all five elements. What are the advantages and disadvantages of each version? Can you effectively convey the discovery both ways?

Exercise 11.6: Book and Film Discoveries

Choose one of your favorite books that has been adapted to film. Read and watch the same discovery in both the book and the film. How are the discoveries treated or expressed differently in the two mediums?

DISCOVERIES AS PAYOFF

Earlier in the book, we talked about the reader-writer contract. At the beginning of a story, promises are made to the reader, promises relating to plot and character, stance and genre. Discoveries help fulfill these promises. While these promises can and should be fulfilled throughout the entire story, big discoveries and shifts are often included at the end of the novel to act as payoff for the reader. Whether it is a twist, a revelation, a momentous action or sacrifice, or a relationship transformed, this is a prize given to the reader as the character's internal and external journeys conclude. In the next chapter, you'll see how discoveries are incorporated at the structural level, in the climax, falling action, and denouement of a story.

When Elizabeth comes to understand the truth about Mr. Darcy and Mr. Wickham, she states, "Till this moment, I never knew myself." Understanding the story of others has helped her discover herself. Storytelling does the same for readers. We become connected to the characters and their aspirations. When they make discoveries about themselves, we often make discoveries about ourselves as well. We are entertained as we read, yes, but we're also rewarded with a better understanding of ourselves and the world.

Chapter Twelve

ENDINGS

"Oh! write, write. Finish it at once. Let there be an end of this suspense. Fix, commit, condemn yourself."

—Mansfield Park

In *Mansfield Park*, Fanny Price spends the entire novel quietly pining for her cousin, Edmund Bertram, even as he pursues Mary Crawford. After refusing to marry Henry Crawford, her uncle sends her back to her parents' house in Portsmouth. While there, she receives a letter from Edmund, who waxes on and on about how much he loves Mary: "I cannot give her up, Fanny. She is the only woman in the world whom I could ever think of as a wife." He spends a large portion of his 1500-word letter debating on how he should approach Mary—should he express his fervent hopes in person or write a letter? He concludes that a letter is *probably* the best option. Fanny is less than pleased:

> "There is no good in this delay," said she. "Why is not it settled? He is blinded, and nothing will open his eyes; nothing can, after having had truths before him so long in vain. He will marry her, and be poor and miserable. God grant that her influence do not

make him cease to be respectable! ... Oh! write, write. Finish it at once. Let there be an end of this suspense. Fix, commit, condemn yourself."

Fanny wants this story to end—she needs this love story to end, even if it ends unhappily for herself and everyone else involved.

Ultimately, as Fanny requests, there must be an end to the suspense. So much of our stories are spent in the beginning and in the rising action, as we build and complicate and layer. But for a story to satisfy, we must bring it to a conclusion. In his *Poetics*, Aristotle writes that "the end is the chief thing of all."[1] While he is speaking specifically of tragedy, this applies to all genres. He also explains that many writers struggle to create a fitting, satisfying ending: "Many poets tie the knot well, but unravel it ill. Both arts, however, should always be mastered."[2]

If the rising action is the complication, the tying of the knot, then the climax must be the knot at its messiest. Both the external and internal journeys come together in crisis. What follows is the unraveling, the picking apart of the knot through the falling action, as each piece of the knot is undone through final conflicts, actions, resolutions, and the denouement. In this chapter, we'll consider the climax, the falling action, and the denouement, and how we can apply Austen's techniques for endings to our own writing.

We'll start by analyzing the ending of *Persuasion*. For Austen's six published novels, no surviving manuscripts exist, except for the original ending of *Persuasion*, which she threw out and rewrote. This manuscript is owned by the British Library, but transcriptions of it can be found in numerous locations, both online and in print books.[3]

The ending of *Persuasion* is set up by two previously discussed chapters. Using Austen's original chapter numbering, these are Chapters 8 and 9 of Volume 2. In Chapter 8 we see the concert in Bath, in which Anne's time is torn between Captain Wentworth and Mr. Elliot. Chapter 9 features the scene in which Mrs. Smith reveals all she knows about Mr. Elliot and his past. In the final

---

1. Aristotle, *Poetics*.

2. Aristotle, *Poetics*.

3. My favorite transcription is found in an appendix of Linda Bree's Broadview Literary Texts edition of *Persuasion*. Many online transcriptions are incomplete; as of this book's printing, the Internet Archive has an accurate one titled "The 'Cancelled Chapters' of *Persuasion*."

paragraphs of this chapter, Anne considers what might have happened should Mrs. Smith not have imparted this knowledge to her:

> Anne could just acknowledge within herself such a possibility of having been induced to marry [Mr. Elliot], as made her shudder at the idea of the misery which must have followed. It was just possible that she might have been persuaded by Lady Russell!

This chapter concludes with Anne's decision that she must tell Lady Russell the truth about Mr. Elliot. From this point, the original ending and the revised, published ending of *Persuasion* diverge.

THE ORIGINAL ENDING (VOLUME 2 CHAPTERS 10 AND 11)

For the original ending, we'll use Austen's original spelling (and spelling errors), punctuation, abbreviations, and paragraphing, which she did not polish for publication.[4]

In Austen's original draft, Anne leaves Mrs. Smith,

> her mind deeply busy in revolving what she had heard, feeling, thinking, recalling & forseeing everything; shocked at Mr Elliot.... The Embarrassment which must be felt from this hour in his presence!—How to behave to him?—how to get rid of him?—what to do by any of the Party at home?—where to be blind?—where to be active?—It was altogether a confusion of Images & Doubts—a perplexity, an agitation which she could not see the end of.

As she walks, she is startled by Admiral Croft. (She has walked, rather unknowingly, near his door.) He believes she has come to speak to his wife; she insists she hasn't; he insists that she must. He takes her upstairs and places her in a room with Captain Wentworth, stating that Mrs. Croft will be down momentarily. As the admiral leaves, he has a hurried conversation with Captain Wentworth, in which he mentions the lease of Kellynch Hall and suggests it as a topic of discussion for Anne and Captain Wentworth.

Embarrassed by the assigned conversational task, a resigned Captain Wentworth proceeds to ask Anne to help with the admiral's

---

4. All quotes from the original ending of *Persuasion* are from Austen, *Persuasion*, ed. Linda Bree, 259-69.

lease of Kellynch Hall. The admiral worries that the lease will be ended due to Anne's engagement to Mr. Elliot. He has also tasked Captain Wentworth with complimenting Anne on said engagement. Anne immediately corrects Captain Wentworth, for she is not engaged:

> "No Sir—said Anne.... You are misin—the Adm¹ is misinformed.—I do justice to the kindness of his Intentions, but he is quite mistaken. There is no Truth in any such report."

This creates quite the reaction from Captain Wentworth. Anne turns to look at him.

> He was looking at her with all the Power & Keenness, which she beleived no other eyes than his, possessed. "*No* Truth in any such report!—he repeated—No Truth in any *part* of it?"— "None."—He had been standing by a chair—enjoying the releif of leaning on it—or of playing with it;—he now sat down— drew it a little nearer to her—& looked, with an expression which had something more than penetration to it, something softer;—Her Countenance did not discourage.—It was a silent, but a very powerful Dialogue;—on his side, Supplication, on her's acceptance.—Still, a little nearer—and a hand taken and pressed—and "Anne, my own dear Anne!"—bursting forth in the fullness of exquisite feeling—and all Suspense & Indecision were over.—They were re-united. They were restored to all that had been lost. They were carried back to the past, with only an increase of attachment & confidence.

Rain forces Anne to stay for dinner, and they explain everything to each other—Louisa and the concert, their emotions and their plans.

Chapter 10 concludes, and then the story moves to Chapter 11, the denouement, which is quite similar to the final, published version. We learn what Anne's family thinks of the attachment; Lady Russell admits she was wrong about Captain Wentworth; Mrs. Clay becomes Mr. Elliot's mistress; and Captain Wentworth helps Mrs. Smith regain her fortune.

As I read the original ending, it feels a little too convenient, a little too easy for Anne and Captain Wentworth to resolve their difficulties. In fact, the entire situation—a chance meeting of the admiral on the street and being forced into a conversation with Wentworth—reads as **deus ex machina**. *Deus ex machina* literally means a god from the machine;[5] it's when a storyteller solves story problems by inserting situations, events, and powers that do not arise naturally from the story and the characters. *Deus ex machina* is most often used during the falling action, and it is in the final chapters that readers find it the least satisfying. Aristotle writes that "within the action there must be nothing irrational" and that "the unravelling of the plot ... must arise out of the plot itself, it must not be brought about by the 'Deus ex Machina.'"[6]

Part of what makes the original ending feel forced is the minor role that Wentworth and Anne play. It is Admiral Croft who tells Captain Wentworth what to say. Wentworth says it, and Anne reacts to his statement. Both Anne and Captain Wentworth respond to what others have done or said; they take only a passive role in their grand emotional reunion. Their decision to become a couple again occurs in a single sentence: "It was a silent, but a very powerful Dialogue;—on his side, Supplication, on her's acceptance." While it's a stylistically well-written sentence, it's also a rather rapid conclusion to almost a decade of separation. Little work is required for Anne and Captain Wentworth to overcome the obstacles in their way.

In this original version, after Mrs. Smith's revelation, we *only* see Anne in scene with Captain Wentworth and the Crofts. While we learn a bit about Anne's family members in the denouement, we never actually see Anne with her family, and we don't see her interact with Mr. Elliot. In a sense, the grand revelation of Mr. Elliot's character has almost no bearing on Anne's actions and behavior.

THE REVISED ENDING (VOLUME 2 CHAPTERS 10, 11, AND 12)

Scholar Linda Bree explains that Austen was "evidently dissatisfied" with the original ending of *Persuasion*, which she had finished on July 18, 1816. And so Austen started the ending anew, replacing the two original closing chapters with the three chapters that

---

5. In a Greek tragedy, sometimes a machine (such as a mechane, an ancient crane) was used to carry a god onto the stage to solve the characters' problems.

6. Aristotle, *Poetics*.
Writers have known that *deus ex machina* is a bad storytelling technique for a long time. We can and should do better.

we read today. It didn't take her long to write a new version—she finished it just nineteen days later, on August 6, 1816.[7]

In the revised, published version of *Persuasion*, events unfold quite differently. Chapter 10 begins as Anne returns to her home and reflects on what she has learned from Mrs. Smith.

> She was concerned for the disappointment and pain Lady Russell would be feeling; for the mortifications which must be hanging over her father and sister, and had all the distress of foreseeing many evils, without knowing how to avert any one of them.... She must talk to Lady Russell, tell her, consult with her.

Anne has always turned to Lady Russell, even after Lady Russell persuaded her to break off her engagement with Captain Wentworth. In her moment of crisis, Anne almost does what she has always done: seek advice and persuasion. If she had done so, it would have been a failure of Anne's internal journey—part of her growth, part of her character arc, is learning to assert herself and trust her own judgment. **In the climax of the novel, when everything is brought to a crisis, the main character should face their own shortcomings that have led to failure at previous points in the story. A satisfying character arc is created when in the conclusion, the character overcomes, circumvents, or deals with their flaws.**

Despite her plan to speak to Lady Russell, Anne does not prioritize it. Instead, Anne makes her own way. That night, Mr. Elliot joins her family for dinner. Unlike in the original version, in which Anne is never forced to apply her new knowledge in her interactions with Mr. Elliot, now she must do so.

> To Anne herself it was most distressing to see Mr. Elliot enter the room; and quite painful to have him approach and speak to her. She had been used before to feel that he could not be always quite sincere, but now she saw insincerity in everything.... It was her intention to be as decidedly cool to him as might be compatible with their relationship; and to retrace, as quietly as she could, the few steps of unnecessary intimacy she had been gradually led along.

---

7. Bree, in *Persuasion*, 224, 259.

He attempts to engage her; he tries to return to the fact that a friend had spoken highly of her long ago; he fails, again and again. Anne knows her father and her sister are still deceived by Mr. Elliot, but she sees no immediate harm in it—in fact, Mr. Elliot's presence seems to prevent Mrs. Clay from fully pursuing Anne's father—so she does not inform them of the truth.

The next morning, Anne is surprised by the arrival of her married sister, Mary Musgrove, and Mary's husband Charles. Anne holds an animated conversation with Charles, in which she learns the fate of Charles's two sisters, Louisa and Henrietta, who had both originally pursued Captain Wentworth but are now happily marrying other men. **The knot is unraveling—we have not yet reached the denouement, but subplots are resolving.**

Instead of visiting Lady Russell, Anne calls upon the rest of the Musgrove party so she may see the elder Mrs. Musgrove and Henrietta. Within thirty minutes, Charles has brought his friends Captain Harville and Captain Wentworth to the hotel. Anne knew this was likely—she knew visiting the Musgroves meant she would interact with Captain Wentworth again.

> Their last meeting had been most important in opening his feelings; she had derived from it a delightful conviction; but she feared from his looks, that the same unfortunate persuasion, which had hastened him away from the Concert Room, still governed. He did not seem to want to be near enough for conversation.

Captain Wentworth does not want to talk to Anne. Being Anne, she does not force it. While she has changed over the course of the novel, her general approach has not, and it does not need to—it is part of her character.

Mary mentions that she sees Mr. Elliot outside the window, talking to Mrs. Clay, and Anne says that it could not possibly be Mr. Elliot, for "he was to leave Bath at nine this morning, and does not come back till to-morrow."

While in the original ending, the revelations of true feelings occurred without hiccups, in this version, Anne has already done something that risks making Captain Wentworth think she wants to marry Mr. Elliot, since why else would she so thoroughly know Mr. Elliot's plans?

> As she spoke, she felt that Captain Wentworth was looking at her, the consciousness of which vexed and embarrassed her, and made her regret that she had said so much, simple as it was.

Even though Captain Wentworth shows no interest in speaking to her, Anne's awareness of him impacts her every word and movement. Mary brings up a scheduling conflict: The Musgroves have been invited by Anne's father to dine with them, the Dalrymples, and Mr. Elliot, but Charles has bought tickets to a play at the same time. While Anne is ostensibly speaking to Mary and Charles, she seizes the opportunity to make her thoughts and feelings known to Captain Wentworth, who is listening:

> "If it depended only on my inclination, ma'am, the party at home (excepting on Mary's account) would not be the smallest impediment. I have no pleasure in the sort of meeting, and should be too happy to change it for a play, and with you."

Finally Captain Wentworth talks to her, and she speaks, for a moment, with feeling, but their conversation is cut short: another interruption. Her sister and father—the disdainful Elizabeth and Sir Walter—arrive, and they specifically invite Captain Wentworth to join their dinner party.

When the chapter ends, a question looms in Anne's mind: Will Captain Wentworth attend the dinner party? Have her words done enough to hint at her feelings?

This chapter is masterful. Anne is an active character. More trials, misunderstandings, and interruptions plague her and Captain Wentworth. They are not allowed an easy, simple resolution. They must fight for it.

Then: Chapter 11. Anne has planned to spend the majority of her day with her sister Mary Musgrove. Others are already present, including Captain Harville and Captain Wentworth, but within two minutes, Captain Wentworth decides to write a letter. Clearly, he does not want to speak to Anne.

After a few minutes, Anne converses with Captain Harville. Even though she is "nearer to Captain Wentworth's table," she feels that he is "not very near." In other words, she does not believe that Wentworth will listen to the conversation.

Captain Harville expresses his shock that Benwick has so quickly moved past his deceased love and fallen in love with Louisa. Anne makes an argument on the constancy of woman's love:

> "We certainly do not forget you as soon as you forget us. It is, perhaps, our fate rather than our merit."

They discuss the subject of men and women's love and constancy, going back and forth. Harville expresses his belief that men's love is stronger: "As our bodies are the strongest, so are our feelings."

Anne replies with an eloquent, emotional speech in which she states that "your feelings may be the strongest, ... but the same spirit of analogy will authorise me to assert that ours are the most tender." Her voice falters as she hints at her own feelings. And then we read,

> A slight noise called their attention to Captain Wentworth's hitherto perfectly quiet division of the room. It was nothing more than that his pen had fallen down; but Anne was startled at finding him nearer than she supposed, and half inclined to suspect that the pen had only fallen because he had been occupied by them, striving to catch sounds, which yet she did not think he could have caught.

Harville asks Wentworth if he has finished his letter, and Wentworth replies that he needs five minutes more. Then Harville and Anne continue their animated conversation, with Anne now aware that Wentworth may be listening.

As their multi-paragraph debate concludes, Anne declares, "All the privilege I claim for my own sex ... is that of loving longest, when existence or when hope is gone."

At this point, much of the party leaves, but before Captain Wentworth does so, he passes Anne a letter. Anne has been active—despite obstacles, she has attempted to express her feelings. And now it is Captain Wentworth's turn to be active, to overcome his own fears and weaknesses. His letter is beautiful and compelling.

> "I can listen no longer in silence. I must speak to you by such means as are within my reach. You pierce my soul. I am half agony, half hope. Tell me not that I am too late, that such precious feelings are gone for ever."

Captain Wentworth gives his letter to Anne, "with eyes of glowing entreaty fixed on her." Illustration by Hugh Thomson, 1897.

After reading Wentworth's letter, Anne is overjoyed, but she struggles to be in the company of the Musgroves. She claims illness, and Charles begins to walk her home. And then, as they're walking, she sees Captain Wentworth. Charles leaves them together.

Unlike in the original ending, when the meeting of Admiral Croft and Anne felt contrived, this meeting between Anne and Captain Wentworth does not: We know that he has recently left, we know that they are both feeling strongly, and we know that he is *still* uncertain of how she will respond to his affections, despite all that she has said to Captain Harville. *Now* Anne and Wentworth exchange words of love and affection, rebuilding that which they once had, but now they are "more tender, more tried, more fixed in a knowledge of each other's character, truth, and attachment; more equal to act, more justified in acting." Like in the original ending, they explain the concert and Louisa and everything else that has come before, but they do so with more of their dialogue in scene, rather than summarized.

Yet this is not the end. We have one final scene in the chapter, the grand party that brings all the characters together: the Elliots, the Musgroves, the Crofts, the Dalrymples, Lady Russell, and Captain Wentworth. Anne does not yet tell everyone of her joy, but she finds the whole evening delightful and too short. She manages to converse with Captain Wentworth several times, and the chapter ends with Captain Wentworth stating, "I must learn to brook being happier than I deserve."

Now we move to the denouement, which, as previously mentioned, is very similar to the original.

As I read both endings, it's clear that Austen made the correct choice in scrapping her original and writing it anew. The new ending:

- Includes much more in scene
- Places more obstacles and misunderstandings in Anne and Captain Wentworth's path
- Takes several scenes rather than a single scene to resolve
- Requires Anne and Captain Wentworth to be active rather than passive
- Forces both Anne and Captain Wentworth to confront their weaknesses
- Does not rely on *deus ex machina*
- Addresses many of the other subplots, even resolving a few of them
- Places Anne in situations where she interacts, in revealing ways, with a range of characters from the book

As Aristotle writes, it's difficult to create a good ending. For me, it's comforting to see a portion of Austen's revision process and to know that she, like most of us, made substantive changes as she revised. The contrast between her original ending—which is adequate—and her published ending—which is spectacular—reveals much of what makes an ending effective.

Exercise 12.1: Best and Worst Endings

Think of two stories, one that had a satisfying and rewarding ending, and another that had an ending that didn't quite work for you. Now go back and analyze the endings—what specifically made the endings effective and ineffective for you as a reader?

Exercise 12.2: Active and Passive Participation in the Ending

Come up with a very basic story that can be expressed in one or two sentences: A character has a small problem, the character tries to overcome the problem, the character faces an obstacle or two, and then the character overcomes the problem. Here's a sample basic story: Annemarie discovers she has no sugar so she goes to the grocery store, but she finds no sugar on the shelves. Somehow, she gets sugar anyway and comes home happy. (If you'd like, you can even use this story.) Once you have a basic story, write the ending of the story two times. (These new endings can be short, just a few sentences each.) In the first version, the main character should take a passive role in the resolution; in the second version, the main character should take an active role. What do you like and dislike about both versions?

THE CLIMAX

The climax is the focal point of the story and the most important turning point. If we consider plot as a pyramid or a mountain, the climax is the peak. Gustav Freytag writes that "the climax … is the most important place of the structure; the action rises to this; the action falls away from this."[8] Some books and theorists define the term *climax* differently than Freytag does, using it to refer to the final scene of intensity and resolution; however, throughout this chapter I will use Freytag's definition, using *climax* to refer to the structural moment when the story shifts from building problems to resolving them. From this lens, the climax is when the internal

---

8. Freytag, *Technique of the Drama*, 105.

and external journeys are brought to a crisis, and any scenes of final intensity and resolution occur later on, during the falling action.

Prior to the climax in *Northanger Abbey*, things seem to be going well for Catherine Morland. She's staying with her friend Eleanor Tilney at Northanger Abbey, and while her love interest, Henry Tilney, cannot always be present, his father, General Tilney, is attentive and seems to approve of their burgeoning relationship. The general takes Catherine to see Woodston, where Henry's new parsonage is located, and we learn Catherine's opinion of it:

> In her heart she preferred it to any place she had ever been.

When she enters the parsonage, she even learns that Henry has "a large Newfoundland puppy and two or three terriers."[9] What could possibly go wrong?

Everything, it turns out. Later, in a scene reminiscent of Catherine's favorite Gothic novels, she hears a noise at her door.

> At that moment Catherine thought she heard [Eleanor] step in the gallery, and listened for its continuance; but all was silent. Scarcely, however, had she convicted her fancy of error, when the noise of something moving close to her door made her start; it seemed as if someone was touching the very doorway—and in another moment a slight motion of the lock proved that some hand must be on it. She trembled a little at the idea of any one's approaching so cautiously; but resolving not to be again overcome by trivial appearances of alarm, or misled by a raised imagination, she stepped quietly forward, and opened the door. Eleanor, and only Eleanor, stood there. Catherine's spirits, however, were tranquilized but for an instant, for Eleanor's cheeks were pale, and her manner greatly agitated.

Eleanor delivers the bad news: Her father is kicking Catherine out of Northanger Abbey. No reason is provided. There is no time to send word to Catherine's family. No servant will accompany her home. Catherine does not even have money to make her way back and must borrow it from Eleanor. Eleanor is upset at the

---

9. I love the humorous lack of specificity on the number of cute dogs.

entire situation and exclaims, "Good God! What will your father and mother say!" The scene is traumatic for both friends.

The climax of a story often includes what Freytag calls "the tragic force." In this scene, the tragic force is clear: General Tilney and his extreme action. This is *the* pivotal turning point in the story. It feels truly irreversible, and it seems that Catherine has lost all chance of fulfilling her want: How can she possibly marry Henry Tilney now? This scene leads to another, which screenwriter Blake Snyder would call the "dark night of the soul" and which I like to call the "night of despair":[10]

> Catherine's swelling heart needed relief. In Eleanor's presence friendship and pride had equally restrained her tears, but no sooner was she gone than they burst forth in torrents. Turned from the house, and in such a way! Without any reason that could justify, any apology that could atone for the abruptness, the rudeness, nay, the insolence of it. Henry at a distance—not able even to bid him farewell. Every hope, every expectation from him suspended, at least, and who could say how long? Who could say when they might meet again? And all this by such a man as General Tilney, so polite, so well bred, and heretofore so particularly fond of her! It was as incomprehensible as it was mortifying and grievous.

Some characters experience their deepest, darkest moment in the same scene as the climax or directly after. Others experience it during the falling action, or at another point in the novel. Yet even if a character does not experience true despair, they should face obstacles during the climax and falling action that make them feel that they cannot possibly achieve their want.

And so, Catherine climbs into a carriage with her bags, her external journey seeming to end in failure.

In *Mansfield Park*, the climax—the point where everything is brought to a crisis—is a multi-scene sequence in which Henry Crawford proposes and Fanny refuses despite the urgings of her uncle. It takes all of Fanny's will and courage to stand up to her uncle and his anger. Near the end of a lengthy conversation, in

---

10. Snyder, *Save the Cat!*, chapter 4.

which Sir Thomas is in turn shocked, disbelieving, silently angry, and argumentative, Sir Thomas forcefully tells Fanny,

"And I should have been very much surprised had either of my daughters, on receiving a proposal of marriage at any time which might carry with it only *half* the eligibility of *this*, immediately and peremptorily, and without paying my opinion or my regard the compliment of any consultation, put a decided negative on it. I should have been much surprised and much hurt by such a proceeding. I should have thought it a gross violation of duty and respect. *You* are not to be judged by the same rule. You do not owe me the duty of a child. But, Fanny, if your heart can acquit you of *ingratitude*—"

Sir Thomas lectures Fanny.
Illustration by C. E. Brock, 1908.

He ceased. Fanny was by this time crying so bitterly that, angry as he was, he would not press that article farther. Her heart was almost broke by such a picture of what she appeared to him; by such accusations, so heavy, so multiplied, so rising in dreadful gradation! Self-willed, obstinate, selfish, and ungrateful. He thought her all this. She had deceived his expectations; she had lost his good opinion. What was to become of her?

"I am very sorry," said she inarticulately, through her tears, "I am very sorry indeed."

"Sorry! yes, I hope you are sorry; and you will probably have reason to be long sorry for this day's transactions."

If this is Fanny's test of character, she is victorious. She has transformed from passive to active, and she fights for what she wants, or, more accurately, against what she doesn't want. While Sir Thomas is tempted to relent, he does not. And Fanny loses everything. She is sent to a home that does not feel like home: dirty, loud, and conducive to sickness.

Instead of using a single climax, some stories have what Freytag calls a "double apex."[11] This seems to be the case in *Emma*. The first climax or peak is when she learns that Frank Churchill has been secretly engaged to Jane Fairfax—this throws everything she thought she knew into question. There's a bit of falling action, and then we have the second climax or peak, which is slightly higher than the first: Mr. Knightley might love Harriet Smith.

Emma has been wrong before. She was wrong about Mr. Elton and his supposed affections to Harriet. She was wrong in her treatment of Miss Bates, especially at Box Hill. These turning points and more minor events spur Emma to change. Over the course of the novel, she overcomes her prejudices against a family named the Coles, who she at first considers "of low origin, in trade, and only moderately genteel"; ultimately, Emma accepts a party invitation from them. Emma decides not to interfere in Harriet's pursuit of love after the ball (thus setting aside her initial character want of matchmaking), she repairs her relationship with Miss Bates, and she attempts to reach out to Jane Fairfax.

Yet in and of themselves, these actions are insufficient. Her external journey as a matchmaker and her internal journey of

---

11. Freytag, *Technique of the Drama*, 132–3.

transformation must be brought to a crisis. And indeed, the double climax brings her to this crisis: Frank Churchill, who she supposed was in love with her, has been secretly engaged to Jane Fairfax this entire time. And Harriet loves Mr. Knightley, and he may love her.

This second climax puts everything on the line: Emma finally understands herself and others, and yet it seems that she is about to lose the one thing—the one person—she actually wants.

The climax raises the stakes to their highest point in the entire novel, where the main character has the opportunity to either gain or lose everything. In many cases, it's also a test of character.

Earlier in the novel, Emma would have attempted to change Harriet's mind, by either convincing Harriet that she should not pursue Mr. Knightley or by persuading her that Mr. Knightley does not truly care for her. The temptation to do so must be strong, but instead of reverting back to her old self in an attempt to get what she wants, Emma tells Harriet,

> "Harriet, I will only venture to declare, that Mr. Knightley is the last man in the world, who would intentionally give any woman the idea of his feeling for her more than he really does."

Emma might lose what she really wants, but at least now she is a better person. At the climax, she seems to have failed her external journey, but she has succeeded at her internal journey of transformation.

When crafting a climax for your story, it's important to create a scene with enough weight and strength to bridge the rising and falling action. This climax should deal with the novel's theme, and the character's wants, and both the internal and external journey. The climax tends to be one of the memorable moments of a story, largely because everything is now at stake for the characters.

Exercise 12.3: Losing Everything

Spend a minute or two brainstorming a character and their want. Skip writing the character's entire story—instead, write a brief climactic scene in which that character knows that they could lose everything that they most care about. Include a tragic force and show how the character is tested.

Exercise 12.4: Evaluating Your Climax

Consider one of your own stories that you've either drafted or outlined. Make a list of the stakes at the climax of the story. What is at stake for the main character? What could be lost? What could be gained? Do these stakes reflect both the character's internal and external journeys? What are the stakes for other characters in the story?

Reflect on your answers and consider how to revise or improve your climax.

THE FALLING ACTION

The falling action is the portion of the story from the climax until the final resolution. At the climax, everything has been brought into question; now, everything of importance must be resolved.

Austen uses a wide range of approaches to falling action in her novels. As we saw in our analysis in Chapter 1, in the falling action of *Pride and Prejudice*, Mr. Darcy proves himself by finding Lydia and Wickham and quietly financing their marriage. Meanwhile, Elizabeth is a support to her family. After Lydia's marriage, Elizabeth successfully manages an encounter with the now-married Mr. Wickham. Then Mr. Darcy brings Mr. Bingley and Jane back together, and the **final suspense** is raised: Will Mr. Darcy and Elizabeth resolve their differences and find happiness? After interactions filled with distance and silence, Mr. Darcy leaves. Lady Catherine visits, and Elizabeth withstands her verbal attacks. The **resolution**—when the major questions of the plot are resolved—is when Mr. Darcy returns again, he and Elizabeth open up to each other, he proposes, and she accepts.

In *Northanger Abbey*, Catherine Morland and Henry Tilney take a different sort of role in the ending. Consider the scenes in the falling action:

Chapter 29 Scene 1	Catherine makes the long journey home; her mind is filled with thoughts and reflections.
Chapter 29 Scene 2	Catherine reaches home and finds happiness in her home and with her family.
Chapter 29 Scene 3	Catherine visits the Allens and is comforted by them but once again feels despair.
Chapter 30 Scene 1	In a multi-day, montage-like scene, Catherine struggles to function.
Chapter 30 Scene 2	Henry arrives and explains himself (including his affection for Catherine) and his father (including the false information that led to General Tilney's behavior).
Chapter 31 Scene 1	Henry asks Catherine's parents if he can marry her, and they conditionally give permission, dependent on General Tilney giving his consent. Henry and Catherine are forlorn but not surprised.
Chapter 31 Scene 2	In a mini-scene, Catherine and Henry write each other clandestine letters.
Chapter 31 Scene 3	Eleanor is married and solicits her father's permission for Catherine and Henry.

Henry's character is shown by his willingness to incur the wrath of his father by standing up for Catherine and doing right by her.

Catherine's role in the falling action ties directly to her internal journey, about learning to read and judge other people. During the falling action, she wonders if she might have been banished from the abbey due to her own actions. She recognizes that she did, at one point, suspect General Tilney of either murdering or locking up his wife. Yet after reflection, she concludes that this is her "only offence." She correctly decides this knowledge could not have reached the general, for it was only known by Henry, and "Henry could not have betrayed her."

This reasoning shows great progress in Catherine's ability to read and judge character: She judges herself and Henry Tilney with accuracy, although she still does not know how to judge General Tilney.

It's not many days before Henry Tilney comes to visit. He explains (but does not justify) his father's behavior. In essence, his father was first misinformed (by John Thorpe, of all people!) that Catherine was extremely wealthy. Then, Thorpe informed him that Catherine was actually very poor, which was false but led to the general's overreaction. This masterfully ties back to the subplot of Catherine's relationship with John Thorpe. Because of what we know of Thorpe's character, the obstacle of the climax feels like it has risen naturally out of the narrative; this also provides a neat (though painful) conclusion to their relationship.

After Henry explains his father's misconceptions, Catherine uses her judgment once again:

> Catherine ... heard enough to feel that in suspecting General Tilney of either murdering or shutting up his wife, she had scarcely sinned against his character, or magnified his cruelty.

Catherine's internal journey—her ability to read other people—has reached its conclusion. She has learned to read people, and she has learned the pitfalls *and merits* of using her literary texts to help her do so. After all, it was her propensity for Gothic literature that led her to see past the General's politeness and to his true domineering and cruel character.

The Morlands are surprised by Henry's request to marry their daughter, but they consent. Illustration by C. E. Brock, 1907.

There is no final suspense in which we wonder if Henry and Catherine will resolve their problems—in fact, they don't even bring about their own resolution. Henry's sister Eleanor does, through a conveniently rich marriage and her persuasive powers. This works in part because of Eleanor and Catherine's friendship, as well as Eleanor's guilt at enacting the terrible will of her father. It is also effective because of the story's stance. The narrator provides further commentary on stories as she pokes fun at the hasty conclusion:

> The anxiety, which in this state of their attachment must be the portion of Henry and Catherine, and of all who loved either, as to its final event, can hardly extend, I fear, to the bosom of my readers, who will see in the tell-tale compression of the pages before them, that we are hastening together to perfect felicity.

As the narrator confesses, we know this will end happily, so why spend pages or chapters on it? The true battle—the transformation brought about by Catherine's internal journey—has already occurred: Catherine has learned to read people.

While the falling action of *Northanger Abbey* shows Catherine's transformation, in *Mansfield Park* it highlights Fanny's continuing powerlessness. As discussed in Chapter 3, in *Mansfield Park*, the double inciting incident raised two main questions:

- Will Fanny find a home?
- How will the arrival of the Crawfords impact Fanny and the Bertrams?

During the falling action, these questions receive the focus. Fanny is unable to find any sense of home at her parents' house, yet Sir Thomas does not allow her to return. Henry Crawford visits Fanny and is kind to her, but she does not encourage his addresses.

Fanny is not physically present for the other pivotal events that explore these questions and the consequences of the characters' choices. Instead of participating in or witnessing these family changes and developments, she learns of them through reading letters and the newspaper: one of her cousins becomes deathly ill, one has an affair and is disgraced, and another elopes. Throughout the falling action, Fanny reverts to being a passive character, writing letters but largely disconnected. She is passive even when

Edmund asks for her advice about how to propose to Mary Crawford: Fanny does nothing to warn him of her true nature, nothing to discourage him from his planned course of action, nothing to tell him of her feelings.

Fanny learns of Maria's disgrace by reading her father's newspaper. Illustration by C. E. Brock, 1908.

The moment of final suspense arises when Fanny hears the news about her married cousin Maria running off with Henry Crawford. It seems that not only has she lost all happiness and security, but so have the people that she cares about:

> What would be the consequence? Whom would it not injure? Whose views might it not affect? Whose peace would it not cut up for ever?

This final suspense continues for days, with no further letters. But then, Edmund writes, explaining that,

My father is not overpowered.... He is still able to think and act; and I write, by his desire, to propose your returning home.

This is the resolution Fanny had hoped for. She returns home—for now she sees Mansfield Park as home—and this time, she brings her dear younger sister Susan with her. Once there, Fanny provides support, quietly making everyone happier and more comfortable. Only when Edmund talks of his separation from Mary Crawford—in the final paragraph of the falling action—does Fanny "feel at liberty to speak openly" and share what she knows of Mary's character. The scene (and the falling action) ends with the line "Fanny's friendship was all that he had to cling to."

Freytag writes that in the falling action, we should see "only great strokes, great effects. Even the episodes which are now ventured, must have a certain significance, a certain energy."[12] Every moment of the falling action in *Mansfield Park* possesses this weight and significance. This is also true in *Sense and Sensibility*, a novel in which the "great strokes" of the falling action interweave Elinor's external and internal journeys.

Colonel Brandon asks Elinor to speak to Edward Ferrars. Illustration by Chris (Christiana) Hammond, 1899.

12. Freytag, *Technique of the Drama*, 134.

When Edward loses his inheritance because of his engagement to Lucy Steele, Colonel Brandon decides to give him a living. It's partly out of the goodness of his heart, but he does not truly know Edward. His real reason is that he knows of Edward's friendship with the Dashwoods. Unfortunately for Elinor, he decides that the only proper thing would be for her to inform Edward of this great gift. This is the falling action's final test of Elinor's character: will she help others even if it harms herself?

Elinor agrees to deliver the news. She decides to write a letter, for "it was at least preferable to giving the information by word of mouth," but then is interrupted by Edward himself, for Mrs. Jennings told him that Elinor needed to speak with him. What follows is a beautiful, painful scene in which Elinor is the source of giving happiness and hope to the man she loves, so that he can marry a woman who has personally wronged her. Elinor insists that she "had no hand in it," but she knows that Edward believes her responsible. When the shocked Edward leaves to offer the Colonel thanks, we read,

> "When I see him again," said Elinor to herself, as the door shut him out, "I shall see him the husband of Lucy."
>
> And with this pleasing anticipation, she sat down to reconsider the past, recall the words and endeavour to comprehend all the feelings of Edward; and, of course, to reflect on her own with discontent.

Elinor performs an incredibly difficult task, and in so doing, we see the strength of her character. In the words of Freytag, during the falling action, the opposition "beats upon the soul of the hero." But we also see that "the greater the pressure the [writer] lays upon [the characters] from without, so much higher the power becomes with which they battle against it."[13]

Ultimately, Elinor loves Edward too much to see him miserable, even if giving him happiness will bring misery to herself.

This action leads directly to the next major event of the falling action: the final suspense, in which it seems impossible for Elinor to achieve her wants. The Dashwoods' manservant sees Lucy Steele, but she is no longer Lucy Steele—she is a married Mrs. Ferrars,

---

13. Freytag, *Technique of the Drama*, 133, 166–67.

and sitting in a carriage with her new husband. She gives a message to the Dashwoods that after their trip, "they'd be sure and call."

The servant tells Mrs. Dashwood that Mr. Ferrars is married.
Illustration by Hugh Thomson, 1896.

This is Elinor's lowest moment. Her immediate emotions upon hearing this news are so strong that the narrator distances herself from them, pulling away from her point of view to focus on Mrs. Dashwood's and Marianne's reactions to Elinor's emotions.

Then, in the next chapter, we are given access to Elinor's thoughts:

> Elinor now found the difference between the expectation of an unpleasant event, however certain the mind may be told to consider it, and certainty itself. She now found, that in spite of herself, she had always admitted a hope, while Edward remained single, that something would occur to prevent his marrying Lucy; that some resolution of his own, some mediation of friends, or

some more eligible opportunity of establishment for the lady, would arise to assist the happiness of all. But he was now married; and she condemned her heart for the lurking flattery, which so much heightened the pain of the intelligence.

To the surprise of all the Dashwoods, Edward comes to visit. In the ensuing conversation, it becomes clear that Lucy Steele did *not* marry Edward Ferrars. Rather, she married his brother, Robert Ferrars. The ultimate resolution occurs in the next chapter, when Edward proposes to Elinor and she accepts. This happy resolution is actually brought about in part because of Elinor's kindness. The living offered by Colonel Brandon to Edward was clearly not enough of a temptation for Lucy Steele in comparison to the future she could have with Robert Ferrars. Yet Colonel Brandon's living,

Edward proposes to Elinor.
Illustration by Chris (Christiana) Hammond, 1899.

while not actually quite enough for Edward and Elinor to live off of, provides enough assurance of future possibilities that they can become engaged.

In *Emma,* the falling action consists of only a chapter and a half of Emma's interactions and reflections. She spends time alone and speaks with Mrs. Weston, and she realizes all the ways she has wronged Harriet, Jane Fairfax, and others. She spends a scene caring for her father, who, in the poor weather, "could only be kept tolerably comfortable by almost ceaseless attention on his daughter's side." By this point, she has both accepted her errors and come to a conclusion:

> Marriage, in fact, would not do for her. It would be incompatible with what she owed to her father, and with what she felt for him. Nothing should separate her from her father. She would not marry, even if she were asked by Mr. Knightley.

Then, the final suspense and the resolution occur in the same scene. Mr. Knightley joins Emma for a walk. She believes that he means to tell her of his plans to marry Harriet Smith; instead, he wants to console Emma because Frank Churchill is marrying another. Ultimately, they reveal their true feelings to each other and become engaged.

In Austen's six novels, we see a wide range of approaches to the falling action. In some of the novels, the falling action is only a few scenes; in others, it's almost an entire volume. Most of her characters are more active in the resolution, but a few, like Fanny Price and Catherine Morland, are less involved. Austen's novels show us that there are many good ways to end a story. While none of these are hard and fast rules (and Austen herself breaks some of them), the following are principles we learn from Jane that we can apply to our own stories:

- The falling action is generally shorter than the rising action. Only essential scenes should be included.
- Subplots are often resolved during the falling action (though some don't receive resolution until the denouement).
- During the falling action, we should resolve both the internal and external journeys. The resolution of one might lead to the other, or they might resolve at the same time.

- There should be tests of character: We must see who the main character has become.
- The falling action should contain more struggle for the characters: Even now, after all the characters have been through, the resolution cannot be too easy.
- Including a deep low point can make a following high point feel sweeter and more powerful by contrast.
- By the end of the falling action, the core problems, conflicts, and questions that the characters have faced throughout the story should be resolved.

As previously quoted, Freytag wrote that in a story, we want to see "the accomplishment of a deed and its reaction on the soul."[14] This accomplishment of a deed occurs, with finality, in the falling action, and we see the soul's reaction to this accomplishment both in the falling action and in the denouement.

Exercise 12.5: One Thing Solves Another

In stories, often solving one thing allows the character to solve another. For instance:

- A test of character or a healing of a relationship can give a character the tools, abilities, or knowledge to solve a practical or physical problem.
- Solving a practical or physical problem can give a character the ability to heal a relationship or help them resolve a larger character problem.

Brainstorm the following:

- Three practical or physical problems a character might need to solve in a story. These can be big or small.
- Three character or relationship problems that a character might need to deal with in a story. For instance, this could be a character flaw, a weakness, or a fractured relationship.

Now choose one item from both lists (a practical/physical problem and a character/relationship problem). Come up with at least one idea of how solving one of these problems could help the character solve the other problem.

---

14. Freytag, *Technique of the Drama*, 104.

Exercise 12.6: A Test Score

Consider two fictional college students who both receive a good grade on a final paper or a final exam. For one student, achieving this goal is only a moderate challenge, while for the other, it is a grand triumph against all odds. Brainstorm details about both characters, who they are, and why this class was easy or difficult for them. Also list what this grade means to the student and the sorts of obstacles this student had to overcome to achieve success. Reflect on these two characters and the sorts of stories that could be crafted about them. For the character that struggled less, what is a success that would be more challenging for them to achieve?

Exercise 12.7: Falling Action Analysis

For a story that you have drafted, make a chart of every scene in your falling action. How many scenes did you include? What occurs in each scene? How does each scene impact the characters, the plot, the subplots, or the key relationships? Which scenes include tests of characters? After creating the chart, find something to improve in your falling action.

THE DENOUEMENT

Before the denouement, the main plot problems are resolved: Emma, Elizabeth, Anne, Elinor, and Catherine are engaged, and Fanny has returned to Mansfield Park. The internal journeys are also largely resolved: The characters have changed and are now in a different, happier state than at the beginning of their novels.

Yet all is not finished. While short stories do not always need denouements, most novels require them. So much has been built up in terms of characters and relationships, plots and subplots, that a few final scenes or chapters are necessary in order to finish unraveling the story. For instance, in *Sense and Sensibility*, Edward Ferrars is still at odds with his family, which means he and Elinor may not have sufficient income to wed. Marianne's happiness is still at stake, and a permanent home for their mother and youngest sister is not guaranteed. In *Pride and Prejudice*, we wonder how Elizabeth's parents will respond to her engagement and how their marriage will impact Mr. Darcy's relationships with family and friends.

All this must be handled in the denouement.

After learning that Elizabeth and Mr. Darcy plan to marry,
"Mrs. Bennet sat quite still...unable to utter a syllable."
Illustration by Hugh Thomson, 1894.

THE PRIMARY ROLE OF THE DENOUEMENT IS TO FINISH THE MAIN CHARACTERS' STORIES.

In the denouement of *Mansfield Park*, the Bertrams suffer regrets because of their life choices. Fanny marries Edmund, and her sister becomes the replacement family helper. Eventually, Dr. Grant dies, and Edmund becomes the rector at Mansfield Park, giving them more financial security and bringing them back into the daily lives of their family members. In *Persuasion*, Sir Walter decides that Captain Wentworth is wealthy enough—and handsome enough—to marry Anne. Anne's sister Mary finds true joy in Anne's marriage. And Lady Russell comes to admit her past mistakes and approve of Captain Wentworth.

In *Sense and Sensibility*, Edward reconciles with his mother, though Elinor loses the position of favorite daughter-in-law to the fawning Lucy. Elinor and Edward marry even though improvements on their house have not been finished by Colonel Brandon. In *Emma*, Mr. Woodhouse is unsurprisingly disturbed by Emma's desire to marry (he hates marriages and change), but he is pleased by Mr. Knightley's decision to move to their home, rather than take Emma with him to Donwell Abbey.

In *Northanger Abbey*, even though Catherine and Henry must wait months to marry, the narrator believes "that the General's unjust interference, so far from being really injurious to their felicity, was perhaps rather conducive to it, by improving their knowledge of each other, and adding strength to their attachment." Not only does their story conclude, but we see the direct role that their struggles played in creating the positive resolution.

THE DENOUEMENT CAN EXPLAIN THAT WHICH HAS, UP TO THIS POINT, NOT BEEN EXPLAINED.

In *Mansfield Park*, we learn of how and why Henry Crawford seduced Fanny's married cousin, Maria: He had been "ruined by early independence and bad domestic example, indulged in the freaks of a cold-blooded vanity a little too long." He wanted the married Maria to treat him the same way she did when she was only engaged, and so he attempted to overcome her resentment. The narrator expresses a belief that if Henry Crawford had not pursued Maria, he might have continued to improve; Fanny might have eventually agreed to marry him.

IN SOME NOVELS, THE DENOUEMENT CAN BE USED TO SHOW HOW THOROUGHLY THE MAIN CHARACTER HAS CHANGED.

In *Emma*, Emma converses with Jane Fairfax and they resolve their differences. Jane attempts to explain her behavior during her secret engagement and apologizes for it:

> "You are very kind, but I know what my manners were to you.—
> So cold and artificial!—I had always a part to act.—It was a life
> of deceit!—I know that I must have disgusted you."

In reply, Emma says,

> "Pray say no more. I feel that all apologies should be on my side.
> Let us forgive each other at once."

Later, Emma speaks to Frank Churchill, and he also explains
himself and his behavior, concluding that "it would have been a
much better transgression had I broken the bond of secrecy and
told you every thing." Without hesitation, Emma replies, "It is
not now worth a regret."

THE DENOUEMENT ALSO WRAPS UP ANY REMAINING SUBPLOTS THAT ARE
YET TO BE RESOLVED. IT CAN HIGHLIGHT RELATIONSHIPS AND SHOW THE
CONCLUDING POINT OF A RELATIONSHIP ARC. AT TIMES, THE DENOUE-
MENT PROVIDES A GLIMPSE OF ALL THE KEY PLAYERS IN A STORY.
Emma and Harriet's relationship is crucial throughout *Emma*.
Yet by the end of the falling action, their friendship has distance.
After Emma's engagement, Harriet avoids her, and Emma finds
herself grateful for this avoidance. Yet Harriet's story is not over:
Mr. Knightley learns that Harriet has become engaged to Robert
Martin. She inherits a small fortune from her father, who publicly
states his parentage. Mr. Knightley expresses his belief that Harriet's friendship with Emma actually helped Harriet become a better,
more refined person, though Emma still feels regret over her negative interference in Harriet's life. Ultimately, Emma and Harriet
reconcile, and Emma attends Harriet's wedding.

In *Sense and Sensibility*, some time passes, and then Marianne
marries Colonel Brandon.

> Colonel Brandon was now as happy, as all those who best loved
> him, believed he deserved to be;—in Marianne he was consoled
> for every past affliction;—her regard and her society restored
> his mind to animation, and his spirits to cheerfulness; and that
> Marianne found her own happiness in forming his, was equally
> the persuasion and delight of each observing friend. Marianne
> could never love by halves; and her whole heart became, in

time, as much devoted to her husband, as it had once been to
Willoughby.

In Austen's denouements, crucial characters, relationships, and
subplots generally receive at least a few sentences and sometimes
entire paragraphs and scenes.

IN THE DENOUEMENT, A NEW STASIS IS ESTABLISHED.
Prior to the inciting incident, the world is in stasis. The inciting incident disrupts the trajectory of the characters, sending them
on internal and external journeys. The denouement creates a new
normal, putting the world, once again, at rest. We can picture Elizabeth Bennet continuing in happiness at Pemberley.
Sense and Sensibility also closes with the sense that the characters' lives will progress in a stable, positive way:

> Among the merits and the happiness of Elinor and Marianne,
> let it not be ranked as the least considerable, that though sis-
> ters, and living almost within sight of each other, they could live
> without disagreement between themselves, or producing cool-
> ness between their husbands.

By the end of each of Austen's novels, the stories feel satisfy-
ingly complete. But being Jane Austen, she is not content to give
her characters unadulterated happiness.

WHILE THE DENOUEMENT CREATES A NEW STASIS FOR THE CHARACTERS,
EVERYTHING NEED NOT BE PERFECT. A COMPLICATION OR TENSION
CAN BE ADDED. THE DENOUEMENT CAN INVITE FURTHER THOUGHT
AND REFLECTION OR LEAVE AN OPENING FOR FUTURE FRICTION OR
PROBLEMS.
Emma closes with happiness that hints at future tension in
the town of Highbury. Mrs. Elton does not attend Emma's wedding, but from what she hears of it, she concludes that it was "all
extremely shabby, and very inferior to her own." While Emma
and Mr. Knightley experience complete marital happiness, there
is a snake in the garden.
Northanger Abbey also ends with ambiguity. A questionable
lesson is given, in conjunction with yet more commentary on
storytelling:

> I leave it to be settled, by whomsoever it may concern, whether the tendency of this work be altogether to recommend parental tyranny, or reward filial disobedience.

While *Persuasion* ends with Anne and Captain Wentworth happy, it also ends with a potential twist, a complication:

> Anne was tenderness itself, and she had the full worth of it in Captain Wentworth's affection. His profession was all that could ever make her friends wish that tenderness less, the dread of a future war all that could dim her sunshine. She gloried in being a sailor's wife, but she must pay the tax of quick alarm for belonging to that profession which is, if possible, more distinguished in its domestic virtues than in its national importance.

Readers in Austen's time would notice the temporal clues spread throughout the novel: They would know that not long after the novel's conclusion, Napoleon Bonaparte escaped from the Isle of Elba, putting England, once again, at war, and Captain Wentworth's life at risk.[15]

Mansfield Park has perhaps the most complicated ending of Austen's novels. In the denouement we learn that Fanny is "happy in spite of everything," for "she was returned to Mansfield Park, she was useful, she was beloved; she was safe from Mr. Crawford," and her uncle begins to treat her with "increased regard." Sir Thomas is miserable, Edmund is miserable, and Maria is in permanent disgrace. It is only in the denouement that Edmund learns to stop regretting Mary Crawford and begin caring for Fanny. We *never* see them in scene together as this transformation occurs—we must take their relationship at the narrator's word. Sir Thomas also begins to treat Fanny as a daughter, but once again, this is part of the denouement, and we never see it in scene.

Some scholars and readers argue that *Mansfield Park* is actually a tragedy, in which characters do not overcome their flaws. As a result, they meet bitter ends.[16] Even though Fanny gets what she has come to want—a secure place in Mansfield Park and Edmund as her husband—her story can still be read as tragic. She marries

---

15. Fortunately for Anne, most of the resulting military action occurred on the continent rather than at sea.

16. Groff, "Jane Austen's Boldest Novel Is Also Her Least Understood."

In the denouement, we learn that after spending time with Fanny, Edmund "had so well talked his mind into submission as to be very tolerably cheerful again." Illustration by Hugh Thomson, 1897.

a man who only wanted another and becomes part of the system that hurt and oppressed her.[17] Other readers point to the Bertrams' wealth, which derives from the slave trade, arguing that the ending is tragic because Fanny becomes complicit.[18] On the other hand, scholar Paula Byrne argues that the ending provides redemption for the remaining Bertrams who live at Mansfield Park—they have allowed Fanny to change them and improve them for the better.[19] Regardless of how you read the ending of *Mansfield Park*, it is complicated and filled with nuance.

⁝⁞

So much happens in a novel that after the falling action—after the major problems have been resolved—we need a little longer with the characters. Austen's denouements tend to be short, ranging from the few paragraphs of *Northanger Abbey* to the several chapters that end *Emma*. The length is less important than the essence. The denouement wraps up loose ends and gives us an opportunity to see the characters in their new, changed state.

Exercise 12.8: Writing the Denouement in Scene and Through Summary

In *Emma,* the denouement is shown largely in scene—we see several sequences in which Emma interacts with other characters. These scenes wrap up subplots and give a sense of Emma's life moving forward. In *Mansfield Park,* the denouement consists of summary by the omniscient narrator, without anything in scene.

Write the denouement of a story two ways. In the first, rely heavily on showing the denouement in scene; in the second, rely heavily on summary. You can do this with a novel you're writing, with the ending of a fairy tale, or with any other story. What are the advantages and disadvantages of both denouements?

---

17. You could even argue that rather than liberating her sister Susan by bringing her to Mansfield Park, Fanny takes part in the subjugation of Susan. It is important to note that Susan was unhappy at home and is happy running around doing whatever Lady Bertram asks of her; however, her role is still to run around and do whatever Lady Bertram asks of her.
18. Bird, "The Darker Side of Jane Austen."
19. Byrne, *The Real Jane Austen,* 27.

Exercise 12.9: Subplot Tracking

Subplots can resolve at any point in a story. In most novels, a few subplots resolve during the rising action, while most of the subplots resolve during the climax, the falling action, and the denouement.

Choose one of your favorite novels. Make a list of all the major sub-plots (these can include relationships, side quests, smaller goals, the wants of other characters, etc.). Now make a chart to track when each of the subplots resolves. How do these resolutions correlate with the main character's internal and external journeys?

A SATISFYING CLOSE

At the end of a story, we want our readers to feel satisfied. Whether our goal is to move our readers to joy or tears, to provide them with catharsis or entertainment, the ending is the last chance we have to spend with the reader. Just as receiving a phone call with tragic news at the end of a good vacation can color our memories of the entire trip, so too can the ending of our stories color the entire reading experience.

One of Jane Austen's juvenile writings was titled "The beautifull Cassandra, a novel in twelve chapters."[20] Like many of her early works, it's a parody, and unlike most novels, it's less than 400 words. It begins when the main character, Cassandra, falls in love with a bonnet. Cassandra goes on a journey with this bonnet, traveling to and fro without paying carriage drivers, devouring "six ices" (ice creams), once again without paying for them, and having other mishaps and adventures. After seven hours of adventure, Cassandra returns home.

---

20. Austen, "The beautifull Cassandra," 81–83.
Austen's unpublished writings tend to have a lot more misspellings than her published, polished works, something I find supremely comforting when I misspell words.

> She entered it and was pressed to her Mother's bosom by that
> worthy Woman. Cassandra smiled and whispered to herself "This
> is a day well spent."[21]

Whether our stories end with joy or tragedy, with everything resolved or with nuance, we want the reader to finish the book and think, "This is a day well spent." Our stories have worth in part because we have brought the reader on a journey: They have traveled far through character and plot, through setting and emotion. As the main character completes their internal and external journey, the reader feels empowered to continue on their own life journeys.

---

21. Austen, "The beautifull Cassandra," 83.

CHAPTER THIRTEEN

STYLE

"He has neither genius, taste, nor spirit.... His understanding has no brilliancy, his feelings no ardour, and his voice no expression."
—*Sense and Sensibility*

I n *Sense and Sensibility*, Marianne Dashwood places great weight on a person's style and manner of speaking, as we see in her above criticism of Colonel Brandon. For her, one's ability to express ideas passionately and in a compelling way is intrinsically connected to the value of the message and the value of the speaker. This preludes Marshall McLuhan's famous statement, first made in 1964, that "the medium is the message."[1] Like Marianne Dashwood, for McLuhan, the form of a message and its content are inseparable.

This form of a message or manner of expression is often called style. After masterclasses from Austen on plot and character, emotion and setting, it's worth considering what she can teach us about style, our overall approach at a macro and micro level. Style has

---

1. McLuhan first used the term in his book *Understanding Media: The Extensions of Man*. It's also the point of his later book, *The Medium is the Massage*. (Yes, "massage," not "message." Legend has it that the book was originally titled *The Medium is the Message* but the typesetter misspelled it as *Massage*; McLuhan thought it was a hilarious commentary and decided to keep it that way.)

been defined in many ways and often feels intangible. As readers, we can recognize good style and bad style, but it can be difficult to pinpoint what makes a style bad or good. It can be even more difficult to define or develop one's own style as a writer.

Miss Steele. Illustration by Chris (Christiana) Hammond, 1899.

We see some styles as correct or appropriate for particular circumstances and others as ill-suited. In *Sense and Sensibility*, Miss Steele (Lucy's older sister) often speaks incorrectly, either in her choice of subject matter or the very way in which she talks. At times, Lucy feels embarrassed and tries to correct her. Elinor views Miss Steele's style as defined by "vulgar freedom and folly." In Miss Steele's dialogue, we can immediately see how her style of speaking does not match upper-class society:

"Nay, my dear, I'm sure I don't pretend to say that there an't. I'm sure there's a vast many smart beaux in Exeter; but you know, how could I tell what smart beaux there might be about Norland; and I was only afraid the Miss Dashwoods might find it dull at Barton, if they had not so many as they used to have. But perhaps you young ladies may not care about the beaux, and had as lief be without them as with them. For my part, I think they are vastly agreeable, provided they dress smart and behave civil. But I can't bear to see them dirty and nasty. Now there's Mr. Rose at Exeter, a prodigious smart young man, quite a beau, clerk to Mr. Simpson, you know, and yet if you do but meet him of a morning, he is not fit to be seen. I suppose your brother was quite a beau, Miss Dashwood, before he married, as he was so rich?"

One focus of style is the rules of expression: matching the expectations of a particular audience, avoiding errors of word choice and grammar, following prescriptions on the ways that punctuation should and should not be used. Just as there are expectations among Austen's characters for proper speech, style guides for writing, like APA and MLA, create sets of rules for individual choices that are meant to be universal for an organization or discipline of study. This creates consistency (we can rely on the fact that the works cited of a scientific paper will include the same details, in the same manner, about each work), and it also forwards the values of an organization (the year of a publication is prioritized in scientific citations, because in a scientific discipline, age and relevance go hand in hand).

Yet style is more than conventions and rules of usage. Theorists Seymour Chatman and Samuel R. Levin argue that style is "the totality of impressions which a literary work produces."[2] Some consider style as ornamentation, rhetorical figures and devices hung on a work like ornaments on a tree. For others, style is an expression of self. Others argue that "ideas exist wordlessly and can be dressed in a variety of outfits depending on the need or occasion."[3] Style can feel distinctive for an author; just as a person's clothing style may carry across different outfits and seasons and even years,

---

2. Glenn and Goldthwaite, *The St. Martin's Guide to Teaching Writing*, 200.
3. Glenn and Goldthwaite, *The St. Martin's Guide to Teaching Writing*, 200.

a writer's style might transcend individual publications and even genres. Or, like with a clothing style, a writer's style may change over time.

Throughout *Sense and Sensibility*, it is not only Marianne who is preoccupied with the question of style. The narrator and numerous characters analyze the "style of life" and "style of living" of individuals, and it becomes clear that a certain style of living (with servants, updated furnishings, and travel) requires a certain amount of income. We read that the Middletons' home was large and they "lived in a style of equal hospitality and elegance." This is more than just their house and its attributes—it's their approach toward other people. Throughout the novel, style is dependent on a person or place's defining characteristics: the most important and salient features.

The novel also addresses different styles of letter writing. As we saw in Chapter 4, Sir John's letters are warm and friendly, and it is not just what he says, but how he says it, that leaves that impression. Later in the novel, Edward criticizes Lucy Steele's letters. Upon showing one to Elinor, he says, "This is the only letter I ever received from her, of which the substance made me any amends for the defect of the style." Generally, not only is her style defective, but so is the substance. In this case, the substance has exceeded expectations. Like Marianne, Edward seems to make a connection between the interior contents and the exterior packaging.

Yet Austen does not allow us to simply accept this conclusion on style. Sometimes, a character has correct, fashionable outward style, without the substance to match. In London, Elinor visits a busy shop for an errand. Pressed on time, she chooses a counter with only one customer, hoping that the man will notice her and politely wrap up his purchase. But then we read,

> The correctness of his eye, and the delicacy of his taste, proved to be beyond his politeness. He was giving orders for a toothpick-case for himself, and till its size, shape, and ornaments were determined, all of which, after examining and debating for a quarter of an hour over every toothpick-case in the shop, were finally arranged by his own inventive fancy, he had no leisure to bestow any other attention on the two ladies, than what was comprised in three or four very broad stares; a kind of notice which served to imprint on Elinor the remembrance

of a person and face, of strong, natural, sterling insignificance, though adorned in the first style of fashion.

Later, Elinor learns that this man is none other than Edward's brother Robert. Just as fashionable attire cannot make up for Robert's personality, in our own works, a well-crafted or fashionable literary style cannot make up for a lack of storytelling. The converse is also true: A good story, even if in common or unstylish trappings, can still have merit.

In *Sense and Sensibility*, at Edward's first introduction, the narrator observes, "He was not handsome, and his manners required intimacy to make them pleasing." Marianne expresses reservations to her mother about Edward's style, both in terms of presentation, personality, and speaking. Marianne states that "there is something wanting," that Edward lacks grace, that he reads in a spiritless way, that "he has no real taste," and that "his eyes want all that spirit, that fire, which at once announce virtue and intelligence." Further, he admires Elinor's art "as a lover, not a connoisseur."

Marianne experiences pain as she listens to Edward reading aloud. Illustration by Chris (Christiana) Hammond, 1899.

Later, his brother Robert also criticizes his style:

> "Poor Edward! His manners are certainly not the happiest in nature. But we are not all born, you know, with the same powers,—the same address. Poor fellow! to see him in a circle of strangers! To be sure it was pitiable enough; but upon my soul, I believe he has as good a heart as any in the kingdom."

Edward's style of speaking and presentation may never rival that of Willoughby, yet he is a good match for Elinor. And while at first Marianne prefers Willoughby's expressive, emotive style, she ultimately marries Colonel Brandon and finds value in a more muted approach to expression.

In *Sense and Sensibility*, more than one speaking style has merit; the same is true of different "style[s] of beauty." Similarly, there is no one correct beautiful style that should be used by every author.

Today, plain, unornamented styles are particularly valued. George Orwell famously said, "Never use a long word where a short one will do," and other authors and teachers eschew the use of all adverbs, and sometimes even adjectives.[4] Modern sentences and paragraphs tend to be shorter than those used by Austen. Yet even if we write shorter sentences or focus on concision, there is still room for stylistic variation. And many modern authors still use long words and sentences, as well as ornamentation, to achieve their storytelling goals. Regardless of what style we adopt, there is much we can do to develop and refine our styles and much that we can learn from Austen on how to do so.

While an entire book could be written on Austen's style and her use of stylistic devices, we'll take a more focused approach. Each of the elements we discussed in the stance chapter—including point of view, tone, diction, and showing and telling—can be considered a part of style. In this chapter we'll analyze Austen's use of sentence structure, rhythm, and punctuation as part of her style kit, and we'll discuss the principles for applying her techniques to our own stories.

---

4. Orwell, "Politics and the English Language."

SENTENCE STRUCTURE AND RHYTHM

So much of the joy that comes from reading Austen is due to her use of sentence structure and rhythm. While we often think of rhythm in poetry, rhythm is also an innate part of prose. Language—even written language—is inherently connected to speech, to sound, and to verbal expression. It's clear from Austen's letters that she realized this: Whenever she critiqued the writing of others, she talked of reading their works aloud, and it's likely that she did so for her own writing as well. While prose should generally not be as marked as poetry—for example, it should not necessarily use iambic pentameter or overflow with literary devices—the general principles are the same. Sentence structure and rhythm determine our reading experience.

Let's analyze a sentence from *Pride and Prejudice*. Elizabeth has been invited to spend time at Pemberley, and she is conversing with Miss Darcy, Miss Bingley, and several other women. She feels conflicted because she doesn't know if Mr. Darcy is present. Consider how the rhythm and the syntax convey emotion and anticipation:

> She wished, she feared, that the master of the house might be amongst them; and whether she wished or feared it most, she could scarcely determine.

There's a rhythmic repetition—"she wished, she feared"—and then both verbs are repeated after the semicolon, and we feel ourselves waffling with Elizabeth. Structurally, the sentence is balanced, yet it conveys imbalance and uncertainty.

Elizabeth and the Gardiners watch out the window as Mr. Darcy approaches the inn. Illustration by Hugh Thomson, 1894.

In another passage, after leaving Pemberley, Elizabeth and her aunt Mrs. Gardiner avoid speaking about the subject that most interests them both:

> They talked of his sister, his friends, his house, his fruit, of everything but himself; yet Elizabeth was longing to know what Mrs. Gardiner thought of him, and Mrs. Gardiner would have been highly gratified by her niece's beginning the subject.

The first clause contains a list, which moves from higher to lesser importance—sister, friends, house, and fruit. The list omits the word *and*, explaining that they're speaking of "everything but himself." The omission of "and" helps create a building sensation, as they move further and further from the ideal subject. The semicolon invites us to consider how the latter half of the sentence relates to the first, and indeed, in the second half of the sentence, we find that Mr. Darcy truly is forefront in both of their minds. Their focus on Mr. Darcy is presented by repeating Elizabeth and Mrs. Gardiner's names, but it's not just a straightforward repetition of Elizabeth and Mrs. Gardiner thinking about Mr. Darcy; the second time, their names are repeated in reverse order—Elizabeth-Mrs. Gardiner, Mrs. Gardiner-Elizabeth (with a variation—instead of repeating Elizabeth's name, the word "niece" is substituted).

In this, as in the previous example, Austen takes advantage of sentence structure and rhythm by creating patterns and expectations. In studying pattern recognition, psychologists and neuroscientists have found that patterns are an essential way that our brains process and store information. Of particular relevance to writing are the studies on music.

A 2011 study in *Nature Neuroscience* explains that when a person finds pleasure in music, it is accompanied by physical changes in the body, including in breathing patterns, heart rate, and body temperature. Some of the pleasure comes at the big moments of musical resolution, but pleasure is also built during the anticipation period. And anticipation is only possible if the listener understands musical patterns. Following standard patterns engages the listener, but the researchers also found that "delaying the predicted outcome" and "violating expectations" can actually increase the listener's emotional investment.[5]

In other words, structure and patterns make sense of a musical work, but it is the changes and variations and that which is unexpected that make us *love* a particular musical work. Difference and distinction draw us in.

As readers, we also crave patterns, both at the macro level of plot structure and at the micro, sentence level, which we'll focus on here. Reading pleasure comes from following, varying, and occasionally breaking sentence patterns.

There are many standard sentence patterns in English, the most basic of which is the following:

Subject + Verb

---

5. Salimpoor et al., "Anatomically distinct dopamine release," 261.

To that, we can add direct and indirect objects. We can insert modifiers before, after, or even between subjects and verbs. We can combine two independent clauses into a single sentence, or we can combine an independent clause and a dependent clause. We can build sentences of one or two words or sentences of over a hundred. These patterns make language comprehensible, but they're also structures that can and should be played with. As we play with structure and rhythm, we impact the content of the story and how it is received.

On September 15, 1813, Jane Austen wrote a letter to her sister Cassandra, but she had a defective pen. This pen made it more difficult to write, and it consciously impacted her sentence style.

> Edward finds his quarters very snug and quiet. I must get a softer pen. This is harder. I am in agonies. I have not yet seen Mr. Crabbe. Martha's letter is gone to the post.
>
>   I am going to write nothing but short sentences. There shall be two full stops in every line. Layton and Shear's is Bedford House. We mean to get there before breakfast if it's possible; for we feel more and more how much we have to do and how little time. This house looks very nice. It seems like Sloane Street moved here. I believe Henry is just rid of Sloane Street. Fanny does not come, but I have Edward seated by me beginning a letter, which looks natural.[6]

It's almost jolting to read Jane Austen writing so many short sentences since her normal writing style leans toward long, developed sentences. We also see how tedious a paragraph can become when every sentence is of similar length and begins in similar ways. Yet even though her pen makes it difficult to write more than a short phrase, Austen begins varying her sentences, adding a semicolon in one spot, a dependent clause in another, and beginning the sentences in different ways. The prose feels more Austenesque, the letter more alive.

In our own writing, it's important to vary the sentence length in our paragraphs in order to avoid a clunky, unnecessarily repetitive feel and to create a more pleasurable reading experience. Sometimes I naturally vary my sentences, yet at other times I must consciously

---

6. Jane Austen to Cassandra Austen, September 15, 1813. *Letters of Jane Austen*.

do so during revisions. Here are a few techniques that can help you improve your sentence length and rhythm:

- **Read a passage aloud.** It's much easier to notice sentence and paragraph rhythm when we hear it. It can also be useful to have someone read your writing aloud to you—they won't correct a sentence for what you meant to say, in terms of focus, rhythm, clarity, or punctuation.
- **Look for emphasis.** Where do the sentences and paragraphs place the focus? Does the sentence structure emphasize the most important content? Often, there is a natural emphasis or weight at the end of a sentence or the end of a paragraph.
- **Count the number of words in each sentence.** If all the sentences are a similar length, see if you can use different structures, break them in different ways, or combine two sentences.

Even when Austen uses primarily long sentences, her paragraphs are filled with variation. She often uses the contrast in sentence length to create emphasis. For instance, in *Northanger Abbey*, after Catherine's friend Isabella becomes engaged to her brother James, Isabella begins to treat James differently, for she is no longer trying to win him. Most notably, she flirts readily with Henry Tilney's elder brother, Captain Tilney:

> But when Catherine saw her in public, admitting Captain Tilney's attentions as readily as they were offered, and allowing him almost an equal share with James in her notices and smiles, the alteration became too positive to be passed over. What could be meant by such unsteady conduct, what her friend could be at, was beyond her comprehension. Isabella could not be aware of the pain she was inflicting; but it was a degree of wilful thoughtlessness which Catherine could not but resent. James was the sufferer. She saw him grave and uneasy; and however careless of his present comfort the woman might be who had given him her heart, to *her* it was always an object. For poor Captain Tilney too she was greatly concerned.

This passage contains six sentences, each of different word length, in the following order:

- 40 words
- 18 words
- 25 words
- 4 words
- 29 words
- 9 words

The excerpt begins with a long sentence (at 40 words) and has three medium-length sentences (at 18, 25, and 29 words). These long and medium sentences are contrasted by two short sentences:

James was the sufferer.

For poor Captain Tilney too she was greatly concerned.

Because of their relative shortness, these sentences receive more emphasis—they draw the reader's notice. From a storytelling standpoint, these two sentences mark Catherine's growing awareness that she must learn to better read people. She cannot always trust the motives of others; she must make her own judgments. Here, she begins to do so because of her concern for the well-being of others. One short sentence about James. One short sentence about Captain Tilney. She has yet to fully apply this judgment to others' motives for her, yet through the sentence variation, we sense Catherine's progress on her internal journey.

Emphasis can be created not just in varying sentence length but also in varying the length of paragraphs. In *Pride and Prejudice,* as Elizabeth tours Pemberley she feels quite self-conscious. She's forced to reflect on how highly the servants value Mr. Darcy's character. When Elizabeth and her aunt and uncle leave Pemberley, they run into Darcy—twice. Note how long each paragraph is, starting with the paragraph in which Elizabeth leaves the house:

- Paragraph 1: 37 words (Elizabeth and the Gardiners leave Pemberley.)
- Paragraph 2: 52 words (They look back and glimpse Mr. Darcy.)

- Paragraph 3: 72 words (Mr. Darcy notices Elizabeth and speaks to her.)
- Paragraph 4: 207 words (Elizabeth and Mr. Darcy converse, and Elizabeth reflects.)
- Paragraph 5: 25 words (Mr. Darcy struggles; he leaves.)
- Paragraph 6: 235 words (The Gardiners talk about Darcy while Elizabeth feels all the emotions.)
- Paragraph 7: 187 words (Elizabeth doesn't really pay attention to the scenery.)
- Paragraph 8: 25 words (Elizabeth decides to act normally.)
- Paragraph 9: 487 words (They go into the woods and meet Mr. Darcy a second time.)

The first four paragraphs create a building sensation as the lengths of the paragraphs increase. We move from leaving the place that embodies Mr. Darcy, to seeing the man himself, to speaking with him. Then, a sudden drop, with a paragraph of 25 words:

> At length, every idea seemed to fail him; and after standing a few moments without saying a word, he suddenly recollected himself, and took leave.

Darcy's struggle to know what to do and how to act is emphasized by the use of this short paragraph. This is followed by two longer paragraphs, in which Elizabeth's feelings are greatly developed. While she converses with her aunt and uncle in a compelling setting, we don't learn much of either the conversation or the setting: The focus is on Elizabeth's thoughts. This is followed by another short paragraph, also of exactly 25 words:

> At length, however, the remarks of her companions on her absence of mind roused her, and she felt the necessity of appearing more like herself.

Both 25-word paragraphs begin with the words "at length," and both involve a character trying to move past their romantic feelings and behave in a socially acceptable manner. The parallels between these paragraphs paint Elizabeth and Darcy as similar—equal—and set up the next paragraph, the longest paragraph, what the entire scene has built to, as Elizabeth and Mr. Darcy meet and speak again. Both characters, in their short paragraphs, have attempted to move away from each other (physically or emotionally). But now, a lengthy paragraph brings them back together. The entire chapter is a masterclass in style and sentence structure and variation and how they can be used to compellingly convey a story.

Every single passage of Austen could be analyzed for sentence structure and rhythm. Most of the time, we enjoy and benefit from these techniques subconsciously—they subtly impact the reading experience. Yet on occasion, I like to read a favorite scene or book with a focus primarily on style. Paying conscious attention to the choices an author makes in terms of sentence structure and rhythm, from a micro to a macro level, tends to improve my own ability to write compelling sentences with emphasis, variability, and deeper meaning.

Exercise 13.2: Sentence Imitation

Find a compelling sentence, with beautiful rhythm, a pointed focus, or a noteworthy technique. This sentence could be by Austen or another author.

Imitate the sentence in structure or form. You can do a close imitation, sticking to particular rhythms and forms, or you can write a loose imitation, using a general technique in your own way.

Now repeat the exercise as many times as you'd like.

Exercise 13.3: Varying Sentence Length

Write a paragraph about your day. As you do so, focus on creating variation in your sentence lengths. It's important to note that sentences with close to the same number of words (for example, if they all have seven, eight, or nine words) will all feel about the same length to readers—greater contrast is needed for it to feel rhythmically different. Try to use variation to create emphasis: In addition to creating more subtle variations, you might also use one very short sentence among medium and long sentences or one very long sentence among medium and short sentences.

Once you've finished, read the paragraph aloud to get a feel for the rhythm you've created.

Exercise 13.4: Content and Paragraph Breaks

Analyze a scene that you have written that is particularly important in your story. Consider how you could break the paragraphs differently. What is the overall structure and feel of the scene? What are you building to? Can you use the rhythm of the paragraphs, and variation between the paragraphs, to reflect the content?

Exercise 13.5: Read Your Manuscript Aloud

Follow Austen's example and read your work aloud! You can do so for a short story, a chapter, or an entire book. As you do so, mark corrections and changes, and feel free to pause and revise. Many writers find this easier to do with a printed copy of the manuscript, but you can also do it digitally. This can be a time-intensive revision technique, but it's often the best way to catch errors and improve sentence structure and rhythm.

Exercise 13.6: Stylistic Analysis

Choose three books by different authors that you like who all share the same genre (ideally, this should be the genre you write). Each of these books should be recent—published within the last five to ten years. Choose two to three pages of each book to analyze.

First, look for standout sentences in each book, in terms of structure, rhythm, or content. Copy down each sentence in a notebook, and then jot down a few notes on what makes each sentence effective.

Second, analyze sentence length and variation for your selection. It might be helpful to make a chart as follows:

BOOK 1 TITLE:	PAGE NUMBERS ANALYZED:
Paragraph 1	
Paragraph length (total number of words):	
Number of sentences:	
Length of each sentence:	
Average sentence length:	

Document this information for each paragraph in the passage.

Once you've done this for each of the paragraphs, do a few more calculations for the section as a whole:

Overall	
Average sentence length:	
Shortest sentence:	
Longest sentence:	
Shortest paragraph:	
Longest paragraph:	

Once you've analyzed the first book, do the same for two to three pages from the other two books you selected. What do you learn about each author's style based on their similarities and differences? What do you learn about the genre?

Bonus step: Take several pages of your own writing and do the same analysis, first looking for standout sentences, and second, analyzing for sentence length and variation. How does your own story align with and diverge from the other authors in your genre?

This exercise can be labor intensive, and it may force you to use a calculator. However, I have found it to be one of the most useful exercises to improve my own writing.[7]

PUNCTUATION

Inseparably connected to sentence structure and rhythm is punctuation. Punctuation influences how a text should be read and interpreted, and it can create the rhythm we desire in our sentence structures. Punctuation marks can also imitate the natural pauses of speaking.

Often punctuation is dismissed as mere mechanics. When I've taught first-year writing classes at various universities, punctuation is often seen as a necessary evil—important in order to make

---

7. This exercise was inspired by an exercise in Martha Kolln's *Rhetorical Grammar* (34–35), which was itself inspired by a study by Edward P. J. Corbett

writing comprehensible, but miserable for both teachers and writers. Then I read the book *Rhetorical Grammar*, which posits that grammar and punctuation are powerful tools to achieve writing goals, less about restrictions than opportunities.[8] Austen uses punctuation joyfully, experimentally, and masterfully, and we can as well. (Note: Some conventions for punctuation marks have changed in the last two hundred years, and some editions of Austen modernize the punctuation. For the passages quoted in this section, I've used the punctuation from the first editions of her novels.)

Austen wields even the most commonplace punctuation to great effect. The period is the most ubiquitous mark and the first punctuation children learn in school. We use periods so frequently that we often forget their power. Periods indicate a pause, a *full stop*. In Austen's hands, a period can create breath, add emphasis, show something is complete, and even disrupt.

In *Persuasion*, while Anne is staying at her sister Mary's cottage, she learns that Captain Wentworth has agreed to join them for breakfast. But then the event changes locations. Notice the power of the periods in both ending and building thoughts, and notice how the periods combine with commas in the final sentence to emphasize Anne's feelings and reflections:

> Anne understood it. He wished to avoid seeing her. He had enquired after her, she found, slightly, as might suit a former slight acquaintance, seeming to acknowledge such as she had acknowledged, actuated, perhaps, by the same view of escaping introduction when they were to meet.

The first two periods create a strong emphasis on her realization: The full stop after "he wished to avoid seeing her" symbolizes that their relationship is also at a full stop. The final sentence is long but to the same effect: The commas build up the distance between them, layering their difficulties as their meeting is postponed. The periods and commas are also intrinsically connected to the rhythm of the paragraph.

As seen in the above passage, Austen shows a keen awareness of the impact of punctuation. Let's consider three overarching lessons that she can teach us on using punctuation in our own storytelling.

---

8. Kolln, *Rhetorical Grammar*.

1. USE PUNCTUATION WITH PURPOSE.

Use punctuation not only to create clarity and conform to standard conventions and correctness, but also to:

- Show *how* a character is speaking
- Express character
- Create emphasis and focus our attention
- Provide commentary

In *Emma*, three em dashes are used in Harriet's dialogue to convey her nervousness as she tells Emma that she likes Mr. Knightley and thinks he might return the sentiment:

> "Therefore, it seems as if such a thing even as this, may have occurred before—and if I should be so fortunate, beyond expression, as to—if Mr. Knightley should really—if *he* does not mind the disparity, I hope, dear Miss Woodhouse, you will not set yourself against it, and try to put difficulties in the way."

These em dashes capture not only the pauses in Harriet's speech, but the way she attempts to build to her point and keeps backing away from it, due to her fear of her friend's reaction.

Austen often uses commas or semicolons with **parallel structure** by giving items in a list the same format or by using a similar structure on opposite sides of a semicolon. This improves readability, and for semicolons, it creates **balance** between the two halves of the sentence, inviting us to draw a connection between them. In *Sense and Sensibility*, Austen uses a loose parallel structure in multiple sentences to compare and contrast Sir John and his wife, Lady Middleton:

> Sir John was a sportsman, Lady Middleton a mother. He hunted and shot, and she humoured her children; and these were their only resources. Lady Middleton had the advantage of being able to spoil her children all the year round, while Sir John's independent employments were in existence only half the time.

This paragraph is followed by two sentences that run in a reverse parallel to each other in terms of both content and punctuation.

Let's read the sentences first and then analyze them in terms of structure and content:

> Lady Middleton piqued herself upon the elegance of her table, and of all her domestic arrangements; and from this kind of vanity was her greatest enjoyment in any of their parties. But Sir John's satisfaction in society was much more real; he delighted in collecting about him more young people than his house would hold, and the noisier they were the better was he pleased.

The first sentence talks about what brings Lady Middleton delight, uses a comma, talks more about her delight, uses a semicolon, and then talks about what brings her the greatest joy. You could write this:

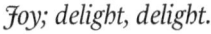

Delight, delight; joy.

The second sentence focuses on Sir John, but reverses the order. First, it talks about Sir John's overall satisfaction, or his joy, and then uses a semicolon. This is followed by something that delights him, a comma, and more detail about what delights him. You could write this:

Joy; delight, delight.

Sir John raises a glass to Elinor Dashwood.
Illustration by Hugh Thomson, 1896.

Thus, in these two sentences, Austen sets up a reverse parallel structure (*Delight, delight; joy. Joy; delight, delight.*) that allows the narrator to elaborate on the differences between the two individuals and posit Sir John's approach as superior: After all, his "satisfaction in society was much more real."

Austen often plays with punctuation and grammar to create a more focused, intense effect. For instance, in *Pride and Prejudice*, after Lydia and Wickham have run away, Elizabeth says to Jane,

> "Assistance is impossible; condolence, insufferable."

The semicolon creates **balance** between the two halves of the sentence, once again inviting us to draw a connection between them. This is coupled with the **omission** of the verb after the semicolon. By substituting the "is" with a comma after condolence, it places more emphasis on the statement and focuses us on the consequences. No one can help them or Lydia, and the inadequate condolences of others only have the power to cause more suffering.

Normally, a full independent clause needs to be on each side of a semicolon. Yet for hundreds of years, authors have artistically used this same sentence construction: the omission of a verb after a semicolon in two phrases with parallel construction. The frequency of this sentence construction makes it a rather standard nonstandard usage. If it became an extremely regular construction, it might lose its power, but for now it's an effective and common enough variation on the norm. As we discussed in the context of sentence structure and rhythm, we're engaged as readers when our expectations are disrupted.

In *Sense and Sensibility*, a double em dash is used to describe Edward Ferrars:

> But he was neither fitted by abilities nor disposition to answer
> the wishes of his mother and sister, who longed to see him dis-
> tinguished—as—they hardly knew what.

There is only a single word between the double em dash. The sentence could be written without the em dashes: "... who longed to see him distinguished, but they did not know as what" or "... who longed to see him distinguished, though how he should distinguish himself was less clear." Yet both would be inferior, and less

Austen's style. We see the movement, we feel them making their judgment, and the quick double em dash catches them in their thoughts, their inability to make him into something that would suit them. This punctuation provides commentary about Edward, his mother, and his sister, and reveals insights into his mother's and his sister's character.

Like Austen, we should use punctuation marks with purpose.

2. AT CRUCIAL MOMENTS IN THE STORY, PARTICULARLY THOSE OF GREAT EMOTIONAL INTENSITY, A GREATER NUMBER OF PUNCTUATION MARKS CAN BE USED TO MORE POWERFULLY CONVEY ACTIONS AND EMOTIONS. INNOVATIVE USES OF PUNCTUATION CAN ALSO BE APPROPRIATE FOR THESE DISTINCTIVE MOMENTS.

In Chapter 7, as we discussed emotions, we saw how effectively Austen uses punctuation to give emotional clues to the reader. Let's look at another example, this time from *Sense and Sensibility*. In this passage, Elinor tries to convince Marianne to not jump to too many conclusions about her relationship with Edward. Marianne's excessive exclamations demonstrate how thoroughly Elinor has failed at her objective:

> "I do not attempt to deny," said [Elinor], "that I think very highly of him—that I greatly esteem, that I like him."
>
> Marianne here burst forth with indignation—
>
> "Esteem him! Like him! Cold-hearted Elinor! Oh! worse than cold-hearted! Ashamed of being otherwise. Use those words again, and I will leave the room this moment."

The exclamation marks both convey Marianne's emotions and create a window into who she is as a person.

Now let's consider a passage in *Persuasion* where Austen uses a number of punctuation marks: periods, commas, em dashes, exclamation marks, semicolons, and colons. While Captain Wentworth manages to escape breakfast with Anne, he cannot avoid her forever, and ultimately, he stops by the cottage. This is Anne and Wentworth's momentous first re-meeting, and it requires substantive punctuation. The passage begins with "a thousand feelings rush[ing] on Anne," and the subsequent punctuation helps us feel these thousand feelings as we watch their actions.

Mary, very much gratified by this attention, was delighted to receive him; while a thousand feelings rushed on Anne, of which this was the most consoling, that it would soon be over. And it was soon over. In two minutes after Charles's preparation, the others appeared; they were in the drawing-room. Her eye half met Captain Wentworth's; a bow, a curtsey passed; she heard his voice—he talked to Mary, said all that was right; said something to the Miss Musgroves, enough to mark an easy footing: the room seemed full—full of persons and voices—but a few minutes ended it. Charles shewed himself at the window, all was ready, their visitor had bowed and was gone; the Miss Musgroves were gone too, suddenly resolving to walk to the end of the village with the sportsmen: the room was cleared, and Anne might finish her breakfast as she could.

"It is over! it is over!" she repeated to herself again, and again, in nervous gratitude. "The worst is over!"

Semicolons stack a series of behaviors—Anne and Captain Wentworth's eyes meeting, and a brief bow and curtsey before his attention is given to others. Wentworth's subsequent actions are stacked between more semicolons. A double pair of em dashes capture an almost claustrophobic sensation felt by Anne: "The room seemed full—full of persons and voices—but a few minutes ended it." And then repeated exclamation marks emphasize the repetitious statements from the normally soft-spoken Anne as she gives release to all that has been wrapped up inside her: "It is over! it is over! … The worst is over!"

Using distinctive punctuation, or large amounts of punctuation, can be a powerful way to capture character emotions and place emphasis on important scenes.

3. You don't have to rigidly follow traditional usages or rules of punctuation.

There are many standard deviations from the normal conventions. You can use punctuation even when it's not strictly necessary, and you can also break the rules of punctuation for effect.

In the following excerpt from *Persuasion*, the comma in the first sentence is grammatically unnecessary:

Her brother and sister came back delighted with their new acquaintance, and their visit in general. There had been music, singing, talking, laughing, all that was most agreeable; charming manners in Captain Wentworth, no shyness or reserve; they seemed all to know each other perfectly, and he was coming the very next morning to shoot with Charles.

Without the first comma, the first sentence would read,

Her brother and sister came back delighted with their new acquaintance and their visit in general.

It's customary to avoid unnecessary punctuation, and the sentence works grammatically without the comma. It's not in dialogue, so the comma isn't imitating a natural pause in speech. Yet the comma serves to focus the sentence on *their new acquaintance*. The comma makes the "visit in general" more of an afterthought: It is Captain Wentworth that delights, and the comma reveals this to the reader.

One of the more common ways Austen departs from traditional punctuation usage is in lists. For example, if you're using commas in a list, the standard convention is to use a conjunction (often the word *and*) directly before the final item in the list. While Austen follows this convention in the majority of cases, at times she departs from it to shift the focus, the meaning, and the reading experience. Take, for example, this sentence from *Mansfield Park* that describes Maria Bertram:

Henry Crawford had destroyed her happiness, but he should not know that he had done it; he should not destroy her credit, her appearance, her prosperity too.

Austen omits the conjunction. Instead of "He should not destroy her credit, her appearance, and her prosperity too," we read, "He should not destroy her credit, her appearance, her prosperity too." Without an "and," Maria's resolve feels more final.

Some rule-breaking uses of punctuation and grammar are common enough that they have their own names. In this case, **asyndeton** is the term for omitting a conjunction before the final item. In other novels, Austen uses it for different effects. First, *Northanger Abbey*:

They arrived at Bath. Catherine was all eager delight;—her eyes were here, there, every where, as they approached its fine and striking environs.

The asyndeton makes us feel like Catherine's eyes, flitting here, there, everywhere without pause. In *Pride and Prejudice*, Elizabeth tells Mr. Wickham that she saw Colonel Fitzwilliam and Mr. Darcy for three weeks while they stayed at Rosings. She asks Wickham if he knows Colonel Fitzwilliam, and the asyndeton in the first phrase emphasizes the sudden, visible shifts in Wickham's facial expressions:

> He looked surprised, displeased, alarmed; but with a moment's recollection and a returning smile, replied, that he had formerly seen him often; and after observing that he was a very gentlemanlike man, asked her how she had liked him.

Elizabeth and Mr. Wickham discuss Colonel Fitzwilliam.
Illustration by C. E. Brock, 1895.

Austen also uses the reverse technique: **polysyndeton**, the use of extra conjunctions in a list. She uses this technique more rarely, but also to great effect. In *Persuasion*, the narrator describes Anne's older sister Elizabeth, and the additional *and*s emphasize the passage of time and how long Elizabeth has been performing her household duties:

> For thirteen years had she been doing the honours, and laying down the domestic law at home, and leading the way to the chaise and four, and walking immediately after Lady Russell out of all the drawing-rooms and dining-rooms in the country.

As writers, we should use devices such as asyndeton and polysyndeton sparingly; excessive unusual or distinctive uses of punctuation and grammar dilute their effect. Yet they—or even more experimental uses of punctuation and grammar—can be a useful seasoning for a scene.

Another nonstandard technique that Austen uses is not finishing her sentences. Seventeenth-century rhetoricians called this technique **aposiopesis**, meaning "to be silent." In these cases, we don't receive the ending we expect. At times, we're not given the anticipated punctuation mark (a period, question mark, or exclamation mark); at other times, the thought or idea does not have a chance to reach its predicted conclusion.

The most common place in which Austen does not finish a sentence is in dialogue, especially when characters interrupt each other. For instance, in *Emma*, Mrs. Weston and Emma argue about Frank Churchill's behavior:

> "Nay, dear Emma, now I must take his part; for though he has been wrong in this instance, I have known him long enough to answer for his having many, very many, good qualities; and—"
>
> "Good God!" cried Emma; not attending to her.

We also find aposiopesis when a character does not finish a thought or statement, leaving something unsaid. They might avoid stating something aloud or shift to a more socially acceptable statement. For instance, in *Pride and Prejudice*, Elizabeth tells Darcy what she has just learned from Jane's letters about Lydia and Wickham:

> "They are gone off together from Brighton. *You* know him too
> well to doubt the rest. She has no money, no connections, noth-
> ing that can tempt him to—she is lost forever."

Elizabeth never finishes the thought. "She has no money, no
connections, nothing that can tempt him to—" We are left hang-
ing. She might have said, "Nothing that can tempt him to marry
her. Nothing that can tempt him to do the right thing. Nothing
that can tempt him to treat her as of worth." But Elizabeth can't
say these things. Instead, she abandons her original sentence and
states the larger problem: *She is lost forever*.

Almost any convention or rule of punctuation and grammar
can be broken effectively—if done purposefully and sparingly, with
the reader in mind. If it feels accidental, unnatural, or excessive,
the reader will judge the writer as inept.

Austen clearly knows how to construct a sentence, yet at several points in *Emma* she uses **fragments**: incomplete sentences
without both subject and verb, or sentences that cannot stand on
their own. When Emma finds out that Frank Churchill has been
secretly engaged for the entire time they have known each other,
Emma declares,

> "How could he tell that he might not be making me in love with
> him?—very wrong, very wrong indeed."

Emma continues to ruminate, and as she does, she uses more
sentence fragments:

> "Mrs. Smallridge, too! Jane actually on the point of going as
> governess! What could he mean by such horrible indelicacy?
> To suffer her to engage herself—to suffer her even to think of
> such a measure!"

Austen also uses fragments outside of the dialogue, in the narration, to emphasize Emma's shock—even in Emma's mind, she
cannot put together a complete sentence:

> The rest of the day, the following night, were hardly enough
> for her thoughts.—She was bewildered amidst the confusion
> of all that had rushed on her within the last few hours. Every

moment had brought a fresh surprise; and every surprise must be matter of humiliation to her.—How to understand it all! How to understand the deceptions she had been thus practising on herself, and living under!—The blunders, the blindness of her own head and heart!

Punctuation is often a subtle part of writing style. But how you use punctuation, which marks you prefer, when you use more concentrated punctuation, and when and how you depart from norms and conventions all influence your writing as a whole.

Exercise 13.7: Punctuation Imitation

Choose one of your favorite sentences or paragraphs quoted from Austen in this section. Use this example as a model. Try to imitate the sentence's punctuation and grammar, but with your own content.

Like Exercise 13.2, this exercise is particularly useful for expanding your ability to write a wider variety of sentences. To extend this exercise, find your own sample sentences to emulate, from Austen or other authors.[9]

Exercise 13.8: Emotional Punctuation

Take a scene you have written that is a moment of great importance or emotional intensity. Revise the scene, trying to use more punctuation, a greater variety of punctuation, or punctuation in more distinctive ways.

Once you're finished, read both versions of the scene. Does the punctuation help carry the weight of the scene? Which changes do you want to keep, and which changes don't help the story?

---

9. A great resource that includes excellent sample sentences and exercises is *The Art of Styling Sentences* by Ann Longknife and K. D. Sullivan. Not only have I worked through the book myself, but I've assigned it as a textbook in college writing classes.

FEELING STYLISTICALLY CONFIDENT

Style is formed by the hundreds and thousands of individual choices made during the process of writing a story. We often think about it as the *form* of the storytelling. Style includes the stance, the use of language, and the sentence structure and rhythm. Moments of distinction and rhetorical devices also contribute to style, as do humor and irony; we'll discuss these techniques in depth in Chapters 14 and 15.

It's easy for style to feel overwhelming. It can be difficult to explain your own style or define what you'd like your style to be. At times, you might even feel like your style is inferior, inadequate, or unworthy. In *Mansfield Park*, Fanny questions her own writing style.

The scene is such: Henry Crawford has used his uncle's connections to secure a promotion for Fanny's beloved brother. This, of course, makes Fanny overjoyed. However, Henry immediately explains that he arranged this because of his feelings for Fanny. To her disbelief and horror, he proposes to her. Understanding his character, Fanny does not believe he actually desires to marry her, and she manages to leave his presence. But later in the day, Henry returns, with a letter from his sister Mary Crawford. Mary writes Fanny, congratulating her on her brother's promotion and encouraging her to marry Henry.

Fanny is shocked by the letter, and she doesn't believe that either Mary or Henry would want her to join their family. Moreover, she cannot believe that they are serious; "their habits and ways of thinking" seem so opposed to this sort of action, and she sees "all her own demerits." Before Henry leaves, he asks her to write a note in reply to Mary. Under pressure, Fanny obliges:

> She went accordingly to the table, where she was in the habit of writing for her aunt, and prepared her materials without knowing what in the world to say. She had read Miss Crawford's note only once, and how to reply to anything so imperfectly understood was most distressing. Quite unpractised in such sort of

note-writing, had there been time for scruples and fears as to style she would have felt them in abundance: but something must be instantly written; and with only one decided feeling, that of wishing not to appear to think anything really intended, she wrote ... in great trembling both of spirits and hand.

In her note, she expresses her gratitude to Mary for the congratulations on her brother's promotion, but she also dismisses the proposal and asks Mary not to mention it again. Finally, Henry leaves, and she reflects in more depth on the inadequacies of her writing style:

> She had no doubt that her note must appear excessively ill-written, that the language would disgrace a child, for her distress had allowed no arrangement; but at least it would assure them both of her being neither imposed on nor gratified by Mr. Crawford's attentions.

While Fanny feels that her writing is inadequate, as a reader, I find her response particularly suited to the occasion. Her rushed reply and lack of planned arrangement only makes it feel more genuine. Often, Fanny censors herself, not making her true opinions known. Yet in this letter, she stands up for herself and her thoughts, beliefs, and feelings. With more time and planning and crafting, that could have been lost. By using the immediate style at hand, without refining or questioning it, she is more open and direct.

In 1809, Jane Austen's sister Cassandra read part of Jane's work to Fanny Austen, who highly complimented it. After learning of this, Jane wrote to Cassandra, saying,

> I am gratified by her having pleasure in what I write, but I wish the knowledge of my being exposed to her discerning criticism may not hurt my style, by inducing too great a solicitude.[10]

Austen feared that she would lose or change her style if she worried too much about gaining the approval of others. Because style is, in part, a matter of taste, we can't please every reader, reviewer, or critique group member.

---

10. Jane Austen to Cassandra Austen, January 24, 1809. *Letters of Jane Austen.*

It can be useful to revise for style, to learn new stylistic techniques, and to consciously refine our writing style. But it's also possible to be too caught up in style. Like Fanny, sometimes what we need to say is best expressed when we're not focusing on how we're saying it. And like Austen, we can listen to others' feedback, but we also need to trust our own instincts and tastes and not be overly swayed by outside voices. As we mature as writers, our styles—the things that define us and make our writing distinct and powerful—will develop naturally.

CHAPTER FOURTEEN

DISTINCTION

"Jane Fairfax was very elegant, remarkably elegant…. Her height was pretty, just such as almost every body would think tall, and nobody could think very tall; her figure particularly graceful; her size a most becoming medium, between fat and thin, though a slight appearance of ill-health seemed to point out the likeliest evil of the two. Emma could not but feel all this; and then, her face—her features—there was more beauty in them altogether than she had remembered; it was not regular, but it was very pleasing beauty. Her eyes, a deep grey, with dark eye-lashes and eyebrows, had never been denied their praise; but the skin, which she had been used to cavil at, as wanting colour, had a clearness and delicacy which really needed no fuller bloom. It was a style of beauty, of which elegance was the reigning character, and as such, she must, in honour, by all her principles, admire it:—elegance, which, whether of person or of mind, she saw so little in Highbury. There, not to be vulgar, was distinction, and merit."

—*Emma*

In *Emma*, much of what makes Jane Fairfax beautiful and admirable are the attributes that distinguish her from the other women in the area. She's taller than average (though fortunately not too tall!). She's not as thin or as fat as others—she's a medium, but with "a slight appearance of ill-health" that marks her as different. Her deep grey eyes make her stand out, and her skin, while paler than that of other young women, has "a clearness and deli-cacy." As the narrator explains, her beauty "was not regular, but it was a very pleasing beauty." Jane's most salient trait, to Emma, is her elegance—both her physical elegance, and the elegance of her mind, which is seen "so little in Highbury." In Jane Fairfax, we see "distinction, and merit."

Jane Fairfax. Illustration by Hugh Thomson, 1896.

The most memorable styles are distinctive in some way. A person seen as stylish often wears clothes that feel original or are seen as superior in quality or brand. Their clothes might be fashion-for-ward or incorporate retro styles and vintage clothing. They might combine normal apparel in irregular ways, or they might stand out by adopting a classic look, uninfluenced by the trends of the day. It is the same with writing: We value distinctions in style. Austen's style is admirable because it shines, it moves us—her words and sen-tences and constructions carry us in ways that not all writing does.

In *Poetics*, Aristotle writes that "the perfection of style is to be clear without being [commonplace]."[1] He goes on to explain that it's a difficult balance to strike. "A certain infusion, therefore, of [distinctive] elements is necessary to style; for the strange (or rare) word, the metaphorical, the ornamental, and the other kinds [of devices] will raise it above the commonplace." Yet at the same time, we don't want to lose clarity or use so many devices that it becomes ludicrous, laughable, or grotesque. "By deviating in exceptional cases from the normal idiom, the language will gain distinction; while, at the same time, the partial conformity with usage will give perspicuity," or in other words, make the writing easy to understand.[2]

Throughout this section we'll consider techniques for distinction that we can incorporate in our own works. It's important to note that Austen didn't overuse any of these devices, and we should also avoid the temptation to do so. As Strunk and White write in their classic work, *Elements of Style*, "Use figures of speech sparingly." They go on to give an example: "The simile is a common device and a useful one, but similes coming in rapid fire, one right on top of another, are more distracting than illuminating."[3]

We're going to examine some of Austen's major approaches to creating distinctive writing, including substitution and repetition, as well as other rhetorical devices she uses, from anastrophe to zeugma. You can read this chapter from start to finish, or you're welcome to treat it as a reference. For many of the less common devices, definitions are quoted or paraphrased from Gideon Burton's online encyclopedia, *Silva Rhetoricae*. For devices without a reference, the definitions are my own.

---

1. Aristotle, *Poetics*.
In his translation, Butcher translates the final word in the sentence as "mean," but it's been over a hundred years since his translation, and now we rarely use the adjective "mean" to signify "shabby, lowly, or commonplace." Thus, for clarity, I've used the word "commonplace."
2. Aristotle, *Poetics*.
3. Strunk and White, *The Elements of Style*, 80.

SUBSTITUTION

Substitution is replacing an object, person, name, concept, or action with something else in order to better convey it or to inject additional commentary or insight. Austen often uses substitution to convey emotions, illuminate character, create irony, and focus us on important details.

Austen uses seven core rhetorical devices that substitute one thing for another. You'll find some of them familiar, like euphemism and metaphor; others, like periphrasis, are less well-known but just as well used by Austen. Each of these devices can be used in our own works.

EUPHEMISM: using a friendlier term for something that's typically unpleasant

In *Sense and Sensibility,* euphemisms are used to refer to old age and death. When we meet Colonel Brandon, we learn that

> his appearance however was not unpleasing, in spite of his being in the opinion of Marianne and Margaret an absolute old bachelor, for he was on the wrong side of five and thirty.

In this case, the unpleasant statement is included immediately before the euphemism: Colonel Brandon is "an absolute old bachelor." The addition of the euphemism creates irony, providing a commentary on Marianne and Margaret's perspective. In the chapter that follows, first Mrs. Dashwood adds a euphemism of her own, and then Marianne uses yet another euphemism, as they speak about death while avoiding the word.

> "My dearest child," said her mother, laughing, "at this rate you must be in continual terror of *my* decay; and it must seem to you a miracle that my life has been extended to the advanced age of forty."
>
> "Mama, you are not doing me justice. I know very well that Colonel Brandon is not old enough to make his friends yet apprehensive of losing him in the course of nature."

ANTONOMASIA: "substituting a descriptive phrase for a proper name, or substituting a proper name for a quality associated with it"[4]

In *Pride and Prejudice*, Elizabeth returns home after learning of Lydia and Wickham's elopement. Upon arriving at the house, she immediately goes to her sister Jane:

> Elizabeth, as she affectionately embraced her, whilst tears filled the eyes of both, lost not a moment in asking whether anything had been heard of the fugitives.

Lydia and Wickham's names are substituted with "the fugitives," which is how Elizabeth now sees them.

In *Sense and Sensibility*, instead of calling Willoughby by name, Margaret sometimes calls him "Marianne's preserver." This characteristic—that he saved Marianne—is forever associated with him in her mind.

PERIPHRASIS: using a roundabout way to describe something, which creates emphasis or context; closely related to antonomasia

In *Persuasion*, instead of being referred to as Charles Hayter, he is sometimes referred to as the "eldest son," which creates for him a certain amount of consequence:

> While the Musgroves were in the first class of society in the country, the young Hayters would, from their parents' inferior, retired, and unpolished way of living, and their own defective education, have been hardly in any class at all, but for their connexion with Uppercross, this eldest son of course excepted, who had chosen to be a scholar and a gentleman, and who was very superior in cultivation and manners to all the rest.

In *Pride and Prejudice*, when Mr. Collins proposes to Elizabeth, he refers to Lady Catherine in a roundabout way that shows how important she is in his life:

> "My reasons for marrying are, first, that I think it a right thing for every clergyman in easy circumstances (like myself) to set the example of matrimony in his parish; secondly, that I am

---

4. "Antonomasia," in Burton, *Silva Rhetoricae*.

convinced it will add very greatly to my happiness; and, thirdly, which perhaps I ought to have mentioned earlier, that it is the particular advice and recommendation of the very noble lady whom I have the honour of calling patroness."

Lady Catherine de Bourgh. Illustration by C. E. Brock, 1895.

Metonymy: substituting a word or a term with something that is related and commonly associated with it

In *Mansfield Park*, Henry Crawford declares,

> "I think too well of Miss Bertram to suppose she would ever give her hand without her heart."

Giving one's hand is commonly associated with marriage, and the heart is commonly associated with being in love, so he uses two substitutions to elegantly state that Miss Bertram wouldn't marry if she weren't in love.

Throughout the novel, Mansfield Park is often used to refer to the physical location: the building and its grounds. But Mansfield Park is also used as a substitute to refer to the Bertram family and the society that they keep at Mansfield Park; this is another use of metonymy.

Synecdoche: using a part of something to stand in for the whole item (or, occasionally, using the whole of something to represent a part of it)

In *Mansfield Park*, synecdoche is used to talk about wealth: A few exclusive items are used to represent all the luxuries that one would ideally possess. Mary Crawford says,

> "A large income is the best recipe for happiness I ever heard of. It certainly may secure all the myrtle and turkey part of it."

Later, Henry Crawford comments on the living that Edmund Bertram is about to take:

> "I am glad to hear Bertram will be so well off. He will have a very pretty income to make ducks and drakes with, and earned without much trouble."

Myrtle, turkey, ducks, and drakes symbolize wealth and luxuries to Mary and Henry Crawford.

Metaphor: using the properties of something else to help the reader better understand the properties of the original item, concept, or person

In *Pride and Prejudice*, after the tides turn against Wickham we read,

> All Meryton seemed striving to blacken the man, who, but three months before, had been almost an angel of light.

Calling Wickham an angel of light reveals how positively the town formerly perceived Wickham and adds extra emphasis to how far he has fallen. The metaphor also has religious connotations.

"The spiteful old ladies"

"The spiteful old ladies" of Meryton; they condemn both Mr. Wickham and Lydia Bennet. Illustration by Hugh Thomson, 1894.

In *Northanger Abbey*, as the narrator describes Catherine's uneventful journey to Bath, she uses a verb in a metaphorical way:

> Neither robbers nor tempests befriended them.

Befriended implies a sort of closeness or connection that could have been gained—this sort of experience would have been seen as a benefit by our adventurous heroine!

In *Mansfield Park*, food is used three times as a metaphor for something that inspires thought in Fanny. In nature, Fanny finds "food for a rambling fancy." Edmund and Miss Crawford's flirtations create "sorrowfull food for Fanny's observation." And when Fanny is kicked out of Mansfield Park, a letter provides "great food for meditation … and chiefly for unpleasant meditation." Using food as a metaphor makes Fanny's thoughts feel very physical.

SIMILE: a type of metaphor that uses the words *like* or *as* to make a comparison, once again inviting us to understand the attributes of one thing by substituting it with the attributes of another thing

In *Persuasion*, Sir Walter learns that his future tenant, Admiral Croft, has been stationed in the Indies.

> "Then I take it for granted," observed Sir Walter, "that his face is about as orange as the cuffs and capes of my livery."

This simile reveals much about Sir Walter's character and his perceptions of the Navy.

At a different point in the book, Anne reflects on her relative, Mr. Elliot:

> She had a great wish to see him. If he really sought to reconcile himself like a dutiful branch, he must be forgiven for having dismembered himself from the paternal tree.

Later, she learns more about Mr. Elliot's conduct from her friend Mrs. Smith, but she has no immediate opportunity to speak with him:

> Mr. Elliot's character, like the Sultaness Scheherazade's head, must live another day.

This final simile is also an **allusion**, a reference to a work outside of the text that readers are likely familiar with and that adds to the reader's understanding.

Exercise 14.1: The Perfect Metaphor

It's easy to create metaphors—with a little effort, almost anything can be turned into a metaphor for something else. But Aristotle writes that it's hard to create a truly good metaphor, in which the connections and resemblances between the two items or things are revelatory. According to Aristotle, being able to do so is "the mark of genius."[5]

Choose a person that you know and create four metaphors that explain something about their personality or one of their characteristics.

Now evaluate your metaphors: Which one is the most expressive, useful, and apt? What makes it superior to the others?

Exercise 14.2: Playing with Substitution

Choose a passage that you have written. It could be a paragraph or a full scene. Rewrite the passage, trying to incorporate as many types of substitution as possible:

- Euphemism
- Antonomasia
- Periphrasis
- Metonymy
- Synecdoche
- Metaphor
- Simile

What is the effect of using substitution? How does it change the passage? Which substitutions improved the passage, and which did not?

Note which type of substitution you found most challenging. As a bonus exercise, write more examples that use this sort of substitution.

---

5. Aristotle, *Poetics*.
Austen uses her metaphors sparingly, but when she does so, they always feel genius to me.

REPETITION

Repetition is repeating or restating sounds, words, or phrases for effect. Most of the time repetition should be avoided in writing; unintentional repetition is almost always grating to the reader, and even intentional repetition can feel redundant and unnecessarily repetitive. (I will leave it to you to decide if the repeated uses of the words "repetition," "repeating," and "repetitive" in the previous two sentences were wise!) However, when used well, repetition can be powerful. Austen often uses it in moments of intense emotion and revelation. She also uses it as a form of wordplay, to provide clever commentary, and to create emphasis.

There are seemingly endless types of repetition; we'll consider just a few.

ALLITERATION: repeating the same sound at the start of multiple words

Alliteration draws attention to the phrasing, and when well used, it can be soothing or jarring, witty or memorable. It can also provide insight or commentary.

Several related figures of speech deal with using similar sounds, including **sibilance** (repetition of the *s* sound), **assonance** (repeating vowel sounds), and **consonance** (repeating similar consonant sounds). These repeated sounds do not have to be at the start of words; they can also occur within words.

Most of the time when Austen uses alliteration, she uses memorable two-word phrases, such as "**d**eepest **d**isgrace" in *Pride and Prejudice*. In *Mansfield Park*, Mrs. Norris tells Fanny, "You must be the **l**owest and **l**ast," two negative, insulting words that both begin with the letter *l*. Normally, *l* creates a soft, friendly sound, but not when Mrs. Norris uses it. In *Sense and Sensibility*, when Marianne talks about marriage positively, she uses the phrase "**f**uture **f**elicity"; when she speaks of it negatively, she uses hard *c* sounds—"**c**ompact of **c**onvenience."

At times Austen does use longer alliterations. In *Pride and Prejudice*, Mrs. Bennet moans, "**S**uch **s**pasms in my **s**ide." In *Mansfield Park*, Henry Crawford wants to give Fanny the news that her brother has returned, but she has already received a letter with the information: "All those **fine first f**eelings, of which he had hoped to be the exciter, were already given." And at times we find consonance, such as in *Sense and Sensibility*, when Marianne and Margaret are "attracted by the par**t**ial **sun**shine of a **sh**owery **s**ky." Using multiple *sh* and *s* sounds draws attention to the artistry of the landscape and creates an artistic parallel in the words.

POLYPTOTON: "repeating a word, but in a different form"[6]

This is particularly effective for providing commentary, elaborating on or exploring an idea, or making a strong point.

In *Pride and Prejudice*, Mrs. Bennet declares, "if they are not married already, *make* them marry." Married and marry are two forms of the same word, and repeating it in different forms adds emphasis to what Mrs. Bennet sees as the only solution for the Wickham-Lydia problem.

Not long later in *Pride and Prejudice*, we see two forms of the word anxiety:

> Every day at Longbourn was now a day of anxiety; but the most anxious part of each was when the post was expected.

The second usage clarifies the first, elaborating on what makes every day a day of anxiety.

In *Mansfield Park*, when Fanny sees her brother for the first time during his visit, she is overjoyed, yet the joy is complicated:

> It was some time even before her happiness could be said to make her happy, before the disappointment inseparable from the alteration of person had vanished, and she could see in him the same William as before, and talk to him, as her heart had been yearning to do through many a past year.

What a telling commentary that expresses so much emotion: "It was some time ... before her happiness could be said to make her happy."

---

6. "Polyptoton," in Burton, *Silva Rhetoricae*.

SYNONYMIA: a different sort of repetition, in which it is not words that are repeated, but ideas; specifically, the use of multiple synonyms in the same sentence

Synonymia is useful for creating emphasis, exploring a depth of feeling, or providing a lens into a character's perspective.

In *Mansfield Park*, Miss Crawford uses several synonyms for the word *happy* when speaking to Fanny:

> "Come, come, it would be very un-handsome in us to be severe on Mrs. Rushworth, for I look forward to our owing her a great many gay, brilliant, happy hours."

Gay, brilliant, and happy are all synonyms in this context, and it emphasizes that one of her priorities in a relationship is what she hopes to receive from it—she already anticipates receiving many hours of happiness from Mrs. Rushworth.

REPEATING WORDS AND PHRASES: There are endless ways to repeat words and phrases, including **anadiplosis** (repeating the final word or phrase of a sentence at the beginning of the next), **anaphora** (repeating words at the beginning of sentences or phrases), **epistrophe** (repeating words at the end of sentences or phrases), **antanaclasis** (repeating the same word, but with an implied different meaning), **epizeuxis** (repeating a word multiple times in a row, with no other words between), **traductio** ("repeating the same word variously throughout a sentence or thought"), **epanodos** (repeating the same words to reemphasize a point or provide more information; sometimes the words in a phrase are repeated in reverse order, such as in the idiom "what's mine is yours, and what's yours is mine"), and **diacope** ("repetition of a word with one or more between, usually to express deep feeling").[7] The possibilities are endless for how these and other types of repetition can be used. And as long as they are saved for key moments and used with care, they can create a multitude of effects.

---

7. "Figures of Repetition," in Burton, *Silva Rhetoricae*.
All of these definitions for figures of repetition are either direct quotations or paraphrases from Burton's incredible *Silva Rhetoricae*. For "epanodos," Burton focuses on the implications of this sort of repetition for an audience rather than focusing on the reverse order, which some definitions favor.

Most of Austen's chapters contain very little repetition; she often saves repetition for scenes of great intensity or import, and then she uses it in concentrated form. One such scene occurs when Elizabeth tells Mr. Darcy that Lydia has run off with Wickham:

"When I consider," she added, in a yet more agitated voice, "that *I* might have prevented it! *I* who knew what he was. Had I but explained some part of it only—some part of what I learnt, to my own family! Had his character been known, this could not have happened. But it is all, all too late now."

"I am grieved, indeed," cried Darcy: "grieved—shocked. But is it certain, absolutely certain?"

Elizabeth speaks to Mr. Darcy after learning of Lydia's elopement.
Illustration by Hugh Thomson, 1894.

Elizabeth's distress at her own responsibility builds as she repeats the word *I*. She uses short, somewhat broken sentences, full of em dashes and asides and repetition: "It is all, all too late now." Darcy also uses repetition in his reply, repeating *grieved* twice, and then providing a contrasting emotion: *shocked*. Then he repeats the word *certain* with another word in between, because he can't quite believe it. Later in the scene he uses repetition in his phrasing ("what has been," "what has been,") as he asks Elizabeth a question:

> "And what has been done, what has been attempted, to recover her?"

As part of her response, Elizabeth says,

> "Nothing can be done; I know very well that nothing can be done."

As the scene continues, Elizabeth laments,

> "When *my* eyes were opened to his real character, oh! had I known what I ought, what I dared to do! But I knew not—I was afraid of doing too much. Wretched, wretched mistake!"

In *Emma*, repetition is also used to express high emotion, such as when Harriet says to Emma,

> "Such a change! In one moment such a change! From perfect misery to perfect happiness."

In *Mansfield Park*, as Fanny and Miss Crawford walk through the gardens, enjoying the improvements made to them, Fanny expresses her joy:

> "Perhaps, in another three years, we may be forgetting—almost forgetting what it was before. How wonderful, how very wonderful the operations of time, and the changes of the human mind!"

At another point in the novel, Mr. Crawford exclaims that he was never happier than when working on the play. Fanny's repetition conveys her condemnation and emphasizes her reflections:

With silent indignation Fanny repeated to herself, "Never happier!—never happier than when doing what you must know was not justifiable!—never happier than when behaving so dishonourably and unfeelingly! Oh! what a corrupted mind!"

Exercise 14.3: Different Forms and Different Synonyms

Practice using two of the less common types of repetition: polyptoton and synonymia.

Create at least two sentences that include polyptoton (using the same word in multiple forms; for example, using anxious and anxiety in the same sentence, or family and familial).

Create at least two sentences that include synonymia (using multiple synonyms for the same word). Try to make sure the use of synonymia doesn't make the sentence feel redundant—you might, for instance, choose synonyms which add new insight or express something about a character. This can be used in narration or in dialogue.

Exercise 14.4: Repetition in an Intense Scene

Write a short scene that feels intense for at least one of the characters. Use repetition of words and phrases to capture that intensity—in dialogue, in the narration, or in both.

OTHER DISTINCTIVE FIGURES OF SPEECH

In addition to substitution and repetition, Austen plays with language in many other distinctive ways, using a number of other stylistic and rhetorical devices. Here are a few that can also be useful to writers today:

ANASTROPHE: reversing the normal word order, which changes the rhythm and allows the writer to add extra details to supplement the adjective; often done by placing an adjective after a noun, rather than before

In *Pride and Prejudice*, after reading Jane's letters about Lydia, Elizabeth reflects,

> She was wild to be at home—to hear, to see, to be upon the spot to share with Jane in the cares that must now fall wholly upon her, in a family so deranged; a father absent, a mother incapable of exertion, and requiring constant attendance.

Instead of "deranged family," the narrator uses "family so deranged"; instead of "absent father," "a father absent"; instead of "incapable mother," "a mother incapable of exertion, and requiring constant attendance."

CORRECTIO: when an individual corrects themselves;[8] often occurring in dialogue, though it can also occur in narration

In *Northanger Abbey*, Miss Tilney corrects herself to make it sound like she is close to both of her brothers, rather than just one:

> "I have no sister, you know—and though Henry—though my brothers are very affectionate, and Henry is a great deal here, which I am most thankful for, it is impossible for me not to be often solitary."

---

8. "Correctio," in Burton, *Silva Rhetoricae*.

In *Sense and Sensibility,* Elinor attempts to explain to Marianne why she is not putting all her hopes into a relationship with Edward. She corrects herself to make her doubts seem smaller:

> "In my heart I feel little—scarcely any doubt of his preference."

OXYMORON: juxtaposing two opposites or extremes

In *Northanger Abbey,* General Tilney speaks of Mr. Allen, who he falsely believes is rich:

> "He is a happy man!" said the general, with a look of very happy contempt.

Happy contempt is an oxymoron—the words are opposites, expressing very different emotions. This reveals the general's envy and also his satisfaction that if his son marries Catherine (who he believes will inherit Mr. Allen's fortune), then at least his son will have access to this wealth.

General Tilney pacing. Illustration by C. E. Brock, 1907.

In *Mansfield Park*, Miss Crawford uses an oxymoron when she doesn't receive the reaction she expects from Edmund and Mrs. Grant:

> "Upon my word," cried Miss Crawford, "you are two of the most disappointing and unfeeling kind friends I ever met with! There is no giving you a moment's uneasiness."

This use of an oxymoron—"disappointing and unfeeling kind friends"—creates humor and makes Miss Crawford likable, for even when she's feeling contrary, she expresses it in a light and entertaining manner.

CLICHE: a trite, overdone, and overused phrase

Sometimes cliched phrases began as innovative metaphors or original insights, but through repetition over years, decades, and centuries of use, they lost all meaning. Generally, cliches should be avoided.

In *Sense and Sensibility*, Marianne explains why and how to avoid cliches:

> "It is very true," said Marianne, "that admiration of landscape scenery is become a mere jargon. Every body pretends to feel and tries to describe with the taste and elegance of him who first defined what picturesque beauty was. I detest jargon of every kind, and sometimes I have kept my feelings to myself, because I could find no language to describe them in but what was worn and hackneyed out of all sense and meaning."

When Austen *does* use cliches, it is to comment or critique them, or to characterize an individual as the type of person who would use cliches. In *Sense and Sensibility*, Marianne inquires of Sir John to learn more of Mr. Willoughby.

> "Aye, aye, I see how it will be," said Sir John, "I see how it will be. You will be setting your cap at him now, and never think of poor Brandon."
>
> "That is an expression, Sir John," said Marianne, warmly, "which I particularly dislike. I abhor every common-place phrase by which wit is intended; and 'setting one's cap at a man,' or

'making a conquest,' are the most odious of all. Their tendency is gross and illiberal; and if their construction could ever be deemed clever, time has long ago destroyed all its ingenuity."

The use—and abuse—of cliche becomes a key part of Marianne and Sir John's relationship, and it shows how opposed Marianne is to a relationship with Colonel Brandon.

"Dear, dear, Norland! when shall I cease to regret you"

Marianne says her goodbyes to Norland.
Illustration by Chris (Christiana) Hammond, 1899.

PERSONIFICATION: assigning the attributes of a person to something that is not a person (such as an object or place), often in order to reveal a character's relationship with the item or to create insight into a character's current state

In *Sense and Sensibility,* when the Dashwoods leave Norland, Marianne laments the loss of her home:

"Oh! happy house, could you know what I suffer in now viewing you from this spot, from whence perhaps I may view you
no more!"

Marianne sees the house as happy, though a house is not alive
and cannot feel emotions. Yet the house was a happy place for her,
and she feels that if it could sense emotions, it would understand
her suffering at having to leave it behind.

ZEUGMA: using a word to perform two different functions at the
same time; often employing a single verb to "yoke" or connect two
different types of nouns, thus using both a literal and metaphorical meaning of the verb

The most commonly cited example of Austen's use of zeugma
is found in *Pride and Prejudice*:

Yet time and her aunt moved slowly—and her patience and her
ideas were nearly worn out before the *tête-à-tête* was over.

This sentence uses zeugma twice. In "time and her aunt moved
slowly," it couples a physical and a metaphorical movement. The
slowness negatively impacts Elizabeth, creating a need for a second
use of zeugma in the sentence: Both Elizabeth's patience and her
ideas are worn out.

Another use of zeugma occurs near the end of *Pride and Prejudice*, after Bingley and Darcy have returned to Meryton, but before
any engagements have occurred. Bingley and Darcy have called
on the Bennets, and Mrs. Bennet has spent the time being kind
to Bingley and rude to Darcy. She wants to invite them to dine,

but, though she always kept a very good table, she did not think
anything less than two courses could be good enough for a man
on whom she had such anxious designs, or satisfy the appetite
and pride of one who had ten thousand a year.

On the subject of food, the verb *satisfy* is commonly used with
a noun such as *appetite*, but here, Mrs. Bennet worries about satisfying both his *appetite* and his *pride*. From her perspective, both
seem like equally daunting tasks.

One scholar, Octavia Cox, talks about how Austen's uses of zeugma act as a joke, both creating humor and adding insight.[9] We see this in an example from *Sense and Sensibility*. After Elinor and Edward's marriage, the narrator writes,

> They had in fact nothing to wish for, but the marriage of Colonel Brandon and Marianne, and rather better pasturage for their cows.

Cox explains, "Jane Austen uses zeugma here to jokily link together the serious—the welfare of Marianne and Colonel Brandon—and the comically domestic—better pasturage." While this linking is funny, in this, Cox sees some "latent cynicism. ... Colonel Brandon, after all, is the master of the Delaford estate and their patron. He is the owner of Delaford parsonage, the home of Elinor and Edward Ferrars." The use of zeugma to yoke marriage with better pasturage might imply that "they hope there might be a direct link between the two, that the former might lead to the latter."[10]

Zeugma fits well with Austen's storytelling stance and often adds humorous yet poignant commentary.[11]

PARALIPSIS: talking about something by stating that you won't talk about it; the very act of doing so draws attention to it[12]

Paralipsis can provide a way for characters to talk about something they shouldn't talk about. When used by narrators, it often creates irony.

In the final chapter of *Mansfield Park*, the narrator states, "Let other pens dwell on guilt and misery." Then the narrator immediately spends several paragraphs discussing the guilt and misery of a number of the story's characters.

In *Pride and Prejudice*, Elizabeth asks Mr. Wickham about Mr. Darcy's character:

---

9. Cox, "Jane Austen's Zeugma Jokes."

10. Cox, "Jane Austen's Zeugma Jokes."

11. We already discussed another example of zeugma in Chapter 8; in *Persuasion*, Anne is placed into a carriage by Captain Wentworth's "will and...hands."

12. "Paralipsis," in Burton, *Silva Rhetoricae*. This technique is sometimes called apophasis, though Burton distinguishes between the two terms.

"I have no right to give *my* opinion," said Wickham, "as to his being agreeable or otherwise. I am not qualified to form one. I have known him too long and too well to be a fair judge. It is impossible for *me* to be impartial."

It is clear that Mr. Wickham sees Mr. Darcy as not agreeable. His use of paralipsis to refuse to give his opinion only emphasizes it. Wickham then goes on to speak more of Mr. Darcy, explaining that it is Darcy's pride, selfishness, and spite that cost Wickham his inheritance.

Even if a character or the narrator immediately moves on to a new subject after stating that they won't talk about it, the point has been raised and attention drawn.

Exercise 14.5: Sampling Techniques

Choose at least three of the techniques discussed in this section that you either haven't used before or have used only rarely:[13]

- Anastrophe
- Correctio
- Oxymoron
- Zeugma
- Personification
- Paralipsis

Write sample sentences that use the techniques.

---

13. Note that I omitted cliches. Almost no writer needs to practice using cliches; instead, we must practice spotting them and removing them from our works. I often ask my critique partners to mark any cliches that I've included. Inevitably, I use them more than I'd like to.

OTHER APPROACHES TO DISTINCTION

Over the past centuries, rhetoricians have defined and codified hundreds of rhetorical devices that are used in speech and writing. This chapter contains just a tiny portion of the techniques used by authors, though, as a writer myself, these are some of the techniques that I find most useful.[14] We'll talk about more techniques for distinction in the next chapter when we discuss humor and irony. But distinction doesn't have to come by using a device with a fancy name inspired by Greek or Latin. Any time that you use language in an unexpected or unusual way, with a particular or focused effect, it acts as a figure of speech, separating the passage from the norm (whether it's the norm within the text or the norm in comparison to other writers). What makes a particular author's writing distinctive is an essential component of their style.

In an earlier chapter, we discussed Austen's juvenile nonfiction work, *The History of England*.[15] The text feels distinct on multiple levels—different than most histories (it is, after all, a pastiche) and different than her other works (she mostly wrote fiction). Even within the text, there are moments of distinction that stand out. In particular, I love the side commentaries the narrator makes. For example:

> During his reign, Lord Cobham was burnt alive, but I forget what for.

And:

> One of Edward's Mistresses was Jane Shore, who had a play written about her, but it is a tragedy & therefore not worth reading.

I also love the moments where Austen uses **direct address** to speak directly to the reader:

---

14. If you'd like to explore more techniques, I highly recommend wandering through Burton's *Silva Rhetoricae*.
15. Austen, *History of England*.

I suppose you know all about the Wars between him & the Duke of York who was of the right side; if you do not, you had better read some other History, for I shall not be very diffuse in this, meaning by it only to vent my Spleen *against*, & shew my Hatred *to* all those people whose parties or principles do not suit with mine, & not to give information.

At times Austen varies, and instead of speaking to the reader, speaks about the reader:

It would be an affront to my Readers were I to suppose that they were not as well acquainted with the particulars of this King's reign as I am myself. It will therefore be saving *them* the task of reading again what they have read before, & *myself* the trouble of writing what I do not perfectly recollect, by giving only a slight sketch of the principal Events which marked his reign.

Throughout the entire text, *The History of England* calls attention to its own distinction. Austen's novels generally use moments of distinction more subtly—as readers, we are meant to immerse ourselves in the storytelling, and rhetorical devices that are used (such as polysyndeton and metaphor) enhance the reading experience without drawing too much attention to themselves. As we write our own stories, we must choose how much distinction we want to use. Most of Austen's novels are like Jane Fairfax, who is described as tall for a woman, but not too tall—the novels use elements of distinction to stand out and yet do not overuse distinction to depart too far from normal conventions and usage.

Exercise 14.6: Varying Levels of Distinction

Choose an everyday task, like going grocery shopping or responding to work emails. Write a paragraph describing this task **without using any figures of speech or distinctive language**.

Now write a new paragraph describing this same task, this time using **as much distinctive language as possible**. Fill your text with figures of speech and other creative uses of language, sentence structure, and punctuation.

Finally, **write something in between**, with a style that Aristotle, Strunk and White, and Austen would approve of. It should include a few moments of distinction. If you'd like, you can reuse your favorite parts of the two original paragraphs.

Reflect on what you like and dislike about each of the paragraphs.

Exercise 14.7: Revising for Distinction

Revise a scene that you have written for a short story or a novel. Find one or two spots where it would be powerful to incorporate one of the figures of speech from any section of this chapter.

Exercise 14.8: The Distinction of a Favorite Author

Choose one of your favorite authors (besides Jane Austen). Make a list of some of the big-picture elements that make their writing stand out to you—things like plot or character or how they play with a genre.

Now look at their writing on a more granular level. Choose a scene or a chapter and look at what makes their writing distinct. This could be in terms of how they use sentences and paragraphs, their approach to adjectives and adverbs, and any rhetorical devices they use (like substitution, repetition, and other techniques discussed in this chapter).

Reflect: How do the big picture and more granular elements of distinction work together to contribute to your reading pleasure? Which elements seem to be most important for this author?

CHAPTER FIFTEEN

HUMOR AND IRONY

"Mr. Darcy is not to be laughed at!" cried Elizabeth. "That is an uncommon advantage, and uncommon I hope it will continue, for it would be a great loss to *me* to have many such acquaintance. I dearly love a laugh."

"Miss Bingley," said he, "has given me credit for more than can be. The wisest and best of men,—nay, the wisest and best of their actions,—may be rendered ridiculous by a person whose first object in life is a joke."

"Certainly," replied Elizabeth, "there are such people, but I hope I am not one of *them*. I hope I never ridicule what is wise or good. Follies and nonsense, whims and inconsistencies, *do* divert me, I own, and I laugh at them whenever I can."

—*Pride and Prejudice*

One of the most loved attributes of Austen's novels is her use of humor. Austen often uses humor in the same manner as Elizabeth in *Pride and Prejudice*—not to constantly tell a joke or to make everyone and everything ridiculous, but rather to point out the follies, nonsense, whims, and inconsistencies of people and society, and to do so in a way that brings laughter and amusement. The first two lines of the novel rely on this type of humor:

> It is a truth universally acknowledged, that a single man in possession of a good fortune must be in want of a wife.
>
> However little known the feelings or views of such a man may be on his first entering a neighbourhood, this truth is so well fixed in the minds of the surrounding families, that he is considered as the rightful property of some one or other of their daughters.

The narrator creates humor by pointing out a nonsensical contrast between the extreme assumptions society makes about a single man and the man's own feelings and views.

We've discussed humor, in some form or fashion, in many of the previous chapters, including those on character, stance, and relationships. While most Western narratives include characters and a plot, there are plenty of stories that do not include humor or only use it in rare moments. However, humor is powerful, and it is one of Austen's favored tools. By examining how Austen creates humor (and a related tool, irony), we can better choose when to use it in our own stories and be more equipped to do so.

Numerous books describe how to create humor, detailing a myriad of techniques and approaches. But from Austen, let's consider three primary techniques and their effects.

1. HIGHLIGHT INCONGRUITIES AND ABSURDITIES

The eighteenth-century Irish philosopher Francis Hutcheson explored the causes and effects of humor in three letters to the editor that he later published in book form as *Reflections upon Laughter*. In the second letter he wrote,

> That then which seems generally the cause of Laughter, is "the bringing together of images which have contrary additional ideas, as well as some resemblance in the principal idea: this contrast between ideas of grandeur, dignity, sanctity, perfection, and ideas of meanness, baseness, profanity, seems to be the very

spirit of burlesque; and the greatest part of our raillery and jest is founded upon it."[1]

Following Hutcheson's lead, numerous other scholars have considered this idea of incongruity or absurdity as a way to create humor. Something incongruous is unexpected: It does not match either itself, a related item, or our expectations. Immanuel Kant wrote that "in everything that is to excite a lively convulsive laugh there must be something absurd."[2]

As we saw previously, the opening lines of *Pride and Prejudice* rely on incongruity. In *Sense and Sensibility*, so does the narrator's description of Marianne:

> Her face was so lovely, that when in the common cant of praise she was called a beautiful girl, truth was less violently outraged than usually happens.

Humor is created by personifying truth, conjuring an unexpected, somewhat absurd image of truth being angry any time a girl is called beautiful. At another point, the narrator presents John Dashwood as follows:

> He never wished to offend anybody, especially anybody of good fortune.

This wry commentary defies convention, by moving us in one direction through praise, and then pulling out the rug underneath it by using a qualifier that breaks the original statement by showing its untruths and absurdities.

In his third letter on laughter, Hutcheson argued that "men have been laughed out of faults which a sermon could not reform."[3] Humor, especially in the hands of Jane Austen, is an effective and palatable form of societal critique, a way for her to poke fun at the faults of her society.

---

1. Hutcheson, *Reflections upon Laughter and Remarks upon the Fable of the Bees*, 19.
2. Morreall, "Philosophy of Humor."
3. Hutcheson, *Reflections upon Laughter*, 35.

2. USE WIT

The Cambridge Dictionary defines wit as "the ability to use words in a clever and humorous way."[4] Another dictionary defines it as "mental sharpness and inventiveness" or "a natural aptitude for using words and ideas in a quick and inventive way to create humor."[5] In 1711 in *The Spectator*, Joseph Addison wrote that wit is the "resemblance and congruity of ideas" or words that provoke delight and surprise.[6] Sometimes wit is produced through **wordplay** or by using words in innovative, insightful, and clever ways.

In *Sense and Sensibility*, the narrator wittily plays with definitions:

> As a house, Barton Cottage, though small, was comfortable and compact; but as a cottage it was defective, for the building was regular, the roof was tiled, the window shutters were not painted green, nor were the walls covered with honeysuckles.

This adds humor while shining insight into the Dashwood women's new living conditions.

Many of Austen's most beloved characters are skilled at quips and witty remarks. In *Pride and Prejudice*, Mr. Bennet makes derisive comments toward his daughters. His wife protests,

> "Mr. Bennet, how can you abuse your own children in such a way? You take delight in vexing me. You have no compassion on my poor nerves."
>
> "You mistake me, my dear. I have a high respect for your nerves. They are my old friends. I have heard you mention them with consideration these twenty years at least."

Mr. Bennet frequently makes these sorts of witty remarks. His clever, funny, and quick statements both entertain us and draw us to him. We forgive Mr. Bennet's faults and failures as a father partly because of Elizabeth's affection for him, but also because his wit makes him likable. This is a common effect of creating a witty character. When used by the narrator, wit can impact the tension and help the reader connect to the storytelling voice.

---

4. *Cambridge Dictionary*, "wit."
5. *New Oxford American Dictionary*, "wit," 1984.
6. Addison, *The Spectator in Three Volumes*.

Mr. and Mrs. Bennet. Illustration by Hugh Thomson, 1894.

3. Use Humor in Situations with Pain and Failure

Many of the funniest moments in Austen's novels are those that are the most painful for the characters. In his novel *Following the Equator*, Mark Twain wrote, "The secret source of Humor itself is not joy but sorrow."[7]

---

7. Twain, *Following the Equator*, chapter 10.
Mark Twain despised the works of Jane Austen, despite the fact that, like him, she was a great humorist. I like Twain and his writing, but I think he was being petty, so in petty vengeance I'm putting his name in my Jane Austen book.

When Mr. Collins proposes to Elizabeth, her feelings are "divided between distress and diversion." Even chapters later, as Elizabeth reflects on the proposal, she "had only to suffer from the uncomfortable feelings necessarily attending it, and occasionally from some peevish allusion of her mother." The proposal causes immediate and prolonged distress for Elizabeth, and some pain and awkwardness for Mr. Collins (we read that after Elizabeth's refusal, "his pride was hurt"). Yet coupled with this distress—woven throughout the scene—is "diversion." Elizabeth responds to her pain and struggle by noticing its humor, and the proposal scene often brings laughter to readers.

As discussed in Chapter 10, on setting, Mr. Elton's carriage proposal in *Emma* ends up being painful both for him and for Emma. After the proposal, they remain trapped together in the carriage, filled with "swelling resentment, and mutually deep mortification." The situation is not funny for the characters, but it's written in such a way as to amuse and delight the reader. Mr. Elton is drunk; Emma shocked. Mr. Elton tries to take Emma's hand; she pulls it away. He tries and fails again, creating physical humor. The characters' extreme reactions to each other delight and surprise the reader, and the fact that they are confined to a small moving box only adds to the hilarity.

Persuasion uses less overt humor than some of her other works, and yet Austen still sets up painful situations in a way that creates amusement. For Anne Elliot, seeing Captain Wentworth and Louisa Musgrove together reminds her of loss: She once held Wentworth's affection, and now he gives it to another. One of the worst moments is when Captain Wentworth and Louisa Musgrove think they are alone; Anne overhears their conversation, protected only by "a bush of low rambling holly." Wentworth praises Louisa for her firmness in decision-making and talks earnestly to her of the happiness of a hazelnut. Meanwhile, Anne "feared to move, lest she should be seen." Wentworth and Louisa flirt while Anne hides feet away—this proximity and possibility of discovery and the absurdity of the hazelnut and the bush create a situation of subtle humor for the reader. We sense an incongruity of character in Anne's behavior, for in this moment, Anne believes that the only thing worse than hearing this conversation would be for them to know that she has heard it.

Anne overhears their conversation.
Illustration by C. E. Brock, 1909.

Humor is a powerful way to address pain and loss and to confront the harsh realities of life. Humor helps some characters, like Elizabeth, deal with their struggles. It can also make difficult situations more palatable, digestible, or enjoyable for the reader, giving hope in the darkness.

Exercise 15.1: Revising for Humor

Select an unhumorous passage from your writing (unpublished or published) that includes a painful or difficult situation or that ends in failure. Rewrite the passage to incorporate humor. (If, by some chance, every single passage you have *ever* written already includes humor, then do this exercise with a nonhumorous passage by a classic author.)

Exercise 15.2: Falling Over

Write a paragraph in which a character falls down again and again and again. This version should not be funny—it might even be tragic.

Now write a new paragraph in which a character falls down again and again and again, but this time, incorporate humor. (Note: The character doesn't necessarily need to find it funny, though the reader should.)

Afterward, reflect. What techniques did you use to make a negative situation humorous?

Exercise 15.3: Three Incongruities

Make a list of threes: three objects you use regularly; three people in your life; three places you often visit; and three of your common tasks. Now set a timer for five or ten minutes. For as many of the items on your list as you can, either create an absurdity or incongruity, or brainstorm a witty statement a character could say about the item.

IRONY

Closely related to humor is irony, and Austen also frequently employs irony throughout her books. According to the *Encyclopedia of Rhetoric*, "Irony's general characteristic is to make something understood by expressing its opposite."[8]

In *Sense and Sensibility*, Mrs. Dashwood makes a list of all the many things she wants to improve in Barton Cottage, which includes knocking out walls, expanding rooms, adding parlors, and making the stairs wider. Then the narrator comments,

> In the mean time, till all these alterations could be made from the savings of an income of five hundred a-year by a woman who never saved in her life, they were wise enough to be contented with the house as it was.

The narrator posits these alterations as forthcoming "from the savings of an income of five hundred a-year by a woman who never saved in her life," clearly meaning that there will never be enough funds for these changes. In many ways, this use of irony is more poignant and expressive of Mrs. Dashwood's follies than if a realistic statement was used to directly point out her weaknesses.

Time and time again, we see that in Austen's hands, irony can be used to point out characters' inconsistencies. In another passage in *Sense and Sensibility*, Marianne plays Lady Middleton's pianoforte. The music she uses

> perhaps had lain ever since in the same position on the pianoforte, for her ladyship had celebrated [her marriage] by giving up music, although by her mother's account, she had played extremely well, and by her own was very fond of it.

What is the truth here? The irony might lie in the fact that she isn't as fond of the pianoforte as she expresses. Yet I'm inclined to think that the irony might be more subtle. It's possible that the narrator is correct in expressing that Lady Middleton played well

---

8. Oesterreich, "Irony."

and truly enjoyed playing. So what truth is revealed? In the world of Austen's characters, marriage is the state most sought-after by single women: It is the ultimate goal, the thing that should bring happiness and security. Yet in choosing marriage, so many women give up the things they love and value. Therein lies the irony.

As Peter L. Oesterreich explains,

> Irony plays with the possibilities of extreme otherness of speech, of life, or of existence as such. The full range of irony is only intelligible through an awareness of the problematic relationship between the expressed and the intended, between character and statement, and between essence and appearance.[9]

Irony is particularly suited to Austen's storytelling because of her interest in exploring the problematic tensions in society: poverty and wealth, the way in which politeness and civility can mask the inner being and lead to self-censorship, the dependence of women on marriage for survival, the bestowal of clergy positions as gifts to friends and family, gender roles and the differing expectations placed on men and women, etc. The list could be endless. Irony allows Austen to unpack society's contradictions through the use of contradiction, by stating what she does not mean.

There are three primary types of irony: situational, dramatic, and verbal. Austen uses each in her stories.

Situational irony is when the result of an action, behavior, or situation is different than what we would expect given the knowledge that we possess. This is a big-picture type of irony; while it can occur within a single scene, it is often manifested over a broader section of the story.

One example of situational irony is found in *Sense and Sensibility*. Marianne won't even consider Colonel Brandon as a suitor. Because of his age, Marianne believes that if any woman were to marry him, she must "submit to the offices of a nurse." The irony is that not only does Marianne eventually marry Colonel Brandon, but more importantly, that he—the older man—helps to nurse her—the younger woman—back to health. When Marianne is violently ill, Colonel Brandon fetches Mrs. Dashwood. He sits at Marianne's bedside, a silent support. He changes his plans

---

9. Oesterreich, "Irony."

to ensure that she receives proper care. When Marianne is well enough to travel home, he "carefully assist[s]" her into a carriage. While some readers might have expected Marianne to eventually marry Colonel Brandon, him nursing her is a reversal of Marianne and the audience's expectations.

Colonel Brandon visits Marianne when she is ill.
Illustration by C. E. Brock, 1909.

Another type of irony is **dramatic irony**, in which the reader knows things that the character does not. This is a very Shakespearean technique. In Austen's novels, it sometimes occurs with the main character. For instance, in *Pride and Prejudice*, the readers know of Charlotte's engagement to Mr. Collins before Elizabeth finds out. However, more often, Austen uses dramatic irony with supporting characters.

In *Mansfield Park*, the reader knows early on that Edmund Bertram plans to become a clergyman. Mary Crawford finds him attractive and actively pursues a relationship with him. While visiting the Rushworth family home, they enter the chapel. Mary proceeds to mock religion, clergymen, and religious gatherings, saying, "The obligation of attendance, the formality, the restraint, the length of time—altogether it is a formidable thing, and what nobody likes." Of course, Mary doesn't know that Edmund is soon to be ordained. This irony creates tension for the reader—we know Mary's statements are unwise, but she does not. It also creates humor—for the reader, at least—at Mary's expense. When Mary is informed of Edmund's planned career path, she's shocked and chagrined, but she manages to say, "If I had known this before, I would have spoken of the cloth with more respect."

The truth—a truth that neither Mary nor Edmund can see—is that they are ill-suited for each other. Their interests and priorities diverge too greatly in areas that matter deeply to them (for instance, one of Mary's most important values is a high income, and this is less important to Edmund). The dramatic irony reveals this to the audience. Sometimes writers think that tension can only be created by withholding information from the reader, but dramatic irony does the reverse, giving us information that the characters don't have in order to heighten our concern for their futures.

Much of Austen's irony is **verbal irony**, irony that relies on words to express the opposite of that which is stated or to express something that diverges in some way from the truth in order to focus us on the truth.

Mansfield Park is often seen as Austen's darkest, least humorous novel, yet irony abounds. Sometimes, it's easy to conflate irony and humor, because humor is often an effect of irony—but it is only one of many good effects. In the following passage, the narrator of *Mansfield Park* uses verbal irony to comment on Maria Bertram's upcoming marriage to Mr. Rushworth:

> Mr. Rushworth could hardly be more impatient for the marriage than herself. In all the important preparations of the mind she was complete: being prepared for matrimony by an hatred of home, restraint, and tranquility; by the misery of disappointed affection, and contempt of the man she was to marry. The rest might wait. The preparations of new carriages and furniture might wait for London and spring, when her own taste could have fairer play.

The irony is thick and obvious: Maria is running headlong into disaster, fleeing from her miserable home life and *ready* for marriage because of her contempt for the man she is about to marry. If looked at too directly, the situation is utterly depressing. The irony simultaneously lightens and accentuates this feeling of disaster.

A subset of verbal irony is **sarcasm**, when an individual states the opposite of what they mean, often to demonstrate a negative emotion, to mock, to show contempt, or to provide commentary.

In *Mansfield Park*, Fanny is invited to dine out. Mrs. Norris does not believe that Fanny should receive such an honor, and she uses sarcasm in an attempt to make Fanny feel bad for the invitation:

> "And I hope you will have a very *agreeable* day, and find it all mighty *delightful*. But I must observe that five is the very awkwardest of all possible numbers to sit down to table; and I cannot but be surprised that such an *elegant* lady as Mrs. Grant should not contrive better! ... People are never respected when they step out of their proper sphere. Remember that, Fanny."

Austen uses italics to signal Mrs. Norris's manner of speaking. Mrs. Norris emphasizes her adjectives to make her sarcasm ridiculously obvious: She does not actually want Fanny to have an agreeable or delightful time, and she does not believe Mrs. Grant elegant. Fanny is meant to feel small, and she does. After Mrs. Norris's lecture on how to behave, we read that Fanny "thought it perfectly reasonable. She rated her own claims to comfort as low even as Mrs. Norris could."

Irony works well because its commentary suits Austen's narrators. If, as an author, you choose to use irony as a regular technique throughout your story, then it must connect to your story's stance, point of view, and narrator. You can also choose to use it more discreetly in your story, with a few individual instances of situational and dramatic irony, but less use of verbal irony. Or irony can be concentrated in the language and attitude of one or two characters. Ultimately, the use of irony should match your authorial goals. Regardless of how it is used, irony can be a powerful tool "to make something understood by expressing its opposite."[10]

Exercise 15.4: Situational Irony

Find an example of situational irony in a work from an author other than Jane Austen. If possible, try to avoid using the internet. Instead, think about some of your favorite stories (short stories, novels, or films). Is there an action, a behavior, a situation, or a result that defies the expectations set by the story world and the characters?

Once you've found an example, consider the impact of this situational irony on the story.

Exercise 15.5: Dramatic Irony

Write a few paragraphs that create dramatic irony through the use of an omniscient point of view with a strong storytelling voice. The omniscient narrator should give information to the audience, then show a character doing or saying something that they would not do or say if they knew the information.

For instance, you could start with a grand, revelatory statement, such as "It was a beautiful morning on the third of June, and no one in Newton knew that later that day, a tornado would sweep through their town."

As an alternative to omniscient with a storytelling voice, you can use first-person past tense to the same effect. Some first-person narrators consistently adopt a storytelling voice, commenting and reflecting on the events of the past. Other novels do so only for the first sentence or paragraph, then shift to a narrower first person, focused on the time without any omniscient-esque knowledge. In either case, there can be a gap between what the storyteller now knows—and transmits to the reader—and what they knew at the time, thus creating dramatic irony.

Bonus extension: Using any point of view and tense, write a few paragraphs in which the audience knows something that a supporting character (who is *not* a viewpoint character) does not know.

Exercise 15.6: Revising for Verbal Irony

Take a scene that you have written. Find a sentence or a passage that expresses, explains, or describes something without using any irony. Now rewrite this sentence or passage using verbal irony: Express the opposite in order to reveal or convey the information.

What is the impact of using irony? Does irony fit with the overall stance of your story or with a character's attitude/approach to life? Do you prefer the original or the revised version, and why?

OVERSTATEMENT AND UNDERSTATEMENT

Overstatement and understatement are two of Austen's most frequent techniques for creating verbal irony. Rather than revealing the truth by stating its direct opposite, **overstatement and understatement are when the true nature of something is revealed by over- or underexpressing it—stating it as larger or smaller than it is in actuality.** Often, overstatement and understatement create humor in addition to irony. Austen also uses these devices to make revelations about her characters and the narrator.

OVERSTATEMENT

Overstatement is describing something as larger than it is. Generally, the reader is aware that overstatement is being used, which invites the reader to further engage with the text in order to better understand the characters or the situation.

In *Sense and Sensibility*, Mrs. Jennings constantly uses overstatement in her speech, such as when she exclaims, "How attentive she is, to think of every body! … It is as pretty a letter as ever I saw." The narrator also uses overstatement to express Mrs. Jennings's motives and goals:

> Mrs. Jennings … had only two daughters, both of whom she had lived to see respectably married, and she had now therefore nothing to do but to marry all the rest of the world.

The overstatement is obvious and serves to emphasize Mrs. Jennings's single-minded focus on her self-appointed task.

Mrs. Jennings. Illustration by Hugh Thomson, 1896.

Overstatement is a general term that includes many specific techniques. We'll address three of these techniques: auxesis, hyperbole, and bomphiologia.

Auxesis: labeling something with a term that makes it seem larger, stronger, better, more severe, more debilitating, etc., than it actually is

In the first chapter of *Pride and Prejudice*, Mrs. Bennet exerts a great deal of energy trying to convince her husband to call upon Mr. Bingley, so their families can officially meet and form a connection. Mr. Bennet vocally refuses, multiple times. In the second chapter, everyone in the family speaks of Mr. Bingley and how they might meet him at the ball.

> "While Mary is adjusting her ideas," [Mr. Bennet] continued,
> "let us return to Mr. Bingley."

"I am sick of Mr. Bingley," cried his wife.

"I am sorry to hear *that*; but why did you not tell me so before? If I had known as much this morning, I certainly would not have called on him. It is very unlucky; but as I have actually paid the visit, we cannot escape the acquaintance now."

When Mrs. Bennet declares that she is "sick of Mr. Bingley," she uses auxesis. *Sick* implies a very negative emotion that Mrs. Bennet does not feel. In truth, she's tired of talking about Mr. Bingley because Mr. Bennet won't visit him. This exaggeration is an attempt to convey her emotions to her husband. Yet she desires the acquaintance greatly, and at Mr. Bennet's confession that he has called upon Mr. Bingley, she is extremely pleased.

HYPERBOLE: extreme exaggeration, making something much larger than it actually is

If you consider truth as a scale, you have truth on one side, auxesis in the middle, and hyperbole on the far side: Auxesis is also an exaggeration, but hyperbole is a much greater one.

TRUTH	**AUXESIS**	**HYPERBOLE**
NO EXAGGERATION	SOME EXAGGERATION	GREAT EXAGGERATION

In *Pride and Prejudice*, after Lydia runs off with Wickham, Mr. Bennet declares to Kitty that not only will he not allow her to go to Brighton, but

"no officer is ever to enter my house again, nor even to pass through the village. Balls will be absolutely prohibited, unless you stand up with one of your sisters. And you are never to stir out of doors, till you can prove that you have spent ten minutes of every day in a rational manner."

Kitty, who took all of these threats in a serious light, began to cry.

This is hyperbole—Mr. Bennet has neither the ability nor the desire to go to such extremes—but Kitty is not sensible enough to recognize it.

BOMPHIOLOGIA: when an individual overstates themselves, through bragging or self-exaggeration;[11] particularly effective in dialogue and can be used to express character

In *Northanger Abbey*, when Catherine first meets John Thorpe, Thorpe exaggerates the distance and speed that his horses have traveled, even when Catherine's brother attempts to reason with him and state the facts. Thorpe then goes on to brag and self-aggrandize. By praising his horse and then his carriage, he is actually praising himself:

> Look at his forehand; look at his loins; only see how he moves; that horse *cannot* go less than ten miles an hour: tie his legs and he will get on. What do you think of my gig, Miss Morland? A neat one, is not it? Well hung; town-built; I have not had it a month.

As he continues to praise the horse, he discloses that he paid fifty guineas—quite the sum—for his carriage:

> "I closed with him directly, threw down the money, and the carriage was mine."
>
> "And I am sure," said Catherine, "I know so little of such things that I cannot judge whether it was cheap or dear."
>
> "Neither one nor t'other; I might have got it for less, I dare say; but I hate haggling, and poor Freeman wanted cash."

He exaggerates his abilities—his ability to get a bargain, his ability to be generous—when he has simply paid more than the carriage was worth. While the conversation discomfits Catherine, she does not judge him for it; she has not yet learned discernment. Thus, John Thorpe's overstatement becomes an important component of Catherine's development and character journey.

UNDERSTATEMENT

Understatement is describing something as less than it actually is. Austen often uses understatement to create commentary; at times her characters use it in an attempt to meet their own goals.

---

11. "Bomphiologia," in Burton, *Silva Rhetoricae*.

In *Northanger Abbey*, when Catherine arrives at the abbey, General Tilney constantly downplays its size and worth. Through Catherine's eyes, we see a grand room with modern adornment and huge windows letting in copious amounts of light.

> The general, perceiving how her eye was employed, began to talk of the smallness of the room and simplicity of the furniture, ... flattering himself, however, that there were some apartments in the Abbey not unworthy of her notice.

When Catherine describes the dining room as noble, the general "acknowledge[s] that it was by no means an ill-sized room." Catherine admires the "elegance of the breakfast set" and the general "confess[es] it to be neat and simple." The narrator even begins to adopt the general's use of understatement: "He led the way across the hall, through the common drawing-room and one useless antechamber."

Throughout these scenes, General Tilney uses understatement because he believes that Catherine is a wealthy heiress. He takes pride in the abbey, but he wants to downplay it in order to seem sophisticated and humble and to show an awareness that much greater wealth is possible. Through understatement, he attempts to woo Catherine for his son.

There are various types and subcategories of understatement, four of which we will consider in more detail: meiosis, anesis, charientismus, and litotes.

Meiosis: a type of understatement in which you give something a name or a label that makes it seem less than it actually is; the opposite of auxesis

One of Austen's classic uses of meiosis is found at the end of *Northanger Abbey*:

> To begin perfect happiness at the respective ages of twenty-six and eighteen is to do pretty well.

"Pretty well" is quite the understatement, yet it fits with the narrator's tone—after all, the narrator has spent Northanger Abbey telling a pastiche and providing commentary on what makes a good heroine and hero. The statement is ironic and humorous and actually makes the point more strongly than saying "To begin perfect happiness ... is incredible and rare," which would feel trite and empty.

In *Emma*, Mrs. Weston talks to Emma about Frank Churchill's secret engagement and the problems his behavior caused in his relationship with Jane Fairfax:

> "The present crisis, indeed, seemed to be brought on by them; and those misunderstandings might very possibly arise from the impropriety of his conduct."
>
> "Impropriety! Oh! Mrs. Weston—it is too calm a censure. Much, much beyond impropriety!—It has sunk him, I cannot say how it has sunk him in my opinion. So unlike what a man should be!"

Emma critiques Mrs. Weston's use of understatement—she worries that trivializing Frank Churchill's behavior ignores its devastating effects.

ANESIS: "adding a concluding sentence [or phrase] that diminishes the effect of what has been said previously"[12]

In *Persuasion*, the narrator paints a picture of the Musgrove parents:

> The father and mother were in the old English style.... Mr. and Mrs. Musgrove were a very good sort of people; friendly and hospitable, not much educated, and not at all elegant.

The first descriptions build up the Musgroves: They are traditional, a good sort of people, friendly, and hospitable. But the final two descriptions diminish the positive effect of the former: They are "not much educated, and not at all elegant."

CHARIENTISMUS: using pleasant or friendly words to deal with a difficult problem, or "mollifying harsh words by answering them with a smooth and appeasing mock"[13]

---

12. "Anesis," in Burton, *Silva Rhetoricae*.
13. "Charientismus," in Burton, *Silva Rhetoricae*.

Near the end of *Pride and Prejudice*, Lady Catherine warns Elizabeth that if she marries Mr. Darcy,

> "Do not expect to be noticed by his family or friends, if you wilfully act against the inclinations of all. You will be censured, slighted, and despised, by everyone connected with him. Your alliance will be a disgrace; your name will never even be mentioned by any of us."

Lady Catherine visits Elizabeth at Longbourn.
Illustration by Hugh Thomson, 1894.

Lady Catherine's words are harsh, but Elizabeth answers them more softly, with a bit of mockery:

> "These are heavy misfortunes," replied Elizabeth. "But the wife of Mr. Darcy must have such extraordinary sources of happiness necessarily attached to her situation, that she could, upon the whole, have no cause to repine."

While Lady Catherine is not appeased (she immediately exclaims, "Obstinate, headstrong girl!"), Elizabeth's softer response to Lady Catherine's harshness demonstrates that she will not allow Lady Catherine to control her emotional reactions or behaviors, whether in speech or marriage.

LITOTES: stating something by "denying its opposite,"[14] a type of understatement that often creates wry commentary and is used frequently by Austen's narrators

In *Northanger Abbey*, Austen introduces Catherine's father by using two litotes:

> Her father was a clergyman ... and he had never been handsome. He had a considerable independence besides two good livings— and he was not in the least addicted to locking up his daughters.

The narrator avoids directly (and uncouthly) describing Mr. Morland as ugly, instead stating, "He had never been handsome." He also gives his daughters large amounts of independence, which is expressed by the fact that he does not lock them up. (Scholar Claire Grogan explains that this is also an allusion to popular novels of the time in which fathers did lock up their daughters.[15])

In *Sense and Sensibility*, Austen uses litotes twice in order to introduce John Dashwood:

> Mr. John Dashwood had not the strong feelings of the rest of the family.... He was not an ill-disposed young man, unless to be rather cold hearted and rather selfish is to be ill-disposed.

The first use of litotes focuses on the fact that he is more reserved than other family members, yet by using litotes to state that he "had not the strong feelings," it focuses the reader on his lack, hinting that this sort of reserve is not necessarily praiseworthy. The second use of litotes ("he was not an ill-disposed young man") is instantly negated by the additional description; it's a clever commentary from the narrator, as being coldhearted and selfish *is* a good way to define being ill-disposed.

---

14. "Litotes," in Burton, *Silva Rhetoricae*.
15. Grogan, footnote to *Northanger Abbey*, 37.

Later in the novel, Sir John apologizes to the Dashwoods that a gathering he has organized will not have a large number of young men:

> They would see, he said, only one gentleman there besides himself; a particular friend who was staying at the park, but who was neither very young nor very gay.

Stating that Colonel Brandon is "neither very young nor very gay" is much more polite than stating that his friend is old and boring.

READER PARTICIPATION

Irony requests active participation on the part of the reader. The audience of the story is not allowed to accept everything at face value. When overstatement and understatement are used, the intent is not to deceive the reader, but rather to engage them and focus them on the actual truth. Like other approaches to irony, overstatement and understatement can be used by individual characters, or by the narrator, as part of the overall stance.

Exercise 15.7: Overstatement and Understatement

Create your own example of each type of overstatement and understatement discussed in this section.

- Auxesis: Have a character or the narrator label something as more than it is.
- Hyperbole: Create an extreme exaggeration.
- Bomphiologia: Create a sentence or paragraph of dialogue in which a character brags or is self-aggrandizing.
- Meiosis: Have a character or the narrator label something as less than it is.
- Anesis: Build something up (a person, a place, an object, etc.), and then add a phrase or sentence that reverses or diminishes the effect of the building.
- Charientismus: Create a two-sentence dialogue in which one character says an insult and the other character responds in a lighter manner or with humorous mocking.
- Litotes: Describe an attribute of someone or something by negating the opposite.

LAUGHTER

Laughter is present in all of Austen's novels. In *Persuasion* and *Northanger Abbey*, it's used less frequently (the word "laugh" or "laughter" occurs in some form in *Persuasion* eleven times and in *Northanger Abbey* sixteen times), while other novels are filled with characters laughing ("laugh," "laughter" or other forms of the word occur forty-four times in *Pride and Prejudice* and forty-nine times in *Emma*).

"Tenderly flirting"

Lydia is excited to journey to Brighton; she pictures herself "tenderly flirting with at least six officers at once." Illustration by Hugh Thomson, 1894.

Like other tools of humor and irony, the use of laughter is a stylistic choice, which may be better suited to some stories than others. In *Pride and Prejudice*, both likable and unlikable characters laugh, for good and bad reasons. When Lydia learns that she—and only she—can go to Brighton with the militia, we read,

Wholly inattentive to her sister's feelings, Lydia flew about the house in restless ecstasy, calling for everyone's congratulations, and laughing and talking with more violence than ever; whilst the luckless Kitty continued in the parlour repining at her fate in terms as unreasonable as her accent was peevish.

Lydia's laughter is insensitive and "violent." And when Lydia runs away with Wickham, she writes a letter explaining what she has done, and she says,

I can hardly write for laughing.

Here, Lydia's laughter is seen by the narrator as inappropriate— she is so dismissive of moral and social norms that she laughs in the face of them.

Elizabeth uses laughter in a broader range of ways. She laughs involuntarily and from joy and diversion.[16] She laughs to conceal her real emotions. And she laughs to deal with hardship. When Mr. Bennet makes negative comments about Mr. Darcy, not knowing what Darcy has done for their family, Elizabeth laughs.

It was necessary to laugh when she would rather have cried.

Near the end of the novel, after she becomes engaged, Elizabeth writes to her aunt Mrs. Gardiner. In her letter, she attempts to convey her extreme level of happiness:

I am happier even than Jane; she only smiles, I laugh.

For Elizabeth, laughter has a certain power that other types of joy cannot possess, and I think this gives us a sense of why Austen uses so much humor and irony throughout all of her novels. Humor and irony can create laughter in the reader, they can create change, they can critique, they can enlighten, and they can create light in the darkness. These techniques might not be appropriate for all stories and situations, but there are certain effects on the audience

---

16. My friend Sarah Chow recently told me a great insight: If characters laugh at a joke or a situation, it invites the reader to laugh and also find it funny.

that can be attained by humor and irony that cannot be achieved through other means.

Humor and irony are present not only in Austen's novels—these same techniques fill her personal correspondence. In one letter to her sister Cassandra, Jane writes, "I hope you will receive the gown to-morrow, and may be able with tolerable honesty to say that you like the color."[17] In another, she references a William Cowper poem ("I am monarch of all I survey,/ My right there is none to dispute/ From the center all round to the sea,/ I am lord of the fowl and the brute")[18] with humorous intent:

> I am now alone in the library, mistress of all I survey; at least I may say so, and repeat the whole poem if I like it, without offence to anybody.[19]

In her letters, there is often a bit of self-mockery, such as when she closes the above letter with

> I have *this* moment seen Mrs. Driver driven up to the kitchen door. I cannot close with a grander circumstance of greater wit.

She is also unafraid of dark humor. When an acquaintance dies, she writes,

> Only think of Mrs. Holder's being dead! Poor woman, she has done the only thing in the world she could possibly do to make one cease to abuse her.[20]

Poor Jane—unable to insult Mrs. Holder because she is dead. She also looks upon aging with a humorous perspective:

> By the by, as I must leave off being young, I find many *douceurs* [pleasures] in being a sort of *chaperon*, for I am put on the sofa near the fire, and can drink as much wine as I like.[21]

---

17. Jane Austen to Cassandra Austen, September 16, 1813. *Letters of Jane Austen*.
18. Cowper, "Verses."
19. Jane Austen to Cassandra Austen, September 23, 1813. *Letters of Jane Austen—Brabourne Edition*.
20. Jane Austen to Cassandra Austen, October 14, 1813. *Letters of Jane Austen*.
21. Jane Austen to Cassandra Austen, November 6, 1813. *Letters of Jane Austen*.

Clearly, Jane Austen lived a life filled with humor and laughter—it was an important part of her key relationships. Scholar Paula Byrne explains that Austen's published novels contained inside jokes to her family members, little humorous references that they would recognize.[22] In 1796, Jane wrote to her sister Cassandra,

> The letter which I have this moment received from you has diverted me beyond moderation. I could die of laughter at it, as they used to say at school. You are indeed the finest comic writer of the present age.[23]

Austen made her family laugh, and they made her laugh in turn. To me, it's clear that Austen's use of humor and irony in her novels is not just a part of the stance she adopted for her fiction; it's an extension of who she was. And every time we put words to a page, even when we adopt stances quite different than our own or write characters unlike ourselves, we do put something of ourselves into our writing.

In the next chapter—the final chapter of this book—we'll take one last masterclass from Jane Austen, by considering more that we can learn from her life that can help us as writers.

---

22. Byrne, *The Real Jane Austen*, 20.
23. Jane Austen to Cassandra Austen, September 1, 1796. *Letters of Jane Austen—Brabourne Edition*.

Chapter Sixteen

A Space for Writing

"I want to tell you that I have got my own darling child from London."
—Letter from Jane Austen to Cassandra, January 29, 1813

On January 28, 1813, *Pride and Prejudice* was officially published. It was Jane Austen's second novel to go out into the world, and she saw it as her "own darling child." She immediately began reading it aloud to a friend, a Miss B., who had dined with them.

> She really does seem to admire Elizabeth.... How I shall be able to tolerate those who do not like [Elizabeth] at least, I do not know.

Like Austen, I am completely unable to tolerate people who dislike Elizabeth Bennet. But besides the humor in her statement, what I'm drawn to is Austen's acknowledgment that not everyone will like her work—of course she wants a happy readership, but she knows that as an artist, you can never please everyone. Austen continues her letter by discussing the errors and shortfalls she sees in her own writing:

> There are a few typical errors; and a "said he," or a "said she," would sometimes make the dialogue more immediately clear; but "I do not write for such dull elves" as have not a great deal of ingenuity themselves. The second volume is shorter than I could wish, but the difference is not so much in reality as in look, there being a larger proportion of narrative in that part. I have lop't and crop't so successfully, however, that I imagine it must be rather shorter than "Sense and Sensibility" altogether.[1]

Sometimes, when I read Austen, I feel so astounded by her genius that I wonder if my own stories are worth telling. But when I read her letters, I see her self-criticism and self-doubt, and I am reminded that artists often question their own work. In response to Jane's letter, Cassandra writes a reply that apparently reassures Jane, for on February 4, 1813, Jane writes again,

> "MY DEAR CASSANDRA,—Your letter was truly welcome, and I am much obliged to you for all your praise; it came at a right time, for I had had some fits of disgust."[2]

Pride and Prejudice is arguably one of the best books ever written in English, and yet the author suffered "fits of disgust." Austen continues the letter by ironically wondering if the novel might be "too light and bright and sparkling." She suggests that her novel could have been improved by "an essay on writing, a critique on Walter Scott, or the history of Buonaparte, or something that would form a contrast, and bring the reader with increased delight to the playfulness and epigrammatism of the general style." Clearly this is in jest—she knew what sort of story she wanted to tell, and she told it well.

In the letter, Jane also notes that she found a printing error in the book (two speeches were combined into one) and that she

---

1. Jane Austen to Cassandra Austen, January 29, 1813. *Letters of Jane Austen.*
2. Jane Austen to Cassandra Austen, February 4, 1813. *Letters of Jane Austen.*

regrets the lack of "suppers at Longbourn." But she also writes, "Upon the whole, however, I am quite vain enough and well satisfied enough."

Every author has to reach this point—where we feel "satisfied enough" with our stories to share them with an audience, realizing that despite our endless hours of writing, there will still be errors and imperfections.

PRIDE

AND

PREJUDICE:

A NOVEL.

IN THREE VOLUMES.

BY THE

AUTHOR OF " SENSE AND SENSIBILITY."

VOL. I.

London:

PRINTED FOR T. EGERTON,

MILITARY LIBRARY, WHITEHALL.

1813.

Title page of the first edition of Pride and Prejudice. *1813.*

In another letter to Cassandra, Jane writes,

> I am not at all in a humour for writing; I must write on till I am.[3]

This is another useful lesson for us today: When Austen did not feel like writing, she kept writing until she *did* want to write. I've personally found that the first fifteen or twenty minutes of writing are the most difficult, but if I do as Jane did and "write on," it gets easier.[4]

In a different letter, she says,

> I do not know what is the matter with me to-day, but I cannot write quietly; I am always wandering away into some exclamation or other. Fortunately I have nothing very particular to say.[5]

While many of our wandering aways are now digital, we too have days where we "cannot write quietly," where we are drawn away by the many other things in our lives.

There's a lot of pressure for writers to always be writing—to always be productive. And it can be discouraging when we don't have time to write or when we put in the time but don't seem to make any progress. Austen struggled with this as well. In another letter to Cassandra she writes,

> I have had a cold and weakness in one of my eyes for some days, which makes writing neither very pleasant nor very profitable, and which will probably prevent my finishing this letter myself.[6]

Yet despite her struggle, she finds a place for optimism and humor. Later in the letter, she says,

> This complaint in my eye has been a sad bore to me, for I have not been able to read or work in any comfort since Friday; but one advantage will be derived from it, for I shall be such a proficient

---

3. Jane Austen to Cassandra Austen, October 26, 1813. *Letters of Jane Austen—Brabourne Edition*.
4. Sometimes, on the days when I least want to write, I set a timer for thirty minutes and tell myself that if I work diligently for that time, I can stop once the timer goes off. But by the time I hit thirty minutes, I usually want to keep going.
5. Jane Austen to Cassandra Austen, June 11, 1799. *Letters of Jane Austen*.
6. Jane Austen to Cassandra Austen, January 8, 1799. *Letters of Jane Austen*.

in music by the time I have got rid of my cold.... Do not be angry with me for not filling my sheet, and believe me yours affectionately,

J. A.

This is, in a sense, an apology for writing a shorter-than-normal letter. Yet Austen's "do not be angry with me" feels like a playful overstatement. Cassandra and Jane were close friends, and so of course Cassandra wouldn't be *angry* that her ill sister had written less than normal. This use of irony feels to me like an invitation for both of them to give themselves more grace for what they can accomplish given their constraints.

Throughout her life, Jane Austen did have many constraints. Historians generally agree that at times Austen grew frustrated with the writing and publication process, and that events in her life made writing more difficult.

Her early years of writing were admittedly very productive. From 1787 to 1793—as a teenager—she wrote what is now called her *Juvenilia*, short pieces of various genres and forms, which she carefully copied into three vellum notebooks when she was seventeen years old.[7]

Some scholars believe that she then wrote the epistolary novella *Lady Susan* from 1794 to 1795.[8] From 1796 to 1798—from the ages of twenty to twenty-two—she wrote what were then called *Elinor and Marianne* and *First Impressions*. Then she wrote (or perhaps finished writing), what was then known as *Susan* but was later retitled *Northanger Abbey*.[9]

By the end of 1799, Jane Austen had completed three full-length novels and (possibly) an epistolary novella. It seems like a fabulous start to a writing career. But then we have this apparent gap: *Sense and Sensibility* (a revised version of *Elinor and Marianne*) wasn't published until 1811.

What happened between 1800 and 1810?

In December 1800, while Jane was taking a trip, her father decided that he was ready to retire—he was seventy years old, after all. When Jane returned to her lifelong home in Steventon,

---

7. Byrne, *The Real Jane Austen*, 53.

8. Byrne, *The Real Jane Austen*, 271.

9. Before her death, she also changed the main character's name from Susan to Catherine.

she was shocked by the news that they were moving to Bath.[10] For various reasons, Austen dreaded this move, feeling rather like her character Anne Elliot:

> She disliked Bath, and did not think it agreed with her; and Bath was to be her home.

Claire Tomalin writes that Jane "had enjoyed Bath as a visitor and used it as a writer, but she had no wish at all to live there." [11]

Their time in Bath was complicated by struggles with finances and housing, and it was interrupted by various lengthy trips. Tomalin argues that moving to Bath "depressed her deeply enough to disable her as a writer."[12] But throughout her time in Bath, she did keep writing and revising. With her, she brought the manuscripts for her three completed novels. She most certainly revised what was then *Susan*,[13] and she likely made revisions on *Elinor and Marianne* and *First Impressions*.[14] Some scholars believe that *Lady Susan* was actually written in its entirety during this period. If Austen did write *Lady Susan* earlier, then at the very least she revised it while in Bath.[15]

Earlier, her father had acted as her literary agent and attempted to sell her books. In 1803, her brother Henry succeeded (with the help of a business associate), selling *Susan* to a London publisher for ten pounds.

Jane Austen received the money. She was going to be a published author.

But the publisher never published the book. Imagine waiting for years, wondering when and if and how your book would actually be published. In 1809, Jane finally received word that they weren't going to publish it—after all, nothing in the contract said they were required to.[16] The publisher offered that she could have

---

10. Worsley, *Jane Austen at Home*, 147.
11. Tomalin, *Jane Austen: A Life*, 173.
12. Tomalin, *Jane Austen: A Life*, 175.
13. *Northanger Abbey*, not *Lady Susan*.
14. Byrne, *The Real Jane Austen*, 165–66.
15. Byrne, *The Real Jane Austen*, 271–72.
16. Byrne, *The Real Jane Austen*, 270–71, 276–77.
It's a common saying in publishing that no contract is better than a bad contract. That said, it's really hard to turn down a publisher who has offered to sell your book; I walked away from the first offer for my debut novel and I was filled with fears—what if no one else

the rights back if she repaid the ten pounds.

I've had personal experiences that let me glimpse, to a small degree, how devastated Jane must have felt. Early in my writing journey, I received second place in a contest for a personal essay I had written. It came with a $200 check, and it was the first time I had ever earned money for my writing. The winning pieces were supposed to be published in an upcoming issue of a literary journal, but issue after issue, my piece didn't appear. I finally emailed them, and they confessed that they didn't like any of the pieces enough to publish them. Ouch. But they gave me back the publication rights (without requiring me to repay the prize money), and I posted the essay on my blog.[17] My own experience left me feeling discouraged, and I can only imagine how much worse it would feel to have this happen for a full-length novel, in a time when an unknown female author had much less power than today. Further, at the time, Austen couldn't repay the ten pounds—a few years earlier, in 1807, Jane's total expenditures for the entire year were just over forty pounds.[18] She certainly couldn't afford to spend a quarter of her yearly budget to repurchase rights for the book.

This, however, was only one of many setbacks Jane faced during this decade.

Her close friend, Anne Lefroy, suddenly and tragically died in December 1804. Jane's father unexpectedly died the next month. While in Bath, Jane had started a novel called *The Watsons*, but at some point after her father's death she abandoned it, perhaps because in the story, she had planned for the main character's father to die, and now it was too difficult to write.[19]

Her father's death led to an extremely difficult financial situation for Jane, her sister Cassandra, and their mother. They became largely dependent on the charity of family members and lived in various locations. One of these homes was in Southampton, where Jane moved in 1806. Lucy Worsley writes that "here, as in Bath, [Jane] would survive rather than thrive."[20]

---

wanted this book or my writing ever again? Fortunately, I only had a few months of worry before receiving a better offer from a different publisher.

17. Later I learned that good contracts for essays and short stories automatically return the rights to authors if pieces aren't published within a year.

18. Worsley, *Jane Austen at Home*, 219.

19. Worsley, *Jane Austen at Home*, 194–98.

20. Worsley, *Jane Austen at Home*, 214.

It's no wonder that in this period of her life, Jane made little progress on her writing.

But then, in 1809, life changed for the better. Her brother Edward had been adopted by distant relatives in Chawton, and when he received his inheritance, he offered a cottage he owned as a residence for his untethered female family members.

Suddenly, Jane Austen had security. She had a home. And she had the space and the time to write.

The cottage where Jane Austen lived in Chawton.
Photograph by R. ferroni2000, 2017.

She revised *Elinor and Marianne*—which she had originally written between 1796 and 1798—and published it as *Sense and Sensibility*. She rewrote *First Impressions* as *Pride and Prejudice*.[21] And then she wrote three new novels: *Mansfield Park*, *Emma*, and *Persuasion*. She began the novel *Sanditon* but did not finish it before her death. Chawton was clearly a place where Jane Austen and her writing thrived.

We each have times and seasons of writing, and it's important to treat ourselves with compassion and understanding. We will

---

21. As previously mentioned, Paula Byrne and other scholars believe it likely that Jane Austen did at least some of the revisions and rewriting on both *Sense and Sensibility* and *Pride and Prejudice* in the period between when she left her home at Steventon and when she arrived at her final home in Chawton. Regardless, Chawton seems to have been a good location for finishing these books and submitting them to publishers.

have times, like the decade in Austen's life, where it is more difficult to write, where life circumstances create additional challenges
for creativity. When we're in survival mode, we need to be patient
with ourselves and our writing. We need to trust that good things
will come and that there will be space in the future for creativity.

I also like to remember that it's okay if certain projects take
time to reach their final form. *Sense and Sensibility* and *Pride and
Prejudice* are two of my favorite novels. And they were not written
quickly. They required writing and re-envisioning and rewriting
over the course of almost two decades.

Exercise 16.1: Your Creative Journey

Write the story of your creative journey. What has led you to be the
writer you are today? Which times and seasons of your life have been
more or less creative? Is there anything from the less creative periods of your life that has helped you with your writing?

Exercise 16.2: An Old Project

Take a project that you set aside, perhaps years ago. Spend a few minutes considering it. If you were going to rewrite it today, how would
you approach it differently?

CREATING A SPACE FOR WRITING

Even when living at Chawton Cottage, Jane Austen could find
writing to be difficult. On September 8, 1816, she wrote a letter
to her sister Cassandra that included the following paragraph:

> I enjoyed Edward's company very much, as I said before, and yet
> I was not sorry when Friday came. It had been a busy week, and
> I wanted a few days' quiet and exemption from the thought and
> contrivancy which any sort of company gives. I often wonder

how you can find time for what you do, in addition to the care
of the house; and how good Mrs. West could have written such
books and collected so many hard words, with all her family
cares, is still more a matter of astonishment. Composition seems
to me impossible with a head full of joints of mutton and doses
of rhubarb.[22]

Company and a busy week made writing more difficult for
Jane Austen. She needed time for herself, time for quiet, and time
without too many obligations. Jane is astonished by Mrs. West,
who balances writing and family cares: "Composition seems to
me impossible with a head full of joints of mutton and doses of
rhubarb."

Most of us have things we need to balance, whether it's family
obligations, a full- or part-time job, school, or endless other responsibilities. These things are part of our lives. They're not going to go
away. But are we letting our heads be "full of joints of mutton and
doses of rhubarb"? Or are we finding some time that is just ours,
where we can let everything else go and give space for creativity?
This is essential, even and especially when life is going well. In the
same letter that mentions Mrs. West, Austen writes about finding
these little pockets of time for her writing: "No morning service
to-day, wherefore I am writing between twelve and one o'clock."

During her years living in Chawton, Jane's family did much to
lift some of her responsibilities in order to give her the time and the
mental space for writing. Jane was responsible for making breakfast
every day, and she was in charge of the tea and the sugar (acquir-
ing these expensive items, keeping them in a locked cupboard, and
dispensing them as necessary). But the others living in the cottage
(her sister Cassandra, her mother, and her friend and housemate
Martha Lloyd) took on the majority of the other household tasks. [23]

In Chawton, Jane often wrote at a small walnut writing table,
only 47 centimeters (18.5 inches) wide. She didn't like others

---

22. Jane Austen to Cassandra Austen, September 8, 1816. *Letters of Jane Austen*.
Here Jane refers to her contemporary, Jane West, who published fiction, poetry, and di-
dactic letters. Jane West was not one of Austen's favorite authors. In a September 28,
1814, letter to her niece Anna, Jane Austen wrote, "I am quite determined, however, not
to be pleased with Mrs. West's 'Alicia De Lacy,' should I ever meet with it, which I hope I
shall not. I think I can be stout against anything written by Mrs. West. I have made up my
mind to like no novels really but Miss Edgeworth's, yours, and my own."
23. Worsley, *Jane Austen at Home*, 237–39.

watching her write or seeing her in-process works, so, according to her nephew, "She wrote upon small sheets of paper which could easily be put away, or covered with a piece of blotting paper."[24] Once, when I attended a guided virtual tour of her Chawton house, the guide explained that several of the windows by the road were boarded up, so passersby on the road wouldn't look in on Jane. Perhaps this also helped her not spend too much time people-watching.

Jane Austen's walnut writing table.
Photograph by Colin Smith, 2019.

Over a hundred years later, a self-admitted Jane Austen fan, Virginia Woolf, wrote that "a woman must have money and a room of her own if she is to write fiction." She lamented that Austen did not have a full room and that she felt she had to cover her work with blotting paper. Woolf continued,

> I wondered, would *Pride and Prejudice* have been a better novel if Jane Austen had not thought it necessary to hide her manuscript from visitors? I read … but I could not find any signs that her circumstances had harmed her work in the slightest. That, perhaps, was the chief miracle about it. Here was a woman about

---

24. "Jane Austen's Writing Table," Jane Austen's House.

the year 1800 writing without hate, without bitterness, without fear, without protest, without preaching. That was how Shakespeare wrote, I thought, looking at *Antony and Cleopatra*; and when people compare Shakespeare and Jane Austen, they may mean that the minds of both had consumed all impediments.[25]

Jane Austen consumed all impediments: She ingested and overcame all her hardships and struggles and losses, and she kept writing.

I don't know a single author who has not faced their own hardships and struggles. Every author I know has had to fight for their own time and space to write. Every author I know has had to say, "Yes, I know I have other responsibilities. I know there are other things I could be doing that would be more profitable or would be seen by others as more valuable. But I am going to find a space for writing in my life."

There have been several times when I have almost abandoned writing, despite my love for storytelling. At these points, it seemed like the process wasn't worth it, that my writing wasn't good enough, and that I faced too many obstacles. Each time, Jane Austen saved me. Her stories inspired me and kept me moving forward.

The most recent time that Austen's works have saved me as a writer was rather recently. I had spent two and a half years—over eight hundred hours—working on a book, putting my heart and soul into a story. And for various reasons, I had to set the manuscript aside. At the same time, because of family needs, I had to give up the office that I'd spent years writing in. My stuff ended up in the basement and my closet, and my desk ended up in the corner of my daughter's bedroom. I saw the spaces for writing in my life shrinking. Every time I wrote, I experienced intense emotional pain, and I wondered if it would be best for me and for those I loved if I just let the physical, mental, and emotional spaces for my creativity continue to diminish until there was nothing left.

Then I saw Jane Austen's novels on my shelf. I thought about the blog I had written years before, titled *Jane Austen Writing Lessons*, and the handful of chapters I had written for a book titled *Write with Jane Austen*. I decided I wanted to finish it—I wanted to write a whole book on the lessons we can learn from Jane Austen's storytelling.

---

25. Woolf, *A Room of One's Own*.

Returning to Austen's works, examining how she writes characters and plots, emotions and settings, transformed me. Her humor and irony helped me see a way forward. Her words and stories lifted me, helping me let go of my fears and making me excited about storytelling again. As I've written this book, I've found my mind brimming with new ideas and possibilities, new directions and techniques and approaches.

It is my hope that you'll also find inspiration from the master storyteller and that by writing with Jane Austen you will be able to tell your own stories without fear.

Appendix A

Objective Correlative (Evoking Emotions Through External Objects)

This mini lesson should be read as a supplement to Chapter 7: Emotions.

A powerful way to evoke emotions—to make them feel real, material, and defined—is through the use of objective correlative, or using external objects that the reader connects with an emotion. And of course, Jane Austen is a master at this.

In Austen's novel *Emma*, Harriet has difficulties with love (largely because of Emma's interference). Due to Emma's encouragement, Harriet falls head over heels for Mr. Elton. She is devastated when she learns that he is actually interested in Emma. Mr. Elton leaves town and comes back with a bride, Augusta Hawkins. A few months later, a ball is held, and even though it is tradition for married men to dance with the unmarried ladies, Harriet is snubbed by Mr. Elton.

After the ball, Harriet comes to visit Emma.

> "It seems like madness! I can see nothing at all extraordinary in him now. … To convince you that I have been speaking truth, I am now going to destroy—what I ought to have destroyed long ago—what I ought never to have kept—I know that very well (blushing as she spoke).—However, now I will destroy it all—and it is my particular wish to do it in your presence, that you may see how rational I am grown."

Harriet then unveils a parcel on which she has written "Most precious treasures." She wants to destroy these treasures, and she wants Emma as a witness.

Inside are two objects. First is court-plaister that Mr. Elton had once played with—today, depending on which continent you live on, you probably call it a plaster, a bandage, or a Band-Aid.[1]

The other object is a "superior treasure," for Harriet finds it even "more valuable, because this is what did really once belong to him." She reveals the object to Emma:

---

1. Do not fear—the court-plaister is unused!

It was the end of an old pencil,—the part without any lead.

Harriet has kept both a piece of court-plaister and an unusable pencil stub *for months* after his marriage to someone else. It's an evocative image, conjuring up a series of emotions for the reader. We feel pity for Harriet, we feel sympathy for her love and her heartbreak as we understand the depth of her feelings, and we feel frustrated with Emma. After all, it is Emma's interference that has caused court-plaster and a discarded pencil stub to be another woman's most prized possessions.

This is classic objective correlative: using an object to create emotions. Interestingly, as readers we have never seen these objects before; neither Emma nor the narrator noticed them at the time, but when Harriet explains the whens and wheres and hows, Emma remembers them. What makes these objects compelling is the sequence of events that occurred before they were destroyed: Harriet could have given them up after a number of previous heartbreaks, such as when, in late December, she learns of Mr. Elton's proposal to Emma, or when, not long after, Mr. Elton marries Augusta Hawkins. But Harriet continues to hold on to these treasures until the events of the ball in early May, which makes their destruction more powerful for the reader.[2]

DEFINING OBJECTIVE CORRELATIVE AND ITS POWERFUL EMOTIONAL IMPACTS

According to scholar George P. Winston, the term objective correlative was coined by the American painter Washington Allston in 1843.[3]

Allston's definition of objective correlative is rather opaque. In his book *Lectures on Art*, he talks about how cabbages are different than cauliflowers—a cabbage can't just change into a cauliflower, for it is a cabbage, and it has its own physical properties and meaning.

Allston then writes,

> So, too, is the external world to the mind; which needs, also, as the condition of its manifestation, its objective correlative. Hence the presence of some outward object, predetermined to correspond to the preexisting idea in its living power, is essential to the evolution of its proper end,—the pleasurable emotion.[4]

---

2. There are many temporal clues in the novel *Emma*, which have been helpfully tracked by scholar Ellen Moody in "A Calendar for *Emma*."

3. Winston, "Washington Allston and the Objective Correlative," 95.

4. Allston, *Lectures on Art*.

In other words, the things that happen inside our heads—and, I would like to add, inside our hearts—are difficult to understand or manifest. It's easy to go about our days and not understand why people make certain choices. It's easy to feel like others don't truly understand our emotions, or like we don't truly understand the emotions of those around us.

This becomes tricky for the writer. How do we take an emotion—something that is inherently abstract, intangible, and in many senses, undefinable—and make it feel real and substantial to the reader? In Chapter 7, we addressed seventeen ways Austen plants emotional clues in order to convey emotions.

Allston doesn't address these approaches, in part because he is a painter, interested in things that can take visual, material form on the canvas. But his advice can be useful for writers as well: He says that what we need to do is manifest the mind—manifest the internal, unfathomable emotion—by finding a concrete, external object that can correlate to what is happening on the inside.

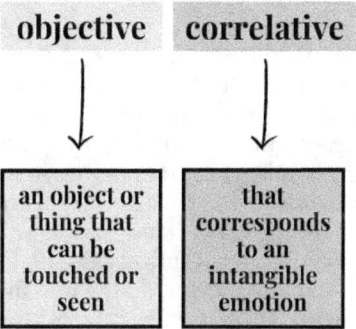

For Washington Allston, objects are "predetermined to correspond" to a "preexisting idea" or emotion, and I agree that some objects have a standard emotion attached to them. For instance, in many Western cultures, a coffin evokes emotions related to sadness and mourning.

Yet we don't automatically associate a bandage or a pencil stub with the powerful emotions that Austen conveys through them. So in order to see the true power of objective correlative, we need a more expansive definition.

While others used Allston's term, it was T. S. Eliot who popularized it in his 1919 essay "Hamlet and His Problems." He writes,

> The only way of expressing emotion in the form of art is by finding an "objective correlative"; in other words, a set of objects, a situation, a chain of events which shall be the formula of that *particular* emotion; such that when the external facts, which must terminate in sensory experience, are given, the emotion is immediately evoked.[5]

---

5. Eliot, "Hamlet and His Problems."

For T. S. Eliot, the emotional meaning of the object is contextual—it's dependent on what happens around it in the poem or story. Objects are part of a situation and a chain of events, and it is these groupings that create a formula for a particular emotion.

Let's consider a few more examples of objective correlative in Austen's work to see how we can apply this to our own writing.

In *Sense and Sensibility*, Marianne sees and reflects on the dead leaves with all the passion of romanticism. The leaves embody Marianne's endless emotions and grief as she loses her home.[6]

In *Mansfield Park*, the play *Lovers' Vows* becomes an object that conveys the emotions of both Fanny and the other characters. This is truly a set of objects: There's the script itself, the assignment of roles, all the weeks of preparation, and of course the physical set that is built and then torn down by Fanny's uncle, leaving the play unperformed.

In Austen's uncompleted novel *Sanditon*, the characters drive past Mr. and Mrs. Parker's old house on the outskirts of Sanditon, which they have left in order to live in a new house, in the heart of the action, so they can pursue Mr. Parker's dreams for the town. Both Mr. and Mrs. Parker see different things in the old house and its gardens—they notice different attributes, and the things they notice and comment upon reveal that they feel very differently about the past, present, and future. While Mr. Parker praises it as "the house of my Forefathers," he remarks that it is "built in a hole" and that he is happy to have moved on. Mrs. Parker, on the other hand, says that it was a "very comfortable House" and comments on the beautiful garden, the places where children can run and play, the desirable shade, and how it is always sheltered from the effects of winds and storms. It is clear that she misses the house and wishes they could return to it, and it is clear that turning Sanditon into a resort town is her husband's dream, not hers.

Austen uses objective correlative with moderation. Her novels are not packed with objective correlative, and not every object included in the novels is meant to evoke an emotion. Yet when she does use this technique, she does so to great effect.

Exercise A.1: Paint or Draw an Emotion

Think of a scene you have written that includes an important emotion (the emotion can be large or small, as long as it is important to the story). Now imagine that you're a painter. Instead of painting the character, you've decided to paint an object that corresponds to their emotion. If you have artistic inclinations (or want to try something new), paint or draw a picture of the object. If not, search for images online to find a representation of the object that best captures your character's emotions.

---

6. The podcast *The Thing About Austen* has an excellent episode about this entitled "The Thing About Marianne's Dead Leaves."

HOW TO USE OBJECTIVE CORRELATIVE TO CONVEY EMOTIONS IN FICTION

There are a number of principles we can take from how Austen uses objective correlative:

1. Objects can be used to correspond to emotions large and small.
2. Some objects are important or evocative in their own right, but many are made important by the attention given to them. The context and history of the object can also help imbue meaning.
3. Within a story, it's important to consider what people do with the objects or how they interact or talk about them.
4. Highlighting the characteristics or attributes of an object can help open up our understanding of the corresponding emotion.
5. The same object can engender different emotions for different characters. While sometimes an object reveals only the emotions of the main character, it can also reveal the emotions of other characters in the story.
6. An object can be used in a single scene (like the pencil in *Emma*) or in a sequence of scenes (like the play in *Mansfield Park*).
7. In addition to revealing the emotions of characters, objects often create emotions in the reader.

We're going to consider one more example from Austen, to further explore the last two points: how an object can be used in a sequence of scenes, and how an object can create emotions in the reader.

USING OBJECTIVE CORRELA-TIVE TO BUILD TO MOMENTS OF EMOTIONAL WEIGHT FOR THE READER

In his definition, T. S. Eliot talked about a **set** of objects and a **chain** of events that *immediately evoke* a particular emotion in the audience.

One of the most effective ways to create a strong emotion in a reader is to build emotion with an object over time.

A great example of this is in *Sense and Sensibility*. As we discussed in Chapter 7, Elinor often keeps her emotions deep inside her, not even sharing them with those closest to her. So how do we know that she is feeling strongly, and how do we as readers feel strongly with her? And how can we draw parallels between Elinor's heartbreak and her sister's heartbreak, even though they are both such different characters? Austen achieves all of this through objective correlative by focusing on locks of hair.

Austen first sets up hair as a meaningful token of affection early in the novel when young Margaret tells Elinor that she saw Willoughby take a lock of Marianne's hair:

> "Last night after tea, when you and mama went out of the room, they were whispering and talking together as fast as could be, and he seemed to be begging something of her, and presently he took up her scissors and cut off a long lock of her hair, for it was all tumbled down her back; and he kissed it, and folded it up in a piece of white paper; and put it into his pocket-book."

Later in the story, Edward—the man Elinor loves—comes to visit. As we discussed in the section on foreshadowing in Chapter 11, he wears a ring that contains a lock of hair. Marianne immediately assumes it belongs to Elinor, and she teases Edward by pretending to wonder if the hair belongs to Edward's sister, Fanny. He blushes and glances at Elinor and claims that the hair does indeed belong to his sister, but Elinor feels confident that the hair is hers, though she wonders how he secretly procured it.

> Edward's embarrassment lasted some time, and … he was particularly grave the whole morning. Marianne severely censured herself for what she had said; but her own forgiveness might have been more speedy, had she known how little offence it had given her sister.

Elinor is secretly pleased that Edward wears her hair in a ring. This is a promise of hope, a promise of affection, a promise that someday they might wed. And all of this emotion is embodied in a lock of hair.

A few chapters later, as the chain of events progresses, Austen once again uses this same lock of hair. This is the prime example of T. S. Eliot's emotional **formula**, for she has set up the object to produce a very specific emotion from the reader.

As we discussed in Chapter 11, when Elinor meets Lucy Steele, Lucy deduces that Elinor is in love with Edward. But Lucy is also in love with Edward, and she wants to mark her territory. Lucy makes Elinor promise not to tell anyone what she is about to share, and then she confides in Elinor that she has been secretly engaged to Edward for four years.

Elinor cannot believe her, but Lucy provides more and more evidence, including dates and places that align with Elinor's knowledge of Edward's whereabouts, a miniature painting of Edward, and a letter written in Edward's hand.

Then Lucy manages to completely decimate both Elinor's and the reader's emotions by bringing back a reference to the key object:

"I gave him a lock of my hair set in a ring when he was at Long-staple last, and that was some comfort to him, he said, but not equal to a picture. Perhaps you might notice the ring when you saw him?"

"I did," said Elinor, with a composure of voice, under which was concealed an emotion and distress beyond any thing she had ever felt before. She was mortified, shocked, confounded.

We too are mortified, shocked, and confounded, and we feel it deeply because these emotions are attached to a physical object. We thought the ring and the hair meant one thing, and to discover without a doubt that they meant something else—this immediately evokes a reaction.

For me, this is the most powerful use of objective correlative in *Sense and Sensibility*, yet Austen continues to use locks of hair for emotional effect by bringing back the other lock of hair: Marianne's.

When Marianne and Elinor spend the season in London, Marianne is snubbed by her love, Willoughby, and Elinor finds Marianne on her bed, completely and violently distraught. Next to Marianne, Elinor discovers a letter from Willoughby, who has returned Marianne's lock of hair.

It is with great regret that I obey your commands in returning the letters with which I have been honoured from you, and the lock of hair, which you so obligingly bestowed on me.

Marianne had asked for him to return her letters and the lock of hair, "if your sentiments are no longer what they were." But she did not actually want her hair back. As she tells Elinor, she thought they were engaged:

"I felt myself," she added, "to be as solemnly engaged to him, as if the strictest legal covenant had bound us to each other."

"I can believe it," said Elinor; "but unfortunately he did not feel the same."

"He *did* feel the same, Elinor—for weeks and weeks he felt it. I know he did. Whatever may have changed him now, (and nothing but the blackest art employed against me can have done it), I was once as dear to him as my own soul could wish. This lock of hair, which now he can so readily give up, was begged of me with the most earnest supplication. Had you seen his look, his manner, had you heard his voice at that moment!"

Marianne rereads Willoughby's letter, and the reference to the lock of hair only makes her more upset:

"It is too much! Oh, Willoughby, Willoughby, could this be yours! Cruel, cruel—nothing can acquit you. ... 'The lock of hair, (repeating it from the letter,) which you so obligingly bestowed on me'—That is unpardonable. Willoughby, where was your

heart when you wrote those words? Oh, barbarously insolent!—
Elinor, can he be justified?"

Once again, Austen employs objective correlative to show the depth of
Marianne's emotion by attaching it to a physical object. And, like Elinor, we
feel deeply for Marianne.

Having built up this chain of events, with this set of objects (the locks of
hair), Austen continues to use them to great effect, bringing up each lock of
hair one additional time.

When Marianne is severely ill and almost dies, Willoughby comes to visit,
and he tries to justify and redeem himself to Elinor. He blames his fiancée
for forcing him to break Marianne's heart and return Marianne's lock of hair.

> "[Marianne's] three notes,—unluckily they were all in my pock-
> etbook, or I should have denied their existence, and hoarded
> them for ever,—I was forced to put them up, and could not even
> kiss them. And the lock of hair—that too I had always carried
> about me in the same pocket-book, which was now searched by
> Madam with the most ingratiating virulence,—the dear lock,—
> all, every memento was torn from me."

Elinor is tempted to absolve Willoughby—his speech is long and passion-
ate, and the way he talks about Marianne's lock of hair is definitely a point in
his favor. Yet he returned it and broke Marianne's heart (and behaved like a
rascal in other ways).

Finally, we return once again to Lucy's lock of hair. After marrying Edward's
brother, Lucy writes one final letter to Edward, saying that she feels no ill will
toward him and that she decided she could bestow her affections elsewhere
since she thought she had lost his. The postscript of the letter reads,

> "I have burnt all your letters, and will return your picture the
> first opportunity. Please to destroy my scrawls—but the ring
> with my hair you are very welcome to keep."

Oh, dear, dear Lucy. You are married to Edward's brother, but you want him
to keep your lock of hair. You want him to treasure and remember you still.

In this case, Austen returns to the hair to create a very different emotion.
We are meant to laugh at Lucy—and this becomes a laugh of relief, and we
do feel relief, for Edward and Elinor have finally come together. Edward and
Elinor are able to read the letter and move past Lucy. As Shakespeare would
say, "All's well that ends well."

Austen does not reveal what Edward actually does with the ring and the
lock of hair, but based on his words to Elinor, and what that lock of hair meant
to Lucy, we can safely assume that he does not keep it.

It amazes me what a simple lock of hair can do in the hands of an author
like Austen. This is one of my favorite uses of objective correlative in literature.

Sometimes I unintentionally incorporate objective correlative in my work, but often I must do so intentionally.

Exercise A.2: An Example of Objective Correlative

Reread one of your favorite stories or rewatch one of your favorite shows and find an example of objective correlative. Is the object used once or as part of a sequence? What is the character's relationship with the object? What emotions does the object reveal, and what emotions does the object create in the audience?

Exercise A.3: An Emotional Sequence

Choose an everyday object: a basketball, a coffee mug, a makeup brush, or anything else. Now outline a sequence that could be used to build emotions related to the object. Plan at least three scenes (or three moments within a single scene) in which it would come into play. What does the object mean for the character? What do you want it to mean for the reader? What could be achieved by building with this object over time?

Appendix B

Establishing Characters Before They Appear in Scene

Most of the time, writers establish characters by showing them in scene. The first time we see a character, they might be engaged in a compelling dialogue that reveals something essential about their nature. They might be performing an action that impacts either themselves or other characters. Or they might be experiencing a moment of tension and drama.

In Chapter 4, we saw the power of showing characters in scene: Readers often feel and understand and accept a character's traits in a deeper way than if they were simply listed by the narrator. In Chapters 1 and 2, we saw how Austen masterfully introduces characters, in part by considering their wants, their needs, and their contradictions. And in Chapter 8, we considered the different techniques Austen uses to establish new and old relationships for the reader.

Yet there is an additional method that Austen frequently uses to introduce and reveal characters to the reader: **establishing characters *before* they appear in scene.**

One of the ways Austen does this is by having her characters think about and reference other characters before they physically appear in the story—sometimes *long* before they physically appear.

For instance, in *Mansfield Park*, Fanny Price is ripped from her home, her town, and her immediate family. When she arrives at Mansfield Park, only her cousin Edmund shows her true kindness, and he gets her to talk about her home. As she does so, we are introduced to William:

> On pursuing the subject, [Edmund] found that, dear as all these brothers and sisters generally were, there was one among them who ran more in her thoughts than the rest. It was William whom she talked of most, and wanted most to see. William, the eldest, a year older than herself, her constant companion and friend; her advocate with her mother (of whom he was the darling) in every distress. "William did not like she should come away; he had told her he should miss her very much indeed." "But William will write to you, I dare say." "Yes, he had promised he would, but he had told *her* to write first." "And when shall you do it?" She hung her head and answered hesitatingly, "she did not know; she had not any paper."

"If that be all your difficulty, I will furnish you with paper and every other material, and you may write your letter whenever you choose. Would it make you happy to write to William?"

"Yes, very."

"Then let it be done now. Come with me into the breakfast-room, we shall find everything there, and be sure of having the room to ourselves."

Fanny continues to think and talk about William throughout the story. He doesn't actually appear in person until about halfway through the novel. Yet he plays an essential role:

- He is the only main character who never hurts Fanny.
- Fanny loves him with all her heart, and his letters and presence bring her joy, as do mere thoughts of him.
- Because of William's visit, their uncle throws a ball, which creates a pivotal scene in the story, as Henry Crawford gives his attentions to Fanny.
- Henry Crawford uses his connections to secure a huge promotion for William, in an attempt to put Fanny in his debt and make her fall in love with him. (A kinder interpretation of Henry is that he secures the promotion because he genuinely cares about Fanny and the people she loves.)

William is introduced to us entirely through Fanny's perceptions of him. Not only does this shape our view of him, but it sets up his role in the story and makes us truly experience Fanny's agony when she must decide what to do. Should she marry Henry Crawford when he proposes to her, especially given what he did for her brother?

Mansfield Park is not the only Austen novel in which she establishes characters before we see them in scene—in fact, she uses this technique in every single one of her novels.

The following chart is not an exhaustive list—other characters are established before they are shown in scene—but it provides a sense of the many ways in which Austen uses this technique.

AUSTEN CHARACTERS WHO ARE ESTABLISHED PRIOR TO BEING SHOWN IN SCENE

Character (Novel)	How the Character is Established	Story Impact
Mr. Elliot (*Persuasion*)	In the first chapter, we learn that he has treated his Elliot cousins poorly, shunning Elizabeth and marrying "a rich woman of inferior birth." He has also "spoken most disrespectfully of them all, most slightingly and contemptuously of the very blood he belonged to." The first time we see Mr. Elliot in scene is slightly before the midpoint of the novel, when he admires Anne at Lyme.	When Mr. Elliot courts Anne, we are skeptical of his intentions because of what we know of his prior behavior. But because it is Elizabeth and Sir Walter who were angry at him, and these characters are also cruel to Anne, Mr. Elliot seems like he could be redeemable.
John Thorpe (*Northanger Abbey*)	When Catherine meets Isabella Thorpe, they realize that they have a prior connection. Catherine remembers "that her eldest brother had lately formed an intimacy with a young man of his own college, of the name of Thorpe; and that he had spent the last week of the Christmas vacation with his family, near London." We see John Thorpe in scene three chapters later.	This prior connection helps the reader to see why Catherine takes so long to read John Thorpe's true character—everything she had learned about him in advance of meeting him was positive.
Mr. Bingley (*Pride and Prejudice*)	Mr. Bingley is discussed in the first chapter as a prospective suitor for one of the Bennet daughters. We see him in scene for the first time at the Meryton assembly.	This builds anticipation for him as a character, so we, like the daughters, long to meet him when he arrives at the Meryton ball.
Mr. Collins (*Pride and Prejudice*)	Mr. Collins is established by Mr. Bennet as the relative who stands to inherit their home. While at this point we don't see him in scene, we hear his words through the letter that he sends to Mr. Bennet. Not long after his letter, he arrives at Longbourn.	Each member of the Bennet family forms a different judgment of Mr. Collins based on his written words. See further discussion in Chapter 8.

Lady Catherine de Bourgh (*Pride and Prejudice*)	Lady Catherine de Bourgh is referenced constantly by Mr. Collins, who reveres her (she is his patroness!). Nuance is added when we learn that she is Mr. Darcy's aunt. We first see her in scene when Elizabeth goes to visit Charlotte after her marriage to Mr. Collins.	Mr. Collins's admiration makes Lady Catherine an intriguing character to the reader—someone we want to meet. Her influence and power foreshadow the end of the novel, when she attempts to convince Elizabeth not to marry Mr. Darcy.
Georgiana Darcy (*Pride and Prejudice*)	Georgiana Darcy is established early on as Mr. Darcy's younger sister. Mr. Darcy writes her long letters, and Caroline Bingley constantly praises Georgiana and wants her brother to marry her. Conversely, Mr. Wickham paints a negative picture of Georgiana, stating that "I wish I could call her amiable. ... She is too much like her brother,—very, very proud." His portrait both skirts and acknowledges his past with her. We also learn about Georgiana from Colonel Fitzwilliam, who is one of her two guardians. Elizabeth teases him about Georgiana likely being "difficult to manage." His response makes Elizabeth realize "that she had somehow or other got pretty near the truth." We see Georgiana Darcy in scene about two-thirds of the way through the novel, when Elizabeth visits Pemberley.	In some respects, Georgiana Darcy is a minor character: We see her very little in scene, and her roles when she is present in scene are rather minor. Yet at the same time, she is a major character: So much of the plot revolves around her and her past relationship with Mr. Wickham, which parallels Mr. Wickham's relationship with Lydia and influences Darcy's and Wickham's behavior. Much of what is established about Miss Darcy serves to foreshadow grand revelations about past events and to foreshadow future incidents.
Frank Churchill (*Emma*)	Frank Churchill is loved and anticipated by (almost) everyone, even though he has never visited. Emma fancies him. Mr. Knightley dislikes and distrusts him, simply because he has not visited his father, Mr. Weston. We first see Frank Churchill in scene a few chapters before the midpoint of the story.	As discussed in Chapter 6, the question of Frank Churchill's character is a driving information gap throughout the novel. A clash between Emma and Mr. Knightley is also established, and we wonder who is correct about Frank's character.

Jane Fairfax (*Emma*)	Jane Fairfax's character is established by Emma, who admits that she has no good reason for not liking her. We see Jane Fairfax through how others speak of her and through her letters to her aunt, Miss Bates. We see Jane Fairfax in scene about a third of the way through the novel, when she arrives to live, once again, with her aunt and her grandmother.	The way in which Jane Fairfax is established highlights the fact that she is a foil to Emma. At the end of the novel, it ends up being significant that Jane Fairfax's return to Highbury predates Frank Churchill's arrival—he has visited not because of his other obligations, but because of her.
Mrs. Ferrars (*Sense and Sensibility*)	Mrs. Ferrars is a constant force in the novel. Her expectations for Edward lead to his misery and control many of his choices. We hear of her through many characters before we meet her. Lucy Steele and Edward hide their engagement in part because of Lucy's belief that "Mrs. Ferrars is a very headstrong proud woman" who would be very angry if she heard of their engagement and would possibly eliminate Edward's inheritance. We only see Mrs. Ferrars in scene in a single chapter that appears almost two-thirds of the way through the novel. In this scene, Mrs. Ferrars meets both Lucy and Elinor for the first time. She is kind to Lucy to be cruel to Elinor.	Mrs. Ferrars influences much of the plot both before and after her single appearance in scene. By mostly appearing through others' accounts, she becomes a larger-than-life mythic force. Lucy's prediction about Mrs. Ferrars is accurate—Mrs. Ferrars disowns Edward on hearing of the secret engagement.

As you can see from these examples, there are endless potential uses for establishing a character before they appear in scene. However, Austen does seem to have a number of core purposes for doing so.

EIGHT REASONS TO ESTABLISH CHARACTERS BEFORE THEY ARE SHOWN IN SCENE:
1. It predisposes us to feel a certain way about unmet characters.
2. It focuses our attention on the character and the role that they will play.
3. It allows a character to influence the plot before they appear physically on the page.
4. It produces an information gap. This can create tension as well as an

expectation and desire for the readers to meet the characters and see them more fully.

5. It foreshadows future events, revelations of past events, and plot twists.
6. It sets up a sense of relationships and can add a community focus to the story—it is not just individual relationships at stake, but an entire community.
7. It draws attention to the lens through which we see characters. The narrator is already providing a way to see the characters and the story, but this draws attention to how we look at a non-present character. As the story progresses, we may either agree or disagree with the lenses that have been used.
8. It reveals information not only about the unseen character, but also about the characters we have already met. We understand our known characters more deeply by how they think and talk about the character who is not yet present.

While there are many other good ways to establish characters, establishing a character before they appear in scene is a multipurpose technique that can be used in powerful ways.

Exercise B.1: Enemy, Friend, Lover

Spend two to five minutes brainstorming a character.

Consider how you could introduce this character without showing them in scene. How would they be talked about by an enemy, by a friend, and by a lover?

You can interpret enemy, friend, and lover in any way you choose. For example, an enemy could be a coworker the character doesn't get along with or a member of a multifamily feud. A friend could be a best friend or a new acquaintance with a shared interest. A lover could be a boyfriend, a spouse, someone involved in an illicit liaison, etc.

Consider also that an enemy, friend, or lover may at times attempt to hide, disguise, or downplay their relationship with the character. If they do so, it may reveal things about both individuals.

Write three brief introductions of the character: one by an enemy, one by a friend, and one by a lover.

Exercise B.2: Character Introductions

Read the first thirty pages of a book or watch the first thirty minutes of a film. Write down every time a character is introduced and how they are introduced (for example, they may be introduced through dialogue, a moment of tension, being referenced by a character who is present on the page, or numerous other methods). Does the story use multiple types of character introductions or mostly one type? How does the manner in which they are introduced impact the audience?

APPENDIX C

CRITIQUING AND REVISING

I've been a member of critique groups for well over a decade, and sometimes I wonder what it would be like to be in a critique group with Jane Austen. We know that as a young writer, she frequently shared her drafts with family members and friends, entertaining them with her stories. We know she revised these pieces, and she surely made changes based on their reactions and their questions.

As a published author, she, in turn, critiqued the writing of others. Her niece, Anna Austen Lefroy, loved to write and asked her aunt for feedback on her works. Between 1814 and 1816, Jane Austen wrote a series of letters to Anna, giving entertaining, helpful, and at times difficult critiques.

One thing that stands out to me is that Austen uses many of the same critiquing methods that I learned in graduate school, when I was studying the best practices for teaching writing.

THE SANDWICH CRITIQUE METHOD: GOOD-BAD-GOOD

In Austen's letters, she never just tells Anna what isn't working; she also gives positive feedback.

In an undated letter, likely from the spring or early summer of 1814, Austen wrote to her niece,

MY DEAR ANNA,

I am very much obliged to you for sending your MS [manuscript]. It has entertained me extremely; all of us indeed. I read it aloud to your Grandmama and Aunt Cass., and we were all very much pleased. The spirit does not droop at all. Sir Thos., Lady Helen and St. Julian are very well done, and Cecilia continues to be interesting in spite of her being so amiable. It was very fit you should advance her age. I like the beginning of Devereux Forester very much, a great deal better than if he had been very good or very bad. A few verbal corrections are all that I felt tempted to make; the principal of them is a speech of St. Julian to Lady Helen, which you see I have presumed to alter. As Lady H. is Cecilia's superior, it would not be correct to talk of *her* being introduced.

It is Cecilia who must be introduced. And I do not like a lover speaking in the 3rd person; it is too much like the formal part of Lord Orville, and I think it not natural. If *you* think differently, however, you need not mind me. I am impatient for more, and only wait for a safe conveyance to return this book.

Yours affectionately, J. A. [7]

This letter uses the classic sandwich technique for critiquing: start with the positive, detail what could be improved, and then end with more positive. In other words, wrap what might be difficult to hear in between things that are working and positive encouragement.

Thus, Jane begins with "It has entertained me extremely" and ends with "I am impatient for more."

At other times, Austen weaves the positive and the negative together. In a letter written on September 28, 1814, Jane analyzes Anna's characters, dissecting which ones are working and which ones need work:

> We like the first chapter extremely, with only a little doubt whether Lady Helena is not almost *too* foolish. The matrimonial dialogue is very good certainly. I like Susan as well as ever, and begin now not to care at all about Cecilia; she may stay at Easton Court as long as she likes. Henry Mellish will be, I am afraid, too much in the common novel style—a handsome, amiable, unexceptionable young man (such as do not much abound in real life), desperately in love and all in vain. But I have no business to judge him so early. Jane Egerton is a very natural comprehendable girl, and the whole of her acquaintance with Susan and Susan's letter to Cecilia are very pleasing and quite in character. But *Miss* Egerton does not entirely satisfy us. She is too formal and solemn, we think, in her advice to her brother not to fall in love; and it is hardly like a sensible woman—it is putting it into his head. We should like a few hints from her better.[8]

She paints a clear picture of strengths and weaknesses: Some of the characters are "pleasing"—they feel natural and likeable—while other characters are cliché ("too much in the common novel style") or "too formal and solemn."

Writing exists with an audience in mind, and as a critiquer, you stand in for the audience, sharing your reactions to the story, as well as your assumptions on how larger audiences will react. Thus, it's useful for Jane to **share both what is working and what is not working**. As writers we clearly need to know what's not working—it's difficult to take a story from our heads and

---

7. Jane Austen to Anna Austen Lefroy, undated letter. *Letters of Jane Austen—Brabourne Edition. Letters to her niece Anna Austen Lefroy, 1814–1816.*

8. Jane Austen to Anna Austen Lefroy, September 28, 1814. *Letters of Jane Austen—Brabourne Edition. Letters to her niece Anna Austen Lefroy, 1814–1816.*

hearts and place it on a page, to convey what we want to convey. An audience reaction can let us know what needs to be improved. But we also need to know what is good about our writing—we need affirmation. In part, this is for self-esteem purposes, but we also need to know what's working well so we keep it in the story. And when a technique is working well, we can emulate it in the rest of the story.

Modern scholar Bill Hart-Davidson recommends using a describe-evaluate-suggest model when giving a critique,[9] and we see Austen using this very approach. She describes what she sees, evaluates it according to the goals of the story, and then, if needed, gives suggestions for improvement.

Thus, she **describes** the character of Henry Mellish as "a handsome, amiable, unexceptionable young man" and then **evaluates** the character according to her metric, feeling like a real person. She writes that he is a type that does "not much abound in real life." The **suggestion** is implied—Anna should make him less "in the common novel style" and pull back on some of his characteristics.

Exercise C.1: Describe-Evaluate-Suggest

Choose something that's not writing that you would normally critique. For example, you might disagree with someone's restaurant choice or vacation plan or the clothes a child has chosen to wear on the first day of school.

Write two versions of a critique. In the first version, be very direct, perhaps stating that it's a bad idea or doesn't work and telling what they should do instead.

In the second version, use the describe-evaluate-suggest framework. First, describe what you see or the choice that is being made. Then, evaluate it according to a framework—hopefully a shared framework. Then make a suggestion. (For example, "That restaurant does have delicious food, but we know we have somewhere to be by 7 p.m. and that's a rather slow restaurant, so it might be better to choose something faster.")

JANE AUSTEN AND CRITICAL DISTANCE

When we consider Austen's few surviving manuscripts, such as the unfinished *Sanditon*, it is clear that Austen revised at multiple stages of the writing process.[10] As I read through the original manuscripts, I see sentences where it seems like Austen wrote part of the sentence, crossed out the middle, and then

---

9. Hart-Davidson, "Describe – Evaluate – Suggest."

10. You can see digitized versions of all of Austen's surviving manuscripts on the website *Jane Austen's Fiction Manuscripts*.

kept going.[11] I also see revisions that were likely made after finishing a scene or a chapter. Words and sometimes entire sentences are crossed out, and new phrases and sentences are squeezed in around the original text.

Yet these are not the only types of revisions Austen made. As we discussed in Chapter 12, on endings, she also made more substantive changes. In the case of *Persuasion*, she scrapped the original ending and wrote a new one. This must have been a difficult decision to make—personally, I am always a little wary of deleting entire scenes or chapters, though I've never regretted doing it.

In one of her letters to Anna, Jane writes,

> I hope when you have written a great deal more, you will be equal to scratching out some of the past. The scene with Mrs. Mellish I should condemn; it is prosy and nothing to the purpose; and indeed the more you can find in your heart to curtail between Dawlish and Newton Priors, the better I think it will be—one does not care for girls until they are grown up.[12]

Austen pinpoints one scene for deletion. She also asks Anna to consider all the scenes between Dawlish and Newton Priors, in order to see what can be cut. Let's return to the sentence **before** these scene-cutting recommendations:

> I hope when you have written a great deal more, you will be equal to scratching out some of the past.

What Austen is recommending is **critical distance.**

Critical distance is giving yourself enough distance or space from your work that you can see it critically and make hard choices about it.

Jane does not want her niece to cut scenes right now—she wants her to do it once she's further through the process and more able to make these bigger sorts of revisions.

I suspect she had this sort of critical distance when she rewrote the ending of *Persuasion*. Another letter written to Anna gives us additional insight. She writes,

> Now we have finished the second book, or rather the fifth. I *do* think you had better omit Lady Helena's postscript. To those that are acquainted with "Pride and Prejudice" it will seem an imitation.[13]

---

11. For example, in the original manuscript of *Sanditon*, it reads, *The severity of the fall was broken by their slow pace & the narrowness of the Lane, & the ~~Travellors beleived found themselves at first only shaken & bruised~~ Gentleman having scrambled out & helped out his companion, they neither of them felt more than shaken & bruised.*

12. Jane Austen to Anna Austen Lefroy, September 9, 1814. *Letters of Jane Austen—Brabourne Edition. Letters to her niece Anna Austen Lefroy, 1814–1816.*

13. Jane Austen to Anna Austen Lefroy, August 10, 1814. *Letters of Jane Austen—Brabourne Edition. Letters to her niece Anna Austen Lefroy, 1814–1816.*

Interestingly, Jane did not make this critique until she had read more—she needed a broader sense of the work in order to see what larger changes needed to be made. This is one of the benefits of finishing a full draft before doing major revisions: Often, we can only tell if things are working when we have a sense of the whole.[14]

One of my personal techniques for creating critical distance is to finish a draft, then give myself at least a few weeks before I start revising it. This allows me to see it more clearly and to separate myself from the work.

Many writing groups—including my own—read a chapter or two of someone's work a month and give feedback on it. But there's certain feedback that can only be given in the context of the whole. While I love the detailed, focused feedback on individual chapters that I receive from my critique group, I always make sure to have other new readers, who haven't previously read a single chapter, read the entire manuscript and give feedback—this allows them to have critical distance as well.

JANE AUSTEN ON WRITING FOR AN AUDIENCE

In Jane's critique letters to her niece Anna, she seems to care a lot about accuracy. In one letter, Jane writes to Anna,

> We are reading the last book. They must be *two* days going from Dawlish to Bath. They are nearly 100 miles apart.[15]

She places emphasis on the word *two*—clearly, Anna did not provide her characters with enough travel time.

In the same letter, she responds to questions that Anna must have asked:

> I am not sensible of any blunders about Dawlish; the library was pitiful and wretched twelve years ago and not likely to have anybody's publications.

Jane had personal experience with the town of Dawlish, while Anna did not; based on her own experiences, she's able to state that Anna's depiction feels accurate. In the same letter, she informs Anna,

---

14. I know a number of authors who won't revise at all until a full draft is complete. If you've never finished writing a full draft of a novel, then this can be a particularly helpful approach. In my current writing process, I make minor revisions as I write, but I try to limit myself until I've finished an entire draft.

15. Jane Austen to Anna Austen Lefroy, August 10, 1814. *Letters of Jane Austen—Brabourne Edition. Letters to her niece Anna Austen Lefroy, 1814–1816.*

There is no such title as Desborough either among dukes, marquises, earls, viscounts, or barons.

Austen either knew her dukes and marquises very well or had access to a book where she could check this information for her niece.

But why does accuracy matter so much to Jane? Why do details about locations, distances, and titles matter?

Later in the letter, Jane gives us a clue when she recommends that Anna change a location:

> Lyme will not do. Lyme is towards forty miles from Dawlish and would not be talked of there. I have put Starcross instead. If you prefer Exeter, that must be always safe.

Jane wants Anna's characters to feel realistic—she wants people in Dawlish to speak of things that would matter to them, not of a town that is too far away. She wants Anna to succeed in capturing people as they really are.

In part, this relates to Austen's approach to storytelling: She uses life—real life—as the canvas for her novels. And with that storytelling framework, if something doesn't feel realistic, it can break the illusion of life for the reader. This is the case even in *Northanger Abbey*, an intentional pastiche that comments on the joys and excesses of the Gothic novel, yet does so by making the characters and situations feel real and possible.

One of Austen's contemporaries, Samuel Taylor Coleridge, writes about the willing "suspension of disbelief" by readers that allows them to enjoy a story. We know something is fiction, and yet we give it "poetic faith"—we invest ourselves in the story.

Breaking the illusion of life can halt the suspension of disbelief, pulling a reader from the story. Jane wrote to Anna that

> your grandmother is more disturbed at Mrs. Forester's not returning the Egertons' visit sooner than by anything else. They ought to have called at the Parsonage before Sunday.[16]

Anna's character, Mrs. Forester, has not met basic societal expectations, and it pulls the reader out of the story. This is not to say that characters cannot break conventions—Austen's characters do all the time, but when they do, it's noticed and commented upon by other characters. For instance, in *Pride and Prejudice*, Lady Catherine is shocked that neither Elizabeth nor her sisters ever received drawing instruction:

> "That is very strange. But I suppose you had no opportunity. Your mother should have taken you to town every spring for the benefit of masters."

---

16. Jane Austen to Anna Austen Lefroy, September 9, 1814. *Letters of Jane Austen—Brabourne Edition. Letters to her niece Anna Austen Lefroy, 1814–1816.*

In *Emma*, Mr. Knightley comments—with exasperation—on the almost ridiculous number of fortunate coincidences that have blessed Frank Churchill:

> Frank Churchill is, indeed, the favourite of fortune. Every thing turns out for his good.—He meets with a young woman at a watering-place, gains her affection, cannot even weary her by negligent treatment—and had he and all his family sought round the world for a perfect wife for him, they could not have found her superior.—His aunt is in the way.—His aunt dies.—He has only to speak.—His friends are eager to promote his happiness.— He had used every body ill—and they are all delighted to forgive him.—He is a fortunate man indeed!"

By calling attention to Frank Churchill's extreme good fortune, it normalizes it within the narrative. At other times, Austen makes something believable by setting up characters, situations, and events in such a way that the unbelievable seems to arise naturally, even if it would be difficult to believe otherwise. For example, in *Mansfield Park*, Sir Thomas returns home right before a major rehearsal of the play *Lovers' Vows* and cancels the play. But this has been set up— it has been foreshadowed—for we know he has been traveling overseas, and we know that the time it takes for ship travel is highly variable. Even further, his tyrannical character has been set up, so his reaction to the play—which might seem extreme for other characters—makes sense within the story's framework.

Often, accuracy helps make the story more readable and meets audience expectations. But at other times, accuracy and audience expectations can collide. Something can match reality yet not be believable to a reader. Jane writes to Anna,

> I have scratched out Sir Thos. from walking with the others to the stables, &c. the very day after breaking his arm; for, though I find your papa *did* walk out immediately after *his* arm was set, I think it can be so little usual as to *appear* unnatural in a book.[17]

This is something I frequently face when writing historical fiction: Something may be historically accurate, but if readers will feel like it's *not* historically accurate, then I probably shouldn't use it. For instance, while working on a story set in the 1870s, I wanted to use the phrase "in her teens," and the phrase had been used regularly for fifty years at that point. Yet it feels like such a modern phrase that it would pull readers out of the story. (It's possible to set something up so readers realize it's accurate and it doesn't pull them out of the story, but most of the time it's only worth doing for important things, not a simple word or phrase.)

---

17. Jane Austen to Anna Austen Lefroy, August 10, 1814. *Letters of Jane Austen—Brabourne Edition. Letters to her niece Anna Austen Lefroy, 1814–1816.*

Austen recognizes that stories are written for an audience, and we must be aware of their needs, understanding, and expectations—even if it sometimes means sacrificing realism and accuracy for believability.

Exercise C.2: The Unbelievable

Make a list of things that have happened to you that readers might find difficult to believe if you put them in a fiction novel.

Choose one of the items on your list. How could you set this up in a way that readers would find it believable?

RESPECTING THE STORYTELLER

One of the other things I notice as I read Jane's letters is the respect that she shows to Anna as a storyteller. She does not assume that she, the person giving feedback, knows better than the writer.

Thus, in the undated letter she writes,

> I do not like a lover speaking in the 3rd person; it is too much like the formal part of Lord Orville, and I think it not natural. If *you* think differently, however, you need not mind me.

In a different letter, at the end of a rather critical paragraph, she writes,

> Excuse the liberty I take in these suggestions.[18]

If I were to receive a critique from Jane Austen, I'd be inclined to apply every piece of feedback without question. But when Austen gives specific feedback, she is careful to frame it as a suggestion. Yes, she is a published author and her niece is not, but she knows that ultimately it's Anna's story. Anna can choose to apply the feedback if she wishes, but Jane does not want her to feel obligated to do so.

This is a healthy attitude to take when giving a critique: The goal is to help the writer revise and tell their own story in their own way, to the best of their abilities. It's not to dominate or to dictate or to encourage the writer to tell the story that *you* would personally tell.

When we receive critiques, it's important to develop the same self-respect that Jane is attempting to engender in her niece: a humility and willingness

---

18. Jane Austen to Anna Austen Lefroy, September 28, 1814. *Letters of Jane Austen— Brabourne Edition. Letters to her niece Anna Austen Lefroy, 1814–1816.*

to improve and be aware of an audience, coupled with a confidence in one's own storytelling and authorial goals.

I wish we had more of Austen's surviving manuscripts so we could peer even further into her revisions, but with the manuscripts we have and her letters to her niece, we get a glimpse of how important critiquing and revising were in her writing process.

Exercise C.3: Respecting the Writer

The next time that you give someone else a critique, consider how you can show respect to them as a storyteller.

The next time that you plan to send your writing to a reader or a critique partner, first write either a personal mantra about your writing, or positive thoughts about yourself as a storyteller or the story that you're about to share. You can acknowledge that the story needs improvement but also show respect to yourself as a writer.

IMAGE SOURCES

Most of the images in this book were created by three late nineteenth-century artists: Hugh Thomson, C. E. Brock, and Chris Hammond.

Hugh Thomson (1860–1920) was an Irish illustrator who used primarily pen and ink. He is known for illustrating all six of Austen's novels, as well as works by Charles Dickens, Elizabeth Gaskell, Shakespeare, and J. M. Barrie.

C. E. Brock (1870–1938) was an illustrator from Cambridge who worked with both ink and watercolor. In addition to illustrating works by Sir Walter Scott, William Thackeray, and George Eliot, he illustrated all of Austen's novels—and some of them he illustrated more than once.

Chris Hammond (1860–1900) was the nom de plume of the female painter and illustrator Christiana Hammond. She illustrated the works of a number of female authors, including Maria Edgeworth, Mary Catherine Rowsell, Dinah Craik, and Elizabeth Gaskell. She only illustrated two of Jane Austen's full novels—*Sense and Sensibility* and *Emma*. She began illustrating *Pride and Prejudice* before her death.

Most of the images included in this book are in the public domain. The remaining images are used through Creative Commons licenses. Details are provided in each source description.

INTRODUCTION

Jane Austen's Writing Case
The British Library. *Jane Austen's Desk (open view 1)*. 2018. Photograph. https://bl.iro.bl.uk/concern/images/67b218b0-4eef-4868-8076-04e054de35eb. Creative Commons License (CC BY 4.0, background removed and converted to black and white).

CHAPTER 1

Emma bringing Mr. Weston and Miss Taylor together
Brock, C. E. *I planned the match from that hour*. 1909. Color illustration. Wikimedia Commons. https://commons.wikimedia.org/wiki/File:Emma_CE_Brock_1909_Vol_I_chapter_I.jpg. Public domain.

Mr. Bingley arrives in Netherfield
Thomson, Hugh. *"He came down to see the place."* 1894. Illustration. Project Gutenberg. https://gutenberg.org/cache/epub/1342/images/i_031.jpg. Public domain.

Mrs. Bennet sends Jane to Netherfield on horseback
Thomson, Hugh. *Cheerful prognostics*. 1894. Illustration. Project Gutenberg. https://gutenberg.org/cache/epub/1342/images/i_069.jpg. Public domain.

While visiting Pemberley, Elizabeth spends several minutes looking at Mr. Darcy's portrait
Brock, C. E. *"She stood several minutes before the picture, in earnest contemplation."*

1895. Illustration. Wikimedia Commons. https://commons.wikimedia.org/wiki/File:Illustration_by_C_E_Brock_for_Pride_and_Prejudice_-_She_stood_several_minutes_before_the_picture,_in_earnest_contemplation.jpg. Public domain.

Mr. Bingley and Mr. Darcy return
Thomson, Hugh. "Mr. Darcy with him." 1894. Illustration. Project Gutenberg. https://gutenberg.org/cache/epub/1342/images/i_433_a.jpg. Public domain.

Lady Catherine informs Mr. Darcy of her conversation with Elizabeth
Thomson, Hugh. "The efforts of his aunt."1894. Illustration. Project Gutenberg. https://gutenberg.org/cache/epub/1342/images/i_477_a.jpg. Public domain.

Elizabeth and Mr. Darcy converse after they become engaged
Brock, C. E. *Now, be sincere; did you admire me for my impertinence?* 1895. Illustration. Wikimedia Commons. https://commons.wikimedia.org/wiki/File:P%26P60-Be_sincere_(BrockNB).JPG. Public domain.

Catherine Morland reading
Artist unknown. *Catherine scaring herself with* Udolpho. 1833. Illustration. Wikimedia Commons. https://commons.wikimedia.org/wiki/File:NACatherinereading.jpg. Public domain.

CHAPTER 2

Emma watches Harriet Smith speak to Mr. Robert Martin
Thomson, Hugh. *Emma was not sorry to have such an opportunity of survey.* 1896. Illustration. Wikimedia Commons. https://commons.wikimedia.org/wiki/File:Emma-frontispice_(ch04).jpg. Public domain.

Maslow's Hierarchy of Needs
Androidmarsexpress. *Maslow's Hierarchy of Needs*. 2020. Graphic. Wikimedia Commons. https://commons.wikimedia.org/wiki/File:Maslow%27s_Hierarchy_of_Needs2.svg. Creative Commons License (CC BY-SA 4.0, converted to black and white).

After her injury, Marianne is approached by Willoughby
Hammond, Chris. *She was scarcely able to stand.* 1899. Illustration. Wikimedia Commons. https://commons.wikimedia.org/wiki/File:Hammond-SS05.jpg. Public domain.

Fanny Price and Mary Crawford
Brock, C. E. *Good, gentle Fanny!* 1908. Color illustration. Wikimedia Commons. https://commons.wikimedia.org/wiki/File:Mp-Brock-20.jpg. Public domain.

Anne and Captain Wentworth speak before the start of the concert
Brock, C. E. *In spite of the formidable father and sister in the background.* 1909. Color illustration. Wikimedia Commons. https://commons.wikimedia.org/wiki/File:Persbrock-19.jpg. Public domain.

Captain Wentworth does something kind for Anne by helping her with her nephew
Thomson, Hugh. *Some one was taking him from her.* 1897. Illustration. Wikimedia Commons. https://commons.wikimedia.org/wiki/File:Thomson-ch9-Aide_bienvenue.JPG. Public domain.

Mr. Woodhouse laments that Miss Taylor has married
Hammond, Chris. *Ah! poor Miss Taylor! 'tis a sad business.* 1898. Illustration. Wikimedia Commons. https://commons.wikimedia.org/wiki/File:Hammond-Emma03_(recadr%C3%A9e).jpg. Public domain.

CHAPTER 3

Sir Walter admires his personal appearance
Brock, C. E. *Few women could think more of their personal appearance than he did.* 1909. Color illustration. Wikimedia Commons. https://commons.wikimedia.org/wiki/ File:Pers-brock-03.jpg. Public domain.

The ill Mary Musgrove greets her sister, Anne Elliot
Brock, C. E. *So you are come at last!* 1909. Color illustration. Wikimedia Commons. https://commons.wikimedia.org/wiki/File:Pers-brock-06.jpg. Public domain.

Fanny as a child, after arriving at Mansfield Park
Brock, C. E. *In vain were the well-meant condescensions of Sir Thomas.* 1908. Color illustration. Wikimedia Commons. https://commons.wikimedia.org/wiki/File:Mp-Brock-03.jpg. Public domain.

CHAPTER 4

Original illustrations for Jane's copy of *The History of England*: Henry IV, Elizabeth I, Mary Queen of Scotts, and Edward IV
Austen, Cassandra. *Henry the fourth.* Circa 1790. Color illustration. Wikimedia Commons. https://commons.wikimedia.org/wiki/File:CassandraAusten-HenryIV.jpg. Public domain.
Austen, Cassandra. *Elizabeth.* Circa 1790. Color illustration. Wikimedia Commons. https://commons.wikimedia.org/wiki/File:CassandraAusten-ElizabethI. jpg. Public domain.
Austen, Cassandra. *Mary Q. of Scotts.* Circa 1790. Color illustration. Wikimedia Commons. https://commons.wikimedia.org/wiki/File:CassandraAusten-MaryQueenofScots.jpg. Public domain.
Austen, Cassandra. *Edward the 4th.* Circa 1790. Color illustration. Wikimedia Commons. https://commons.wikimedia.org/wiki/File:CassandraAusten-EdwardIV. jpg. Public domain.

"Mrs. Elton was first seen at church"
Hammond, Chris. *"Mrs. Elton was first seen at church."* 1898. Illustration. Wikimedia Commons. https://commons.wikimedia.org/wiki/File:Hammond-Emma20. jpg. Public domain.

Elizabeth leaves the others to their walk
Thomson, Hugh. *"No, no; stay where you are."* 1894. Illustration. Project Gutenberg. https://gutenberg.org/cache/epub/1342/images/i_096.jpg. Public domain.

The Bennet family
Thomson, Hugh. *The Bennet family at home.* 1894. Illustration. Wikimedia Commons. https://commons.wikimedia.org/wiki/File:Benethom.gif. Public domain.

Catherine sees everything in the abbey in the light of her Gothic novels
Brock, C. E. *Good God! How came you up that staircase?* 1907. Color illustration. Wikimedia Commons. https://commons.wikimedia.org/wiki/File:Northanger_ Abbey_CE_Brock_Vol_II_chap_IX.jpg. Public domain.

Mrs. Cole is surprised when she sees Jane Fairfax's anonymously-gifted pianoforte
Hammond, Chris. *As soon as she entered the room, had been struck by the sight of a pianoforte.* 1898. Illustration. Wikimedia Commons. https://commons.wikimedia.org/ wiki/File:Hammond-Emma17.jpg. Public domain.

CHAPTER 5

Fanny picks roses
Brock, C. E. *While Fanny cut the roses*. 1908. Color illustration. Wikimedia Commons. https://commons.wikimedia.org/wiki/File:Mp-Brock-06.jpg. Public domain.

Mrs. Norris supervises Fanny's needlework
Brock, C. E. *She worked very diligently under her aunt's directions*. 1908. Color illustration. Wikimedia Commons. https://commons.wikimedia.org/wiki/File:Mp-Brock-10.jpg. Public domain.

Fanny Price refuses Henry Crawford's proposal
Brock, C. E. *"No, no, no!," she cried, hiding her face*. 1908. Color illustration. Wikimedia Commons. https://commons.wikimedia.org/wiki/File:Mp-Brock-17.jpg. Public domain.

Mrs. Ferrars
Hammond, Chris. *Upright even to formality in her figure, and serious even to sourness in her aspect*. 1899. Illustration. Wikimedia Commons. https://commons.wikimedia.org/wiki/File:Hammond-SS18.jpg. Public domain.

Cover of *Sense and Sensibility*
Artist unknown. *Sense and Sensibility by Jane Austen*. 1884. Book cover. British Library. https://www.flickr.com/photos/britishlibrary/11170582744/. Public domain.

Willoughby requests that Elinor listen to his story
Brock, C. E. *Miss Dashwood … I entreat you to stay*. 1908. Color illustration. Wikimedia Commons. https://commons.wikimedia.org/wiki/File:Sands-brock-21.jpg. Public domain.

CHAPTER 6

Catherine Moreland and Isabella Thorpe in Bath
Brock, C. E. *Always arm-in-arm when they walked*. 1907. Color illustration. Wikimedia Commons. https://commons.wikimedia.org/wiki/File:Northanger_Abbey_CE_Brock_Vol_I_chap_V.jpg. Public domain.

Mr. Elliot steps back, and as he does so, he admires Anne
Brock, C. E. *Politely drew back and stopped to give them way*. 1909. Color illustration. Wikimedia Commons. https://commons.wikimedia.org/wiki/File:Pers-brock-13.jpg. Public domain.

Frank Churchill breaks the expectations of Highbury by traveling all the way to London for a haircut
Thomson, Hugh. *Having his hair cut*. 1896. Illustration. Wikimedia Commons. https://commons.wikimedia.org/wiki/File:Emma-ch25_(II,7).jpg. Public domain.

Henry and Mary discuss his plans to break Fanny's heart
Thomson, Hugh. *"And how you think I mean to amuse myself, Mary, on the days that I do not hunt?"* 1896. Illustration. Wikimedia Commons. https://commons.wikimedia.org/wiki/File:Thomson-MP-Ch-22.JPG. Public domain.

Maria Bertram and Henry Crawford upon hearing the news that Sir Thomas has returned
Thomson, Hugh. *"My father is come!"* 1897. Illustration. Wikimedia Commons. https://commons.wikimedia.org/wiki/File:Thomson-MP-ch18.JPG. Public domain.

CHAPTER 7

Marianne's emotional exit
Thomson, Hugh. *Apparently in violent affliction.* 1896. Illustration. Wikimedia Commons. https://commons.wikimedia.org/wiki/File:Sense_and_sensibility_1896_ (118347263).jpg. Public domain.

Willoughby looks at the ground as he speaks
Hammond, Chris. *With his eyes fixed on the ground, he only replied, "You are too good."* 1899. Illustration. Wikimedia Commons. https://commons.wikimedia.org/wiki/File:Hammond-SS09.jpg. Public domain.

Fanny and Henry Crawford open the ball
Brock, C. E. *Conducted by Mr. Crawford to the top of the room.* 1908. Color illustration. Wikimedia Commons. https://commons.wikimedia.org/wiki/File:Mp-Brock-16.jpg. Public domain.

Mr. Darcy declares that Elizabeth is tolerable
Thomson, Hugh. *"She is tolerable."* 1894. Illustration. Wikimedia Commons. https://commons.wikimedia.org/wiki/File:Thomson-PP05.jpg. Public domain.

The five Bennet sisters
Thomson, Hugh. *Not for sale.* 1894. Illustration. Wikimedia Commons. https://commons.wikimedia.org/wiki/File:Thomson-_For_sale.JPG. Public domain.

Mr. Wickham and the other officers arrive at the Phillipses' home
Brock, C. E. *It was over at last, however. The gentlemen did approach.* 1895. Illustration. Wikimedia Commons. https://commons.wikimedia.org/wiki/File:P%26P16-Arriv%C3%A9e_de_Wickham_(BrockNB).JPG. Public domain.

Mr. Darcy asks Elizabeth to read his letter
Brock, C. E. *"Will you do me the honour of reading that letter?"* 1895. Illustration. Wikimedia Commons. https://commons.wikimedia.org/wiki/File:Illustration_by_C_E_Brock_for_Pride_and_Prejudice_-_Will_you_do_me_the_honour_of_reading_that_letter.jpg. Public domain.

Mrs. Dashwood sits through the night with Marianne during her illness
Hammond, Chris. *"Mrs. Dashwood would sit up with her all night."* 1899. Illustration. Wikimedia Commons. https://commons.wikimedia.org/wiki/File:Hammond-Emma20.jpg. Public domain.

CHAPTER 8

Mr. Darcy's first proposal to Elizabeth
Brock, C. E. *"You must allow me to tell you how ardently I admire and love you."* 1895. Illustration. Wikimedia Commons. https://commons.wikimedia.org/wiki/File:Illustration_by_C_E_Brock_for_Pride_and_Prejudice_-_You_must_allow_me_to_tell_you_how_ardently_I_admire_and_love_you.jpg. Public domain.

Caroline Bingley attempts to flirt with Mr. Darcy
Brock, C. E. *"You write uncommonly fast."* 1895. Illustration. Wikimedia Commons. https://commons.wikimedia.org/wiki/File:Illustration_by_C_E_Brock_for_Pride_and_Prejudice_-_You_write_uncommonly_fast.jpg. Public domain.

Emma caring for her father

Thomson, Hugh. *Emma hung about him affectionately.* 1896. Illustration. Wikimedia Commons. https://commons.wikimedia.org/wiki/File:Emma-ch53_(III-17).jpg. Public domain.

The unnamed Lucas boy

Brock, C. E. *"If I were as rich as Mr. Darcy, I would keep a pack of foxhounds, and drink a bottle of wine every day."* 1895. Illustration. Wikimedia Commons. https://commons.wikimedia.org/wiki/File:Illustration_by_C_E_Brock_for_Pride_and_Prejudice_-_If_I_were_as_rich_as_Mr._Darcy,_I_would_keep_a_pack_of_foxhounds,_and_drink_a_bottle_of_wine_every_day.jpg. Public domain.

Mr. Knightley and Emma playing with their young nephews

Thomson, Hugh. *Tosses them up to the ceiling.* 1896. Illustration. Wikimedia Commons. https://commons.wikimedia.org/wiki/File:Emma-ch9_(I-9).jpg. Public domain.

Charlotte asks Elizabeth to visit her

Thomson, Hugh. *"Will you come and see me."* 1894. Illustration. Project Gutenberg. https://gutenberg.org/cache/epub/1342/images/i_210_a.jpg. Public domain.

Charlotte and Mr. Collins

Thomson, Hugh. *"Whenever she spoke in a low voice."* 1894. Illustration. Project Gutenberg. https://gutenberg.org/cache/epub/1342/images/i_195.jpg. Public domain.

Willoughby cuts a lock of Marianne's hair

Thomson, Hugh. *He cut off a long lock of her hair.* 1896. Illustration. Wikimedia Commons. https://commons.wikimedia.org/wiki/File:Sense_and_Sensibility_Illustration_Chap_12.jpg. Public domain.

Harriet cries upon learning that Mr. Elton favors Emma, not her

Hammond, Chris. *"The sight of Harriet's tears."* 1898. Illustration. Wikimedia Commons. https://commons.wikimedia.org/wiki/File:Hammond-Emma14.jpg. Public domain.

Chapter 9

Marianne sends a letter to Willoughby

Hammond, Chris. *Marianne, ringing the bell, requested the footman who answered it, to get that letter conveyed for her to the twopenny post.* 1899. Illustration. Wikimedia Commons. https://commons.wikimedia.org/wiki/File:Hammond-SS13.jpg. Public domain.

Sir Walter and Mr. Shepherd

Brock, C. E. *"The unwelcome hints of Mr Shepherd, his agent."* 1898. Color illustration. Wikimedia Commons. https://commons.wikimedia.org/wiki/File:2pers-01.jpg. Public domain.

Mr. Collins proposes to Elizabeth

Thomson, Hugh. "To assure you in the most animated language." 1894. Illustration. Project Gutenberg. https://gutenberg.org/cache/epub/1342/images/i_161_a.jpg. Public domain.

Mrs. Smith shares one of Mr. Elliot's letters with Anne Elliot

Brock, C. E. *Such a letter, could not be read without putting Anne in a glow.* 1909. Color illustration. Wikimedia Commons. https://commons.wikimedia.org/wiki/File:Pers-brock-21.jpg. Public domain.

Miss Bates speaking to Emma
Thomson, Hugh. *Miss Bates came to the carriage door.* 1896. Illustration. Wikimedia Commons. https://commons.wikimedia.org/wiki/File:Image_taken_from_page_379_of_%27(Emma._New_edition.)%27_(11299328635).jpg. Public domain.

CHAPTER *10*

Those gathered at Box Hill play a rather disastrous word game
Hammond, Chris. *"Ladies and gentlemen, I am ordered by Miss Woodhouse … to say."* 1898. Illustration. Wikimedia Commons. https://commons.wikimedia.org/wiki/File:Hammond-Emma22_(recadr%C3%A9e).jpg. Public domain.

Box Hill, Surrey, with Dorking in the distance
Lambert, George. *Box Hill, Surrey, with Dorking in the distance.* 1733. Oil on canvas. Wikimedia Commons. https://commons.wikimedia.org/wiki/File:George_Lambert_-_Box_Hill,_Surrey,_with_Dorking_in_the_distance_-_Google_Art_Project.jpg. Public domain.

Bath pump room and baths
Artist unknown. *Engraving of the Pump Room and exterior of the baths in Bath.* 1864. Engraving. Wikimedia Commons. https://commons.wikimedia.org/wiki/File:Bath_Pump_Room_%26_Baths.jpg. Public domain.

John Thorpe and Catherine Moreland in a carriage
Thomson, Hugh. *Off they went, without a plunge or a caper.* 1897. Illustration. British Library. https://www.flickr.com/photos/britishlibrary/11240130306/. Public domain.

Miss Bates helps someone less fortunate than herself
Hammond, Chris. *I really believe if she had only a shilling in the world she would be very likely to give away sixpence of it.* 1898. Illustration. Wikimedia Commons. https://commons.wikimedia.org/wiki/File:Hammond-Emma09.jpg. Public domain.

Mrs. Jennings and Sir John speak to Elinor through her window
Hammond, Chris. *"She came hallooing to the window, How do you do my dear."* 1899. Illustration. Wikimedia Commons. https://commons.wikimedia.org/wiki/File:Hammond-SS11.jpg. Public domain.

Mr. Darcy during his first proposal to Elizabeth
Brock, C. E. *"You must allow me to tell you how ardently I admire and love you."* 1895. Illustration. Wikimedia Commons. https://commons.wikimedia.org/wiki/File:Illustration_by_C_E_Brock_for_Pride_and_Prejudice_-_You_must_allow_me_to_tell_you_how_ardently_I_admire_and_love_you.jpg. Public domain.

Mr. Wickham is "surprised, displeased, alarmed"
Brock, C. E. *He looked surprised, displeased, alarmed.* 1895. Illustration. Wikimedia Commons. https://commons.wikimedia.org/wiki/File:Illustration_by_C_E_Brock_for_Pride_and_Prejudice_-_He_looked_surprised,_displeased,_alarmed.jpg. Public domain.

Rose pencil drawing
Rose (Rosa species): flowers and leaves. Pencil drawing. Wellcome Collection. https://wellcomecollection.org/works/s85ugtmt. Creative Commons License (CC BY 4.0, image cropped and converted to black and white).

Steps on the Cobb
Talbot, Chris. *Cobb—Steps onto the Cobb.* 2009. Photograph. https://www.geograph. org.uk/photo/1599557. Creative Commons License (CC BY-SA 2.0, cropped and converted to black and white).

Everyone is shocked at Louisa's injury
Brock, C. E. *The horror of that moment to all who stood around!* 1909. Color illustration. Wikimedia Commons. https://commons.wikimedia.org/wiki/File:Pers-brock-14. jpg. Public domain.

A carriage in "Christmas weather"
Hammond, Chris. *Christmas weather.* 1898. Illustration. Wikimedia Commons. https:// commons.wikimedia.org/wiki/File:Hammond-Emma11.jpg. Public domain.

CHAPTER 11

Henry Crawford helps Fanny with her shawl
Thomson, Hugh. *Put round her shoulders by Mr. Crawford's quicker hands.* 1897. Illustration. Wikimedia Commons. https://commons.wikimedia.org/wiki/ File:Thomson-MP-Frontispice_(ch25).JPG. Public domain.

Colonel Brandon tells Eliza's story to Elinor
Brock, C. E. *Rising hastily walking for a few minutes about the room.* 1908. Color illustration. Wikimedia Commons. https://commons.wikimedia.org/wiki/ File:Sand-brock-15.jpg. Public domain.

Willoughby carries Marianne down the hill after her injury
Brock, C. E. *Carried her down the hill.* 1908. Color illustration. Wikimedia Commons. https://commons.wikimedia.org/wiki/File:Sands-brock-06.jpg. Public domain.

Lucy and Elinor, moments before Lucy reveals her secret
Thomson, Hugh. *Amiably bashful.* 1896. Illustration. Wikimedia Commons. https:// commons.wikimedia.org/wiki/File:Sense_and_sensibility_1896_(118347485). jpg. Public domain.

Mr. Knightley proposes to Emma
Thomson, Hugh. *He stopped to look the question.* 1896. Illustration. Wikimedia Commons. https://commons.wikimedia.org/wiki/File:Emma-ch49_(III-13).jpg. Public domain.

Mr. Knightley and Emma, when he realizes that Emma returns his affections
Hammond, Chris. *"Say 'No' if it is to be said." She could really say nothing.* 1898. Illustration. Wikimedia Commons. https://commons.wikimedia.org/wiki/ File:Hammond-Emma24_(recadr%C3%A9e).jpg. Public domain.

CHAPTER 12

Captain Wentworth gives his letter to Anne, "with eyes of glowing entreaty fixed on her"
Thomson, Hugh. *Placed it before Anne.* 1897. Illustration. Wikimedia Commons. https:// commons.wikimedia.org/wiki/File:Thomson-ch23-Lettre.JPG. Public domain.

Sir Thomas lectures Fanny
Brock, C. E. *"Am I to understand," said Sir Thomas, "that you mean to refuse Mr. Crawford?"* 1908. Color illustration. Wikimedia Commons. https://commons. wikimedia.org/wiki/File:Mp-brock-18.jpg. Public domain.

The Morlands are surprised by Henry's request to marry their daughter, but they consent
Brock, C. E. *Mr and Mrs Morland's surprise … was considerable.* 1907. Color illustration. Wikimedia Commons. https://commons.wikimedia.org/wiki/File:Northanger_Abbey_CE_Brock_Vol_II_chap_XVI.jpg. Public domain.

Fanny learns of Maria's disgrace by reading her father's newspaper
Brock, C. E. *"There!—much good may such fine relations do you."* 1908. Color illustration. Wikimedia Commons. https://commons.wikimedia.org/wiki/File:Mp-Brock-23.jpg. Public domain.

Colonel Brandon asks Elinor to speak to Edward Ferrars
Hammond, Chris. *She was almost read to cry out, "Lord, what should hinder it."* 1899. Illustration. Wikimedia Commons. https://commons.wikimedia.org/wiki/File:Hammond-SS19.jpg. Public domain.

The servant tells Mrs. Dashwood that Mr. Ferrars is married
Thomson, Hugh. *"I suppose you know, ma'am, that Mr. Ferrars is married."* 1896. Illustration. Wikimedia Commons. https://commons.wikimedia.org/wiki/File:Sense_and_sensibility_1896_(118348183).jpg. Public domain.

Edward proposes to Elinor
Hammond, Chris. *His errand at Barton … was a simple one. It was only to ask Elinor to marry him.* 1899. Illustration. Wikimedia Commons. https://commons.wikimedia.org/wiki/File:Hammond-SS21.jpg. Public domain.

After learning that Elizabeth and Mr. Darcy plan to marry, "Mrs. Bennet sat quite still…unable to utter a syllable"
Thomson, Hugh. *"Unable to utter a syllable."* 1894. Illustration. Project Gutenberg. https://gutenberg.org/cache/epub/1342/images/i_486_a.jpg. Public domain.

In the denouement, we learn that after spending time with Fanny, Edmund "had so well talked his mind into submission as to be very tolerably cheerful again"
Thomson, Hugh. *Sitting under trees with Fanny.* 1897. Illustration. Wikimedia Commons. https://commons.wikimedia.org/wiki/File:Thomson-MP-ch48.JPG. Public domain.

Chapter 13

Miss Steele
Hammond, Chris. *"'There now,' said Miss Steele, affectedly simpering 'everyone laughs at me so about the Doctor.'"* 1899. Illustration. Wikimedia Commons. https://commons.wikimedia.org/wiki/File:Hammond-SS16.jpg. Public domain.

Marianne experiences pain as she listens to Edward reading aloud
Hammond, Chris. *"I could hardly keep my seat. To hear those beautiful lines which have frequently almost driven me wild, pronounced with such impenetrable calmness."* 1899. Illustration. Wikimedia Commons. https://commons.wikimedia.org/wiki/File:Hammond-SS03.jpg. Public domain.

Elizabeth and the Gardiners watch out the window as Mr. Darcy approaches the inn
Thomson, Hugh. *Heading to Chapter XLIV.* 1894. Illustration. Project Gutenberg. https://gutenberg.org/cache/epub/1342/images/i_347_a.jpg. Public domain.

Sir John raises a glass to Elinor Dashwood
Thomson, Hugh. *Drinking to her best affections.* 1896. Illustration. Wikimedia Commons. https://commons.wikimedia.org/wiki/File:Sense_and_sensibility_1896_(118347464).jpg. Public domain.

Elizabeth and Mr. Wickham discuss Colonel Fitzwilliam
Brock, C. E. *He looked surprised, displeased, alarmed.* 1895. Illustration. Wikimedia Commons. https://commons.wikimedia.org/wiki/File:Illustration_by_C_E_Brock_for_Pride_and_Prejudice_-_He_looked_surprised,_displeased,_alarmed.jpg. Public domain.

CHAPTER *14*

Jane Fairfax
Thomson, Hugh. *"I am very sorry to hear, Miss Fairfax, of your being out this morning in the rain."* 1896. Illustration. Wikimedia Commons. https://commons.wikimedia.org/wiki/File:Emma-ch34_(II,16).jpg. Public domain.

Lady Catherine de Bourgh
Brock, C. E. *I assure you, I feel it exceedingly.* 1895. Color illustration. Wikimedia Commons. https://commons.wikimedia.org/wiki/File:Lady_Catherine_de_Bourg.jpg. Public domain.

"The spiteful old ladies" of Meryton
Thomson, Hugh. *"The spiteful old ladies."* 1894. Illustration. Project Gutenberg. https://gutenberg.org/cache/epub/1342/images/i_406_a.jpg. Public domain.

Elizabeth speaks to Mr. Darcy after learning of Lydia's elopement
Thomson, Hugh. *"I have not an instant to lose."* 1894. Illustration. Wikimedia Commons. https://commons.wikimedia.org/wiki/File:Thomson-PP19.jpg. Public domain.

General Tilney pacing
Brock, C. E. *It was the air and attitude of a Montoni!* 1907. Color illustration. Wikimedia Commons. https://commons.wikimedia.org/wiki/File:Northanger_Abbey_CE_Brock_Vol_II_chap_VIII.jpg. Public domain.

Marianne says her goodbyes to Norland
Hammond, Chris. *"Dear, dear, Norland! when shall I cease to regret you."* 1899. Illustration. Wikimedia Commons. https://commons.wikimedia.org/wiki/File:Hammond-SS04.jpg. Public domain.

CHAPTER *15*

Mr. and Mrs. Bennet
Thomson, Hugh. *Mr and Mrs Bennet.* 1894. Illustration. Project Gutenberg. https://gutenberg.org/cache/epub/1342/images/i_034.jpg. Public domain.

Anne overhears their conversation
Brock, C. E. *"Here is a nut," said he, "to exemplify."* 1909. Color illustration. Wikimedia Commons. https://commons.wikimedia.org/wiki/File:Pers-brock-11.jpg. Public domain.

Colonel Brandon visits Marianne when she is ill
Brock, C. E. *Colonel Brandon was invited to visit her.* 1909. Color illustration. Wikimedia Commons. https://commons.wikimedia.org/wiki/File:Sands-brock-23.jpg. Public domain.

Mrs. Jennings
Thomson, Hugh. *Both gained considerable amusement.* 1896. Illustration. Wikimedia Commons. https://commons.wikimedia.org/wiki/File:Sense_and_sensibility_1896_(118348067).jpg. Public domain.

Lady Catherine visits Elizabeth at Longbourn
Thomson, Hugh. *Lady Catherine de Bourgh comes to visit Elizabeth*. 1894. Illustration. Wikimedia Commons. https://commons.wikimedia.org/wiki/File:Thomson-PP22. jpg. Public domain.

Lydia is excited to journey to Brighton
Thomson, Hugh. *"Tenderly flirting."* 1894. Illustration. Project Gutenberg. https:// gutenberg.org/cache/epub/1342/images/i_319.jpg. Public domain.

CHAPTER 16

Title page of the first edition of *Pride and Prejudice*
Austen, Jane. *Title page from the first edition of the first volume of Pride and Prejudice*. 1813. Title page. Wikimedia Commons. https://commons.wikimedia.org/wiki/ File:PrideAndPrejudiceTitlePage.jpg. Public domain.

The cottage where Jane Austen lived in Chawton
R. ferroni2000. *Jane Austen house museum*. 2017. Photograph. Wikimedia Commons. https://commons.wikimedia.org/wiki/File:Jane_Austen_house_museum.jpg. Creative Commons License (CC BY-SA 4.0, converted to black and white).

Jane Austen's walnut writing table
Smith, Colin. *Chawton—Jane Austen*. 2019. Photograph. Wikimedia Commons, https://commons.wikimedia.org/wiki/File:Chawton_-_Jane_Austen_-_geograph. org.uk_-_6692601.jpg. Creative Commons License (CC BY-SA 2.0, converted to black and white).

BIBLIOGRAPHY

JANE AUSTEN

Austen, Jane. "The beautifull Cassandra. a novel in twelve Chapters. dedicated by permission to Miss Austen." In *Jane Austen's Manuscript Works*, edited by Linda Bree, Peter Sabor, and Janet Todd. Broadview Editions, 2013.

Austen, Jane. "The 'Cancelled Chapters' of *Persuasion*." 1816. Internet Archive Wayback Machine. Accessed October 13, 2025. https://web.archive.org/web/20250125055033/https://mollands.net/etexts/persuasion/prscancel.html.

Austen, Jane. *Emma: A Novel. In Three Volumes*. 1st ed. Volumes 1–3. 1816. University of Illinois Urbana-Champaign via Internet Archive, 2010. https://archive.org/details/emmanovel01aust.

Austen, Jane. *Emma*. 1815. Project Gutenberg, 1994. https://www.gutenberg.org/cache/epub/158/pg158-images.html.

Austen, Jane. *Fragment of a Novel [Sanditon]*. Originally unpublished, 1817. Project Gutenberg, 2024. https://www.gutenberg.org/cache/epub/74233/pg74233-images.html.

Austen, Jane. *The History of England from the reign of Henry the 4th to the death of Charles the 1st*. Originally unpublished juvenilia, Nov. 26, 1791. University of Chicago. Accessed May 29, 2025. https://penelope.uchicago.edu/austen/austen.html.

Austen, Jane. *Lady Susan*. Originally unpublished, 1794. Project Gutenberg, 1997. https://www.gutenberg.org/files/946/946-h/946-h.htm.

Austen, Jane. *Letters of Jane Austen*. 1892. Project Gutenberg, 2024. https://www.gutenberg.org/files/42078/42078-h/42078-h.htm.

Austen, Jane. *Letters of Jane Austen—Brabourne Edition*. 1906. Pemberley.com, 2011. https://pemberley.com/janeinfo/brablets.html.

Austen, Jane. *Letters of Jane Austen—Brabourne Edition. Letters to her niece Anna Austen Lefroy, 1814–1816*. 1906. Pemberley.com, 2011. https://pemberley.com/janeinfo/brablt16.html.

Austen, Jane. *Mansfield Park: A Novel. In Three Volumes*. 1st ed. Volumes 1–3. 1814. University of Oxford via Google Books via Internet Archive, 2017. https://archive.org/details/JaneAusten-MansfieldPark-1814-v1.

Austen, Jane. *Mansfield Park*. 1814. Project Gutenberg, 1994. https://www.gutenberg.org/files/141/141-h/141-h.htm.

Austen, Jane. *Northanger Abbey: and Persuasion. In Four Volumes*. 1st ed. Volumes 1 4. 1818. University of Illinois Urbana-Champaign via Internet Archive, 2010. https://archive.org/details/northangerabbeyp01aust.

Austen, Jane. *Northanger Abbey*. 1803. Project Gutenberg, 1994. https://www.gutenberg.org/files/121/121-h/121-h.htm.

Austen, Jane. *Persuasion*. Edited by Linda Bree. Broadview Literary Texts, 1998.

Austen, Jane. *Persuasion*. 1818. Project Gutenberg, 1994. https://www.gutenberg.org/files/105/105-h/105-h.htm.

Austen, Jane. *Pride and Prejudice: A Novel. In Three Volumes*. 1st ed. Volumes 1–3. 1813. Opensource via Internet Archive, 2017. https://archive.org/details/

JaneAusten-PrideandPrejudice-1sted-1813-vol1/.

Austen, Jane. *Pride and Prejudice*. 1813. Project Gutenberg, 2013. https://gutenberg. org/cache/epub/1342/pg1342-images.html.

Austen, Jane. *Sense and Sensibility: A Novel. In Three Volumes*. 1st ed. Volumes 1–3. 1811. Duke University Libraries via Internet Archive, 2012. https://archive.org/ details/sensesensibility131aust/.

Austen, Jane. *Sense and Sensibility*. 1811. Project Gutenberg, 1994. https://www.gutenberg.org/cache/epub/161/pg161-images.html.

OTHER

Ackerman, Angela, and Becca Puglisi. *The Emotion Thesaurus: A Writer's Guide to Character Expression*. 2nd ed. JADD Publishing, 2019.

Addison, Joseph. *The Spectator in Three Volumes*. Edited by Henry Morley. 1891. Project Gutenberg, 2014. https://www.gutenberg.org/files/9334/9334-h/9334-h.htm.

Allston, Washington. *Lectures on Art*. Edited by Richard Henry Dana, Jr. 1850. Project Gutenberg, 2020. https://www.gutenberg.org/files/11391/11391-h/11391-h.htm.

Aristotle. *The Poetics of Aristotle*. Translated by S. H. Butcher. Project Gutenberg, 2008. https://www.gutenberg.org/files/1974/1974-h/1974-h.htm.

Bird, Kristen. "The Darker Side of Jane Austen." *CrimeReads*. February 9, 2022. https:// crimereads.com/darker-side-jane-austen/.

Brody, Jessica. *Save the Cat! Writes a Novel: The Last Book on Novel Writing You'll Ever Need*. Ten Speed Press, 2018.

Brownstein, Rachel M. "Endless Imitation: Austen's and Byron's Juvenilia." In *The Child Writer from Austen to Woolf*, edited by Christine Alexander and Juliet McMaster. Cambridge University Press, 2005.

Burton, Gideon. "Description (The Progymnasmata)." *Silva Rhetoricae: The Forest of Rhetoric*. February 26, 2007. https://rhetoric.byu.edu/Pedagogy/Progymnasmata/ Description.htm. Creative Commons License (CC BY 3.0).

Burton, Gideon. "Figures of Repetition." *Silva Rhetoricae: The Forest of Rhetoric*. February 26, 2007. https://rhetoric.byu.edu/Figures/Groupings/of%20Repetition. htm. Creative Commons License (CC BY 3.0).

Burton, Gideon. *Silva Rhetoricae: The Forest of Rhetoric*. February 26, 2007. https:// rhetoric.byu.edu. Creative Commons License (CC BY 3.0).

Byrne, Paula. *The Real Jane Austen: A Life in Small Things*. Harper, 2013.

Cambridge Dictionary. Accessed May 29, 2025. https://dictionary.cambridge.org/ dictionary/english/.

Cowper, William. "Verses, supposed to be written by Alexander Selkirk, during his solitary Abode in the Island of Juan Fernandez." 1782. Eighteenth-Century Poetry Archive, 2015. https://www.eighteenthcenturypoetry.org/works/ o3794-w0130.shtml.

Cox, Octavia. "Jane Austen's Zeugma Jokes: What is zeugma? And how does Jane Austen use it? Literary Analysis." Dr. Octavia Cox, August 5, 2022. Video, 18 min., 52 sec. https://www.youtube.com/watch?v=Y2T32p2gCM0.

Eliot, T. S. "Hamlet and His Problems." *The Sacred Wood*. 1921. Bartleby, 1996. https://www.bartleby.com/lit-hub/the-sacred-wood/hamlet-and-his-problems/.

Etymonline: Online Etymology Dictionary. Updated April 7, 2025. https://www.etymonline.com/.

Freytag, Gustav. *Freytag's Technique of the Drama: An Exposition of Dramatic Composition and Art*. Translated by Elias J. MacEwan. 1894. Google Books, 2010. https://

books.google.com/books?id=nD8PAQAAMAAJ.

Gardner, John. *The Art of Fiction: Notes on Craft for Young Writers*. Vintage Books, 1991.

Glenn, Cheryl, and Melissa A. Goldthwaite. *The St. Martin's Guide to Teaching Writing*. 6th ed. Bedford/St. Martin's, 2008.

Groff, Lauren. "Jane Austen's Boldest Novel Is Also Her Least Understood." *New York Times*. June 27, 2025. https://www.nytimes.com/2025/06/27/books/review/jane-austen-mansfield-park.html.

Grogan, Claire. Introduction and commentary on *Northanger Abbey*, 2nd ed., by Jane Austen. Edited by Claire Grogan. Broadview Literary Texts, 2004.

Hart-Davidson, Bill. "Describe - Evaluate - Suggest: Giving Helpful Feedback, with Bill Hart-Davidson." Eli Review, December 19, 2014. Video, 3 min., 46 sec. https://www.youtube.com/watch?v=KzdBRRQhYv4.

Heath, Chip, and Dan Heath. *Made to Stick: Why Some Ideas Survive and Others Die*. Random House, 2007.

Herrick, James A. *The History and Theory of Rhetoric: An Introduction*. 4th ed. Pearson: 2009.

Hutcheson, Francis. *Reflections upon Laughter and Remarks upon the Fable of the Bees*. Facsimile ed. Garland, 1971.

Jane Austen's Fiction Manuscripts. Accessed May 30, 2025. https://janeausten.ac.uk/.

"Jane Austen's Writing Table." Jane Austen's House. Accessed May 29, 2025. https://janeaustens.house/object/jane-austens-writing-table/.

Kolln, Martha. *Rhetorical Grammar: Grammatical Choices, Rhetorical Effects*. 5th ed. Pearson Education: 2007.

Krotoski, Aleks. "Robin Dunbar: we can only ever have 150 friends at most..." *The Guardian*. March 13, 2010. https://www.theguardian.com/technology/2010/mar/14/my-bright-idea-robin-dunbar.

Le Guin, Ursula K. *Steering the Craft: A 21st-Century Guide to Sailing the Sea of Story*. Mariner Books, 2015.

Lehrer, Jonah. "The Itch of Curiosity." *Wired*. August 3, 2010. https://www.wired.com/2010/08/the-itch-of-curiosity/.

Longknife, Ann, and K. D. Sullivan. *The Art of Styling Sentences*. Barrons Educational Series, 2012.

Maslow, A. H. "A Theory of Human Motivation." *Psychological Review* 50 (1943): 370–396. Classics in the History of Psychology, 2000. https://web.archive.org/web/20170914183817/http://psychclassics.yorku.ca/Maslow/motivation.htm.

McKee, Robert. *Story: Substance, Structure, Style, and the Principles of Screenwriting*. HarperEntertainment, 1997.

Moody, Ellen. "A Calendar for *Emma*." January 3, 2003. http://www.jimandellen.org/austen/emma.calendar.html.

Morreall, John. "Philosophy of Humor." In *Stanford Encyclopedia of Philosophy*, edited by Edward N. Zalta and Uri Nodelman. Revised September 19, 2024. https://plato.stanford.edu/archives/fall2024/entries/humor/.

New Oxford American Dictionary. 3rd ed. Edited by Angus Stevenson and Christine A. Lindberg. Oxford University Press, 2010.

"Newton's Laws of Motion." *Glenn Research Center, National Aeronautics and Space Administration*. Last modified June 27, 2024. https://www1.grc.nasa.gov/beginners-guide-to-aeronautics/newtons-laws-of-motion/.

Obstfeld, Raymond. *Novelist's Essential Guide to Crafting Scenes*. Writer's Digest Books, 2000.

Oesterreich, Peter L. "Irony." *Encyclopedia of Rhetoric*. Translated by Andreas Quintus. Edited by Thomas O. Sloane. Online ed., 2006. Oxford Reference Library.

Orwell, George. "Politics and the English Language." 1946. The Orwell Foundation.

Accessed March 29, 2025. https://www.orwellfoundation.com/the-orwell-foundation/orwell/essays-and-other-works/politics-and-the-english-language/.

Oxford English Dictionary. Accessed December 15, 2024. https://www.oed.com/

Patterson, Janci. "Reaching for Beats." May 2, 2014. https://www.jancipatterson.com/2014/05/02/reaching-for-beats-2/.

Peters, Hayden. *Art of Mourning*. 2005. https://artofmourning.com/.

Salimpoor, Valorie N., Mitchel Benovoy, Kevin Larcher, Alain Dagher, and Robert J. Zatorre. "Anatomically distinct dopamine release during anticipation and experience of peak emotion to music." *Nature Neuroscience* 14, no. 2. (2011): 257–62. ProQuest Central.

Satici, Seydi Ahmet, Recep Uysal, and M. Engin Deniz. "Linking social connectedness to loneliness: The mediating role of subjective happiness." *Personality and Individual Differences* 97 (July 2016): 306–310. https://www.sciencedirect.com/science/article/abs/pii/S019188691530057X.

Slaughter, Elliott. "Dialogue Tags: An Empirical Study." June 20, 2020. https://elliottslaughter.com/2020/06/dialogue-tags.

Snyder, Blake. *Save the Cat! The Last Book on Screenwriting You'll Ever Need*. Michael Wiese Productions, 2005. Kindle.

Snyder, Maria V. "Writing Through the Middle." Accessed May 29, 2025. https://www.mariavsnyder.com/advice/middles.php.

Southam, Brian. *Jane Austen's Literary Manuscripts: A Study of the Novelist's Development Through the Surviving Papers*. Rev. ed. Athlone Press, 2001.

Strunk, Jr., William, and E. B. White. *The Elements of Style*. 4th ed. Longman: 2000.

Temple, Emily. "Kurt Vonnegut's Greatest Writing Advice." *LitHub*. April 11, 2017. https://lithub.com/kurt-vonneguts-greatest-writing-advice/.

The Thing About Austen. Episode 4, "The Thing About Marianne's Dead Leaves." Hosted by Zan Cammack and Diane Neu. July 22, 2021. Podcast, 29 min., 14 sec. https://www.thethingaboutausten.com/episodes/ep-04-the-thing-about-mariannes-dead-leaves.

Tomalin, Claire. *Jane Austen: A Life*. Vintage, 1999.

Twain, Mark. *Following the Equator: A Journey Around the World*. 1898. Project Gutenberg, 2025. https://www.gutenberg.org/files/2895/2895-h/2895-h.htm.

Wade, Karen. "Jane Austen's Social Networks." *The Sea of Books*, July 4, 2017. https://theseaofbooks.com/2017/07/04/jane-austens-social-networks/.

Walton, Jo. "Thud: Half a Crown & Incluing." May 16, 2007. Internet Archive Wayback Machine. https://web.archive.org/web/20111119145140/http://papersky.livejournal.com/324603.html.

Wells, Dan. "Dan Wells on Story Structure, part 2 of 5." S. James Nelson, February 21, 2010. Video, 10 min. https://www.youtube.com/watch?v=mrP-9604BEOM&list=PLzfRuHa21NIzQFrQ6FAq8Pj2IA_SXiwrN&index=2.

Wells, Dan. "Dan Wells on Story Structure, part 4 of 5." S. James Nelson, February 21, 2010. Video, 9 min., 53 sec. https://www.youtube.com/watch?v=0WC_WWEr-Nd8&list=PLzfRuHa21NIzQFrQ6FAq8Pj2IA_SXiwrN&index=4.

Winston, George P. "Washington Allston and the Objective Correlative." *The Bucknell Review* 11, no. 1 (1962): 95–108. ProQuest Central.

Woolf, Virginia. *A Room of One's Own*. 1929. Project Gutenberg Australia, 2020. https://gutenberg.net.au/ebooks02/0200791h.html.

Worsley, Lucy. *Jane Austen at Home: A Biography*. St. Martin's Press, 2017.

Writing Excuses. Season 9, episode 13, "Three Pronged Character Development." Hosted by Brandon Sanderson, Howard Tayler, Mary Robinette Kowal, and Dan Wells. March 30, 2014. Podcast, 20 min., 5 sec. https://writingexcuses.com/writing-excuses-9-13-three-prong-character-development/.

Writing Excuses. Season 9, episode 25, "Adjusting Character Sympathy." Hosted by Brandon Sanderson, Howard Tayler, Mary Robinette Kowal, and Dan Wells. June 15, 2014. Podcast, 18 min., 55 sec. https://writingexcuses.com/writing-excuses-9-25-adjusting-character-sympathy/.

Writing Excuses. Season 17, episode 3, "Chekov's Surprising Yet Inevitable Inverted Gun." Hosted by Howard Tayler, Kaela Rivera, Sandra Tayler, and Megan Lloyd. January 16, 2022. Podcast, 20 min., 10 sec. https://writingexcuses.com/17-3-chekovs-surprising-yet-inevitable-inverted-gun/.

Writing Excuses. Season 17, episode 32, "Everything is About Conflict." Hosted by Dan Wells, Mary Robinette Kowal, Maurice Broaddus, and Howard Tayler. August 7, 2022. Podcast, 17 min., 41 sec. https://writingexcuses.com/17-32-everything-is-about-conflict/.

GLOSSARY

action: outward manifestations of will; what a character does *(see also: want; motive)*

active character: a character who acts and does things in an attempt to achieve their wants and fulfill their needs *(see also: passive character)*

alliteration: repeating the same sound at the start of multiple words *(see also: repetition)*

allusion: a reference to a work outside of the text that readers are likely familiar with and that adds to the reader's understanding

anastrophe: reversing the normal word order; often done by placing an adjective after a noun

anesis: building something up, and then using a statement to diminish or negate the priorly expressed positives *(see also: understatement)*

antagonism: anything that opposes or interferes with a character and their wants and needs, whether a person, an object, a setting, or outside events; by providing struggle, this opposition or interference creates engaging plot events and provides opportunities for character growth *(see also: antagonist; obstacle)*

antagonist: a person who actively opposes the main character and tries to interfere with them achieving their wants and needs, typically over multiple scenes or a large portion of the story *(see also: obstacle; villain)*

antonomasia: instead of using a proper name or noun, using a quality or descriptive phrase *(see also: substitution; periphrasis)*

aposiopesis: not finishing a sentence, thought, or idea

assonance: repetition of vowel sounds *(see also: repetition)*

asyndeton: omitting a conjunction before the final item in a list *(see also: polysyndeton)*

authorial stance: see stance

auxesis: labeling something with a term that makes it seem larger, stronger, better, more severe, more debilitating, etc., than it actually is *(see also: overstatement)*

backstory: the entire history of the characters, their situations, and their communities *(see also: exposition; infodump; incluing)*

bomphiologia: when an individual overstates themselves, through bragging or self-exaggeration *(see also: overstatement)*

character: a fictional person in a story; also, this person's characteristics and essence *(see also: character arc; internal journey)*

character arc: how a character changes over the course of a story *(see also: character; internal journey)* *charientismus:* using pleasant or friendly words to deal with a difficult problem *(see also: understatement)*

cliche: a trite, overdone, and overused phrase

climax: the focal point of the story and the most important turning point; problems build to this moment where everything is at stake, and then begin to resolve after this moment *(see also: tragic force; key turning point)*

complication: the rising action of the story, in which difficulties build on each other *(see also: rising action)*

conflict: tension between characters that is manifest in words or actions *(see also: dialogue; persuasion)*

consonance: repetition of similar consonant sounds *(see also: repetition)*

constructed situation: a storytelling stance in which a character recounts a story with an ambiguous occasion or audience *(see also: natural rhetorical situation; point of view)*

correctio: when an individual corrects themselves

critical distance: when a writer has distance or space from their work that they can see it critically in order to revise

deep point of view: when the reader is immersed as deeply and richly as possible into a single character's perspective *(see also: third person; third-person limited; fly-on-the-wall point of view; point of view)*

denouement: the final section of the story, in which loose ends are tied up and the reader sees the impact of the resolution on the characters *(see also: resolution)*

description: words and phrases that help the reader to visualize people, places, and objects in a story *(see also: setting)*

deus ex machina: when a storyteller solves story problems by inserting situations, events, and powers that do not arise naturally from the story and the characters

dialogue: what characters say and how they say it

diction: the word choice and how it impacts the story *(see also: tone)*

direct address: when the narrator speaks directly to the reader

discovery: new knowledge that is gained by the characters and the readers; this includes reveals, knowledge about others and self, new information, and plot twists *(see also: information gap; foreshadowing)*

distraction: something that draws the attention of the main character away from their core want; a side path on the external journey *(see also: try-fail cycles)*

distinction: differences from the norm, often as an element of style; this includes the use of rhetorical devices, variations of syntax and punctuation, and the way in which techniques like point of view are employed by an author

dramatic irony: when the reader knows things that the character does not *(see also: irony)*

emotion: how a character feels; the internal reaction to outward events *(see also: emotional clues)*

emotional clues: details that help a reader understand what a character feels *(see also: emotion)*

epistolary form: a story told through letters *(see also: natural rhetorical situation; first person)*

ethos: appeals to the authority of the speaker, or to other sources that the listener would find authoritative *(see also: persuasion; pathos; logos; implicit assumption)*

euphemism: using a friendlier term for something that's typically unpleasant *(see also: substitution)*

exposition: establishing the story world in stasis, before change occurs and the story begins *(see also: backstory)*

external journey: the way in which the character interacts with the world; plot *(see also: plot)*

falling action: the portion of the story in between the climax and the denouement; major character and plot problems are resolved *(see also: unraveling)*

familiar setting: a place where a character has spent much time and often feels comfortable *(see also: setting; unfamiliar setting)*

figure of speech: words or phrases used in distinctive or unusual ways to create an effect *(see also: rhetorical devices)*

final suspense: a final test of the characters or a final moment in which it seems that the characters are unlikely to get what they want *(see also: falling action; resolution)*

first person: when the narrator is a character and is telling their story *(see also: point of view)*

fly-on-the-wall point of view: the narrator acts as an observer with no commentary or filter, and no ability to dip into any characters' perspectives *(see also: deep point of view; point of view)*

foreshadowing: setting up surprises and discoveries so they feel like a natural part of the story *(see also: discovery; information gap)*

fragment: an incomplete sentence without both subject and verb, or a sentence that cannot stand on its own

free indirect speech: a method of revealing character thoughts in which the narrative shifts from the slightly more distant perspective of the narrator to placing the reader directly and fully into the character's perspective, thoughts, and visceral experience *(see also: emotion; emotional clues; motive; stream of consciousness; point of view)*

hook: something that captivates and engages the reader and makes them want to keep reading; often at the beginning of a story or at the beginning or end of a chapter

humor: using language to point out the follies, nonsense, whims, and inconsistencies of people and society, and doing so in a way that brings laughter and amusement *(see also: irony)*

hyperbole: an extreme exaggeration; making something much larger than it actually is *(see also: overstatement)*

imitation: consciously using an author or a text as a model in order to learn or practice specific storytelling techniques, approaches, and styles

implicit assumptions: the assumptions or beliefs that undergird an argument and its appeals *(see also: persuasion; ethos; pathos; logos)*

in medias res: starting a story "in the middle of things," after the inciting incident

in scene: when it feels to the reader as if they are present in the scene with the characters; achieved through showing rather than telling *(see also: showing)*

inciting incident: a disruptive force that sets the characters on their journeys *(see also: exposition; rising action)*

incluing: spreading backstory and other information throughout the story, without being over-concentrated in any one scene *(see also: backstory; infodump)*

infodump: an excess of information that pulls the reader out of the narrative *(see also: backstory; incluing)*

information gap: a lack of knowledge that drives characters and the reader to want to learn more *(see also: discovery; rising action)*

internal journey: a changing and progression of the self; character *(see also: want; need)*

interruption: something that halts the forward movement of the internal and external journey *(see also: try-fail cycles)*

irony: expressing the opposite of something in order to enlighten *(see also: situational irony; dramatic irony; verbal irony)*

key turning point: an important scene for the story which serves as a shift or catalyst, creating irrevocable change *(see also: inciting incident; midpoint; climax; pinch point)*

litotes: stating something by, as Gideon Burton explains, "denying its opposite" *(see also: understatement)*

logos: appeals to logic and reason *(see also: persuasion; ethos; pathos; implicit assumption)*

meiosis: a type of understatement in which you give something a name or a label that makes it seem less than it actually is *(see also: understatement)*

metaphor: using the properties of something else to help the reader better understand the properties of the original item, concept, or person *(see also: substitution; simile)*

metonymy: substituting a word or a term with something that is related and commonly associated with it *(see also: substitution; synecdoche)*

midpoint: a pivotal turning point at or near the center of the story; often a major victory or defeat for the characters *(see also: key turning point)*

motive: a driving force or reason behind a character's behavior *(see also: action; character)*

natural rhetorical situation: a storytelling stance in which the act of storytelling feels like it could derive from a real situation for the characters *(see also: constructed situation; epistolary form; point of view)*

need: an often subconscious problem or gap that is a driving force in a character's behavior *(see also: want; character; internal journey)*

obstacle: anything that gets in the way of the character as they go on their journey *(see also: antagonist; villain)*

omniscient point of view: the use of an all-knowing narrator who knows all of the characters' perspectives and the entire plot *(see also: selectively omniscient; point of view)*

overstatement: describing something as larger or more than it is *(see also: auxesis; hyperbole; bomphiologia; irony; understatement)*

oxymoron: juxtaposing two opposites or extremes

paralipsis: talking about something by stating that you won't talk about it; the very act of doing so draws attention to it

parallel structure: using the same grammatical or syntactical format to create continuity

parody: an imitation of a work or a genre, often using absurdity or exaggeration in order to create humor and social commentary

passive character: a character who does not seek after their goals, either because of a lack of will or a lack of agency/power to do so *(see also: active character)*

past tense: events occurred in the past and are later described to the reader *(see also: present tense; point of view)*

pathos: appeals to emotion *(see also: persuasion; ethos; logos; implicit assumption)*

periphrasis: using a roundabout way to describe something, which creates emphasis or context *(see also: substitution; antonomasia)*

personification: assigning the attributes of a person to something that is not a person

persuasion: changing or influencing someone else through the use of language *(see also: dialogue; conflict; ethos; pathos; logos; implicit assumption)*

pinch point: a key moment that applies pressure to the characters and the plot *(see also: key turning point)*

plot: the events, actions, and interactions that occur in a story; the aspects of a story in which a character interacts with the outside world, as opposed to thoughts and transformations that occur within a character *(see also: external journey)*

plot structure: the movement of the characters through a set of events; certain types of movement (such as rising and falling action, with specific moments like an inciting action and a climax) can create certain effects on the story and the reader; plot structure can be used descriptively, to describe how and why a plot works, or prescriptively, creating a map that a writer can follow to achieve particular storytelling results

point of view: the perspective of the narrator; who is telling the story and how *(see also: stance; first person; third person; third person limited; deep point of view; past tense; present tense; omniscient point of view; selectively omniscient point of view; fly-on-the-wall point of view; natural rhetorical situation; constructed situation; unreliable narrator)*

polyptoton: repetition of a word using a different form of the word (for example, a verb and a noun form) *(see also: repetition)*

polysyndeton: the use of extra conjunctions in a list *(see also: asyndeton)*

power: control and influence in a situation *(see also: voice (3); privilege)*

present tense: events occur as the story unfolds and are described as they happen *(see also: past tense; point of view)*

privilege: advantages (often unfair) that are held by particular individuals in a situation *(see also: voice (3); power)*

psychic distance: how near or close the reader feels to the story and its events *(see also: point of view; stance)*

reader-writer contract: an agreement between the reader and the writer; promises are made by the writer (in terms of genre, conflict, themes, stance, plot, etc.) and the reader expects these promises to be kept over the course of the story *(see also: stance)*

red herring: a conclusion that is false or misleading or causes the protagonist to pursue the wrong path *(see also: try-fail cycles)*

relationship arc: the way that a relationship transforms, changes, or develops throughout a story *(see also: relationship)*

relationship: the connections between characters *(see also: relationship arc; conflict)*

repetition: repeating or restating sounds, words, phrases, or ideas for effect *(see also: alliteration; assonance; consonance; polyptoton; sibilance; synonymia)*

resolution: the moment when the major questions of the plot are resolved; often at the final conflict or struggle *(see also: final suspense; falling action)*

revision: the process of re-seeing and re-envisioning a work; making changes both large and small (from plot structure and character arc to sentence- and word-level changes) in order to improve a story and better convey it to an audience

rhetorical devices: specific techniques used to impact an audience, often related to language, words, sounds, and figures of speech; these techniques can be used to persuade or to engage an audience with a story in distinctive ways *(see also: distinction; style)*

rhythm: the sound of a sentence or passage, and the way in which a sentence's structure, through combining words and punctuation, impacts the reading experience *(see also: syntax)*

rising action: the portion of the story in between the inciting incident and the climax; this involves character exploration, relationship development, and the building and complication of plots and subplots with their intrinsic difficulties *(see also: complication)*

sarcasm: when an individual states the opposite of what they mean, often to demonstrate a negative emotion, to mock, to show contempt, or to provide commentary *(see also: verbal irony)*

selectively omniscient point of view: a storytelling narrator who knows everything but selectively focuses on certain perspectives and knowledge in order to best tell the story; or, a storytelling narrator that is only selectively omniscient and does not actually know everything, yet has a broader sense of the story than a single point of view and can dip into multiple perspectives and provide context *(see also: omniscient; point of view)*

setting: the physical location for a scene; its attributes impact the characters and the plot *(see also: familiar setting; unfamiliar setting)*

showing: an immersive storytelling approach in which the reader "sees" the actions and the dialogue as if it is happening before them *(see also: in scene; telling)*

sibilance: repetition of the s sound *(see also: repetition)*

simile: a type of metaphor that uses the words *like* or *as* to make a comparison *(see also: substitution; metaphor)*

situational irony: when the result of an action, behavior, or situation is different than what we would expect given the knowledge that we possess *(see also: irony)*

stakes: what the characters have to lose or gain *(see also: internal journey)* *stance:* the deliberate narrative position adopted by an author, including where the author stands in relation to the story, the characters, and the reader *(see also: reader-writer contract; point of view; tone)*

stream of consciousness: the natural, continuous, not always sequential direction of thoughts, when recorded in a story *(see also: free indirect speech)*

style: the form of a message or manner of expression, including choices made regarding stance, point of view, tone, sentence structure and rhythm, sentence and paragraph length, and rhetorical devices *(see also: distinction)*

subplots: throughlines in a story that are smaller than the main focus of the plot yet still important; these often include the pursuit of smaller wants and needs (or the wants and needs of supporting characters), relationships between a main character and a supporting character, relationships between supporting characters, and side quests; these throughlines generally interconnect with the main plot/external journey and help the character move through their internal journey

substitution: replacing an object, person, name, concept, or action with something else in order to better convey it or to inject additional commentary or insight *(see also: euphemism; antonomasia; periphrasis; metonymy; synecdoche; metaphor; simile)*

subtext: something that is not stated in the text or by the characters but that influences the story and can be observed or sensed by the reader

sympathetic character: a character that is likable or relatable; they are often kind or the reader understands and sympathizes with their actions and perspective *(see also: unsympathetic character)*

synecdoche: using a part of something to stand in for the whole item (or, occasionally, using the whole of something to represent a part of it) *(see also: substitution; metonymy)*

synonymia: repetition of ideas, often through the use of multiple synonyms in the same phrase or sentence *(see also: repetition)*

syntax: the structure or arrangement of a sentence; each language has common sentence structures that are used to create meaning, as well as acceptable variations within these structures

telling: a storytelling approach which forwards the role of the narrator and often includes summarizing or commenting on events, actions, dialogue, characters, etc. *(see also: showing)*

theme: a message, lesson, issue, or topic of interest that is explored in a story; this is often related to what it means to be human, how individuals should act, or how individuals relate to each other

third person: when the narrator is not a character in the plot and is instead an outside voice *(see also: third-person limited; deep point of view; point of view)*

third-person limited: a narrative point of view in which the narrator can tell the story from the perspective of what a single character knows and experiences *(see also: deep point of view; third person; point of view)*

tone: the mood or overall feeling that is conveyed to the reader *(see also: diction; stance)*

tragedy: a story with an unhappy ending for the characters (or in which the characters end at a worse state than they began); this type of story often occurs when characters refuse to grow or change

tragic force: a negative event that occurs at the climax of the story and makes it feel like it will be impossible for the main character to get what they want *(see also: climax)*

try-fail cycles: when a character tries and fails at something multiple times before gaining a victory *(see also: distraction; interruption; red herring; rising action)*

understatement: describing something as less than it actually is *(see also: meiosis; anesis; charientismus; litotes; irony; overstatement)*

unfamiliar setting: a place that is new to a character and possesses unknown physical characteristics *(see also: setting; familiar setting)*

unraveling: the falling action of the story, in which difficulties resolve *(see also: falling action)*

unreliable narrator: a point of view that is incomplete or from a character whose perspective is skewed or otherwise untrustworthy *(see also: point of view)*

unsympathetic character: a character that is unlikable or not relatable; they may act in unkind or cruel ways *(see also: sympathetic character)*

verbal irony: using words to express the opposite of that which is stated or to express something that diverges in some way from the truth in order to focus us on the truth *(see also: irony; sarcasm; understatement; overstatement)*

viewpoint: *see point of view*

villain: an antagonist who causes significant, lasting, and often irreversible harm in the main character's life or in the lives of those the main character cares deeply about *(see also: obstacle; antagonist)*

voice: (1) how a narrator (and by extension, an author) expresses themselves, including their stance, their relationship with the audience, and how they speak and sound (2) the attributes of how an individual character speaks and communicates with others; what makes their dialogue distinctive (3) the ability to speak and tell one's story

want: what a character consciously desires; a driving goal *(see also: need; character; internal journey)*

wit: a clever or sharp use of words and language, often to create humor *(see also: wordplay)*

wordplay: using words in an innovative, insightful, and clever way *(see also: wit)*

zeugma: using a word to perform two different functions at the same time; often employing a single verb to "yoke" or connect two different types of nouns, thus using both a literal and metaphorical meaning of the verb

Index Locorum

This index contains all the quotes and notable references to Jane Austen's six published novels that are used in *Write with Jane Austen*. The index is organized alphabetically by novel. For each novel, there is a list of chapters that are cited in this book.

Each chapter entry includes the following:
- The chapter number, for editions that use continuous chapter numbering. (Many modern editions have eliminated the volume breaks. For example, *Emma* has 55 chapters originally broken across three volumes, with each volume starting again at chapter 1. But modern editions generally number the chapters from 1 to 55.)
- In parentheses, the volume and chapter number for the first edition of Jane Austen's novels and other editions that use the same breaks. (Thus, III.IV means volume 3, chapter 4 in editions that use multiple volumes.)
- A brief description of what occurs in the chapter.
- The page numbers in *Write with Jane Austen* where aspects of this chapter are discussed.

Mansfield Park

Northanger Abbey

Persuasion

Pride and Prejudice

Sense and Sensibility

INDEX

Z

ACKNOWLEDGMENTS

The support of family, friends, and others made it possible for Jane Austen to write and publish. Similarly, this book would not be possible without the endless help and support I've received from so many.

First, thanks to my husband for giving me the original idea that led to this book (he asked, "Why don't you combine your love of teaching writing with your love for Jane Austen's works?").

I am grateful to the readers and friends who said that instead of just writing a blog on the subject, I should write a book. I am also grateful to my agent, Stephany Evans, who believed in this project from the start and was instrumental in refining the book's overall vision and structure.

Thanks to my Kalamazoo writing group, who read some of my early writings on this topic way back in 2019 and then continued to give feedback over the years. Thanks to Julia Wagner, Donna Fuller, Brooke Lamoreaux, and the other writers who organized and attended the Pennsylvania and Kentucky writing retreats; thanks for sharing your thoughts and feedback and knowledge of Jane Austen. This book was also influenced by Jay Whistler, Buffy Silverman, and Isabel Estrada O'Hagin; their insights on writing techniques impacted key chapters (especially the stance chapter!), and their support helped me keep going. Thanks to Chris Nagle for allowing me to audit his Jane Austen adaptations class in 2020; the class strongly influenced my readings of several of Austen's novels.

As always, I owe endless thanks to Sarah Blake Johnson, who read this book multiple times. I can't count the number of times when I asked "Could you possibly read the new version of this chapter?" and she said "Of course!" Her encouragement and her insights as a fellow writer were invaluable. I don't feel like I deserve her as either a mother or a critique partner.

Other incredible readers included Sarah Knapp, who gave detailed feedback on the entire manuscript, Pam Eaton, who drilled down on the plot-related chapters, Sarah Chow, who brought her expertise to the stance, style, and humor chapters, and Cinda Craig, who focused on the character chapters.

My untiring editor, Jeanna Mason Stay, helped me refine my ideas and arguments *and* write with clarity and focus *while* using a modified version of the Chicago style guide. Without her, the book would have contained confusing passages, errors in the footnotes, and seventeen different approaches to lists. I owe her so much, and I now fervently believe that (at least for me) editing fiction is easier than editing nonfiction. Any errors that remain are my own and were likely added after Jeanna's editing passes! Further, any unnecessary commas are because I love unnecessary commas.

Thank you to Marieke Krijnen for her help with complicated Chicago citation questions.

I would also like to thank the 133 backers on Kickstarter who brought this book to life and made it so I could justify including the vintage illustrations. The Kickstarter backers are also responsible for the inclusion of the three appendices and the index locorum. Thanks to Anthea Sharp and Sandra Tayler, who collectively taught me everything I know about running a Kickstarter.

I also need to gave a huge thanks to Melissa Williams Design for the stunning book cover.

My three daughters and my husband were a constant source of support, and I'm grateful for their sacrifices that helped me to prioritize finishing this book.

Finally, I'd like to thank Jane Austen. It truly wouldn't be possible for me to thank her enough for the influence she has had on my life. She has made me both a better writer and a better person.